When Refugees
Go Home

When Refugees
Go Home

AFRICAN EXPERIENCES
Edited by
TIM ALLEN & HUBERT MORSINK

in association with

JAMES CURREY

AFRICA WORLD PRESS

United Nations Research Institute
for Social Development (UNRISD)
Palais des Nations
1211 Geneva 10, Switzerland

James Currey
www.jamescurrey.com
is an imprint of Boydell & Brewer Ltd
PO Box 9, Woodbridge, Suffolk IP12 3DF, UK
and of Boydell & Brewer Inc.
668 Mt Hope Avenue, Rochester, NY 14620, USA
www.boydellandbrewer.com

A catalogue record is available from the British Library

ISBN 978-0-85255-222-3

Typeset in Bembo

DEDICATION
To those who returned
to be forgotten

There at the edge of town
Just by the burial ground
Stands the house without a shadow
Lived in by new skeletons

That is all that is left
To greet us on the home coming
After we had paced the world
And longed for returning.

An extract from 'Home Coming' by Lenrie Peters
Satellites, Heinemann, 1967

Contents

List of Tables
Maps & Figures

Tables

Maps

Figures

Acknowledgements

The editors and the United Nations Research Institute for Social Development are grateful to several organizations and individuals whose contributions have made this volume possible. The Netherlands Government have provided the bulk of the funds for UNRISD's research programme on refugees. The Ford Foundation in New York, the Commission of the European Communities in Brussels and the Office of the United Nations High Commissioner for Refugees in Geneva have helped finance field work among returned refugee populations, and contributed towards the international symposium held at Harare, Zimbabwe, at which first drafts of most chapters were discussed. Thanks are also due to the University of Zimbabwe for co-sponsoring the symposium, and H.E. Minister J.J. Nkomo, Minister of Labour, Manpower Planning and Social Welfare, who made the opening address. The lively participation at the Harare symposium and other UNRISD meetings of researchers, government representatives, and staff of intergovernmental and voluntary organizations from Zimbabwe, Mozambique, Namibia, Botswana, Eritrea, Malawi, Ghana, Chad, Swaziland, Tanzania, Uganda, Sudan, Zambia, Ethiopia, Somalia, Algeria and several other countries has been immensely useful. The editors would additionally like to thank Jo Yates and other UNRISD staff members for providing such efficient logistical assistance, Jeff Crisp of UNHCR for detailed comments on several chapters, and Geoff Sayer and Annelisse Hollmann of the Oxfam and UNHCR photograph libraries for help in locating illustrations.

Note on
UNRISD

The United Nations Research Institute for Social Development (UNRISD) was established to promote in-depth research into the social dimensions of pressing problems and issues of contemporary relevance affecting development. Its work is inspired by the conviction that, for effective development to be formulated, an understanding of the social and political context is crucial, as is an accurate assessment of how such policies affect different social groups.

The Institute attempts to complement the work done by other United Nations agencies and its current research themes include the social impact of the economic crisis and adjustment policies; environment, sustainable development and social change; ethnic conflict and development; refugees, returnees and local society; the socio-economic and political consequences of the international trade in illicit drugs; and social participation and the social impact of changes in the ownership of the means of production.

List of Contributors

Joshua O. Akol teaches geography at the University of Juba, Sudan. He has written a Ph.D. thesis and published several articles about the situation in Southern Sudan following the Addis Ababa Agreement in 1972.

Tim Allen is a lecturer in Development Studies at the Open University, Milton Keynes, and at South Bank University, London. He has carried out anthropological research for many years among populations in the Sudan/Uganda border region. Among recent publications, he has co-edited the text book *Poverty and Development in the 1990s*.

Kwame Arhin is Professor and Director, Institute of African Studies, University of Ghana, Legon. He specializes in Social History, Economic and Political Anthropology, and has published a considerable number of books and papers on West African traders and markets in Ghana and Asante economic, political and social history and organization.

Ammar Bouhouche is a Professor at the Institute of Political Science and International Relations, University of Algiers, Algeria.

Nicholas Van Hear is a researcher at the Refugee Studies Programme, Queen Elizabeth House, the University of Oxford. He has written widely on refugee, migration and development issues. In a study funded by the UK Economic and Social Research Council, he is currently investigating the circumstances which give rise to mass departures of migrant and minority communities worldwide, examining their socio-economic dimensions and consequences, and considering the policy options available to deal with them.

Jeremy Jackson is a lecturer in applied social science methodology at the Centre for Applied Social Sciences (CASS), University of Zimbabwe. He has researched and published papers on rural poverty, food and income insecurity, small-holder contract farming and rural refugees. He is currently working as a socio-economic adviser to the SADCC Zambia–Zimbabwe Fisheries project.

John Baptist Kabera holds a Ph.D. in Population Studies. He was Head of the Geography Department, Makerere University, before being appointed by ILO as the National Adviser on integration of population factors in district development planning in Uganda.

He was editor of the *East African Geographical Review* and has written extensively on refugees, the displaced and migration.

Stella Tandai Makanya teaches at the School of Social Work, University of Zimbabwe. She was a guerrilla fighter in the Zimbabwe liberation war, and writes extensively about refugee issues.

Hubert Morsink is a senior adviser and programme co-ordinator for refugees at the United Nations Research Institute for Social Development, Geneva.

C. Muyanja was based at the Department of Geography, University of Makerere, Uganda. He was researching on Uganda when he died during the preparation of this volume.

Jovito Nunes trained as an economist and worked for a number of years as a journalist, starting Mozambique's first independent news magazine *Economia*. It was in 1989 that he began social research on war, displacement and social change in northern Mozambique.

Rosemary Preston is Research Director of the International Centre for Education in Development at the University of Warwick, U.K. She is currently a Visiting Research Fellow at the Namibian Institute for Social and Economic Research at the University of Namibia, co-ordinating an EEC funded project on the integration of war affected people two years after Namibian independence.

Terence Ranger is Professor of Race Relations at St Antony's College, University of Oxford. He has published several books on Africa, including *Peasant Consciousness and Guerrilla War in Zimbabwe*.

John R. Rogge is Professor and Co-ordinator of the Disaster Research Unit, University of Manitoba. He is a specialist on involuntary migration and has published extensively on refugees and displaced persons in Africa and S.E. Asia. He is author of *Too Many, Too Long: Sudan's Twenty Year Refugee Dilemma* and is editor of *Refugees: a Third World Dilemma*. His current research focus is on reconstruction and development following disasters, especially as this relates to repatriating refugees and displaced persons.

Barry N. Stein is a Professor of Political Science at Michigan State University. Since 1975 he has taught courses on 'refugees, displaced persons, exiles' and has published widely on refugee problems in developing countries. He is co-director of the International Study of Spontaneous Voluntary Repatriation.

Chris Tapscott is a Professor and Director of the Namibian Institute for Social and Economic Research at the University of Namibia. Although focussing primarily on issues of rural development, he has conducted several studies on the reintegration problems of repatriated Namibian exiles.

Ken B. Wilson is a Research Officer with the Refugee Studies Programme in Oxford, specializing in central southern Africa. He has researched and published on both social and human ecological issues associated with the 'African crisis' of drought, economic collapse, war and flight.

1

TIM ALLEN & HUBERT MORSINK
Introduction
When Refugees Go Home

It is generally assumed that most refugees will eventually want to go home, and representatives of the Office of the United Nations High Commissioner for Refugees (UNHCR) have persistently highlighted the need to create conditions favourable for mass return movements (UNHCR, 1981, 1985, 1990; Hocké, 1986). At the 1991 Executive Committee Meeting, the High Commissioner again drew attention to this issue. She saw 1992 as the first year of a decade for voluntary repatriation, and stated that it was a basic aim of the organization to pursue every opportunity to facilitate it. She also reiterated concerns that had been expressed about the life refugees might face when they arrived back in their countries of origin.

Such concerns had been noted frequently at international forums during the 1980s. In 1984, for example, the findings of the Second International Conference on Assistance to Refugees in Africa (ICARA II) had warned that there was a danger of returned refugees becoming 'internally displaced persons', uprooted within their own country, and perhaps aggravating problems such as excessive urbanization. As a consequence, discussions between the UNHCR and the United Nations Development Programme (UNDP) had explored ways in which international action might be promoted beyond the traditional UNHCR mandate to protect refugees in their countries of asylum. This led to the signing in 1987 of guidelines for co-operation between the two organizations, including approaches to returnee programmes.

In 1991 the High Commissioner made it clear that she intended to build upon these decisions. She said that she was determined to act as a catalyst in sensitizing and encouraging governments, development organizations and donors to help ensure that UNHCR's assistance to returnees is complemented by longer term development efforts.

Thus voluntary repatriation has been presented as the best way to resolve the global refugee problem, and good intentions have been voiced about the need to assist returnees for some time after arrival in their countries of origin in order to ensure that they attain viable livelihoods. These statements are surely significant, and can be expected to affect policy making. It is, therefore, rather surprising that very little information has been available about what has happened to those refugees who went home in the past.

In a book-length report written by G.J.L. Coles for a Round Table meeting sponsored by the UNHCR in July 1985, it was noted that 'although voluntary repatriation has been proclaimed as, in principle, the most desirable solution to a refugee situation, it has so far not been examined in any depth by experts or scholars' (Coles, 1985). Two years later, the point was reinforced in a comprehensive survey of the literature on voluntary repatriation between developing countries, undertaken by Jeff Crisp at the behest of the United Nations Research Institute for Social Development (UNRISD) (Crisp, 1987).

Crisp showed that, although the literature was slightly broader than Coles had suggested, almost all of it (including Coles' 1985 report) had focussed on three main themes; international law, political motivations, and logistics. Literature relating to legal matters had explored the principles guiding the international approach towards repatriation, including issues like the basic right of refugees to return to their homeland, the mandatory responsibilities of international organizations, and the question of whether or not the UNHCR should continue to be involved in protecting and assisting refugees after they had repatriated (e.g. ECA, 1968; Coles, 1985; Goodwin-Gill, 1986; Hausermann, 1985; Radley, 1978; Gorman, 1984). Analyses of political factors had often been more polemical in style. They had been particularly concerned with controversies surrounding specific population movements, such as the extent to which repatriation was in the interest of those promoting it rather than the refugees themselves (e.g. Crisp, 1984a, 1984b, 1986a, 1986b; Harrell-Bond, 1985a, 1985b; LCIHR, 1985; Altrows and Racicot, 1985). Studies concentrating on logistics had been essentially descriptions of the way particular operations had been funded and organized (e.g. Coles, 1985; UNHCR, annual; UNHCR, 1973; Pitterman, 1984; Betts, 1974).

A few of these publications and reports were of a high quality, but many large-scale repatriations had hardly been examined at all, and few authors had made any serious attempt to investigate the experiences of the returnees themselves. Moreover, longer term economic and social dimensions had been largely ignored. It is also worth noting that Coles' 1985 report was never officially endorsed or released by the UNHCR, and another report written by him for a UNHCR Round Table in 1989 was similarly 'shelved' (Coles, 1989).

Doubtless, some of the reasons why this literature was so thin and limited in scope had to do with the difficulties involved in studying returnees. Many refugees are distinct groups in that they can claim a legally recognized status, are often surrounded by an alien population, and may be geographically concentrated. In some parts of the world, their lives are regulated on a day-to-day basis by government officials and aid agencies. In contrast, once they have crossed the border into their homeland, returnees are usually dispersed populations, and in practice have tended to be left to their own devices. Moreover, socio-economic ramifications of repatriation cannot be assessed adequately from a short-term perspective. Establishing farms, forming communities, creating local markets, integration into national politics, and rebuilding infrastructures take time. A further problem is that many mass return movements occur in highly unstable situations, sometimes ones of full-scale war. Independent research in these circumstances is likely to be dangerous or impossible.

However, there are also other factors which help explain why this critically important topic was largely ignored until the 1970s and why subsequent writings were limited in scope. These are linked to the nature of international thinking about repatriation since the Second World War.

The initial UN resolutions appertaining to refugees had explicitly mentioned voluntary repatriation as a first solution, and mass returns had occurred in Europe in 1945. But from 1947 until the 1970s it was effectively set aside as a means of resolving the plight of refugees. This was because discussion about it at international meetings was bound up with the far-reaching political implications of the creation of the state of Israel and of the Cold War. Zionist demands for the right of repatriation to a Biblical homeland, and competing

Palestinian demands to repatriate from their refugee camps, made debate about the general issue of returning refugees very sensitive. The fact that the United States and the Soviet Union took up opposed positions over the conflict led to a stalemate situation. The UNHCR was also put in the position of having to resist pressure from East European states to encourage the return of their citizens who had claimed refugee status in the West. The organization was repeatedly accused of not respecting the General Assembly's resolutions emphasizing the importance of voluntary repatriation, and tended to respond by disowning direct responsibility for seeking or carrying out solutions. In practice, approaches to refugee problems during the 1950s and 1960s emphasized integration into other countries.

The important exception was the return of some 200,000 refugees to Algeria in 1962. At the time this was treated as a special case. It was viewed as a spontaneous movement and the issue of returnee protection did not arise (or was not recognized). The governments of France, Algeria, Tunisia and Morocco facilitated the repatriation process, and the UNHCR had only a limited supporting role. Nevertheless, it established precedents which later became significant. First, it became apparent that the integration of returnees into a war damaged economy was not straightforward and might require long-term assistance. Second, in devastated areas, there might be no clear distinction between returnees and people who had been locally displaced due to the fighting. Third, in situations where national states were being created, the permanent settling of refugees in other countries was unlikely to be a generally viable option. Fourth, it was possible to resolve a refugee problem by repatriation in one region without making it necessary to deploy the same approach in other parts of the world.

Discussion of repatriation at an international level remained difficult, but it was clear that many refugees were more like the exiled Algerians had been than they were like Hungarians or Czechoslovakians who had fled the Soviet invasions. In the 1970s, several wars ended, at least temporarily, and further mass returns occurred, such as those to Nigeria between 1970 and 1971, to Bangladesh between 1971 and 1972, to Sudan after 1972, to Angola, Mozambique and Guinea-Bissau between 1975 and 1977, to Zaire in 1978, to Cambodia in 1979, and to Zimbabwe in 1980. As a consequence, voluntary repatriation was finally forced onto the agenda at international gatherings. In the course of the decade, the United Nations General Assembly identified return as the solution to refugee problems in certain circumstances, notably where the principle of self-determination was involved. In effect this encompassed virtually all the major refugee populations. Moreover, the solution came to be expressed 'not in terms solely of the right to choose freely whether or not to return, the traditional formula, but also in the form of the human right to return in safety and dignity – a right to be asserted and implemented' (Coles, 1989: 162).

At the same time, the global refugee problem was becoming worse, and by the early 1980s, donor countries were expressing concern about the increasing levels of funding required for emergency relief. The major refugee crises in Indo-China, Pakistan and northeast Africa had led to an enormous growth in the UNHCR budget. Most of this extra money went on the relief efforts, and there was a relative (though not absolute) decline in expenditure on the promotion of durable solutions. The organization came under pressure to reduce its overall requirements. This, in turn, prompted interest in the possibilities of actually promoting voluntary repatriation, and to a different kind of controversy over the issue.

In several situations the UNHCR's interest in repatriation during the 1980s coincided with an antagonistic attitude towards refugee populations in host countries. In addition

1.1 *The repatriation to Algeria in 1962 established important precedents: Algerian refugees in Morocco in 1960 (UNHCR/548/Stanley Wright)*

1.2 *The UNHCR programme of 'voluntary' repatriation from Djibouti to Ethiopia in the mid-1980s provoked a storm of controversy: transit camp for returnees from Djibouti, 1986 (UNHCR/16031/ H. Hudson)*

to refugees sometimes being a security risk in that they encouraged border violations, the poverty of most refugee receiving states combined with inadequate international assistance meant that refugees were often viewed as being a drain on the local economy. Representatives of the international community occasionally came under pressure to encourage refugees to go back home, and concerns began to be expressed that the UNHCR was becoming involved in repatriation schemes which jeopardized the safety of refugees. Writing about Africa during the 1980s, Coles notes that repatriations 'have taken place when the underlying security or political problems had not been resolved fully with the result that the returns have not always proved durable' (Coles, 1989: 212). Other commentators have been more trenchant. The writings dealing with political motivations noted in Crisp's bibliography examine the cases of Ethiopian refugees in Djibouti, Ugandans in Sudan, and Salvadorians in Honduras. They argue that the shift in the UNHCR strategy during the early 1980s was an abrogation of responsibility and endangered lives (for a general discussion of these findings see Crisp, 1986c).

Partly in response to these criticisms, the UNHCR became more concerned about the lives of refugees following repatriation. In 1985 the Executive Committee affirmed that the organization had a legitimate interest in the consequences of return and should have access to the returnees. Such statements reflected a growing consensus that the internationally accepted role of the UNHCR to protect specific persecuted populations should in some way be formally expanded. But even with the easing of Cold War antagonisms, agreement on a broader mandate was not straightforward. Many states were opposed to establishing systems for long-term monitoring of returned citizens. For some ex-colonies the idea had neo-imperialistic connotations which infringed their hard won national autonomy, while governments wishing to persecute populations obviously resisted any externally imposed restrictions on doing so. Also, human rights activists pointed out that an extension of the UNHCR's mandate to include protection of returnees was potentially counter-productive. It might encourage host countries to make refugees repatriate on the grounds that the international community was committed to guaranteeing safety in their homeland.

These issues were not resolved, and the approach of the UNHCR on the ground often seemed confused. It appeared to be dictated more by hand-to-mouth responses to donor pressure than a set of established principles or detailed knowledge of the local situation. In some parts of the world, the organization continued to facilitate the return of populations to politically unstable locations. In Cambodia this was done in the face of vigorous criticism from other development agencies. Elsewhere, the misjudged efforts to promote repatriation against the wishes of refugees in the early 1980s were set aside in favour of strategies to actively discourage repatriation until security could be guaranteed in the country of origin. A well-documented example of this was the return of an estimated 170,000 Tigrayans to war torn Ethiopia between 1985 and 1987 (Hendrie, 1992). Under US pressure, the UNHCR attempted to prevent the refugees leaving Sudan, and ended up in the ludicrous position of maintaining that the refugees were being coerced when the bulk of them had already repatriated under their own volition.

Repatriation remained a controversial subject, and Coles' 1989 report, which carefully outlined the changes in international thinking about repatriation since 1914, and managed to describe the contradictions in UNHCR policy without overt criticism, was still regarded as too sensitive for distribution. Solutions to situations of large-scale population displacement continued to be negotiated in legal and political terms, without much attempt to find out what had happened to returned refugees once they had disappeared from the spotlight and media attention had moved on to the next crisis. Nevertheless, the international community had become aware that immediate relief and assistance based on humanitarian concerns were not an adequate response. It had become apparent that repatriation in itself may solve nothing if the underlying causes of flight remained unaddressed. Towards the end of his 1989 report, Coles observed that the refugee problem 'has, by common recognition, to be seen now in the light of more general considerations and more long-term factors than interim care and maintenance'. It is increasingly accepted that it is concerned with 'such basic issues as social and economic development' (Coles, 1989: 211).

It was at this time that UNRISD decided to initiate a programme dealing with returned populations. The aim was to investigate socio-economic aspects of particular mass repatriations, and to open this topic up for discussion among informed government officials and aid agency staff. This meant finding out what had actually happened to people during the years following arrival in their former homes, and entailed inviting returned refugees to participate in meetings and commissioning studies which presented returnee experiences from a 'grassroots' perspective.

The programme focussed on the lives of returnees in Africa, and initial findings were presented at a series of week-long international symposiums held in Harare, N'Djamena and Addis Ababa in 1991 and 1992. These symposiums brought together a wide range of returnees, academics, planners, and practitioners for intensive discussions. Many participants found this a new and challenging experience. It involved being exposed to a variety of very different perspectives. Exchanges were lively and sometimes confrontational, but immensely productive. They led to an increased understanding among researchers of the constraints under which governments and aid agencies were working, and to a greater awareness among practitioners that detailed information about the lives of returnees could be very useful, even if this involved a serious questioning of claims about the effects of policies. Many of those who attended revealed an extraordinary level of insight about specific events, and the establishing of contacts between such individuals proved to be one of the most rewarding parts of the project. The chapters of this book are mostly revised versions of papers first presented for discussion in March 1991 in Harare.

Chapters 2 and 3 are overview pieces. John Rogge reviews the extant literature on voluntary repatriation and surveys problems that have arisen in specific situations. He points out that, far from always being a simple and 'optimum' solution, returning to a homeland can be as traumatizing as fleeing into exile. Some returnees may find that life at home has changed for the worse, while second- and third-generation refugees born in exile are likely to find 'home' a strange or even threatening place. Rogge touches on several other issues explored further in Barry Stein's chapter. Stein looks at the links between assistance to return movements and longer term development aid. He has a particular interest in the controversial issue of refugee repatriation during conflict and has co-edited two useful volumes on this topic (Larkin, Cuny and Stein, 1991; and Cuny, Stein and Reed, 1992). He points out that most contemporary 'voluntary repatriations' occur where there has been no change in the regime or the conditions that originally caused flight. Both authors indicate that return is often a response to deterioration of conditions in the country of asylum, not an improvement in conditions at home.

Chapters 4 to 15 describe what has happened to particular groups of returnees in Sudan, Uganda, Zimbabwe, Namibia, Mozambique, Ghana, and Algeria. Although these chapters make observations which might be applicable in many situations and highlight issues of crucial relevance in aid planning, they are rooted in the details of how families have adapted to difficult circumstances, and set about re-establishing their old homes, or in some cases creating communities in their nominal homelands for the first time. Almost all of these chapters deal with repatriated populations. The exception is Chapter 6 by Kabera and Muyanja, which discusses the return of the 'internally displaced' population of Uganda's 'Luwero Triangle' in 1986, following years of genocide in the area. The chapters by Arhin and Van Hear (13 and 14) also differ in that they are not concerned with returning refugees, but with the enforced repatriation of 'economic migrants' to Ghana from Nigeria in the early 1980s.

The final chapter of the book offers some personal reflections on the proceedings at the UNRISD Harare symposium by Terence Ranger, who delivered the closing address at the meeting. This postscript and the overviews by Rogge and Stein address many of the key themes raised in the other chapters. But a few general remarks are worth making here.

The book demonstrates that there is a basic problem with using the label 'returnees'. It becomes particularly acute when attempting to compare one group of returnees with another, or returnees with refugees, or when examining an issue like repatriation in general. We are in fact imposing simplistic categories on complex social situations, and we classify examples which might only be similar to other examples, drawn from elsewhere in the world, in that the same label is used. A similar difficulty can arise with respect to 'refugees', but at least there is a legal definition of a refugee to fall back on. The very notion of 'returnee' is ambiguous, implying conceptions of a homeland and of shared values within a population which may or may not exist.

The chapters by Stella Makanya, Jeremy Jackson, Chris Tapscott and Rosemary Preston show that, for Zimbabweans and Namibians, the long struggles for self-determination and the political activities of resistance movements were instrumental in establishing a collective identity, which at least partially survived in the years following repatriation. But this was not the case for other African populations. The Mozambicans studied by Ken Wilson and Jovito Nunes had more flexible attitudes to nationality, indicating that crossing an international boundary into a neighbouring country and later recrossing into a homeland may not always be the enormously significant events that they seem to outsiders. Similar findings have also emerged from studies of the border regions between Uganda, Sudan, Ethiopia, Eritrea and Somalia presented at the UNRISD symposium in Addis Ababa (Allen, 1993; UNRISD, 1993; Allen, forthcoming). Sometimes migrations may be done repeatedly as a way of making the most of a difficult environment, and, in areas of long-term and unresolved war, there may be no clear distinction between a 'returnee', a 'refugee', a 'migrant' and a 'stayee'. An individual may even switch between these categories depending on whom he or she is talking to, and collective identity may be constructed as much out of the shared experiences of migrations as out of language or a traditional relationship with a particular territory.

Often, what appears to aid workers, journalists or government officials as an event, or a series of linked events (i.e. flight – refuge – repatriation – rebuilding a homeland), may for those caught up in social upheavals be relatively indistinct phases in the ongoing business of gaining a living in trying circumstances. As a result, it is difficult to generalize sensibly about returnees in one region, let alone to do so at an international level. An insight about a specific group of returnees in Zimbabwe is less likely to be of direct relevance in Mozambique than an understanding of the local sociological, political, historical, cultural and economic contexts. The term 'returnee' is helpful in that it directs attention at populations which have persistently been overlooked, but it cannot be used as a defining category in any mechanistic manner. This may seem self-evident, yet it would appear that it is persistently forgotten, sometimes with practical ramifications for the implementation of relief and development programmes.

Evidence presented in this book suggests that, at least as far as Africa is concerned, aid agencies have had a very limited capacity to mitigate the difficulties faced by populations when they are actually on the move, and that, where the UNHCR has attempted to control or co-ordinate events, it has usually been unable to do so. When refugees want to go home, either because life in exile is impossible, or because things in their country of origin have improved, then they will usually do so of their own accord irrespective of directives from United Nations institutions. In any case it seems that in most instances agencies are unable to mobilize adequate resources fast enough to transport thousands of people and their possessions. Even on the occasions that sufficient aid has been allocated, it rarely arrives before the migration has occurred. For example, in Zimbabwe refugees returned after independence in 1980 to participate in elections. The majority did not repatriate via official reception centres, and received no assistance.

In such instances, UNHCR staff have expended considerable efforts in registering and counting returnees. The reason for this seems to have been that aid interventions were assessed in terms of the numbers of people who were supposed to have crossed borders, and not in terms of the outcomes of projects. There was a consequent tendency for agencies to exaggerate (or occasionally underestimate) figures for fund-raising purposes. But even when attempts have been made to collect data objectively it can prove an impossible task. UNHCR staff have been persistently frustrated by the numbers crossing borders informally and by the strategy adopted by some returnees of officially repatriating more than once in the hope of obtaining donated items. Often, reported population figures are no more than guesses and subsequent census data indicate that they are not at all accurate. There is clearly a value in field staff observing events at the borders (in the case of Zimbabwe this brought to light abuses by the Rhodesian security forces), but it is difficult to avoid the conclusion that resources might be better used visiting locations where returnees have actually settled rather than in time-consuming and often ultimately pointless bureaucratic activities at official reception centres.

Several speakers at the Harare symposium were also very critical of a tendency for development workers to treat returnees as one undifferentiated mass, ignoring the needs, aspirations and capacities of individuals, and overlooking economic stratification and the particularities of social groupings. It was pointed out that categories such as 'nationality', 'community' and 'tribe' are commonly applied with little attempt to discover what these identities mean for the people so designated, and they are frequently appended to conceptualizations of target returnee populations in ways that compound misconceptions. Partly as a consequence, even where top down aid schemes are run efficiently in terms of accounting to donors, distribution of relief items and the installation of infrastructure, they may still be largely tangential to the daily concerns of most of those they are supposed to be assisting.

A message would seem to be that efforts to provide relief and protection should be flexible enough to respond to the changing situation on the ground rather than try to direct or regulate it. In most situations there is likely to be a need for development orientated assistance as well as short-term relief, but if resources are inadequate they should probably be concentrated on helping the most vulnerable. This in turn requires an understanding of what is actually happening, because it is not enough to define the vulnerable as infants, the elderly, the disabled and women. Invariably many of those suffering most will be quite specific groups. Those at risk may include an old man without sons, children of a mother for whom no bridewealth has been paid by the father's family, and a woman who had either chosen or been forced to earn money while in exile in ways that violated customs of her people.

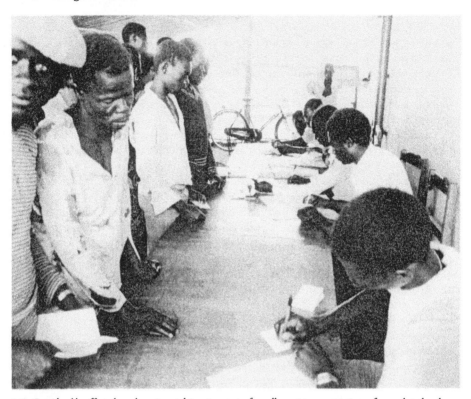

1.3 *Considerable efforts have been invested in attempts to formally register repatriating refugees, but they have been frustrated by the numbers crossing borders informally and by the strategy adopted by some returnees of officially repatriating more than once in the hope of obtaining donated items: Ugandans arriving from Sudan in 1987 (UNHCR/no number/J. M. Goudstikka)*

This all seems to boil down to a plea for the UNHCR and other organizations to treat situations of return on a case-by-case basis. But it is not as simple as that. At the UNRISD symposiums there was a tension between arguments put forward for greater specificity and arguments put forward for greater consistency. Sometimes it was the same participant who would point out that returnees were being treated as homogeneous populations and were being treated differently from one place to another without reference to any internationally agreed principles. In the early 1990s events have brought such tensions into the foreground of global politics with worrying implications.

Partly due to a recognition that repatriations have not always meant an end to refugee problems and that relief efforts for returnees have fallen short of needs, and also partly due to more general shifts in international thinking about population displacement since the easing of Cold War tensions, new strategies have been adopted. For example, in Nicaragua the UNHCR has developed a programme of 'Quick Impact Projects' (QIPs). These are small, rapidly implemented schemes which require one-time investments designed to satisfy urgent needs at a community level, and which have been presented as 'a formula for consolidating durable solutions' (Bonifacio and Lattimer, 1992). QIPs have become an ingredient of other UNHCR returnee programmes, and attempts have sometimes been made to have them taken over by other organizations as part of longer term aid. In Cambodia, for example, the UNHCR has arranged for some 45 QIPs to be supported by

UNDP following the closing of the UNHCR field offices in 1993. A potentially more ambitious approach is being attempted in parts of northeast Africa, where the UNHCR has tried to establish something called a Cross Mandate. Here, the UNHCR is attempting to work as an equal partner with several other agencies, including NGOs. It tries to provide assistance to all the population in devastated locations, irrespective of nationality or of refugee and returnee status. QIPs and the Cross Mandate are significant developments because they do not prioritize the task of numerating and registering refugees and returnees in unstable areas where nationality may be ambiguous, and they move away from the narrow, emergency relief orientation of assistance activities towards some form of integrated response adapted to local needs.

In several respects such experiments seem to be positive initiatives, which reveal that lessons have been learned from past mistakes. However, it is not yet clear that they illustrate the future overall direction for UNHCR planning in situations of mass return. Behind the scenes, major donors have continued to put pressure on the organization to reduce expenditure, and have not supported its involvement in development work. It has been argued that the UNHCR should leave longer term aid to others, notably UNDP and NGOs. To some extent fund raising for QIPs sidesteps this problem by maintaining that the aim is not development, but the setting up of conditions in which development will be possible. The UNHCR thereby seeks to become a 'catalyst' for development, something which relies on close co-operation with implementing partners who will continue operating in the area. Unfortunately, the kinds of tensions between the UNHCR and NGOs described in some of the chapters of this book remain common. Moreover, the 1987 agreement between the UNHCR and UNDP on guidelines for co-operation has not resulted in a standardized way of handing over responsibility following repatriation. In Cambodia it seems that an agreement has been reached, but in other countries this has not been possible. For example, in northwest Uganda during the late 1930s the UNHCR was unwilling to move away from a narrow, emergency relief approach (Allen, 1993). This was partly due to a lack of funds, but field staff argued that UNDP should be responsible for anything to do with development. The fact that UNDP was not operational in the area was dismissed as irrelevant.

Such inconsistencies in the responses of the international community to the needs of returnees are even more apparent when it comes to the crucial issue of protection. Although there has been no official agreement to extend the terms of the UNHCR mandate to include returnees, some kind of protection does seem to be suggested by the presence of UNHCR staff at field offices in areas of return, and by their involvement in operations like QIPs. Furthermore, in the early 1990s, a commitment by the international community to protect some populations within their own countries was manifested by the United Nations' association with military activity in Iraq, Somalia and the former Yugoslavia. Yet, in many awful situations, no action has been taken at all. Support for suffering populations has even been withdrawn because they have moved the 'wrong' way across an international frontier.

For example, in Sudan during the 1980s, hundreds of thousands of people became internally displaced as a result of war, drought and atrocities perpetrated by the government. They received little assistance, in spite of the publication of harrowing accounts of what was going on by Amnesty International and other human rights organizations. Those Sudanese who managed to cross into Ethiopia or Uganda were given support, because they were accepted as proper refugees. However, this was only so long as they did not cross back into Sudan. In 1991, many of the Sudanese refugees in Ethiopia were attacked by the Oromo Liberation Front, and they had no option but to flee into Sudan even though fighting was still continuing in their home areas. Instead of being defined as 'returnees' they were classified as 'displaced people' and both protection and assistance came abruptly to a halt. It has been reported that people subsequently died in their hundreds (Keen, 1992: 31).

Highlighting the plight of the Sudanese is not an argument for abandoning other afflicted groups. The point is that, whatever the humanitarian motivations behind the returnee programme in Nicaragua or Cambodia and the sending of troops to Somalia or Iraq, it cannot be demonstrated that decisions have been made according to universally applied criteria. This results in dangerous ambiguities.

An indirect effect of interventions to help some returnees may be to undermine the rights of refugees. The impression has been given that security may now be guaranteed by the international community within the borders of war torn states. This makes it hard to explain to the governments of

1.4 *Returned populations are sometimes left to starve: a Sudanese returnee from Ethiopia cooking wild grasses for a meal, 1991 (UNCHR/21050/B. Press)*

countries burdened with large refugee populations why they should continue to recognize UN resolutions on refugee status. In situations where the international community is intervening to create 'safe zones', refugee hosting countries may push refugees home, and other countries may refuse to allow them in. When nothing is being done to impose peace, refugee hosting countries may assert that they are being treated unfairly. Governments may legitimately ask why should Somalia be 'restored to hope' and not Mozambique, Angola or Sudan? Refugees may end up being used as pawns in the inevitable squabbles. It also needs to be asked if the UN is really committed to protecting people from their own governments, or from a breakdown of civil society. In the places that intervention has occurred, is the UN in a position to monitor human rights over the long term? What will happen when it pulls out of Cambodia or Iraq?

There are no comfortable answers to such questions, but the extent to which the international community can grapple with the kinds of problems now confronting it depends on the UN being able to occupy the moral high ground and act according to generally accepted rules. Keeping the moral high ground and working within sets of rules are both extremely difficult. Nevertheless they have to be done. When they are not, any influence the UN may have is rapidly undermined. A serious shortcoming of the present unstructured case-by-case approach to internal displacement and mass repatriation is that it can be viewed as serving the ends of the UN's main funders.

The following chapters do not comprise a manual about relief and development policy. Several authors have words of advice based upon the benefits of hindsight in particular places, but these remain personal views, just as the analyses of what has happened after repatriations are personal interpretations. Some of the views expressed involve trenchant criticism of international agencies, including the UNHCR. However, it is worth noting that these same organizations supported much of the research carried out for this volume, and staff also proved willing to rake over the coals of failed programmes, to set aside assumptions of what returned refugees ought to be like, and to participate in frank discussion at the UNRISD symposiums. Such an engagement between academics and practitioners was possible because of shared empathies with the sufferings of particular populations, and because of a point of agreement about what is required of the international community. There is a clear and urgent need for the adoption of a fine-tuned procedural code which can be seen to regulate policy making. This code might broaden the existing UNHCR mandate, but will have to be acceptable to all (or almost all) governments, and to be variegated and sophisticated enough to deal satisfactorily with the complexities on the ground.

Now is a time of uncertainty in international thinking about the return of refugees. There are grounds for concern in that lack of a clear overall strategy has led to confusion in the planning and implementation of assistance. But the present lack of clarity has also afforded a degree of openness about repatriation at international gatherings which has not been possible in the past. It is important for those anxious about the welfare of the world's displaced millions to seize the opportunity to put returnee as well as refugee needs and aspirations on to the agenda of such meetings, and to keep them there by persistent lobbying. It is hoped that these pages may be a contribution to that end.

References

Allen, T. (1993) *Social and economic aspects of the mass 'voluntary' return of refugees from Sudan to Uganda between 1986 and 1992*, a report for UNRISD, Geneva, February.

Allen, T. (ed.) (forthcoming) *In search of cool ground: displacement and homecoming in northeast Africa*, James Currey, London.

Altrows, L. and Racicot, D. (1985) *CCIC observer mission to El Salvador and Honduras, April 21–May 14, 1985*, Canadian Council for International Cooperation, Ottawa.

Betts, T. (1974) *The Southern Sudan: the ceasefire and after*, Africa Publications Trust, London.

Bonifacio, A. and Lattimer, J. (1992) *A primer on Quick Impact Projects: a formula for consolidating durable solutions* (mimeo), UNHCR, Geneva.

Coles, G. (1985) *Voluntary repatriation: a background study*, a report for UNHCR's Round Table on Voluntary Repatriation. International Institute of Humanitarian Law, San Remo.

— (1989) *Solutions to the problem of refugees and the protection of refugees – a background paper*, International Institute of Humanitarian Law, and the UNHCR, Geneva.

Crisp, J. (1984a) 'The politics of repatriation: Ethiopian refugees in Djibouti', *Review of African Political Economy*, Vol. 30: 73–82.

— (1984b) 'Voluntary repatriation programmes for African refugees: a critical examination', *Refugee Issues*, Vol. 1, No. 2.

— (1986a) 'Refugees return to Tigray', *Sudan Information Service Bulletin*, No. 1: 1–3.

— (1986b) 'Ugandan refugees in Sudan and Zaire: the problem of repatriation', *African Affairs*, Vol. 86, No. 339: 163–80.

— (1986c) 'Refugee repatriation: new pressures and problems', *Migration World*, Vol. 14, No. 5: 13–20.

— (1987) *Voluntary repatriation for refugees in developing countries: a bibliographical survey*, UNRISD, Geneva.

Cuny, F., Stein, B. and Reed, P. (eds) (1992) *Repatriation during conflict in Africa and Asia*, Center for the Study of Societies in Crisis, Dallas.

ECA (Economic Commission for Africa) (1968) *Conference on the legal, economic and social aspects of African refugee problems, 9–18 October 1967*, ECA, Addis Ababa.

Goodwin-Gill, G. (1986) *Voluntary repatriation: legal and policy issues*, Queen Elizabeth House, Oxford.

Gorman, R. (1984) 'Refugee repatriation in Africa', *The World Today*, October, 436–43.

Harrell-Bond, B. (1985a) *Some comments on the repatriation programme for returnees in Djibouti*, Queen Elizabeth House, Oxford.

— (1985b) *Imposing aid: emergency assistance to refugees*, Oxford University Press, London.

Hausermann, J. (1985) *International protection of refugees and displaced persons: an analysis of lacunae and weaknesses in the legal and institutional framework for the international protection of refugees and displaced persons and recommendations for its strengthening*, Independent Commission on International Humanitarian Issues, Geneva.

Hendrie, B. (1992) 'The Tigrayan refugee repatriation: Sudan to Ethiopia 1985–1987', in Cuny, Stein and Reed op. cit.

Hocke, J. (1986) *Beyond humanitarianism: the need for political will to resolve today's refugee problem*, text of the Joyce Pearce Memorial Lecture, Oxford University.

Keen, D. (1992) *Refugees: rationing the right to life*, Zed Books, London.

Larkin, M., Cuny, F. and Stein, B. (eds) (1991) *Repatriation under conflict in Central America*, Center for Immigration Policy and Refugee Assistance, Georgetown University, Washington DC.

LCIHR (Lawyers' Committee for International Human Rights) (1985) *Honduras: a crisis on the border*, LCIHR, New York.

Pitterman, S. (1984) 'A comparative survey of two decades of international assistance to refugees in Africa', *Africa Today*, Vol. 31, No. 1.

Radley, K. (1978) 'The Palestinian refugees: the right to return in international law', *American Journal of International Law*, Vol. 72: 586–614.

UNHCR (annual) *Report of the UNHCR*, Economic and Social Council of the United Nations, New York.

—— (1973) *Nursing a miracle: the role of UNHCR in the UN emergency relief operation in South Sudan*, UNHCR, Geneva.

—— (1981) 'Voluntary repatriation' in *Notes presented to the Sub-Committee of the Whole on International Protection by the UNHCR, 1977–1980*, Division of International Protection, Geneva.

—— (1985) *Executive Committee of the High Commissioner's Programme, 36th Session: report of the Sub-Committee of the Whole on International Protection*, UNHCR, Geneva.

—— (1990) 'Repatriation: policy and principles', *Refugees*, No. 72: 10–11.

UNRISD (1993) *Refugees returning home*, report of the symposium for the Horn of Africa on the social and economic aspects of mass voluntary return movements of refugees, Addis Ababa, 15–17 September, 1992, Geneva, March.

2 JOHN R. ROGGE
Repatriation of Refugees

A not so simple 'optimum' solution

Introduction

While many refugee repatriations have run their course without problems and have resulted in a total return of all refugees and their subsequent effective reintegration into their home regions, in other cases, repatriations have turned out to be a most difficult and problematic durable solution to implement. There have been instances where not all refugees have been willing to return; where a home government has been less than welcoming; where a host government has been too forceful in encouraging return; where there has been limited assistance to returnees creating difficulties in reintegration; and there have been cases where, after long periods in exile, returnees have encountered many and complex problems in re-establishing themselves in their traditional areas and societies. For second-generation refugees, such as now exist in many parts of Africa, return to their country of 'origin' does not always necessarily mean 'going home'. Indeed, the Office of United Nations High Commissioner for Refugees (UNHCR) has conceded that repatriation is a most difficult durable solution to implement and that a successful and relatively problem-free return is more often the exception than the rule (Coles, 1985).[1] There is, therefore, much scope for research on repatriation so as to create a better understanding of potential problems and to facilitate better preparedness in the planning and implementation of return movements when circumstances permit.

The principal objective of this chapter is to provide a global overview of the problems arising from mass voluntary repatriations of refugees. It will explore some of the myths and realities associated with repatriations and critically evaluate an array of problems that have arisen from past repatriation exercises or which may be anticipated to arise in future return movements. While the substance of the chapter focusses predominantly upon the African situation, it will also draw upon experiences from other world regions when these are deemed relevant to the African context. Many of the issues and problems considered in this chapter may not necessarily have arisen in Africa; the potential that such problems may arise in future repatriations should, however, not be precluded.

The chapter will also provide a detailed examination of the extent to which repatriation, whether organized or spontaneous, has provided, or has the potential of providing, a

---

[1] This comprehensive 230 page report by Coles was prepared at the request of UNHCR for the San Remo Round Table. The report was, however, never officially endorsed or released by UNHCR.

durable solution to the problem of African refugees. In so doing, it will assess factors influencing the desire among refugees to return home, especially among those who have been in exile for protracted periods, and examine the extent to which return movements have been welcomed and supported or resisted by either host or home governments. A key issue that also needs closer review is that of who determines when a repatriation is possible and is to be initiated – it is not uncommon for the perceptions held by concerned governments, by the international community, and by the affected refugees to differ significantly on this question. Although not refugees in the technical sense, the problems surrounding the repatriation to home regions of *internally displaced persons* must also be considered, especially since such displacements are now very widespread and the numbers involved often run into the millions, and because virtually no research has been conducted on this issue within Africa.

The research literature on repatriation of refugees is relatively thin, especially when compared with that on resettlement of refugees in the West, or even with that dealing with the local integration and settlement of refugees within Africa. Much of the writing on voluntary repatriation produced to date has focussed upon such issues as the political and legal parameters of return movements or the logistics of mass returns. There has been very little emphasis on the socio-economic dimensions of repatriations or its human and psychological implications. This chapter will identify research needs which, if addressed, will hopefully lead to a better understanding of the processes involved in repatriating refugees.

Myths & Realities of Repatriation

Repatriation is one of the three preferred durable solutions to the refugee problem – *local integration and settlement* and *resettlement to third countries of permanent asylum* are the other two. Other 'solutions' which are sometimes adopted, or which materialize for lack of durable solutions, include the protracted restriction of refugees to *holding camps* in which they are kept in conditions of interminable dependency; the forced return or *refoulement* of refugees to their countries of origin; or, in attempts to find their own durable resettlement solution, refugees end up perpetually drifting *in orbit* between countries because they are denied residence status by one potential asylum state after another.

All of these responses/solutions have been experienced by Africa's refugees, albeit some have been much more widespread than others. For example, compared to Southeast Asia or Eastern Europe, where third country resettlement has been the dominant response to refugees, in Africa, third country resettlement has played only a minimal role and is highly unlikely to become any more significant in the foreseeable future. Conversely, while local integration and settlement have been widespread throughout Africa, and there are now many examples of successful absorption and near total integration of refugees in first asylum states, in Southeast Asia and parts of Central America host governments have vociferously opposed any attempts to locally absorb refugees.

As for the less desirable 'solutions', *holding camps*, where little or no attempt is made to move refugees from a state of total care and maintenance towards one of self-support, these can now be found in several parts of Africa, albeit none take on the concentration camp-like appearance of camps for Vietnamese or Khmer in Hong Kong and Thailand respectively. Over the past decade, there have also been a few instances of *refoulement* in Africa, or, at least, of where repatriation has been less than totally voluntary – none of these, however, have been on the scale or have had the tragic consequences of experiences in Southeast Asia

Table 2.1 *Scale & direction of major assisted/recorded repatriations between African states, 1971–90*

Year	Total repatriating throughout Africa	Principal groups of repatriates	Size of group
1971–72	19,271	Zairians from Burundi	7,000
		Zairians from Sudan	1,068
		Zairians from Zambia	9,250
1972–73	92,015	Zairians from Burundi	20,000
		Sudanese from CAR	17,000
		Sudanese from Ethiopia	7,400
		Sudanese from Uganda	25,600
		Sudanese from Zaire	21,000
1973–74	87,826	Sudanese from Ethiopia	14,216
		Sudanese from CAR	16,000
		Sudanese from Uganda	53,000
		Burundians from Rwanda	4,000
1974–75	47,969	Guinea-Bissauans from Senegal	40,000
		Mozambicans from Tanzania	2,000
		Zairians from Tanzania	4,700
1975–76	112,583	Guinea Bissauans from Senegal	74,000
		Mozambicans from Tanzania	37,000
		Mozambicans from Zambia	4,000
1976–77	12,510	Guinea Bissauans from Senegal	10,000
1977–78	22,049	Burundians from Zaire	6,000
		Comorians from various states	16,000
1978–79	190,045	Zairians from Angola	150,000
		Zairians from Burundi	36,000
		Angolans from Zambia	3,000
		Angolans from Portugal	1,000
1979–80	130,757	Zairians from Angola	2,000
		Zairians from Burundi	35,000
		Zimbabweans from Botswana	19,900
		Zimbabweans from Mozambique	11,000
		Zimbabweans from Zambia	20,000
		Eq. Guineans from Cameroon	20,000
		Eq. Guineans from Gabon	15,000
		Ugandans from Tanzania	4,000
1980–81	166,740	Zimbabweans from Botswana	22,000
		Zimbabweans from Mozambique	72,000
		Zimbabweans from Zambia	21,000
		Angolans from Zaire	50,000
1981–82	327,281	Zairians from Burundi	20,650
		Chadians from Cameroon	67,500
		Chadians from Sudan	13,000
		Chadians from other states	69,500
		Angolans from Zaire	46,000
		Ethiopians from various states	110,000
1982–83	146,963	Chadians from Nigeria	3,500
		Chadians from Sudan	2,000
		Ugandans from Zaire	15,000
		Ethiopians from various states	126,000
1983–84	238,612	Zairians from Burundi	2,062
		Ethiopians from Djibouti	35,000
		Chadians from Sudan	1,000
		Ugandans from Zaire/Sudan	200,000
1984–85	206,880	Zairians from Angola	6,800
		Ethiopians from Djibouti	6,200
		Ethiopians from Sudan	170,000

Table 2.1 *(cont.)*

		Ugandans from Sudan	5,833
		Ugandans from Zaire	14,800
1985–86	158,117	Zairians from Angola	6,800
		Ethiopians from Djibouti	7,475
		Ethiopians from Sudan	121,000
		Rwandans from Tanzania	2,000
		Ugandans from Sudan	3,353
		Ugandans from Zaire	14,798
1986–87	253,798	Chadians from CAR	19,775
		Ethiopians from Sudan	150,000
		Ugandans from Kenya	2,600
		Ugandans from Rwanda	30,400
		Ugandans from Sudan	33,000
		Ugandans from Zaire	16,740
1987–88	288,757	Chadians from CAR	16,932
		Chadians from Sudan	15,000
		Ethiopians from Djibouti	3,223
		Ethiopians from Somalia	80,000
		Ethiopians from Sudan	65,000
		Sudanese from Kenya	1,400
		Ugandans from Sudan	100,000
		Ugandans from Zaire	6,000
1988–89	538,735	Burundians from Rwanda	53,000
		Burundians from Zaire	56,000
		Chadians from Cameroon	5,022
		Chadians from CAR	1,326
		Chadians from Sudan	10,500
		Ethiopians from Djibouti	5,671
		Ethiopians from Somalia	8,838
		Mozambicans from Malawi	4,000
		Mozambicans from RSA	20,000
		Mozambicans from Zimbabwe	10,000
		Mozambicans from other states	116,000
		Angolans and Mozambicans from Zambia	1,677
		Angolans from Zaire	4,239
		Ugandans from Sudan	97,646
		Ugandans from Zaire	1,204
		Zimbabweans from Botswana	3,151
		Namibians from Angola	34,765
		Namibians from Zambia	2,696
		Other returnees	103,000
1989–90	470,303	Angolans from Zaire	6,213
		Chadians from Cameroon	3,312
		Ethiopians from Somalia	1,544
		Ethiopians from Kenya	2,831
		Mozambicans from Malawi	3,520
		Mozambicans from other states	208,000
		Namibians from Zambia	3,841
		Namibians from other states	3,993
		Ugandans from Kenya	6,047
		Ugandans from Sudan	226,000
		Rwandans from Kenya	1,966
		Zairians from Angola	3,036
Total	3,511,213		

Source: Various UNHCR reports, especially the annual reports on UNHCR Assistance and Proposed Programmes.

or Central America. And, in Western Europe, there are currently many thousands of Africans who, along with Asians, East Europeans and Central Americans, are helplessly circulating between countries as *refugees in orbit*.

With the exception of the massive repatriation of Bangladeshis from India in 1971, nowhere has repatriation played such a prominent role as it has on the African continent over the past twenty years. The few voluntary repatriations that have occurred in Southeast Asia and in Central America have all been at relatively modest levels and even the ongoing repatriation to Afghanistan remains small-scale because of the continuing risk of conflict and insecurity inside Afghanistan (Sorenson, 1991). In Africa, on the other hand, some 3.5 million refugees have returned home since the early 1970s (Table 2.1)[2] and the prospects of further return movements are favourable in several regions. However, because of the changing nature and causes of refugee movements in other parts of the continent, there is a mounting spectre that a significant proportion of its refugee population is unlikely ever to return – several African states are, essentially, in the process of becoming countries of permanent asylum.

This latter point needs some amplification before we develop in any detail the overall question of repatriation in Africa and the difficulties thereby created. As the refugee problem in Africa developed during the early post-independence era, the principal causes of refugee movements were either due to anti-colonial wars in the remaining bastions of colonial domination or they were due to localized civil wars that were a legacy of the regionalism or the many irrational boundaries that the colonial era had imposed upon Africa. In almost all of these cases, however, it was generally assumed that conflicts would be resolved in relatively short order and the refugees thereby created would all soon return to their countries of origin. There is little or no doubt that the greater majority of African asylum states during the 1960s and 1970s viewed their acceptance of refugees from neighbouring countries as only a temporary phenomenon. In particular, the acceptance of refugees from countries engaged in anti-colonial war was viewed as an expression of solidarity; it was seen as a political statement intended to reinforce the notion of unity and brotherliness among African states. This was certainly also the position taken by the OAU (Goundiam, 1970). Indeed, in adopting its own protocol on refugees in 1969, the OAU emphasized that the acceptance of refugees by one state should not be perceived as a hostile act towards the neighbouring country from which the refugees originated (Weis, 1970).[3]

This near universal position held by African governments that repatriation was the 'natural' outcome of all refugee movements on the continent is now, however, increasingly in need of re-evaluation. The colonial wars and early post-independence civil wars have all run their course; most of the refugees which they produced have long since returned. Today, other sets of causes – political repression and persecution, ideological and/or ethnic conflicts, secessionism, economic oppression and destitution, ecological disasters – are responsible for the flight of most current refugees; such causes are similar to ones which have produced protracted or permanent refugee exoduses elsewhere in the world. Indeed, in some parts of Africa, as is the case in many other world regions, home governments

---

[2] The data presented in this table are subject to considerable conjecture. The major sources, for example, were UNHCR's annual reports on Assistance and Proposed Programmes which give indications of numbers repatriated. However, it is not always clear whether the numbers are for the past year only or for the total ever. Moreover, such numbers are more often than not based upon crude estimates or local government data rather than being based upon enumerations or registrations. Readers should therefore approach this table with considerable caution.

[3] The final recommendations by the OAU on the principles governing repatriations in Africa are summarized in the Appendix (*Source*: Coles, 1985).

are often happy to be rid of the refugees and are thus in no hurry to facilitate any process that would lead to their return. Elsewhere, there have been forcible repatriations of economic 'refugees' (i.e. of people who have fled their home areas because of poverty and destitution); on their return they have much the same needs as other refugee repatriants, yet, because of their status, have virtually no access to external assistance. Any evaluation of the future role of repatriation in Africa must, therefore, commence with a careful and objective appraisal of areas likely to remain temporary vis-à-vis permanent places of asylum for refugees and other displaced persons. Such a review is clearly beyond the scope of this chapter but should, however, be undertaken as soon as possible.

Similar attitudes towards repatriation have traditionally prevailed among the refugees themselves. Until relatively recently, few of Africa's refugees ever saw their exile as permanent. Their exodus was invariably viewed by them as a temporary aberration in their lives; most were passive victims of localized conflicts who simply sought refuge across the nearest border so as not to be caught in a crossfire between warring factions with which few were able or wanting to identify. They intended to return as soon as peace was re-established. None of them expected to still be in exile

2.1 *Over 3.5 million refugees have returned home in Africa between 1971 and 1990: refugees repatriating under UNHCR auspices to Chad in 1981 (UNHCR/11227/I. Guest)*

some two decades later; none anticipated that their children would be forced to grow up in alien environments and cultures: none foresaw that their children's children would never see their ancestral lands; and, in some parts of Africa, few expected that the one-time hospitality, sympathy and receptiveness expressed towards them by local populations among whom they settled would turn to resentment, if not outright hostility.

Today's refugee problems have, clearly, become much more complex and the disruptions caused by flight are much more severe and lasting. Many refugees have now been in exile for over a decade – some for well over two decades – and there is a growing apprehension among many about their prospects of returning. For a variety of reasons, some may not even wish to return if and when the opportunity arises. Others have, in the process of becoming refugees, also undergone major cultural and social transformations, such as becoming urbanized, joining insurgency movements and thereby exchanging their initial political passiveness to one of militancy, or, out of sheer desperation to survive, have adopted anti-social or even criminal lifestyles. All of these conditions will clearly complicate any attempted return to traditional agrarian economies and societies from which the majority originate. While repatriation continues to remain the 'ideal' solution to their dilemma as refugees, for many of Africa's displaced population, the prospect of returning home arouses anxiety or trepidation.

Meanwhile, the international community has been consistent in maintaining a position on the inevitability of repatriation resolving most, if not all, the continent's refugee problems. One manifestation of this position is the very limited response by Western countries to third country resettlement of African refugees – only three Western states[4] have adopted annual 'planning levels' for intake of African refugees, albeit ones which are relatively modest when compared to intake from other Third World regions. For example, compared to the over one million Indochinese who have been resettled in the West over the past decade, less than 35,000 Africans[5] have been successful in getting accepted. The dominant and continuing consensus among most Western governments, and by extension also of most of the international organizations, is that *Africa's refugees are an African problem best resolved in Africa by Africans*. While some limited aid is provided both bi-laterally and multi-laterally to African governments to assist them with this task (and which simultaneously helps absolve the West's collective conscience for lack of doing something more tangible and durable), most of the onus of support for the refugees continues to fall upon the very countries least able to divert chronically scarce resources to implement durable solutions for a refugee problem.

The predominant response by the UNHCR and its many implementing NGO partners over the past quarter century has been to attempt to maintain refugees on agricultural settlements where at least some degree of self-support is made possible until such time as they can return to their country of origin. In almost all cases, such programmes have been implemented as *temporary solutions pending a repatriation*; programmes specifically aimed at the permanent integration and absorption of refugees in their country of first asylum have been few and far between. Tanzania and Botswana remain the only Sub-Saharan African countries to date which have granted permanent residency and citizenship to some of their refugees, albeit a few other states, notably Uganda and Senegal, have recently placed the issue under consideration.

The options open to African asylum states are limited. Local integration and voluntary repatriation are, essentially, the only acceptable or realistic alternatives. When numbers are manageable and there is a high degree of certainty that a return will not be possible, then local integration is an option which many governments are prepared to entertain, especially if assistance to facilitate the process is provided by the international community. However, when numbers run into the hundreds of thousands, when resources are already severely constrained, and when social and political tensions are exacerbated by the refugees' presence, opposition to local integration from both local populations and from political forces mandate that other options be more forcefully explored. Thus, as refugee numbers continue to increase, the pressures to repatriate refugees are building up in many areas. There is, thus, a growing risk that some repatriations may become less than completely voluntary; that they will return refugees to areas ill-prepared or incapable of receiving them; or that they will return refugees to governments less than anxious to receive them and who will have little interest in or commitment to facilitating their reintegration.

It must be recognized, therefore, that, while in most cases repatriation clearly remains the most preferable option, it is all too often taken for granted that the return of refugees

---

[4] The US, Canada and Australia are the only countries which have planning levels for an annual intake of African refugees; recently, these levels have been set around 3,000, 1,000 and 250 respectively. Some European countries also admit a limited number of African refugees, but do so only on an individual case basis rather than by 'quota'.

[5] Of whom some 24,000 have gone to the US.

to their country of origin is a 'natural' and thus a 'problem-free' process. This is undoubtedly one of the most misleading myths surrounding the process of repatriation. Much of the remainder of this chapter, therefore, will address the problems associated with the repatriation process and suggest that in most cases it is *anything but a simple 'optimum' solution*.

Overview of Repatriations

Throughout history, most refugee movements have tended to result in permanent exile of the displaced populations. Norwood (1969) effectively demonstrated this with his exhaustive treatise on religious refugees throughout history, as did Simpson (1939) with his review of Europe's refugees during the inter-war years, and Proudfoot (1956) and Vernant (1953) with their examinations of the population displacements brought about by the Second World War. Indeed, in Simpson's view, repatriation was so unlikely an occurrence as to be almost insignificant as 'a practical instrument of solution'.[6] Since the Second World War, such a view has been given further credibility as few of the major refugee movements have tended to lead to subsequent repatriations; most Palestinians and Tibetans have now been in exile for some four decades, the massive forced transfers of Hindus and Muslims following the partition of India became permanent, few East European refugees settled in the West are likely to return despite recent radical changes in Eastern Europe, exiles from North Korea residing in South Korea or Chinese who fled to Hong Kong or Taiwan show no indication of wishing to repatriate, and it is highly unlikely that many of the Indochinese dispersed since the end of the Vietnam War will ever go home.

Yet, despite the apparent 'permanency' of most modern refugee movements, there have been some very notable exceptions to the 'norm', producing significant repatriations within Africa, elsewhere in the Third World, and even to some European countries.[7] The most detailed evaluation of these repatriations in terms of the political and legal conditions which facilitated them is a study prepared for UNHCR's Round Table on Repatriation at San Remo in 1985 (Coles, 1985). This study did not, however, address the question of the manner in which refugees repatriated, nor did it attempt to evaluate their diverse experiences in reintegrating into their home areas. Indeed, such studies are still few and far between, albeit some attempts are currently being made to redress this deficiency in our understanding of the repatriation process.[8]

Of the three durable solutions, repatriation is clearly the least researched; this is evidenced by the dearth of substantive research papers and reports (see Bibliography). One likely reason for this relates to the widespread assumption that, because repatriation is the most desirable outcome of a refugee problem, it is also the least problematic and hence one not generating high research priorities. The few studies that have recently been

---

[6] Simpson (1939) wrote '. . . deliberate repatriation on a large scale is scarcely relevant in a discussion of practical instruments of solution . . . voluntary return of refugees to their home countries will occur on so small a scale as to not affect the refugee problem itself'.

[7] For example, some 18,000 Hungarians (or about 10 per cent of the outflow of refugees in 1956) had returned to Hungary by 1960; thousands of Spaniards and Portuguese returned from exile following the end of Fascist rule in the early 1970s; and some 17,000 Greeks returned after the downfall of the Papadopoulos government in 1974.

[8] One of the most extensive of the studies currently underway is that by Cuny and Stein who, with the assistance of the Ford Foundation and some other agencies, have commissioned a number of case studies of spontaneous repatriations in the Third World.

produced, however, show that this is a myth (for example Akol, 1986, 1987; Crisp, 1984a, 1984b, 1986, 1987; Cuny and Stein, 1988; Rabe, 1990; Rogge, 1990a, 1990b, 1991; Rogge and Akol, 1989; and Wood, 1989), that repatriation is anything but problem-free and that there is a dire need for a much better understanding of the conditions under which refugees return, whether spontaneously or as part of an organized process, and how their rehabilitation and reintegration can be more effectively facilitated.

There is also the problem of inadequate data on repatriation, especially for repatriations that are spontaneous rather than assisted. While the UNHCR has some data on cases it has assisted, such data are essentially limited to accounts of expenditures. Only in recent years have any attempts been made to undertake pre-repatriation assessments of areas into which repatriations are expected, such as for the currently anticipated return of Cambodians (UNHCR, 1990). Post-return surveys of the reintegration process have seldom been undertaken; indeed, there continues to exist heated debate about the point at which the agency's mandate and responsibility for refugees ends following a repatriation. Moreover, it is often difficult to readily identify returnees once back in their home countries because of their dispersal or, in many cases, because returnees deliberately seek not to be identified as former refugees. More will be said about this later.

Before proceeding to an examination of the problems associated with repatriations, it is useful to review briefly some of the major repatriation exercises that have taken place both in Africa and elsewhere. Such a review will be especially useful in placing the role that repatriation has played in Africa into an overall global context.

Some Significant Non-African Repatriations

Certainly, the most significant modern repatriation in terms of sheer numbers was that of the Bangladeshis returning from India following Bangladesh's secession from Pakistan in late 1971. As the civil strife in East Pakistan intensified throughout 1971, culminating in a brief all-out war in early December, some 10 million Bengalis sought refuge across the border in India. From the outset, the Indian government was categorical that it was only granting temporary asylum to the 'evacuees' and that the 'transit relief camps', assisted by the UN, would be available only until the disturbances ended. Within days of the creation of Bangladesh, a massive repatriation exercise was underway. It took only two-and-a-half months to complete the repatriation of 10 million; for example, by late January, 1972, over 200,000 were crossing the border daily. Many refugees returned under their own power since the distance to their home villages was short. Assistance, in the form of rations, transport, and sometimes cash, was provided to returnees. The speed and success of the repatriation was due to a number of factors such as the short duration of exile, the short distances that refugees had fled, the lack of any serious disruption during the conflict to the physical and economic infrastructure in Bangladesh, and the fact that a return within a relatively short time-frame had been anticipated by all parties throughout the crisis. Few of the problems associated with longer term exile, such as those which will be discussed later in this chapter in connection with some of Africa's repatriations, had the opportunity of developing during the Bangladeshi refugee crisis.

There have been several other significant repatriations within Asia; a brief summary of four of these follows. In 1975, following the collapse of the Kurdish rebellion and the Algiers Agreement between Iraq and Iran, some 100,000 Kurds repatriated to Iraq from Iran following an Iraqi amnesty. The failure of the Kurdish rebellion had removed the reason for most refugees to be in Iran, and Iran was glad to see an end to the security risk which the refugees presented. The International Committee of the Red Cross (ICRC) assisted with the return and international observers reported that the returnees were well-treated and that the Iraqi authorities were making genuine efforts to reintegrate the returnees. However, Kurdish reports suggested that some returnees were persecuted and even executed, and that many were forced to settle in areas that were not traditional Kurdish homelands (Coles, 1985). Such diverse views about conditions of returnees are not uncommon and illustrate the need for detailed and independent follow-up investigations. The impacts and needs of the recent Kurdish repatriation, where close to a million Kurds were involved, are only beginning to be fully assessed (Rogge, 1991). This current repatriation also illustrates the attendant risks of repatriating people into a zone of continuing insecurity.

In late 1978, some 200,000 Burmese Muslims, who had earlier fled to Bangladesh claiming persecution by Burmese authorities, began to return to Burma. Most were Rohinyas from Arakan Province where a Muslim insurgency had been underway for some time. This repatriation took place a little over a year following the refugees' arrival; it was complicated by the fact that the Burmese maintained that the refugees were originally from Bangladesh, having been moved into Burma during the colonial era (Elahi, 1987). Only after protracted negotiations between the two governments did Burma finally concede to a repatriation plan. However, when the plan was implemented there was near total resistance among the refugees to returning.[9] Most were fearful of what awaited them on return – some 10,000 even slipped away from the refugee camps so as not to have to return. Only after rations to the camps were curtailed and general living conditions allowed to seriously deteriorate did the majority decide to repatriate. This suggests that the repatriation was primarily a bi-lateral exercise between the two governments and that the refugees' perceptions and will were essentially of little or no consideration. A UNHCR mission visiting the areas of return some two years following the repatriation, however, reported that the majority had reintegrated to a level of self-sufficiency comparable to local people.

Following the Vietnamese invasion of Cambodia and the defeat of the Khmer Rouge in early 1979, Cambodians fled across all three borders; the largest number sought refuge along the Cambodian side of the Thai border. Thai policy was to keep the refugees at the border,[10] although for a brief period in late 1979 it allowed some to cross into Thailand. Famine inside Cambodia brought more to the border during 1980 – at the peak of the crisis, close to a million displaced Khmer were being assisted in camps along the Thai–Cambodian border and inside Thailand. The greater majority spontaneously repatriated into the interior during the second half of 1980 and throughout 1981, as did the majority who had fled to Vietnam and Laos. Those who remained at the border were forced inside Thailand in the mid-1980s by a Vietnamese offensive against the resistance forces which had become established in the border camps. These refugees are expected to repatriate now that the four factions which make up Cambodia's convoluted political scene have reached a settlement. The significance of the repatriation of the early 1980s is that most returned with virtually no assistance from either the international community or Cambodian authorities and were able to reintegrate themselves into a society, economy, and infrastructure that had been devastated by the five-year administration of the Khmer Rouge (Rogge, 1990a). Moreover, it has frequently been suggested by observers who were at the border in the early 1980s that had the international relief effort phased itself out

---

[9] After two-and-a-half months, only 5,300 had returned compared to the 50,000 that the plan had envisaged (Coles, 1985).
[10] One of the worst episodes of forced repatriation took place at this time – some 45,000 Khmer were pushed back across a heavily mined border; as many as 10,000 did not survive this ordeal (Greve, 1987).

Table 2.2 *Principal countries of assisted/recorded repatriation 1971–90*

Country of return	Number of returnees
Angola	118,045
Burundi	119,000
Chad	228,367
Equatorial Guinea	35,000
Ethiopia	907,291
Guinea-Bissau	124,000
Mozambique	400,520
Namibia	45,295
Sudan	155,616
Uganda	777,421
Zaire	297,566
Zimbabwe	168,151

Source: UNHCR.

when the crisis abated,[11] many of the remaining refugees would have returned to the interior and today's refugee problem might have been on a much smaller scale.

An ongoing repatriation, and one that has the potential of becoming the costliest and most complex return movement ever, is that of Afghan refugees returning from Pakistan and Iran. Over 5 million Afghans remain in exile despite the withdrawal of the Soviet forces from Afghanistan more than two years ago. Continuing conflict between government and Mujahidin forces, as well as between rival factions among the Mujahidin, have precluded any large-scale return, although elaborate plans have been drawn up by the UNHCR (1989a) and the concerned governments (Wood, 1989). While both Pakistan and Iran would like to lessen their burden of support of the refugees, neither country is exerting undue pressure on the refugees to repatriate to what essentially remains a conflict zone. Certainly, the majority of refugees remain to be convinced that it is safe for them to return. A joint study by the Refugee Policy Group, Washington, and the Disaster Research Unit, Winnipeg, undertaken during the summer of 1991, has evaluated the current extent of repatriation and associated problems faced both within Afghanistan by returnees and in border areas in Pakistan by prospective returnees (Sorenson, 1991; and Refugee Policy Group, 1991).

These few examples from Asia illustrate many of the issues and complexities associated with repatriations which need to be examined in the African context. The questions which need addressing include:

- under what circumstances can and should refugees be returned to conflict zones?
- who determines whether it is safe for refugees to return?
- under what circumstances can or should people be 'forced' to participate in an 'organized' repatriation?
- how does one define 'voluntariness' for repatriations?
- what is the relationship between the success of a repatriation exercise and the length of exile?
- what conditions promote large-scale spontaneous repatriations?
- under what conditions can or should services in refugee settlements be withdrawn in order to induce repatriation?
- should refugees always be free to return to the destinations of their choice?
- what can be done to reduce the risks to people returning to former conflict zones where mines and other unexploded munitions abound?

[11] There have been few, if any, refugee situations where the international assistance efforts have been on a scale comparable to that in Thailand. At the height of the crisis in early 1980, for example, there were 95 NGOs servicing refugees at the border.

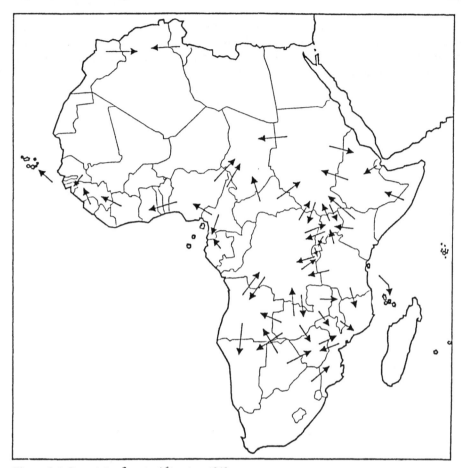

Figure 2.1 *Repatriation flows in Africa since 1960*

Some Major African Repatriations

The scale, time-frames and directions of Africa's major repatriations over the past 20 years are summarized in Tables 2.1 and 2.2 and Figure 2.1. Both tables are compiled from UNHCR's annual reports (UNHCR, annual) and hence are not completely accurate or comprehensive since these reports' primary purpose is to summarize UNHCR's programmes and its past and anticipated expenditures rather than provide any detailed enumeration of refugees or returnees.[12] In the absence of any other comprehensive and readily available documentation on repatriation, however, they do serve a useful function

---

[12] For example, this source of data provides no specific numbers on the repatriation of Angolans or Mozambicans in the mid-1970s, yet it is clear that many refugees did return at that time.

in identifying the principal movements and providing at least some summary enumerations. For the balance of this section of the chapter, some of the major and/or more significant repatriations will be briefly summarized in order to identify problems and concerns that have become associated with Africa's repatriation experience.

Africa's earliest repatriation was that of some 200,000 Algerians returning from Tunisia and Morocco following the Algerian peace settlement in 1962. This was the first major refugee crisis produced by anti-colonial war; it was also to set the scene for how African asylum states would respond to refugees arriving from neighbouring countries. From the outset, repatriation was accepted by all parties (the governments of Tunisia, Morocco, and France, the administration in Algeria, the Front de Libération National (FLN), the UN, the Red Crescent, and the refugees) as the only realistic solution to the crisis. It was also UNHCR's first major involvement with African refugees as part of the tripartite repatriation commission. Following the Evian Agreements, the actual repatriation went relatively smoothly and quickly and, because of the full co-operation of the refugees, took only a little over three months to complete. Before leaving Morocco and Tunisia, returnees were provided with rations and received medical checks. Transport was provided to pre-determined crossing points at the Algerian border from where they were taken to their villages by Algerian authorities. Once back, a major problem of reintegration and rehabilitation was faced because most of the refugees returned to areas which had been seriously affected by the war. In delivering assistance with the reintegration process, a zonal approach was adopted where little distinction was made between, returnees and others in the area since all were deemed in need of help. Holborn (1975), in her monumental study of the earlier work of the UNHCR, suggests that this Algerian experience was the first to draw attention to the special needs that refugees in Third World countries generate.

While the Algerian repatriation was underway, several other refugee crises were developing in Africa and in at least two of these repatriations were also being attempted. However, in neither case were the attempts successful; in 1961, Portuguese authorities in Angola unsuccessfully tried to coax back refugees who had fled to Zaire and to resettle them in strategic hamlets – *aldeomentos* – and in 1964, Sudanese authorities signed a repatriation agreement with Uganda, declared an amnesty for returnees, and proposed a plan to resettle repatriating refugees in peace villages protected by the army – only a few hundred refugees ever opted to participate in this programme. In both these cases, reluctance to return was primarily because of continuing conflict in the regions. Also, in both cases, the refugees had little faith in the resettlement plans proposed by their respective governments, and, indeed, remained fearful for their safety. Examples such as these point to one of the basic issues that need addressing in any repatriation, namely, how do refugees perceive the safety of return vis-à-vis the governments' position on the issue in both the countries of asylum and origin.

Much the same sort of response was initially experienced by Sudanese refugees in 1972 after the Addis Ababa Agreement was concluded; many chose to remain in exile for up to two years following the commencement of repatriation because of an apprehensiveness about security and freedom from retribution. Only after the experiences of earlier returnees made it abundantly clear that it was indeed safe to return did the balance decide to repatriate (Akol, 1986). In contrast, the repatriation of some 60,000 following the end of Nigeria's civil war in 1970 was completed relatively quickly and successfully. It was also achieved without UNHCR assistance.[13] The success of the repatriation can be attributed

---

[13] UNHCR's assistance for Nigerian refugees was not requested by neighbouring governments since they did not officially recognize the fleeing Ibos as refugees. Consequently this repatriation never features in any UNHCR data on African repatriation despite the large numbers involved.

primarily to the conciliatory gestures of the Federal authorities; the Federal armed forces went to great lengths to gain the confidence of local populations in recaptured areas and were also the principal vehicle through which government reconstruction assistance was provided.

The repatriation experiences in the four Portuguese colonies following independence in the mid-1970s differed widely. In the case of Guinea-Bissau and the Cape Verde Islands,[14] the majority of refugees returned within months of independence and rapidly reintegrated into their home areas. Some 5,000 Guinea-Bissauans chose to remain in Senegal's southern Casamance Province where they had become self-sufficient and more or less fully integrated into host communities; many had been former soldiers in the Portuguese army and thus had good reason to fear returning after independence. The Senegalese government placed no pressure on these refugees to return. Likewise, the majority of Mozambicans also returned from Tanzania, Zimbabwe, Malawi and Zambia. Much of the repatriation was spontaneous. However, their return and reintegration were complicated by the severe devastation which the war had wrought on their home areas. It was not surprising, therefore, that some subsequently migrated back to their former refugee villages in southern Tanzania where they had achieved a high degree of self-sufficiency during their exile. There was also considerable resistance to returning among those refugees politically opposed to Frelimo; UNHCR eventually accepted their continuing exile and their recognition as refugees was maintained despite the repatriation agreement with Mozambique. As in Senegal, the Tanzanian government did not pressure any of these refugees to return. In Angola's case, independence was followed by a civil war fuelled by foreign intervention in the region and hence few refugees were willing or able to repatriate. Moreover, the refugee issue became interminably entangled in the internal politics of post-independence Angola; each of the three factions accused the others of using refugees to attain political ends. The fact that many of the refugees in Zaire were openly supportive of the National Front for the Liberation of Angola (FNLA) did not help make their return a high priority for the Popular Movement for the Liberation of Angola (MPLA) government. (More will be said later in the chapter about home governments' reluctance to receive refugees back.) The repatriations from these former Portuguese colonies are good illustrations of the diverse manner in which governments of refugees' countries of origin can respond and how their attitudes and policies can affect the desire among refugees to return (Coles, 1985).

The 1980s and early 1990s have seen the greatest developments in African repatriations; about 75 per cent of all repatriations have taken place during this time. Among the most significant were the repatriations to Zimbabwe and to Chad at the beginning of the decade, the return to Ethiopia[15] and to Guinea[16] in the middle of the decade, the return to Uganda throughout most of the decade, the recent repatriation of Namibians and the ongoing repatriation of Mozambicans. The circumstances of these repatriations and their respective reintegration experiences will not be discussed in this section; rather, specific issues and experiences drawn from these repatriations will be used in subsequent sections of the chapter as illustrations of problems associated with massive return movements.

[14] In addition to returning refugees, the Cape Verde Islands also had to absorb a large number of 'evacuees' from Angola who were forced to leave Angola following its independence. While not recognized as refugees, these 'evacuees' (as well as ones evacuated to Portugal) were assisted under the 'good offices' provision of UNHCR.

[15] Primarily of drought displacees rather than political refugees.

[16] Few of the two million refugees which had left during Sekou Touré's rule were ever recognized as refugees in their country of asylum and thus do not appear in UNHCR statistics. Indeed, it appears that in many cases the principal motivating factor was economic rather than political. UNHCR did provide some limited assistance to some of the quarter million who chose to return in 1984 and 1985.

2.2 Africa's earliest repatriation followed the Algerian peace settlement in 1962: Algerian refugees in Tunisia (UNHCR/no number/S. Wright)

2.3 Transport bottlenecks often limit the effectiveness of assistance programmes in situations of mass repatriation: a UNHCR lorry laden with Chadian returnees boards the Chari ferry, 1981 (UNHCR/11228/I. Guest)

Organized Versus Spontaneous Repatriation

While UNHCR has always recognized as part of its mandate the need to ensure that refugees are not forced back against their will to their countries of origin, its responsibility for and involvement in repatriation exercises, especially in terms of longer term assistance in the process of reintegrating refugees within their country of origin, were less than clearly defined until recently.[17] Moreover, for a variety of reasons, the agency has often been unable or unwilling to participate in voluntary repatriations. For example, refugees who do not register with UNHCR, or whose country of asylum does not officially recognize them as refugees, may not receive any assistance when they spontaneously return simply because the agency is not party to their movements or no governments request that assistance be provided. Elsewhere, the authorities controlling an area into which refugees are returning may not be recognized by the UN and, as such, cannot be directly dealt with by UNHCR. Alternatively, where a country of origin identifies returnees as part of an insurgent movement and does not, therefore, sanction their return, UNHCR is clearly unable to assist them. Internally displaced refugees who return to home areas are a special problem; international agencies cannot provide any assistance or protection during displacement or on return unless invited to do so by the national government. And there have been several instances where refugees fear that by returning through 'official' channels they will be identified by local authorities or local residents as returnees, and that such identification may place them at a disadvantage or even at risk.

Given these diverse conditions, repatriations can take many different forms in terms of degrees of voluntariness in returning, the levels of assistance provided to the returnees, the receptiveness to the returnees, and their subsequent success in re-establishing themselves on their return. Much of the literature and data base on repatriations tends to focus specifically on return movements organized and/or assisted by the international community, and much of the information we have is concerned specifically with the legal and/or political parameters of such repatriations. However, it is now generally recognized that the spontaneous repatriation of refugees is often on a much greater scale than organized repatriation under UNHCR sponsorship – Coles (1985) suggests that spontaneous repatriations may be ten times greater – yet our data base and understanding of the processes and problems of spontaneous repatriations remain very limited.

Organized repatriations can only proceed within the legal and statutory framework of international law and the 1951 Convention. UNHCR is, therefore, tied in the level of its involvement; it must always work within the constraints set by both the country of origin and the country of asylum. Unless the political will for a repatriation exists on both sides of a border, the agency's ability to implement an effective repatriation exercise is limited. UNHCR also has the responsibility of ensuring that any such return movement is completely voluntary; refugees must be seen to have access to the information necessary for making informed decisions, individually or collectively, on whether a return is in their best interest. There is considerable concern among some observers about whether UNHCR, in its negotiations with national governments over the implementation of repatriations, has always remained fully cognizant of the perceptions and will of the refugees. Certainly, there was a widespread criticism levelled at the agency's role in the repatriation of Ethiopians from Djibouti (Crisp, 1984a; Goodwin-Gill, 1989); it was also very evident in its activities along the Thai–Cambodian border during 1979 and 1980 (Shawcross, 1984; Rogge, 1990a).

[17] The Round Table at San Remo was a major milestone in the agency's deliberations on its response to repatriation.

The array of legal parameters surrounding organized repatriations has recently, and very succinctly, been summarized by Goodwin-Gill (1989) and thus will not be discussed in this chapter. It is clear that many of the recent organized repatriations, both within and outside Africa, have proceeded with the full co-operation of returnees. However, in any mass repatriation, the principal raison d'être of the exercise can quickly become one of *numbers moved at minimum costs* and the human cost and impacts of the migration are thereby lost in the bureaucracy and among the accountants. Elaborate plans for channelling returnees through 'collection centres' to 'processing centres' to 'transit centres' to 'reception centres' and finally to 'dispersal centres' may look very impressive on paper, but, to unpoliticized rural refugees simply wanting to return home with minimal fanfare, they can be formidable and intimidating hurdles. Moreover, when at the outset there remains concern or apprehension among refugees about whether the time is really the most appropriate for returning, heavily bureaucratized channels involving seemingly endless documentation and many uniformed officials, or even the military, may act as a deterrent rather than as a stimulus for return. Alternatively, refugees may simply choose to avoid such official channels altogether and decide instead to return spontaneously.

A related factor is the time-lag that generally prevails between the resolution of a conflict and the mobilization of an official repatriation programme.[18] There may also be a time-lag between an official peace settlement and the refugees' acceptance of it or of the amnesty for them that such a settlement may include. No matter how well prepared, it takes time for governments and the international community to put a repatriation plan into operation. Many refugees, in their desperation to return, will not wait for an official programme to be implemented. For some, getting back early may be seen as advantageous in gaining access to land or other means of production. For others, returning before the 'official' wave may be seen as the most effective way of avoiding the label of 'returning refugee'. A good illustration of this problem is the current situation along the Thai–Cambodian border where the majority of refugees are clearly very anxious to return after lingering for the best part of a decade in border camps. While UNHCR's contingency plans for the repatriation are ready and the agency is expecting to assist the greater majority of the 350,000 refugees in returning, it is likely that many – perhaps as much as a third – will go back independently and precipitously once the outcome of the peace settlement between Cambodia's four political factions, and especially of the role the Khmer Rouge will play, is clearly established. In a situation such as this, therefore, it is critical that (a) a number of safe routes through the heavily mined border areas be identified and maintained for returnees well in advance of the return, and (b) that a plan for zonal reintegration assistance is targetted by the international community to areas where refugees are likely to return. These needs are common to all spontaneous repatriations.

Because spontaneous repatriation is so widespread, there are a number of issues which urgently need to be researched. These include:

- how to better determine in advance of a repatriation those who are most likely to return spontaneously and why they choose this option.
- what levels of information do refugees have or need in order to determine whether they will return independently?
- under what conditions are spontaneous repatriants the most vulnerable of returnees and thus those in greatest need of assistance or, alternatively, when are spontaneous repatriants the

[18] In fairness to UNHCR, it must be emphasized that, in most instances where massive repatriations are anticipated, repatriation plans are usually drawn up by the agency well in advance of a final settlement of the conflict. For example, an elaborate Repatriation Plan (UNHCR, 1989b), together with a detailed Absorption Study (UNHCR, 1990) of the areas into which refugees are expected to repatriate, was in place long before the final settlement of the Cambodian conflict was achieved.

most adjusted and resilient and thus needing only minimal or even no assistance?
- what sort of pre-departure assistance, if any, can be provided to those likely to return independently?
- how does one implement zonal assistance programmes benefiting both returnees and local people, yet retain the capacity to specifically target the most vulnerable returnees?
- which agencies and types of programmes are the most appropriate for assisting returnees?

Many of these issues, especially those associated with the pre-departure and the return phases, are currently being examined by the Ford Foundation funded International Study of Spontaneous Repatriation led by Cuny and Stein (1988). A parallel research initiative of UNRISD (Morsink, 1990) has placed emphasis on issues associated with the post-return phase, including the positive and negative impacts of official policies after return, the capacity of returnees to take care of themselves, and the contributions they can make to the development of the areas of return.[19]

There is one other form of repatriation that we also need to be cognizant of; in lieu of a better term, we will call it *periodic repatriation*. There are many parts of Africa where refugees have crossed a border but remain close to it in anticipation of a speedy return. In many cases, they remain in the same ethnic region or remain in areas into which they may have traditionally migrated on a seasonal basis. Indeed, for many Africans, the question of 'where is home?' is one which complicates the basic issue of refugee status to a much greater degree than anywhere else in the world. For such refugees, their sojourn is periodic; during flare-ups of conflict they cross the border, returning when conditions permit – perhaps returning only during the rainy season when there is usually a lull in fighting which allows a crop to be cultivated in their home areas – only to move back across the border during subsequent hostilities. Such movements are almost always spontaneous and the migrants are unlikely to be accorded refugee status in their country of periodic asylum. Some of the movements out of Chad are good illustrations of this, as were the movements of Beni Amer out of Ethiopia into eastern Sudan in the 1960s. While such migrants are usually able to survive without external assistance, the very nature of their ephemeral existence reduces their access to basic services in both home and asylum areas and thereby increases their level of vulnerability. Whether it is possible to provide assistance to such refugees and, if so, what type of assistance is most appropriate are questions that need to be addressed.

The Desire to Return

It was suggested in an earlier part of this chapter that almost all refugees and host governments in Africa have assumed that their exile is temporary and that eventually all will be able to go home. This has produced an implicit acceptance of the fact that all of Africa's refugees *desire* to return. In most cases this is undoubtedly true, but there are several qualifications to this generalization which need to be considered. It is evident that, in many other parts of the world, refugees view their exile as a permanent event from the outset; even if the conditions which caused their exile were to change, it is very unlikely that they would return. There are also many examples where refugees resist returning despite the fact that their home governments have extended an amnesty to them to return and their country of asylum wants them to go back. It is useful, therefore, to reflect on the extent to which such conditions of resistance, or even total opposition, to returning prevail among African refugees.

[19] Most of the field studies of the UNRISD study have been conducted in partnership with local scholars and research institutes.

The desire to return to the country of origin is to a large extent a reflection of how refugees identify themselves vis-à-vis their home areas. In this context, Kunz (1981) suggested that there are three basic categories of refugees. First, there are those who hold a firm conviction that their opposition or antagonism to events at home, which caused them to seek asylum, is shared by the majority of their compatriots. Thus, they are likely to retain a strong bond with their home areas – Kunz referred to such refugees as *majority identified refugees*. While Kunz did not address the issue of repatriation, it is suggested here that such refugees are clearly the ones most likely to want to repatriate when the cause of their exile is removed. It is also clear that many of Africa's refugees fall into this category. A second category is that of refugees who, on leaving their home areas, feel alienated from the rest of their homeland population, and probably also feel discriminated against. As such, they become irrevocably estranged from their fellow citizens. Such refugees may be referred to as *events related refugees*; they are less likely to have a strong desire to return home, especially if there have not been any fundamental changes to the social or political systems which alienated them on the one hand, or if they have become economically and/or socially integrated in their country of asylum on the other hand. In Africa, examples of such refugees can be drawn from areas where ethnic conflict was a principal cause of exile, such as among Rwandan and Burundian refugees in Tanzania. A third category identified by Kunz – *self-alienated refugees* – is that of refugees who exile themselves for a variety of individually held beliefs and philosophies. These are people who alienate themselves rather than society alienating them; they are the least likely ever to want to return. This category is perhaps more relevant to non-African refugee situations.

Length of time in exile, degrees of integration in the area of asylum, the pressures exerted by authorities for the refugees to return, the measure of physical disruption in home areas, and the extent to which political change has occurred in their country of origin are the principal sets of variables affecting attitudes regarding repatriation. The first two of these are often closely correlated. The third may be a reaction to the first two. The fourth may be downplayed or even ignored in attempts at governmental levels to achieve a repatriation, and, as has previously been suggested, there may be significant differences in perceptions among refugees vis-à-vis governments and international organizations regarding the fifth variable.

A key issue which needs to be examined for any impending massive repatriation is that of the information refugees have about their home areas and the sources of that information. Refugees in close proximity to the border, and where it is possible to make frequent visits into their home regions, will clearly be better informed about the safety or risks of returning than those at a distance from the border and wholly dependent upon secondary sources. When there are political motivations for having refugees return, or when the refugees are controlled by political fronts in opposition to the government in their country of origin, and who may be reluctant to see their population base reduced through some refugees repatriating, the information base provided the refugees may be limited or deliberately distorted. Refugees agreeing to repatriate 'voluntarily' on the basis of misinformation fed them are anything but voluntary returnees. Consequently, we need to understand much more about the basis on which refugees make their decisions to return, whether individually or collectively; what sets of information do refugees primarily base their decisions to return on and what are the sources of information they most depend upon?

The host government, the home government, the international community, and the political fronts in exile all play a role in influencing or even determining the refugees' desire to return. The manner in which a host government responds to a potential repatriation will depend greatly on the degree to which the refugees are believed to be positively or negatively impacting upon the asylum area. If the goal is to be rid of refugees but not be seen to be forcibly repatriating them, then an array of passive measures such as reducing services, restricting, income-generating opportunities, limiting freedom of movement and association, etc., can all be implemented to influence the refugees' willingness to repatriate. Conversely, if the refugees are well integrated and making valuable contributions to regional economies – which might even be disrupted by the refugees' withdrawal – then the home governments may actively encourage refugees to remain.

With respect to the government in the country of origin, the type of signals it sends out to the refugees will greatly influence their desire to return. Clearly, the removal of a government whose activities caused the refugees to seek exile will usually be sufficient to attract refugees back; this is especially so when the new government is known to be sympathetic to the refugees or to their causes. But what if the political situation has not changed or if the fighting is over but the same authorities remain in control? Blanket amnesties for the refugees to return may be declared, but are these sufficient to entice reluctant returnees back? For example, Mobutu's periodic amnesties to refugees have failed to bring many Zairians out of exile. In most such cases, refugees tend to adopt a 'wait and see' attitude; a few courageous or desperate souls may return and the rest of the refugees wait to see how they fare. Again, this is where it is critical that an accurate flow of information to the remaining refugees is facilitated.

International agencies, whether large organizations or small-scale NGOs, have the potential of playing a major role in ensuring that good, reliable information flows are instituted and maintained. In theory at least, they have nothing to lose or gain from disseminating correct information. Also, refugees often place a high degree of trust in agency workers; they are often more likely to believe them than local officials or visiting officials from their home country. In reality, however, the information flows emanating from international agencies are sometimes contradictory or are based upon misguided philosophies.[20] In extreme cases, they can also be self-serving. The personnel of some NGOs, especially among the smaller or missionary based agencies, is often relatively inexperienced or has only a limited understanding of the many complex underpinnings of a refugee movement; the very high turnover of agency personnel exacerbates this situation.

International agencies can also influence the desire to return by the scale and nature of the services they deliver. The levels of services available in refugee camps may sometimes be so superior to those available in their home areas that refugees are unwilling to leave the camps despite a strong desire to go home. Making the decision to wind down camp services when refugees are still present is not an easy task for an NGO nor is it easily justified to the distant population from whom funding for its humanitarian operations is derived. Yet such strategies may sometimes be necessary and desirable because of the longer-term benefit in achieving a durable solution for the refugees in their home country. Unfortunately, a few NGOs are extremely reluctant to let go of their refugee clients.

Exiled political fronts also have a significant influence on refugees' attitudes towards returning. This is especially the case when their credibility and international recognition as a political force are contingent upon the numbers of people the fronts are seen to represent, irrespective of whether the population is politically active or passive. The danger in such a situation is that political fronts may actively discourage refugees from returning, either indirectly by such activities as disseminating misinformation about the risk of

---

[20] For example, many observers have suggested that the majority of Khmer refugees entering Thailand in 1980 and early 1981 were expecting to eventually return. It was only after well-meaning NGO workers promoted the idea of third country resettlement that many Khmer began to favour such an option.

returning, or directly by physically preventing their return. Such relationships between political fronts and populations under their control may even be extended when mass repatriations take place, in that returnees are forcibly channelled by the fronts into areas which they control in the home country. To date, such conditions have not been too common in Africa; they do exist, however, among some Afghan refugees and are especially a risk for Khmer refugees returning from the Thai–Cambodian border.[21]

Economic Issues & Problems

In any repatriation, economic reintegration and rehabilitation are key issues, irrespective of whether returnees are spontaneous, coming back under the umbrella of UNHCR, returning to traditional rural homes, or repatriating to the cities. In virtually every case, repatriation implies some measure of economic disruption and subsequent readjustment. Some degree of assistance is usually needed to facilitate the process. However, this is not unique to repatriating refugees; all migrants face such disruptions and need to readjust. Indeed, it has been argued that migrants from whatever cause usually bring with them a will to succeed which is born of the difficulties which led them to move in the first place (Mollett, 1991). They are willing to work harder and wait longer to reap the reward of their labour than are people who have lived all their lives in one place and without ever being disturbed. For repatriating refugees, this process of economic adjustment and reintegration is contingent upon a number of variables: length of time in exile, level of self-sufficiency or dependency while in exile, skills or knowledge acquired while in exile, income-generating opportunities or means of production available in home areas, individual or zonal reintegration assistance provided, degree of voluntariness in returning, and individual commitment and/or tenacity to re-establishment.

In attempts to measure economic success following repatriation, it is important to establish a basic parameter, namely, whether reintegration is to be achieved at the level prevailing at the time of exile or at levels experienced at the time of repatriation in the country of asylum. This becomes an especially important issue when refugees have been in exile in a relatively developed area and are repatriating to a much less developed region or one that has been totally devastated by war. It is also important to appreciate that it will take time to fully reintegrate, especially if there have been major disruptions in the home area which limit access to the means of production or if the refugees have been kept in a high degree of dependency while in exile and thus have difficulty readjusting to fending for themselves. All too often, we attempt to measure 'success' too early and as a result arrive at false conclusions. When examining the economic adjustment of immigrants, we readily accept that it may take as long as 10 to 15 years, i.e. not until the second generation, yet for returnees who have often been much more disrupted and traumatized than other migrants, we expect them to fully re-establish themselves within a much shorter time-frame, if not immediately upon returning. This protracted time-frame required for adjustment applies as much to social reintegration as it does to economic reintegration.

Refugees' levels of self-sufficiency or dependency while in exile have an important bearing upon the subsequent pace of economic reintegration. It is clear that there is a great variance in the degree to which refugees in Africa become self-sufficient, whether spontaneously settled or living on organized settlement schemes (Rogge, 1985a). In

---

[21] Various reports during 1990 suggested that as many as 100,000 refugees may have been forcibly repatriated by the three political fronts, and particularly by the Khmer Rouge, into areas inside Cambodia controlled by each front.

some cases they become fully integrated into regional economies and have standards of living equal, and sometimes even superior, to those of local residents. When the option of repatriation presents itself, such refugees must make the difficult choice of whether to forgo what they have attained and start anew in their home area. From a strictly economic standpoint, they may, therefore, be reluctant to leave. If the authorities in asylum areas give them little choice but to leave, then the question becomes one of the extent to which they can transfer their economic self-sufficiency with them to their home areas. Are they permitted to or is it physically feasible to bring back livestock, tools or vehicles, foodstocks, other capital goods, or currency? If so, then the process of economic reintegration will be relatively smooth and rapid and little reintegration assistance will be required. If, on the other hand, they are restricted from transferring their wealth, as was apparently the case among many Angolan returnees from Zaire, or more recently among Iraqi Kurds returning from Iran, then there will be strong resistance to returning. Reluctant migrants seldom make successful settlers, even if it means 'going home'.

A key issue in this context is which refugees achieve high degrees of self-sufficiency in exile. Two factors determine this. First, refugees achieve self-sufficiency by being able to do what they did before – for example, they resume life in exile as peasant cultivators. They are able to do this because they are given access to land, tools and seed. Thus, the migration into exile was only temporarily disruptive; in the same way, a return migration will also be disruptive, but providing that access to the means of production is also available on return then traditional economies will be re-established relatively quickly. This is clearly the ideal scenario for rural to rural refugees. A second factor is one of individual tenacity. In any population there are those who achieve and those who do not. Differences in levels of self-sufficiency achieved within a single refugee community are in large part a reflection of personal ability and tenacity. It follows, therefore, that refugees who have been economically successful in exile will usually be the ones with the best prospects of re-establishing themselves on return.

Refugee settlements are notorious for the dependency they breed among their population. Nowhere is this more forcefully demonstrated than in the Khmer refugee camps along the Thai–Cambodian border where no attempt has ever been made to introduce even minimal measures of self-reliance; Thai refugee policy opposed such a strategy. The notion that refugees are helpless casualties of events beyond their control, and are therefore in need of care and maintenance, is deeply ingrained in much of the aid-providing community as well as among many host governments. Although it has been demonstrated that refugees are fully capable of achieving self-reliance without much external assistance (Harrell-Bond, 1986), in many parts of Africa, refugees remain heavily dependent upon aid agencies for virtually all their basic day-to-day needs. Such dependency also includes having others make all decisions on their behalf. Repatriating such refugees, and having them become economically viable in their home areas, is, therefore, a problem of more than simply providing them with land and/or other means of production. Getting people to break out of a welfare syndrome acquired during many years in refugee settlements and to make decisions for themselves again is a major task confronting any repatriation exercise;[22] in some cases it may be impossible. It is clear that the longer the time in

---

[22] In a recent study of internally displaced refugees from southern Sudan living in rural care and maintenance camps in Kordofan Province, between 10 and 20 per cent of young adult males I interviewed indicated that, despite the deplorable conditions in the camps, they would probably remain there as long as they were able to, even though others in the camp were spontaneously repatriating to the South or were leaving to seek work on nearby Arab farms (Rogge, 1990b).

exile in a state of acute dependency, the greater will be the difficulty in achieving economic reintegration on return.

The extent to which home areas were devastated or decayed during the period of exile will, clearly, affect both the refugees' willingness to return home and their subsequent success in re-establishing themselves. If the cause of the exile was a protracted war, then much of the infrastructure may be destroyed, villages may have been abandoned, and agricultural lands reverted back to 'bush'. It is, therefore, not just the refugees that are in need of rehabilitation. The time-lag between the heavy inputs needed in rehabilitating basic infrastructure, rebuilding villages, reclearing land and otherwise making it usable again, and the production of any meaningful output and/or profit from the land may be too long for some returnees to withstand. As is suggested in Figure 2.2, this time-lag may be of several seasons' duration and disillusionment may well set in before outputs reach the anticipated level. Alternatively, returnees

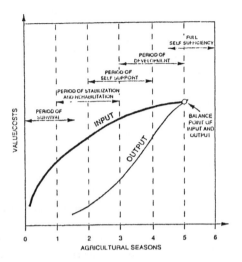

Figure 2.2 *Stages in the process of reintegration of rural refugees*

may be driven to the urban area out of a sheer desperation to survive. Figure 2.2 illustrates the urgent need for aid to tide returnees through the period of deficits in output; it also strongly suggests that such assistance may be necessary for more than just the immediate post-repatriation period.

Moreover, if the refugees are returning to areas where an insurgency is still underway, or to areas which were associated with an insurgency, government response to returnees may be less than welcoming and hence it may not be willing to commit the funding necessary for rehabilitation. Returnees to both northern Mozambique and Southern Sudan during the 1970s were faced with extremely difficult conditions in their home areas making their re-establishment a slow and frustrating process. It can also be argued that in both these cases government agencies could have done much more to facilitate the process. Many of the current refugee crises will also face such difficulties if and when repatriation occurs.

A related issue is that of refugees having to reintegrate into a radically different political-economic system from that existing before going into exile, or that which was adjusted to during exile. Such changes may have completely restructured the system of land tenure; lands to which refugees once had claim may now be held by others, systems of co-operative or communal land tenure may have replaced freehold systems, or the control of all agricultural land and production may now be entirely vested in the state. Likewise, large estates which once provided agricultural employment may have been replaced by small-scale freehold plots or tenancies, greatly reducing or even eliminating the demand for agricultural labour. Adjusting to change of this kind will take time. Indeed, such changes may greatly exacerbate the difficulty of gaining access

2.4 *The devastation caused by war may affect the willingness of refugees to return home: destroyed buildings in N'Djamena, 1981 (UNHCR/11233/N. van Praag)*

to any land and hence accelerate the returnees' move to urban areas. Moreover, if either the populations who stayed in home areas instead of fleeing into exile or new populations migrating into the refugees' home areas during their absence subsequently took over lands formerly owned or used by the refugees, then the reintegration process will clearly be exacerbated. Indeed, returnees may well be unwelcome or their return even resisted; there has been little or no research on the question of how 'stayees' respond to returning refugees. Even when land is available, access to the other means of production may be limited or non-existent. For example, internally displaced southern Sudanese who repatriated to the South in 1990 encountered such an acute scarcity of all resources – seed, tools, and even fish hooks – that few local residents in areas of return were in a position to provide even the most minimal levels of assistance in helping them re-establish their livelihood.[23] In the absence of any external source of assistance, these returnees were rendered totally vulnerable. Clearly, in cases such as this, external inputs are absolutely critical.

Repatriating to a former war zone has a further economic implication. Land may be too dangerous to use because of unexploded munitions and mines. It may also be pockmarked with bomb craters and require substantial labour inputs for levelling before it can be used. On the other hand, acute land scarcity may force people to utilize such lands

---

[23] Many returnees alleged that the Sudanese military stripped them of all tools and seeds, ostensibly to prevent them getting into 'rebel' hands, as they crossed from government-controlled areas into the Sudan People's Liberation Army (SPLA)-controlled areas. Many observers, however, suggest that the Sudanese military was fully cognizant of the destabilizing impact that a repatriation of empty-handed returnees into SPLA areas beset by acute shortages of everything would have.

and accept the attendant risks. While land shortage has not yet surfaced as a major problem in Africa, it is one currently faced in Afghanistan, Cambodia and Iraqi Kurdistan. In the longer term, it could well be faced following any massive repatriation to Eritrea, Angola, or to other long-term war zones.

A lengthy exile, together with a high level of dependency, creates another potential problem for returnees, and especially for those who have grown up within the confines of a refugee settlements. This is the problem of lack of experience with agricultural practices. Returning to rural areas implies reintegration into an agricultural economy; becoming a self-sufficient peasant farmer capable of making correct decisions and implementing appropriate risk-mitigating strategies is not something acquired overnight. Peasant farmers acquire such skills from childhood through working the farms of their parents or kinfolk. It is a skill that extends well beyond the basic mechanics of planting and weeding maize, sorghum, cassava, yams or rice; a successful farmer must also be able to understand his soil, correctly interpret signals given by weeds, read the weather and accurately anticipate the rains. Moreover, being a peasant farmer requires a tenacity and endurance which, if not learned from childhood, may be difficult to instil into young adults, especially if they have spent much of their adolescence and early adulthood in semi-idleness in refugee settlements. Many such refugees may well opt to proceed to urban areas on return to their countries of origin despite the fact that they also lack the skills needed to make their reintegration there any easier.

In contrast to the above scenarios, there have been instances where the refugee experience has led to the acquisition of new skills, the introduction to new farming techniques or crops, and the opportunity to become better educated than had the refugee not gone into exile. In such cases, a repatriation can have very positive impacts upon areas of return, especially if the newly acquired skill and/or experiences can be implemented in home areas. For example, Southern Sudanese who spent much of the 1960s in exile in organized refugee settlements in Uganda were introduced to many new cropping techniques and other income-generating opportunities which were transferred to Sudan on repatriation. This resulted in these refugees achieving relatively good economic returns vis-à-vis other refugees who had spent the war internally displaced in the 'bush' and who continued practising 'traditional' economies after they returned (Akol, 1986).

Being introduced to new concepts and attitudes while in exile may also accelerate the urbanization process. Africa is in the midst of urbanization; rural push factors are intensifying everywhere and urban pull factors, whether illusionary or real, are universal. The refugee experience may well be the catalyst which displaces people from home areas and, once displaced, will result in refugees continuing their migration until they reach the urban area. While few refugees were considered urban refugees in the 1960s, or even during much of the 1970s, the 1980s have seen an ever-increasing number gravitating spontaneously, and often illegally, to the cities. How best to cope with such refugees when they repatriate is little understood. There has been no substantive research on whether repatriating and simultaneously urbanizing refugees encounter more or less problems than other rural to urban migrants. However, the psychological impacts of having become a refugee, the possible long-term dependency ingrained while in exile, and the lack of acquisition of urban-applicable skills must together place the refugee at considerable disadvantage, if not outright vulnerability, in the cities. On the other hand, refugees who successfully adjusted in urban areas while in exile, and perhaps even acquired some tangible skills and/or capital, should be able to do likewise on repatriating. Unfortunately, this rationale applies equally well to those who acquired 'anti-social' or 'criminal' skills while in exile.

Repatriation usually also has economic impacts upon the areas from which refugees depart. Little attention is, however, paid to such potential impacts when plans for repatriation are drawn up. The most obvious impact is that of eliminating the cost of supporting the refugees. The support of large refugee concentrations requires that an array of economic systems develop; much of the local population, many businesses and agencies benefit from these systems. Regional economies adjust to the needs which the refugee communities generate. This is particularly the case in areas where refugees have been located on well-serviced and organized settlements and kept in a high state of care and maintenance. The very presence of a large refugee community will likely bring significant external (hard-currency) funds into an area. Expatriate workers servicing refugees will also create new and relatively affluent markets. Farms and businesses become dependent upon the labour provided by the refugees; some businesses may even develop or expand specifically because of the availability (and cheapness?) of refugee labour. Local populations may also become dependent upon some of the services, such as clinics, which are provided for refugees but are also made accessible to local populations. The subsequent departure of a large refugee population may, therefore, have a considerable array of negative economic impacts at both local and regional levels. For example, how would the large-scale mechanized grain farmers fare in eastern Sudan if all the Ethiopian/Eritrean refugees, on which their farms have become almost wholly dependent for labour, were to depart overnight? No research has been undertaken on such issues.

Social Issues & Problems

All migrants are required of necessity to make at least some attempt at economic adjustment and integration. Not to do so may mean failure to survive. In contrast, social adjustments are made by choice, albeit the pressures to adjust or to remain distinct may vary substantially from place to place. Length of residence is usually one of the most significant variables in the social adjustment process; second-generation migrants are invariably more integrated into the host community than were their parents. The research literature on this is plentiful.

In examining repatriations, problems of readjustment and reintegration are not uncommon, despite the fact that the migrants are *returning* to their home areas rather than *leaving* them. As with some of the other problems associated with repatriation, all too often the fact that there may be problems of social reintegration among returnees is discounted or even repudiated. Yet refugees are migrants and, as such, invariably take some steps to adapt to their asylum areas. The longer the exile, the greater are the chances of refugees taking on at least some of the social and cultural characteristics of their hosts. Second-generation refugees, of which there are now many in Africa, are born into an alien society and culture and are, therefore, even more likely to adopt local ways and attitudes. This is particularly the case when they are integrated into local school systems. Thus, repatriation often requires a considerable degree of readjustment; for second-generation refugees, returning to their parents' country of origin does not necessarily mean 'going home'.

After lengthy periods in exile, not only have refugees adopted coping strategies and social attitudes different from those existing before leaving, their home areas may also have undergone very significant changes during their absence as a result of new government policies or due to other external influences. Thus repatriants may well find the home society significantly changed on their return. An extreme example of such conflicts in social and cultural reintegration is that currently being faced by the impending repatriation to Cambodia. All three political fronts in exile have imbued their population with radically different values; the Khmer Rouge continue to uphold their extreme principles of utopian agrarian communism, the Sihanoukists foster a traditional Khmer society dominated by a near-feudal royalty, and the Khmer People's National Liberation Front (KPNLF) proffer a Western-style laissez-faire society and democracy. Repatriation will send all three factions into a Cambodian society that has also evolved significantly during the past decade of Vietnamese control and which bears little or no resemblance to the Cambodia of the 1960s or to any of the societal visions held by the exiles. Such extreme problems of readaptation are not likely to be faced by any of Africa's repatriations, although long-term exiles from Angola or Ethiopia will certainly find significant differences if ever they are to return home.

The reception accorded to returnees by local populations, and hence the degree to which they are accepted, welcomed, and assisted in re-establishing themselves may also vary considerably. In most cases in Africa, refugees have been welcomed back, especially when they are returning among kinfolk. Spontaneously settled refugees who remained in border areas and therefore were likely to have maintained close contact with kin in home areas are usually at an advantage in this regard. However, if refugees are viewed as having 'deserted' during times of crisis, or if they have been associated with insurgency movements with which the local population has little sympathy, or perhaps has even been harassed by, then the reception may well be hostile and/or little or no assistance provided in helping the refugees readjust. Likewise, if refugees return to their home areas where, after a lengthy period of exile, others have moved in independently or under government direction to occupy abandoned lands and villages, tensions between returnees and locals may well erupt. Such problems may become particularly acute when repatriations are spontaneous or are not condoned by the government.

Under an organized repatriation, potential conflicts between returnees and locals over land or over other social/political issues may be diffused by channelling population movements into areas where repatriants may be more readily absorbed. However, in many parts of Africa, such strategies are not always readily implemented because of the close association between land and ethnicity.

People returning from organized settlement schemes where they have become accustomed to basic services provided by an array of refugee-servicing NGOs may have difficulty readapting in home areas where services are less well developed, or perhaps even nonexistent. This is particularly the case with health services. Moreover, the problem is more than one of simply having less access to primary health care. While vaccinations, disease vector control, and improved water supplies in refugee settlements may create a healthier environment and a healthier population in exile, they may also reduce the natural immunity which people have to endemic diseases. Such immunity will be needed if refugees return to areas lacking in primary health care or controlled water supplies. Indeed, many infants and young children may only be alive because of the availability in the settlements of drugs and other support services to them or to their mothers; these may not be available on repatriation. Much the same can be said for support services for other vulnerable groups – the physically handicapped or the psychologically traumatized – who may only be able to survive because of the availability of assistance. Absence of or serious deficiencies in services in areas of repatriation can become a major catalyst for secondary migration of returnees to the city. Consequently, this is an area where zonal-directed post-repatriation assistance can play a major role. Such assistance will

2.5 *The provision of education to refugees in exile is crucially important, but it is sometimes forgotten that this depends more on a supply of trained teachers than it does on school buildings: Mozambican refugee school in Zambia, 1968 (UNHCR/1518/Jean Moln)*

2.6 *Life can be particularly difficult for women following repatriation: Ethiopian returnees from Somalia, 1991 (UNHCR/21027/A. Hollmann)*

also benefit local populations and, in so doing, may increase their receptiveness to the returnees.

Education is clearly a very important service provided for refugees in exile. In many cases, refugees have been able to access levels of education that are superior to those available at home. For example, because of the civil war, almost a whole generation of Southern Sudanese were denied basic education during the 1960s with the exception of those who had become refugees or who had become internally displaced into the North. Following the repatriation in 1972, refugees who had received some education while in exile were in great demand by government and other employers and hence had little difficulty achieving rapid economic reintegration. Herein also lies an important distinction between refugees who are settled on organized schemes and those who integrate spontaneously; the latter are often at a disadvantage in gaining access to educational facilities and hence have fewer opportunities on repatriating. In some cases, education for refugees has extended beyond the basics to include vocational or even professional training – again such levels are most readily available to refugees on organized settlements, or, sometimes, to those who have spontaneously settled in urban areas.

A problem that may arise on repatriation is one of whether the educational qualifications or vocational certificates gained in exile will be recognized in the home country. Radically different curricula may exist. Alternatively, languages of instruction (and even scripts) may have been different. Some returning refugees may not even have had the opportunity of learning the official language of their country of origin. In most refugee settlements in eastern Sudan for example, Ethiopian/Eritrean refugees are taught by Sudanese teachers using a Sudanese curriculum in Arabic language and script. Thus, reintegration into a Tigrinya or Amharic educational environment will clearly not be an easy transition for students to make. Likewise, Angolan refugees are exposed to a French-based education in Zaire, while in Zambia they are exposed to an English one. In neither case are they receiving any formal instruction in Portuguese. There has not been any detailed research on the impacts which diverse and unrelated educational systems have had on returning refugees.

There are a number of other factors which may complicate social and cultural readjustments on return. Adopting a different religion while in exile may cause problems on return. Marriage to someone outside the refugee community may present difficulties when repatriation becomes possible, especially if the spouse does not want to move. Female refugees marrying indigenous men may run into difficulty if they want to return and their husbands do not; it could mean giving up their children. For other females, the limited options for survival in exile may have forced them to adopt 'anti-social' coping strategies. The stigma of having had to resort to prostitution, for example, may follow the returnee home and preclude her being able to return to her home village. In such cases, women have little choice but to drift to urban areas where they are forced to continue to ply their trade.

One final issue that warrants consideration is the need to rebuild the emotional fabric of many refugees following repatriation. Becoming a refugee is for many synonymous with losing their self-esteem and self-confidence.[24] By going into exile, refugees surrender most of the social and cultural networks that normally provide support in times of adversity. On top of that, they may become subject to violence and corruption, and, in some cases, even take on guilt feelings that they have survived when many of their kin may have perished. In the confines of refugee settlements, they may experience a

---

[24] It is not coincidental, for example, that the Arabic term for refugee – *laji* – means the 'downtrodden'.

breakdown of traditional family life and values such as a basic trust in others or respect for their elders. Alternatively, among spontaneously settled refugees in urban areas, the sheer necessity and desperation to survive may radically modify parental attitudes to children; petty theft by children becomes a means of augmenting family resources and is, therefore, rewarded rather than admonished. For many returning refugees, therefore, this psychological atrophy must be better understood so that the necessary support networks can be augmented.

Gender Issues & the Problems of Vulnerable Groups

An almost totally unresearched area in refugee studies is that of the diverse impacts of the refugee experience, including repatriation, upon women and vulnerable groups.[25] Both the adjustments women must make to life in exile and their subsequent needs to readjust on repatriation must be better understood by all involved in refugee assistance or administration.[26] Women's traditional roles, responsibilities and supportive networks become dramatically altered by involuntary migration, especially when the migrations also mean separation from husbands and kin. Extended family networks from which women normally draw much of the strength and support for their onerous roles in traditional society may be completely lost; instead women become isolated, dependent upon themselves, solely responsible for children in the absence of fathers, subject to exploitation, and, in many cases, also to emotional and physical/sexual abuse. For many women, becoming a refugee sets in motion an almost continuous process of balancing traditional values with a new 'sense of self' imposed by the refugee experience.

Perhaps the single most important impact upon women refugees, and especially on those who become 'heads of households', is the change in family values, expectations and responsibilities. They are forced into completely new sets of decision-making roles. They gain new powers of determination regarding the allocation of resources. Their traditional roles as mothers are transformed by the need to survive; they are forced to become the sole providers of material and emotional stability for their children. The need to strive for economic self-sufficiency outside of a traditional system becomes an indispensable variable promoting their new 'sense of self'. Loneliness and a feeling of abandonment are common. The net effect of all these changes is that they are subject to much emotional and psychological upheaval.

Opportunities for self-support for women are usually very limited. On organized settlements they may, as heads of household, gain access to plots of land along with other refugees, but all too often they end up without the other means of support needed to become self-sufficient cultivators. Some engage in day labour if such options exist; others attempt to survive through informal sector activities such as marketing, running food stalls, or brewing (sometimes illegally) traditional beers and liquors. Domestic work among indigenous households is often the only form of permanent employment available, but exploitation is rife, wages are low, hours are long, and physical abuse is common.[27]

[25] The attached bibliography shows the paucity of research in this field. Indeed, even the journalists writing for UNHCR's *Refugees* magazine have given the issue only cursory attention. I wish to acknowledge the insights on this issue gained from conversations with two of my graduate students, Ms Dodo Motsisi and Ms Julianna Herfst.
[26] Some recent reports have begun to address this issue including UNICEF (1990), Thorn (1991), and Mocellin, Motsisi and Wiest (1991).
[27] Non-Muslim refugees seeking refuge in Muslim countries are especially disadvantaged since many options open to refugee women elsewhere are not available to them in strict Muslim societies (see Rogge (1985b) for discussion of this as it affected Eritrean women in eastern Sudan).

Out of sheer desperation, and because of a total lack of other viable options, many refugee women are forced to resort to prostitution.

Such severe disruptions among women refugees clearly have serious implications when repatriation occurs. Alienation from traditional systems has often reached non-reversible levels. This is especially the case for younger, single women. Unlike their male counterparts, few women are likely to have learned readily applicable skills while in exile. Many will not even have had an opportunity for education, which, had they not gone into exile, they might well have had at home. Finding lost kin, and being accepted by them given the non-traditional attitudes, values, and even manner of dress acquired while in exile, may also present a problem. As a result, many women may well drift into the anonymity of urban areas on return where they are forced to resort to marginalizing activities.

The question of how to facilitate the reintegration of women refugees must be given a much higher priority in any repatriation plan. More attention must be paid to how better to prepare female refugees for repatriation through the provision of special skills-upgrading programmes before departure. Community and social support programmes must also be developed to assist women prior to departure as well as at their destinations. Effective programmes do exist in some refugee arenas; what is needed is a better sharing of experiences and ideas.[28] Here is a niche where the NGOs can provide a valuable service.

Aside from women, there are several other groups which are made acutely vulnerable through the refugee experience. The elderly, especially those separated from their traditional extended family support networks, the orphaned or otherwise separated children, and the handicapped are all groups requiring special assistance and consideration in any repatriation exercise. In refugee settlements, effective support services for these groups are usually provided by NGOs; they allow the refugees to persevere. In most instances, the severely handicapped, such as quadriplegics (war injured), the blind, and the mentally incapacitated, are totally dependent upon NGO support services in the settlements. Once they repatriate, however, access to such services may not be possible and consequently their fingerhold on survival is lost. Only those able to return to villages where kinfolk are able to provide the levels of assistance previously obtained from the NGOs are likely to survive. However, the demands this places upon kin may be too much for some to withstand, especially when they too are in the process of rehabilitation. Again, a sharing of experiences of how such vulnerable groups have been dealt with elsewhere will help develop more viable strategies for coping with vulnerable groups repatriating in Africa. Academic research in this area is also needed.

There is one additional group of returnees that need special consideration, namely, demobilized soldiers/resistance fighters. While not vulnerable in the same sense as the groups discussed above, these young adults often have a particularly traumatic experience in reintegrating. Their expectations are almost always much greater than the reality of the situation awaiting them on return. Lack of applicable skills is one problem, unless they are inducted into the home army on return. They may be subjected to suspicion or even overt hostility on return, especially if they are returning to areas controlled by their former antagonists. In some cases they may have been members of undisciplined cadres and have become used to 'living off the land'; the possession of a gun gave them the 'right' to take what they needed. Rehabilitation of such returnees is thus as much a

---

[28] In the Khmer border camps in Thailand, a very effective programme of this type has been instituted – the Khmer Women's Association. This programme is funded by the UN, but implemented entirely by refugee women; it provides skills training, adult literacy programmes, child care support, and an array of social and psychological (based upon traditional concepts and medicines) support services. One of its objectives is specifically to prepare women for repatriation.

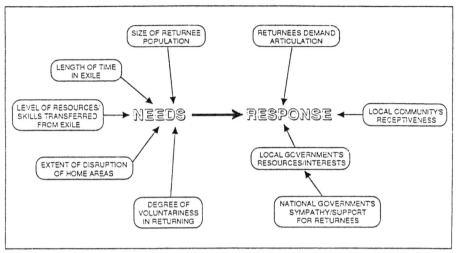

Figure 2.3 *Determinants of responses to refugee repatriations*

process of instilling new sets of values as it is of finding suitable means of income generation.

Implications & Conclusions

This chapter set out to summarize the diverse issues and problems that relate to repatriation of refugees. It has primarily drawn upon experiences with returnees in Africa and, to a lesser extent, in Asia. It has not attempted to address in any detail the question of programmes for returnees once back in their country of origin; this is clearly a subject for another chapter. However, by way of conclusion, it is useful to look at some of the policy implications of massive repatriations, and to establish the relationships between the *needs* of returnees as outlined in this paper and the factors governing the *response* to those needs once refugees are back in their home country.

Figure 2.3[29] attempts to summarize this relationship between *need* and *response* as it relates to the repatriation process. The levels of *need* which returnees have are a product of five sets of variables; all have been discussed in this chapter. Size of returnee populations is a self-evident issue; the larger the return, the greater are the pressures created and the needs that must be addressed. While repatriations of individuals are constantly being facilitated throughout the continent and elsewhere in the world by UNHCR, Africa has especially been required to deal with large-scale mass repatriations. The length of exile is a particularly critical variable. On the surface, long periods in exile may not change the underlying desire to go home, but do produce an array of personal adjustments to the conditions of life in exile, many of which may not even be perceived by the refugee, which, on return, exacerbate the process of reintegration. Resources and skills acquired in exile are clearly a positive force in the reintegration process if they can be transferred and adopted in the home areas. However, when no resources are transferred, or when

[29] This figure is adapted from Pitterman (1987).

the refugees return from conditions of long-term total dependency, the need for assistance with reintegration will be substantial. In turn, this variable relates to the extent to which returnees are required to reintegrate within areas that have been severely disrupted by conflict. While returnees may well have the capacity to adjust, they may not be able to do so, or do so quickly enough to be able to survive, due to a totally destroyed economic, social or physical infrastructure. In such cases the needs are for rehabilitating the home areas rather than specifically rehabilitating the refugees. Zonally targeted assistance is thus essential. Lastly, the question of degree of voluntariness among returnees must also be given more attention. Governments of countries of origin may want refugees to return for political reasons, governments of countries of asylum may want refugees to leave to reduce costs or localized tensions, the international agencies want to be seen to be effecting durable solutions, and, in the process, the will and perceptions of the refugees are often relegated to secondary considerations. Success of any migration and settlement venture is in large part contingent upon the level of co-operation of the affected population; there have been few, if any, successful examples of relocation and resettlement programmes where the settler community was made up of reluctant participants. There is no indication that it is any different in the case of repatriations.

In the country of origin, the *response* to a repatriation exercise is also affected by several sets of variables. One set is the extent and effectiveness of the returnees' ability to articulate their needs. This is contingent upon many factors, including their distance from the centre of government, their numbers, their level of organization and/or administration, and their past and present relationship with the powers in government. The levels of assistance available to returnees at the local level is clearly a reflection of the resources available to local governments – usually very limited – and the interests and sympathies which local officials have in the returnees. In this context, there may be breakdowns in communicating the needs of the returnees to the authorities at the regional or national level who may have the capacity to mobilize appropriate interventions. On the other hand, when the national government is not overtly sympathetic to a repatriation it is unlikely to provide any meaningful response. Lastly, the receptiveness of the local population also affects the nature of responses returnees encounter. If local chiefs, for example, are supportive of the return, then an array of response strategies will be available from within the community. For rural refugees returning to their home areas, this is obviously the ideal scenario. If there is no support, or if local people are hostile to the returnees, then the reintegration process will be seriously impeded.

External interventions are also important in the reintegration process, especially when local resources are limited. International organizations and NGOs both have a role to play in *monitoring* the needs which returnees have and in *sensitizing* the authorities to those needs. This is especially the case where repatriations have been spontaneous. They are also often the only ones with the appropriate resources and skills to be able to respond to those needs. The key issue here is one of how such assistance is best targeted – specifically at the refugees or zonally to regions where refugees are known to have returned. Given that many returnees are anxious to reintegrate as quickly as possible without being labelled 'refugees', or perhaps may even be fearful of such identification, zonal assistance strategies are often the most desirable. Moreover, zonally targetted responses benefit *all* the population in a region and thus may serve to foster the reintegration process by making local people more receptive and supportive of a repatriation. On the other hand, many returnees have very specific needs which can only be met through individually targetted responses. Clearly this is a complex issue and one we need to address by further research.

APPENDIX
Final Recommendations of the OAU on the Principles Regarding Repatriation (1967)

1. That the essentially voluntary character of repatriation is respected in all cases and no refugee be repatriated against his will;
2. That the country of asylum, in collaboration with the country of origin, make adequate arrangements for the safe return of refugees requesting repatriation;
3. That the country of origin, on receiving back refugees, facilitate their resettlement and grant them the full rights and privileges of nationals of the country and subject them to the same obligations;
4. That refugees who voluntarily return to their country be in no way penalised for having left it for any of the reasons giving rise to refugee situations. That whenever necessary an appeal should be made through the Administrative Secretary General of the OAU inviting refugees to return home and giving assurance that the new circumstances prevailing in their country of origin will enable them to return without risk and take up a normal and peaceful life without fear of being molested or punished, and that the text of such appeal should be given to refugees and properly explained to them by their country of refuge;
5. That refugees who freely decide to return to their homeland, as a result of such assurances or on their own initiative, should be given every necessary assistance by the country of refuge, the country of origin, and by the voluntary agencies, the international and inter-governmental organisations to facilitate their return;
6. That, in conformity with Article 1.C.5 of the United Nations Convention of 1951, refugee status ceases to apply to any person if the circumstances as a result of which he became a refugee cease to exist;
7. That every possible step should be taken to eliminate the causes, whatever they may be, which have forced refugees to leave their country;
8. That the country of origin should help returning nationals to resettle and to take up a normal and peaceful life, with the help of international organisations where necessary, and that all the planning and executive facilities contemplated for the integration of refugees in their country of asylum should, whenever possible, be made equally available to them when they return to their homes;
9. That inter-governmental committees for aid to returning refugees should be set up, consisting of representatives of countries of origin and of countries of asylum and also of representatives of refugees and of international organisations, with the approval of the governments concerned;
10. That the United Nations General Assembly should adopt a resolution broadening the terms of reference of the UNHCR to enable it to assist governments in their endeavour to aid former refugees who have returned to their homeland; and
11. That an inter-African Committee for Refugee Migration should be set up to deal with the transport of refugees from one country to another.

N.B. The first five paragraphs of this recommendation were subsequently adopted with *ad verbatim* as Article V of the OAU Convention Governing the Specific Aspects of Refugee Problems in Africa which was adopted by the OAU Assembly of Heads of State and Government in Addis Ababa on 10 September 1969.

References

Akol, J. O. (1986) *Migration and repatriation: case studies of some affected rural communities in Southern Sudan*, unpublished PhD dissertation, University of Manitoba, Winnipeg, Canada.

— (1987) 'Southern Sudanese refugees: their repatriation and resettlement after the Addis Ababa Agreement' in J. R. Rogge (ed.) *Refugees: a Third World dilemma*, Rowman and Littlefield, Totowa, NJ: 143–58.

Coles, G. (1985) *Voluntary repatriation: a background study*, a report for UNHCR's Round Table on Voluntary Repatriation, International Institute of Humanitarian Law, San Remo.

Crisp, J. F. (1984a) 'The politics of repatriation: Ethiopian refugees in Djibouti', *Review of African Political Economy*, Vol. 30: 73–82.

— (1984b) 'Voluntary repatriation programmes for African refugees: a critical examination', *Refugee Issues*, Vol. 1, No. 2.

— (1986) 'Ugandan refugees in Sudan and Zaire: the problem of repatriation', *African Affairs*, Vol. 86, No 339: 163–80.

Cuny, F. and B. Stein (1987) 'Voluntary repatriation in action', *Refugees*, No. 47: 30.

— (1988) 'Prospects and promotion of spontaneous repatriation' in G. Loescher and L Monahan (eds) *Refugees and international relations*, Oxford University Press, New York: 293–312.

Elahi, K. M. (1987) 'The Rohinya refugees in Bangladesh: historical perspectives and consequences' in J. R. Rogge (ed.) *Refugees: a Third World dilemma*, Rowman and Littlefield, Totowa, NJ: 227–32.

Goodwin-Gill, G. (1989) 'Voluntary repatriation: legal and policy issues' in G. Loescher and L. Monahan (eds) *Refugees and international relations*, Oxford University Press, New York: 255–91.

Goundiam, O. (1970) 'African refugee convention', *Migration News*, Vol. 19(2): 7–12.

Greve, H. S. (1987) 'Kampuchean refugees between the Tiger and the Crocodile: international law and the scope of one refugee situation', unpublished PhD dissertation, University of Bergen, Bergen, Norway.

Harrell-Bond, B. (1986) *Imposing aid: emergency assistance to refugees*, Oxford University Press, London.

Holborn, L. W. (1975) *Refugees: a problem of our time. The work of the UNHCR*, Scarecrow Press, Metuchen, NJ.

Kunz, E. F. (1981) 'Exile and resettlement: refugee theory', *International Migration Review*, Vol. 15: 42–51.

Mocellin, J., D. Motsisi, and R. Wiest (1991) *Desk study on the needs of women and children in emergency situations*. Report for UNDP/UNDRO, Disaster Research Unit, University of Manitoba, Winnipeg.

Mollett, J. A. (ed.) (1991) *Migrants in agricultural development*, Macmillan, Basingstoke.

Morsink, H. (1990) 'UNRISD and its research into social and economic aspects of mass voluntary return of refugees from one African country to another', unpublished UNRISD, Geneva.

Norwood, F. A. (1969) *Strangers and exiles: a history of religious refugees*, Abingdon Press, Nashville.

Pitterman, S. (1987) 'Determinants of international refugee policy: a comparative study of UNHCR material assistance to refugees in Africa, 1963–1981' in J. R. Rogge (ed.) *Refugees: a Third World dilemma*, Rowman and Littlefield, Totowa, NJ: 15–36.

Proudfoot, M. J. (1956) *European refugees, 1939–1952: a study of forced migration*, Northwestern University Press, Evanston, Ill.

Rabe, P. (1990) *Voluntary repatriation: the case of the Hmong in Ban Vinai*, Indochinese Refugee Information Centre, Occasional Paper Series, No. 2, Chulalongkorn University, Bangkok.

Refugee Policy Group (1991) *Repatriation to Afghanistan: trends and prospects* (provisional title), Refugee Policy Group, Washington, DC.

Rogge, J. R. (1985a) 'Africa's displaced population: dependency or self-sufficiency' in J. I. Clarke, M. Khogali and L. A. Kozinski (eds) *Population and development projects in Africa*, Cambridge University Press, Cambridge.

— (1985b) *Too many, too long: Sudan's twenty year refugee dilemma*, Rowman and Allenheld, Totowa, NJ.

— (1990a) *Return to Cambodia: the significance and implications of past, present and future spontaneous repatriation*, Report to the International Study of Spontaneous Repatriation, The Intertect Institute, Dallas, 150 pp.

— (1990b) *Relocation and repatriation of displaced persons in Sudan*, Report to the Minister of Relief and Displaced Persons Affairs, Government of Sudan, UNDP (Emergency Unit), Khartoum, 70 pp.

— (1991) *Report on the medium and longer term resettlement and reintegration of displaced persons and returning refugees in the proposed Kurdish autonomous region of Iraq*, UNDP, New York, 51 pp.

Rogge, J. R. and J. O. Akol (1989) 'Repatriation: its role in resolving Africa's refugee dilemma', *International Migration Review*, Vol. 22(2): 184–200.

Shawcross, W. (1984) *The quality of mercy: Cambodia, holocaust and modern conscience*, Andre Deutsch, Ltd, London.

Simpson, J. H. (1939) *The refugee question: a report of a survey*, Oxford University Press, London.

Sorenson, J. (1991) *Afghan refugees in Pakistan: prospects for repatriation*, Disaster Research Unit, University of Manitoba, Winnipeg, 56 pp.

Thorn, L. (1991) *From rice truck to paddy field*, Report for UNHCR on Cambodian women in Thai refugee camps.

UNHCR (1989a) *Plan of action for Afghan repatriation*, Geneva.

— (1989b) *Proposal for 'Cambodian Repatriation' Plan*, Bangkok, Thailand.

— (1990) *Absorption capacity study*, Phnom Phen, Cambodia.

— (annual), *Report of the UNHCR*, Economic and Social Council of the United Nations, New York.

UNICEF (1990) *Cambodia: the situation of women and children*, New York.
Vernant, J. (1953) *The refugees in the post-war world*, George Allen and Unwin, London.
Weis, P. (1970) 'The convention of the OAU governing specific aspects of the refugee problem in Africa', *Journal of Human Rights*, Vol. 3: 464–90.
Wood, W.B. (1989) 'Long time coming: the repatriation of Afghan refugees', *Annals of the Association of American Geographers*, Vol. 79(3): 345–69.

3

BARRY N. STEIN
Ad hoc Assistance to Return Movements
& Long-term Development Programmes

This chapter examines the 'actual' and 'desirable' link between assistance to returnees and development assistance. There is a tremendous gap between principle (the desirable) and practice (the actual) with regard to aid to returnees. There is little dissent on the desirability of development-oriented aid to both the refugees and the local population in the local areas where refugees return. Unfortunately, virtually no one is willing to do it or pay for it. In practice returnee regions are neglected. The failure of the international community with regard to development-oriented refugee assistance is much broader than the arena of repatriation. It also includes a failure to provide development aid to refugees and their host communities during exile.

This chapter will deal with two matters: (1) the level and types of aid given to returnees in the course of a return movement; and (2) development aid to the local areas of return, including the region and its physical infrastructure and, most importantly, aid to the local population who may have stayed in place or have been internally displaced. The links between assistance to returnees and development assistance will be examined in terms of both what is considered desirable by governments and the international community and what is actually being done in historical and present terms. I will also examine the larger subject of refugee aid and development of which development aid to returnees is only a part.

Before getting to these issues, there are three vital background matters to examine: (1) the nature of the contemporary refugee crisis; (2) the problem of repatriation under conflict; and (3) the crisis in African development. These background factors set the context for actual and desirable assistance to returnees and decisively influence international practice.

The Contemporary Refugee Crisis

The Executive Committee of the Office of the United Nations High Commissioner for Refugees (UNHCR) has indicated that 'the majority of today's refugees are persons who do not fall within the "classic" refugee definition in the UNHCR Statute' (UNHCR, 1985). Rather they are 'persons who have fled their home country due to armed conflicts, internal turmoil and situations involving gross and systematic violations of human rights'.

'Classic' refugees are caused by government action and there is a strong political element inherent in their situation. Refugees flee because of a controversy between themselves and their government. Because the basic bond between citizen and government has been broken, 'fear has taken the place of trust, and hatred the place of loyalty' (Grahl-Madsen, 1966). Trifles do not cause refugees, and refugees cannot easily pick up and go home until substantial changes occur or until there is a change in the regime that originally caused them to flee. A continuing controversy over politics, race or religion may mean that prospects for the refugees' return will remain poor for a considerable length of time.

But, today, most refugees are externally displaced persons rather than 'classic' refugees. They are not necessarily fleeing a controversy that personally involves them. Often they are getting out of harm's way rather than fleeing from persecution. Many who flee from a land suffering from a protracted, low-intensity conflict may be fleeing from a proximate cause rather than the conflict itself. Years of conflict lead to adjustments and experience that provide some degree of safety for individual civilians. The final push toward a mass exodus is not generally the direct result of the familiar conflict, but a last-straw change in conditions such as a famine, drought or other natural calamity, or increased fighting that is too close for comfort. Such displaced persons may not fear their government, or whoever normally controls their region. They may well be unafraid and willing to return home to an insecure land if the proximate cause has eased even though the low-intensity conflict persists.

Repatriation Under Conflict[1]

The contemporary international beliefs and principles regarding repatriation assume that return to one's homeland will be purely voluntary, will be assisted and monitored by governments and international agencies under the terms of a tripartite agreement between UNHCR and the governments of the refugees' country of origin and the country of asylum, and that the refugees' complete safety and socio-economic integration will be assured. For example, at the 1990 meeting of UNHCR's Executive Committee, the representative of the Holy See indicated the

> need to ensure that voluntary repatriation – the best solution to uprooting – really was voluntary. In order to do that refugees must be told what opportunities for reintegration into their home countries they would actually have, and it must be ensured that they could return in complete safety (UNHCR, 1990c).

Unfortunately, it is the rare refugee situation that will allow for such orderly and organized return. International activities based on the above assumptions may be irrelevant for the needs of most refugees.

The changing nature of refugee problems has altered the contemporary practice of voluntary repatriation. For a while during the 1960s and early 1970s many refugees were able to repatriate after the successful conclusion of struggles for independence and liberation from colonial rule. However, for more than a decade, most refugee-producing conflicts have involved the newly independent states and have been based on issues of internal

[1]Voluntary repatriation has been studied relatively little. Several studies are now underway at the Refugee Policy Group and at the United Nations Research Institute for Social Development (UNRISD). The study – International Study of Spontaneous Voluntary Repatriation – on which this chapter is based is the oldest. It was supported by the Ford Foundation, the Intertect Institute, Michigan State University, Georgetown University's Hemispheric Migration Project, and the Canadian International Development Agency. Both the Refugee Policy Group and the University of Manitoba have assisted the study. Complete or partial case studies include Afghanistan, Cambodia, Sri Lanka, Ethiopia, Burundi, Guatemala, El Salvador, and Nicaragua.

nation-building, revolutionary change, or conflicts with neighbours. This has caused, in the words of former High Commissioner Hartling, 'the massive arrivals of refugees in low-income countries where often no durable solutions are at hand' (Hartling, 1983).

Today, most voluntary repatriations occur under conflict, without a decisive political event such as national independence, without any change in the regime or the conditions that originally caused flight. Countless individual refugees and sizeable groups of well-organized refugees return home in the face of continued risk, frequently without any amnesty, without a repatriation agreement or programme, without the permission of the authorities in either the country of asylum or of origin, without international knowledge or assistance, and without an end to the conflict that caused the exodus. Such returns raise serious questions of coercion and protection. Returning refugees to their homelands under circumstances of conflict will require new thinking about ways to aid return movements and areas of return. Implementation of a development assistance project under conflict conditions in the area of return may be nearly, if not totally, impossible.

The refugees are the main actors in the contemporary practice of voluntary repatriation. They are the main decision-makers and participate in determining the modalities of movement and the conditions of reception. Refugee-induced repatriation is a self-regulating process on the refugees' own terms. The refugees apply their own criteria to their situation in exile and to conditions in their homeland and will return home if it is safe and better by their standards.

Recent Repatriations
Below are brief descriptions of recent repatriations to Namibia, Mozambique, Ethiopia, Burundi, and Uganda. Only the first example, Namibia, fits the conditions for orderly and organized, internationally assisted repatriation. The other repatriations are more ambiguous and disorderly. Where the returns are organized, that organization is induced and controlled by the refugees.

Namibia
Joyous occasions are relatively rare when dealing with refugee problems. One such date was 21 March 1990 when Namibia became independent after decades of struggle. In anticipation of independence, 43,387 Namibian refugees were repatriated by UNHCR from Angola, Zambia, and 40 other countries. The refugees were registered while in exile, airlifted home, processed in reception centres, given rehabilitation assistance by a number of international agencies, and one year of food rations and material assistance to facilitate their integration into local society.

Mozambique
Mozambique is not as fortunate as Namibia; independent since 1975, it continues to be racked by a nightmarish civil war. The Renamo (Mozambican National Resistance) insurgency practises terror tactics against civilians, with many instances of massacre and mutilation of innocents. Mozambique has produced over one million refugees and a roughly equal number of internally displaced persons. Yet, in 1990, UNHCR (1990d) reported that 4,400 refugees returned to Mozambique with UNHCR assistance, but that 'as of 31 December 1989 . . . the number of returnees from Malawi, South Africa, Tanzania, Zambia and Zimbabwe was 208,000 persons, the great majority of whom had returned *spontaneously*'. The lion's share, 98 per cent of the Mozambican refugees, returned of their own accord, with little or no international assistance, to a homeland in conflict.

Burundi

In August 1988, ethnic violence, between the minority but politically dominant Tutsi and the majority Hutu, broke out in northern Burundi resulting in the deaths of over 5,000 villagers and soldiers and in the flight of some 50,000 refugees to southern Rwanda. Although this violence was only the latest in a long-standing conflict between Burundi's two major ethnic groups, which has resulted in thousands of deaths and hundreds of thousands of refugees, this time the result was different. By the end of 1988 almost all of these refugees had returned home. The returns were mostly refugee-induced, only a few thousand of the last returnees were transported by UNHCR or otherwise significantly assisted. The returns were in response to a number of constructive and conciliatory actions taken by the Government of Burundi and to an effective Tripartite Commission, which also had constructive co-operation from Zaire. The Government of Burundi has continued to pursue a policy of ethnic reconciliation. 'It made substantial changes in the education system and the civil service, as well as undertaking structural economic reform. The level of interethnic tension has been significantly reduced, but many steps remain to be taken' (US Department of State, 1990).

3.1 *People survive as best they can in the most awful circumstances: returning to an area of Mozambique liberated from Renamo, 1987 (AIM/9733/39/Sergio Santimano)*

Uganda

The initial flow of Ugandan refugees into Sudan began after the fall of Idi Amin in 1979. Through 1982, the number of Ugandans in Sudan grew to over a quarter of a million, as civilians fled the guerrilla war being waged in the northwest of their country and the abuses perpetrated by the Uganda National Liberation Army (UNLA). Although the UNHCR assisted some Ugandans to return home in 1984 and 1985, the vast majority remained in Sudan until after Museveni's National Resistance Army (NRA) defeated the UNLA and seized Kampala in January 1986.

The NRA take-over led to an improved security situation in much of Uganda, but it was not this development that prompted a mass repatriation so much as the outbreak of war in Sudan. Many of the Ugandans have established relatively affluent livelihoods in Sudan, and were unwilling to return to Uganda with all its political uncertainties. However, in April 1986 there were armed attacks on refugee settlements on the East Bank of the Nile, and several thousand refugees had no option other than to flee back to Uganda. The UNHCR and other international aid agencies became involved in assistance programmes, providing some transport and reception facilities. However, over 200,000 Ugandans remained on the West Bank of the Nile in Sudan until the fighting between the Sudan People's Liberation Army (SPLA) and Sudan government forces spread into their vicinity. Only when life became impossible did they too flee back into Uganda. Most had returned by the end of 1989, and were accompanied by several thousand Sudanese refugees. Studies of the relief operations in the area indicate that they were generally unsuccessful and that people had to manage as best they could in very difficult circumstances (Harrell-Bond and Kenyeihamba, 1986; Allen, 1993).

Tigray
In 1985, some 68,000 Tigrayan refugees returned from Sudan to Ethiopia at the height of the drought and famine, during a period of stepped-up military activity. The first returns occurred while massive numbers were still evacuating central Tigray. The return was aided by the indigenous Relief Society of Tigray (REST) and 'protected' by the Tigrayan People's Liberation Front (TPLF). Both UNHCR and the United States Government actively opposed the return and limited the aid others could give to the returnees. Only Sudan gave limited assistance. Despite great fears, most refugees returned home in good health, but without adequate agricultural inputs to securely re-establish themselves. Indeed, in 1986 even larger numbers (77,000) returned, some with limited international assistance. By the end of 1987, 164,000 of the original 190,000 Tigrayans to enter Sudan had returned home (Hendrie, 1990).

Of the repatriations described above, only the Namibian repatriation and, to a much lesser degree, the Burundi return fit contemporary international assumptions, beliefs and principles regarding return. The Tigray, Uganda, and Mozambique returns, and many other in Africa, are returns to ambiguous or conflictive political conditions. In the last few years almost one million African refugees have returned home, only about 100,000 of them through orderly and organized, internationally assisted repatriation.

In the last few years UNHCR has made significant efforts to promote voluntary repatriation more actively. In several Central American repatriations UNHCR undertook innovative measures to protect refugees, remain in contact with all parties, and promote return. Nonetheless, despite its importance as a durable solution, voluntary repatriation, particularly under conflict, is a difficult solution for UNHCR to implement. Given the irregular nature of many contemporary refugee movements, a large number of refugees never register with UNHCR while in the country of asylum. The forces controlling the area to which the refugees return may not be those of the sovereign government recognized by the UN. Countries of origin often assume returnees are part of an insurgent movement and thus refuse to approve their return. Many refugees fear that going through official channels to repatriate and being 'turned over' to their government would put them in danger or mark them as suspect. Lastly, although UNHCR's tripartite approach to repatriation is useful and important in a few cases, its pace is often slow and does not reflect the refugees' own pace and criteria for decision-making. In many situations, refugees return on their own rather than wait for formal action by UNHCR.

Varieties of Repatriation
Generally, if international agencies and governments do not initiate, manage and organize a voluntary repatriation, the international agencies refer to it as an unorganized or

3.2 *A flight from refuge: Ugandans returning from Sudan following attacks on refugee settlements in 1986 (UNHCR/no number/J. M. Goudstikka)*

spontaneous repatriation. However, as the Tigray repatriation shows most clearly, the failure or inability to provide international repatriation assistance does not mean there is a lack of organization. REST, TPLF, and the Sudanese Commissioner for Refugees (COR) provided substantial organization. They had woefully inadequate resources, unfortunately, due to the lack of international participation.

To a certain degree, it is better to avoid labelling types of repatriation and to concentrate instead on examining the range of repatriation experiences. It is useful to think of types of repatriation as lying along several continuums or spectrums. Amongst the possible continuums would be (1) whether a repatriation is unassisted or organized and by which actors; (2) the degree to which a repatriation is purely voluntary, encouraged, induced, or forced; (3) whether it is an individual, small group, or more sizeable collective return; and (4) a political conflict spectrum reflecting the degree to which there has been a significant change in the original cause of flight. Today, most repatriation occurs under far from ideal conditions. The repatriations occur under conflict and raise serious questions of coercion and protection. When refugees return under conflict, it greatly complicates the provision of long-term development aid to areas of return.

Some of the points along a repatriation under political conflict spectrum would be: (1) return after fundamental political change such as independence (Zimbabwe, Namibia); (2) return after a political settlement or major political change (Nicaragua); (3) return after a political settlement that does not end the political conflict and which leaves the contending parties with substantial political and military power (Afghanistan, Sri Lanka, Angola); (4) return to areas not controlled by the government of the country of origin (may be controlled by a rival political force or by local forces) (Tigray, Afghanistan, El Salvador, Mozambique); (5) return to a country controlled by the government that originally caused the flight (Guatemala); (6) return caused by deteriorating political security conditions in the host country (the post-1985 return from southern Sudan to Uganda, the 1989–1991 return from Somalia to Ethiopia); and (7) forced return of refugees to a conflict zone (Khmer Rouge controlled areas of Cambodia).

African Development Crisis

In 1989 the World Bank released another in a series of reports on Africa's continuing economic crisis. This crisis is, of course, important in its own right, but it also has an impact on the willingness of donor governments and development agencies to provide development assistance. The World Bank reported:

> Sub-Saharan Africa has now witnessed almost a decade of falling per capita incomes and accelerating ecological degradation . . . In the past decade six countries have slipped from the middle-income to the low-income group. If overvalued exchange rates were taken into account, more would have slipped.
> In many African countries the administrations, judiciaries, and educational institutions are now mere shadows of their former selves.
> Equally worrying is the widespread impression of political decline. Corruption, oppression, and nepotism are increasingly evident. These are hardly unique to Africa.
> Sometimes the military have deposed unpopular regimes. But often this has led to more, not less, state violence and lawlessness. Occasionally it has led even to civil war. These disruptions have driven many to become refugees, both directly by threatening lives and indirectly by making drought and other natural calamities harder to cope with. Sub-Saharan Africa, with one-tenth of the world's population, now accounts for about a third (or almost 4 million) of the world's officially recognized refugees. In addition the region has another 12 million or so displaced persons. (World Bank, 1989)

Africa's economic crisis means that development assistance to local areas of returnee influx will only be possible with funding by the international community. When refugees return under conflict to states run by corrupt and violent regimes, such international assistance is unlikely.

The World Bank view of African governments and of development in Africa is shared by many donor governments and other international agencies. Even African countries that are at peace and neither host nor cause refugees are seen as failing with regard to development. The willingness to aid repatriation regions cannot be divorced from this negative viewpoint which holds that Africa's elites have 'hijacked' the process of development. Whatever may be the 'desirability' of development programmes for returnee areas, it is unlikely that it will produce 'actual' programmes without rigorous efforts to ensure that the benefits reach the intended beneficiaries.

By definition, development-oriented returnee programmes will pass through the government of origin. If the government that originally caused the exodus is still in power, or if the refugees are self-repatriating to areas not controlled by their government or to areas where conflict continues, then there will be great reluctance on the part of donors and development agencies to deal with the offending origin government.

'Desirable' Aid to Return Movements & Areas of Return

The international community has adopted a series of principles, declarations, conclusions and reports which address the issue of the desirability of development-oriented assistance to facilitate the reintegration of returnees and the area to which they return. The most important of these international decisions are the 'Principles for Action in Developing Countries' (UNHCR, 1984), the 'Declaration and Programme of Action of the Second International Conference on Assistance to Refugees in Africa' (ICARA II) (UN, 1984), and the Report of the Meeting of Experts on Refugee Aid and Development (UNHCR, 1983). These principles regarding the desirability of development-oriented repatriation assistance were clarified and modified in 1989–90 in the context of the UNHCR financial crisis. In all of these discussions and conclusions development-oriented reintegration assistance has been treated as part of the larger issue of 'Refugee Aid and Development'.

Unfortunately, despite all this effort, the concept of refugee aid and development is still ill-defined. The failure to achieve a clear definition is directly related to a fundamental split between donor states and host states (and, to a lesser degree, origin states) about the nature and purpose of and responsibility for refugee assistance. This fundamental split about refugee assistance is far more than a terminological dispute; it is one of the root causes of the 1989–90 funding crisis of UNHCR which has sharply diminished global refugee protection and assistance.

UNHCR has drawn attention to the definitional difficulties caused by the 'plasticity' of the concept of development but has also noted that:

> this elusiveness of the concept 'development' partially disappears once the dialogue becomes more concrete in terms of 'refugee aid' and 'development assistance'. This is especially so, if each of these terms is understood in the sense they are given in the *Principles for Action in Developing Countries*, adopted by the thirty-fifth session of the Executive Committee (1984), namely, refugee aid is 'what refugees need to help themselves' and development assistance is 'what disadvantaged local people need'. *Obviously, these two descriptions do not stand up to close scrutiny.* [emphasis added] (UNHCR, 1989a)

The concept of refugee aid and development emerged in the late 1970s – it has earlier roots – precisely because of the failures of the traditional refugee assistance system that was narrowly focussed on life-sustaining, relief-oriented refugee assistance. What was apparent then was that giving only relief and emergency assistance to refugees leads to dependency, a life in limbo, and a heavy burden on the least-developed countries. Failure to pursue a durable solution means that life-sustaining, care and maintenance assistance becomes open-ended and expensive.

The problem with defining refugee aid and development is less a difficulty with the meaning of the words or the concept and more an issue of who is responsible for refugees and of institutional arrangements. Before getting to those issues, however, it is best to note the five key elements that define refugee aid and development. These five elements are present in both the declaration made at the second International Conference on Assistance to Refugees in Africa (ICARA II) and in the UNHCR's *Principles for Action in Developing Countries*. Refugee aid and development assistance is aid that:

(1) is development-oriented from the outset;
(2) moves refugees toward self-reliance and self-sufficiency;
(3) helps least-developed countries cope with the burden that refugees place on their infrastructure;
(4) may include the local population in the impacted area in the assistance programme; and
(5) is consistent with the national development plan of the host country (Stein, 1981; Aga Khan, 1981).[2]

On the more specific issue of the desirability of development-oriented aid in areas of return, the 1983 Meeting of Experts on Refugee Aid and Development elaborated several key points which have been accepted by the international community. First, reintegration assistance should include the population in the affected area. Second, development aid to areas of origin might encourage more repatriation. Lastly, reintegration assistance is more than merely returning refugees to their homes; successful reintegration will require long-term development assistance beyond the scope of UNHCR's mandate. The Experts stated:

> In the case of large-scale voluntary repatriation, an enduring international commitment to help, or even developmental investments for the benefit of returnees that would also benefit their compatriots in the affected areas, may well be needed to achieve successful reintegration. The returnees are likely, as a result of their ordeal, to be among the most needy elements in the country, but having been uprooted, they are also more likely to be receptive to development initiatives and new techniques.
>
> When there are indications that more refugees would seek repatriation if economic conditions in their areas of origin were better, and particularly where a large-scale exodus of refugees from a low-income area results not only from persecution or conflict, but also from economic deprivation or destruction . . . undertake projects or programmes which might encourage voluntary repatriation of greater numbers.
>
> To achieve the ultimate aim of successful reintegration of returnees into their society, rehabilitation assistance will often be required well beyond the initial period during which

---

[2] The ICARA II *Declaration*: 'For solutions to last, assistance to refugees and returnees must aim at their participation, productivity and durable self-reliance; it should be development-oriented as soon as possible and, in the least developed countries, it should take into account the needs of the local people as well'.

'. . . programmes should be development-oriented and . . . be linked to existing or planned economic and social development schemes for the area or region.'

The *Principles*: 'development-oriented projects are required that would generate work opportunities and . . . long-term livelihoods for refugees and local people in a comparable situation, through activities which . . . contribute to the overall development of the area.

'The projects should be consistent with existing and planned development schemes for the area.'

UNHCR can provide it. [It would be] . . . appropriate for UNHCR to alert . . . suitable developmental organizations and interested governments to the need for continued rehabilitation assistance beyond the scope of its own programme. (UNHCR, 1983)

Several recent repatriation programmes have reflected these points. Aid to the local population is needed because: 'Ethiopia was not merely a least-developed country, but also one of the poorest of the poor . . . The life of a considerable proportion of the local population was no better than that of the refugees whom Ethiopia was striving to assist' (UNHCR, 1990d). Further, the conflicts that produce refugees normally affect many other segments of the population. Nicaragua noted:

the task of national reconstruction had to be undertaken after a war which had affected approximately one third of the population, including 354,000 displaced persons, 40,000 repatriated persons, 7,500 refugees, 18,000 members of the demobilized resistance, excluding their families, 30,000 demobilized soldiers and some 80,000 civilians who had fled the country. (UNHCR, 1990e)

To attract returnees, the Afghan repatriation programme seeks: 'to put in place a set of incentives designed to redress the balance of humanitarian and economic services between areas of asylum and areas of origin of the Afghan refugees' (UNHCR, 1990e).

Types of Reintegration Assistance

Recent repatriation programmes, proposed or implemented, for Sri Lanka, Somalia, Ethiopia, Mozambique, and Afghanistan indicate the types of repatriation and reintegration assistance that are needed.

Sri Lanka's programme was 'designed to promote the resettlement of Sri Lankan returnees and afford assistance to internally displaced families'. 'In the longer term, the programme envisaged the rebuilding of infrastructure in affected areas and financial aid, vocational training and, where necessary, land for the returnees. Restoring damaged infrastructure was essential to the reintegration of refugees . . . for the benefit not only of target groups of refugees but also of local communities' (UNHCR, 1990e).

Somalia's rehabilitation programme was developed by a December 1989 joint mission to Somalia by officials of UNHCR, the European Community (EC), the World Bank and the United Nations Development Programme (UNDP) and approved by a Tripartite Commission. The refugee-affected areas project aimed at strengthening essential services in towns and other communities; protection of natural resources by rehabilitating the environment; and enhancement of marketing potential and encouragement of production by reinforcing basic infrastructure in the rural areas (UNHCR, 1990d).

The above programme for Somalia was part of an agreement with Ethiopia that included an effort to repatriate voluntarily 160,000 Ethiopian refugees from Somalia. Ethiopia noted that:

the onerous burden . . . was multidimensional and too heavy for Ethiopia to bear on its own . . . The rehabilitation assistance being provided to returnees must also be augmented with assistance for sustained development in the spirit of ICARA I and II and the report of the IFAD/UNHCR mission in the Ogaden so that it would in the long run benefit not only the refugee and returnee communities but also the local population at large . . . The future of the refugees lay in the hands of the international donor community. Neglect of such vital areas of assistance as education, training and development was a matter of grave concern. (UNHCR, 1990d)

Mozambique's reintegration programme is more modest, focussing on providing for the basic needs of the returnees 'in the sectors of food, transport, shelter, water, sanitation and health, agricultural assistance, education, income generation and agency support' (UNHCR, 1990d).

Afghanistan's approximately six million refugees in Pakistan and Iran are currently the world's largest refugee problem. Despite the withdrawal of Soviet troops in 1989 a massive repatriation has not yet materialized. Nonetheless, extensive contingency plans have been made for the return movement and development assistance inside Afghanistan. Priority activities focus on the rehabilitation of community infrastructure including: 'promotion of crop production; repair to water channels; underground irrigation canal cleaning; basic repairs to access roads; repairs to public buildings, such as warehouses, silos, etc.; and provision of construction materials' (UNHCR, 1989c).

The above programmes indicate that merely getting refugees home is not enough. Desirable and necessary repatriation assistance must include not only the returnees, but also the local areas of return, and in most cases the whole civil society. While assistance has to address the immediate basic needs of the returnees, it must also rebuild or restore the comr unity and economic infrastructure and essential services as well as repair the damage to the environment. Provision of land to returnees, restoration of agricultural land and services, and the encouragement of production and marketing are likely to be necessary. Massive problems and conflicts produce massive refugee flows. The reintegration of mass returnees involves major rehabilitation and development activities requiring international funding. An evaluation of the Nicaragua returnee programme indicates the difficulty when reintegration assistance is limited.

> The future waves of returnees would find the original network of communities . . . sufficiently re-established to absorb their return, but no more. The question was now the need for the socio-economic reactivation of the region as a whole.
> UNHCR was conscious of the limitations of their own programs as well as the urgent need for the next stage to begin . . . [They] had created the minimal conditions, a starting point, from which integral development aid could then begin. (Barry, 1990)

'Actual' Reintegration Assistance

In practice, despite agreement in principle, actual reintegration assistance, either to the process of return or as development-oriented aid, falls far short of what is desirable. Three main problems limit actual reintegration assistance: operational issues regarding which international agency should provide development-oriented assistance; a lack of funding for reintegration assistance; and a fundamental difficulty related to repatriation under conflict which leads to the 'insufficiency of the development approach alone' (Gallagher and Diller, 1990) to resolve problems relating to returnees. The operational issue is difficult but not insurmountable. However, sufficient funding for reintegration assistance in conditions of repatriation under conflict is highly unlikely.

Operational Issues

For many years there has been an informal belief that UNHCR assistance to repatriation should be time-limited, generally to a period of less than one year. Repatriated refugees are no longer refugees, they have re-established a relationship with their country. UNHCR's role in their reintegration is thus limited.

The problem with development-oriented reintegration assistance is that it involves development aid and UNHCR is not a development agency. Consistently, the Executive Committee has indicated that UNHCR can be a catalyst and prime mover initiating development-oriented assistance but someone else must take on and finish the job. The prime candidate for this role has always been the UNDP. The *Principles for Action in Developing Countries* (1984) state that:

- UNHCR, while being the focal point for durable solutions, should not assume the role of a development agency . . . the High Commissioner's role should be essentially that of a catalyst and co-ordinator: he should initiate suitable projects, promote their development by a competent organization . . . and then promote their financing.
- Development projects aimed essentially at repairing or improving . . . economic or social infrastructure . . . should as a rule be handled by UNDP and/or other developmental organizations. (UNHCR, 1984)

Bradford Morse, then Administrator of UNDP, told ICARA II that 'UNDP stands ready' to actively participate, to ensure that developmental projects 'will be co-ordinated with other development activities of the UN system . . . and integrated into the development plans and programmes of the countries concerned' (Morse, 1984).

However, in terms of institutional mandates, UNHCR's mandate does not overlap or touch UNDP's mandate. This gap in mandates meant that from 1984 until 1989 there was a vacuum regarding refugee aid and development. Indeed, it was not until after UNHCR's extraordinary Executive Committee session in 1990 that UNDP's Governing Council took action 'recognizing that relief, rehabilitation, reconstruction, and development, are part of the same continuum' and encouraged UNDP 'to play an active role in assisting concerned Governments . . . to take into account the problems of refugees . . . in their development plans and programmes' (UNDP, 1990a and 1990b).

As welcome as this UNDP decision is, it still leaves a structural and institutional gap. At a 1989 Executive Committee session then Deputy High Commissioner Dewey noted:

The fourth myth was that international development agencies should play a more active role in the funding and implementation of the material assistance activities needed to increase the viability of lasting solutions . . . However, those agencies would need to undergo fundamental structural and procedural changes before that new distribution of tasks could be put into effect. *They would need to acquire an operational capacity, primarily by using NGOs [non-government organizations as executing partners, as well as a rapid response capability in order to take over from UNHCR. All that would take time.* [emphasis added] (UNHCR, 1989b)

At its fortieth session (1989) the Executive Committee strongly reined in UNHCR's development activities. It reached 'Conclusions and Decisions on Refugee Aid and Development' that echoed the earlier *Principles* but then added conclusions on 'Sharing of Responsibility for Operational Activities Relating to Refugees':

(1) Recalling the particular responsibilities assigned by the United Nations General Assembly to UNDP in matters pertaining to development.
(2) Calls on the High Commissioner to establish in his operation programmes, a distinction on the one hand between tasks that relate directly and essentially to his mandate, namely international protection, assistance and the search for durable solutions and, on the other hand, the tasks that could be undertaken in whole or in part by other agencies of the United Nations system . . . in particular development initiatives.
(3) Calls on the High Commissioner to . . . establish, in relation to activities that do not derive directly from his mandate, especially those dealing with development, a close working relationship between UNHCR and the relevant agencies of the United Nations system . . . that will assure an agreed division of responsibilities and arrangements for the financing of these activities.

3.3 *There have been high level discussions about international assistance for returned refugees, but many populations are overlooked: Sudanese refugees fleeing back into their war-torn country following attacks on refugee settlements in Ethiopia, 1991 (UNHCR/21051/B. Press)*

3.4 *Short-term aid is often focussed on relief efforts and the rebuilding of facilities, but longer-term development programmes are needed to restore the social networks essential for investment, trade, increasing agricultural production and the re-establishing of communities: construction site for a child welfare centre in Mozambique, 1977 (UNHCR/7172/S. Vieira de Mello)*

(4) Requests in this regard, the High Commissioner to enter into consultations as soon as possible with UNDP . . . to examine the conditions and modalities of an appropriate implementing mechanism, for development projects relating to refugees. (UNHCR, 1989a)

In an intervention typical of the donors regarding repatriation assistance, Canada indicated that:

by drawing a clear distinction between his own mandate and those of other agencies the High Commissioner was ensuring that he would conserve his resources for use in situations which clearly fell within his mandate. For example, UNHCR should have the lead responsibility for the repatriation and safety of South African refugees and exiles . . . leaving their later resettlement mainly to South African organizations. (UNHCR, 1990a)

UNDP

The international community clearly intends for UNDP to step in and fill the gap created by the restrictions placed on UNHCR. UNDP has been courted, cajoled and recruited to take a leading role in refugee-related development assistance. In 1983, at the initiative of the Secretary-General, UNDP was brought into the ICARA II process. Struggling at the time with an 'unparalleled downturn' in its own resources UNDP was a hesitant, reluctant and uninterested participant. Only in 1990 did UNDP's Governing Council finally take action on refugee aid and development. However, the policy paper prepared for UNDP's Governing Council offers a view of refugee aid and development which is unacceptable to most donor countries.

There is one development process in a given country . . . It is the country and its Government who bear the main responsibility for its own development. Although refugees are a special case . . . they are not the only ones affected . . . Accordingly, it is for the country and its government to determine the position and role refugees can and should play in the development process. (Denes, 1990)

UNDP's troubles in the 1980s in some ways parallel UNHCR's financial crisis. The problem that caused the donors to withhold support was that the developing countries had taken control of UNDP's country programmes. Although UNDP negotiates the use of the IPF (indicative planning figure) for each country, its power was limited to 'recognizing the sovereignty of the recipient country in determining its own priorities' (UNDP, 1982). Thus the country programme is 'based on what projects the government would like UNDP to fund in line with its national development objectives' (US General Accounting Office, 1990). The donor response to UNDP's compliance with recipient's wishes was to give UNDP meagre support and to shift funding elsewhere. The United States General Accounting Office report is not encouraging in its view of UNDP.

The Program is not fulfilling its designated role as the central funding channel and coordinating body for U.N. technical assistance . . . For the most part, other U.N. projects are not coordinated or integrated into an overall country plan . . . Other U.N. agencies operate independently and have their own mandates. About 4,700 Program-funded projects . . . are small and scattered, they have limited impact on the priority development needs of recipient countries. (US General Accounting Office, 1990)

In circumstances of repatriation under conflict, where the basic breach between the returnees and homeland may not have been closed, it is doubtful that low-income countries of origin will use their IPF monies for the benefit of returnees of suspect loyalty.

Further, UNDP's structural constraints – lack of an operational capacity and a long project gestation period – suggest caution in viewing it as protector and provider for returnees.

Some hope does emerge, however, from UNDP's experience in working with Central American refugees in the context of the 1989 International Conference on Central American Refugees (CIREFCA) and its 1990 follow-up session. UNDP is managing and co-ordinating the Development Programme for Displaced Persons, Refugees, and Returnees in Central America (PRODERE) which, 'with its total cost of $110 million (mostly contributed by Italy), is the largest single operation ever undertaken by UNDP' (Denes, 1990). PRODERE has good prospects because it is linked with the momentum towards regional peace and development that has been gathering since the August 1987 Esquipulas II agreement, commonly known as the Arias Peace Plan. 'PRODERE originated . . . as an alternate means of assistance to uprooted peoples . . . aim[s] at promoting self-sustained development through grassroots projects . . . in conflictive zones' (Gallagher and Diller, 1990).

UNDP and the entire UN system are able to work effectively on PRODERE, up to a point, because there is a regional peace movement and the concerned countries are willing to integrate the refugees and returnees. The great problem confronting the international community in the future will be how to take care of returnees when the country of origin is not willing to reintegrate them or lacks control of the region to which the refugees have returned.

Failure to Fund Reintegration

Many repatriation and returnee reintegration programmes in Africa and on other continents are not being properly funded by the international community. At the 1990 Executive Committee, Sweden noted: 'because of lack of contributions, ongoing repatriation programmes were being hampered or even halted' (UNHCR, 1990b).

At the same meeting, Angola protested that approximately 29,000 Angolan refugees, who continued to live in poor conditions without any status remained to be repatriated from Zaire. It noted that:

> A two-way repatriation between Angola and Zaire began by air in September 1989. Nearly 6,500 Angolans and over 3,000 Zairians had been repatriated when the operation was temporarily suspended in March 1990 as a result of financial constraints and operational considerations. More Angolan refugees are wishing to repatriate . . . if political developments and resources permit.
>
> Financial and logistical difficulties encountered in supplying basic food and minimum construction and agricultural materials to the returnees to ensure their smooth reintegration in Angolan society, necessitated the suspension of the operation. (UNHCR, 1990d)

Tragically, in Shaba, many of the Angolan refugees who had hoped to repatriate had 'abandoned their fields and sold their possessions'.

Mozambique is experiencing both a continued exodus and some voluntary repatriation. The returnees go to safe areas in Mozambique where there are opportunities for integration.

> The overall aim of the programme was to facilitate the reintegration of the returnees. Basic needs were provided to new returnees and in the sectors of food, transport, shelter, water, sanitation and health, agricultural assistance, education, income-generation and agency support.
>
> The poor response to the 1989/90 appeal led to disruptions in the smooth flow of assistance

that is critical to the success of any repatriation/returnee exercise. Due to lack of funds, activities in the returnee programme could concentrate only on providing emergency food/relief supplies and limited agricultural inputs. Sectors such as water, health and sanitation could not be covered and the activities of the NGOs . . . were severely affected. (UNHCR, 1990d)

Repatriation programmes to Somalia, Ethiopia, Nicaragua, Afghanistan, and elsewhere are all suffering from a lack of funds. 'Unfortunately, there were no signs of forthcoming aid. . . . And there were no other UN agencies willing to work in these regions' (Barry, 1990).

There is strong evidence that the international community is failing to provide both ad hoc assistance to returnees and developmental aid to returnee areas. This failure is both financial and organizational. Not only is the funding inadequate, but the implementation measures and identification of responsible agencies are also lacking. It appears that as refugees return home the international community loses interest in their cause and needs, and the community's attention shifts elsewhere. There are many complaints by countries of origin – Nicaragua, Angola, Mozambique – that the extensive political and military aid that went to the destabilizing activities of refugee warriors and exile groups has not followed them home. There appears to be something askew with a system that can provide guns to exiles but fails to provide the same individuals with seed and tools after they have returned home. The problem, however, is that often refugees do not return home in peace.

When refugee assistance moves from humanitarian aid toward development aid there is a shift in leverage in favour of the donors. Humanitarian aid has a compelling dramatic immediacy about it that makes it difficult for donors to stand on the sidelines. Lives are at stake and aid rushes in. Development-oriented refugee assistance, on the other hand, is after the emergency, conditions have stabilized, the danger is past, and, whatever the compelling arguments in favour of development aid, the drama and urgency are missing. Donors asked to fund unsatisfactory projects can sit on their purses. Countries of origin must take serious account of donor views if their projects are to go forward.

Conflict & Development

Refugee problems demand durable solutions. A genuinely durable solution means integration of the refugees into a society, such as reintegration in the country of origin after voluntary repatriation. A durable solution, reintegration, is not assured in cases of repatriation under conflict. The basic bond between citizen (refugee) and government (of origin) has not been repaired, trust has not yet taken the place of fear, and loyalty the place of hatred. Most repatriation is occurring without a basic change in the government that originally caused the flight.

In most of the African repatriations that have occurred in the past few years, the country of origin is not at peace. In Chapter 2, Rogge lists approximately one million returnees since 1988 to Burundi, Chad, Ethiopia, Mozambique, Angola, Uganda, Namibia, Rwanda, Zaire, and Zimbabwe. Of these, only Burundi, Namibia, and Zimbabwe are at peace or welcomed the refugees home in a spirit of significant reconciliation.

Repatriation under conflict is refugee-induced or stimulated. It is self-repatriation motivated by the refugees' desire to achieve relative security and some degree of control over their lives. Repatriation decisions may have little to do with the actions and policies of the government of their homeland; refugees may be fleeing insecurity or hopelessness in their host country or returning to home regions not controlled by the government of origin. Many refugees practise ebb and flow repatriation – where they follow a strategy of return and departure to an unsettled region that experiences a cycle of peace and turmoil.

As a system of sovereign states, the UN system is constrained to provide development aid through governments. In the case of development-oriented reintegration assistance that would mean the aid would pass through the hands a government of origin that has played little or no role in advancing a durable solution.

In the debates about refugee aid and development and development-oriented reintegration assistance there are two points of view regarding the nexus between peace and development. One view holds that development assistance is necessary to the achievement of peace, that without programmes addressing the 'the underlying social and economic structural deficiencies' (Gallagher and Diller, 1990) of a society, political power differences cannot be resolved. The other view holds that development assistance is nearly impossible without peace. The political settlement must precede, rather than follow, the assistance. The donor community, as indicated by its unwillingness to fund reintegration assistance in situations of repatriation under conflict, follows the peace before development view.

Gallagher and Diller (1990) have outlined four factors, among others, that are responsible for the failure of the development alone approach in Central America. These factors are:

(1) social and political polarization in areas of conflict,
(2) potential for harmful rather than beneficial results of assistance,
(3) insufficient political resolve on the part of governments, and
(4) limited accountability for projects undertaken.

Repatriation under conflict is by far the most common form of contemporary repatriation. In many cases the returnees and the government have made no effort to resolve their political conflicts. In some cases the refugees are clearly hostile to their government or are returning to areas controlled by insurgent forces. 'In El Salvador returnees and displaced persons reside in areas of armed conflict, and any development effort on their behalf is inevitably influenced by national security concerns' (Gallagher and Diller, 1990). Implementation of development programmes in areas of high polarization is nearly impossible.

'The development approach has proved harmful in circumstances where development programs have been used by the government or military as tools of repression' (Gallagher and Diller, 1990). Development projects can be used for counter-insurgency, to force the relocation of suspect populations, to aid in the pacification of regions. Development assistance in situations of conflict could be used to harm the intended beneficiaries. In 1985, Ethiopia's programme to relocate hundreds of thousands of people from the highlands to the lowlands was severely criticized:

> Refugee movement to the Sudan has also been triggered by a program which the Ethiopian government says is a response to the famine . . . Western organizations and governments . . . have criticized the program saying its real purpose is to remove the population from dissident areas. Authorities have reportedly forced people onto resettlement trucks at gunpoint or by withholding relief food. (US Committee for Refugees, 1986)

When the population to receive aid consists of enemies, suspects, or former enemies it is easy to doubt the political resolve of the country of origin. The lack of resolve stems from an ambivalence toward the returnees arising from the mixture of security and humanitarian concerns. Especially in circumstances of internal competition for resources it would take a government firmly committed to reconciliation to direct programmes to those whose support is not assured. Lastly, reflecting the conflict that caused the refugee flow, there may be deep splits within the governing elements in the government of origin. In Guatemala, conciliatory measures promoted by the civil authorities were routinely undercut by military actions.

Refugees located in conflictive areas may be viewed with suspicion by the origin government, but they may benefit from their ability to articulate their needs, from their identity and cohesiveness as a threatened community, and from political support both within their homeland and from outside groups that may have assisted them during their exile. Refugees have demonstrated an impressive ability to organize collectively. They may bring home new leaders and skills. The *masivas* to El Salvador represent a model of repatriation whereby the repatriates are organized to protect and promote their collective interests (Fagen and Eldrige, 1990).

One potential argument in favour of investing developmental funds in returnee areas is the possibility of greater investment success in projects involving migrants. This is an understudied subject, but there are findings (Keller, 1975) which suggest that refugees are altered by the exile experience. Besides developing new skills and attitudes they have been forced out of the social and cultural systems that may have constrained them. In the trial of exile, many have discovered unsuspected strengths and confidence, become more aggressive and willing to take risks. The activities of aid agencies during exile may have enhanced the refugees' organizational and problem-solving skills.

With regard to desirability of development aid, as distinct from short-term return assistance and efforts to restore or rehabilitate destroyed or damaged facilities to their pre-exile level of functioning, to the local areas where refugees return an added complication is the fact that the presence of returnees does not necessarily convert a region into a desirable focus for development activities. In an environment of great and numerous human needs and intense competition for scarce development resources, investment strategies need to be carefully devised to produce national benefits. A region of refugee return is not necessarily the most potentially productive area or a suitable focus for infrastructural assistance. Such development projects might be the wrong project in the wrong place with the wrong needs, thus skewing the national development plan. This is not to argue against development assistance to returnee regions, but to remind those whose primary concern is refugee assistance that the presence of repatriated refugees is just one of many factors that need to be evaluated in the course of development decisions.

Conclusion

What is described above is a very unsatisfactory situation. The ability of refugees to take matters into their own hands and organize repatriations is a hopeful sign. But often they are forced into this position by hopelessness, danger, and lack of assistance. Iran has charged that: 'For the refugees, reduced assistance constituted an attempt to force them to return to their country'. What is the connection between malnourished refugee children in Malawi and 'spontaneous repatriation' to Mozambique? The *masivas* to conflict zones in El Salvador grew out of the hostile, hopeless situation in the closed refugee camps in Honduras. Attacks on refugee settlements in southern Sudan have driven hundreds of thousands of refugees back to Uganda.

The international community has failed to provide durable solutions for millions of refugees. It compounds this failure by failing to promote and support voluntary repatriation effectively. At the 1990 Extraordinary Executive Committee of UNHCR, several countries of origin, such as Angola, Ethiopia, and Somalia, complained bitterly that 'refugees were awaiting the helping hand of the international community in order to return home' but the funding crisis had reduced repatriation programmes.

In principle, voluntary repatriation is the most desirable durable solution. The international community is on record as supporting not only the return home of refugees but also development-oriented assistance to promote reintegration and to reconstruct homelands and regions of return.

In practice, however, much remains to be done. Actual assistance to voluntary repatriation and reintegration is meagre. Part of the difficulty is a lacuna in the mandates of international agencies. UNHCR cannot provide development assistance and no other agency stands ready to provide and implement development-oriented reintegration programmes. UNDP may evolve to fill this role, but its progress in this direction has been slow and reluctant. UNDP's ability to attract funding for reintegration projects will depend on much greater accountability by countries of origin with regard to the use of international monies.

The heart of the problems with repatriation and reintegration assistance is the nature of contemporary returns. Most returns take the form of repatriation under conflict without a resolution of the political issues that originally caused an exodus. A lack of peace, failure to reconcile, and continuing conflict are not conducive to long-term development programmes. Donor governments are singularly unimpressed by the argument that development assistance can precede and produce peace. Their 'show me' attitude demands progress towards political reconciliation by the governments of origin before investments will be made.

Repatriation is not a panacea. Where is 'home' for those in exile for thirty years or for those born in exile? Hostile, ill-prepared homelands still embroiled in conflict are not ideal arenas for reintegration and protection.

In October 1990, Rwandan refugees from Uganda invaded their homeland. For thirty years the Rwandans had lived in Uganda; in the mid-1970s UNHCR declared their settlements had achieved self-sufficiency. However, neither the original refugees nor their children were given citizenship. In the early 1980s the settlements were attacked by Ugandans and many refugees fled, temporarily, to Rwanda. The 1990 invasion by the younger generation of Rwandan refugees was the product of thirty years of statelessness, hopelessness, pain, and frustration.

The dilemma is that no durable solution is offered to most refugees. Confronted with this harsh reality many refugees explore the possibility of going home. In the absence of coercion, repatriation is a self-regulating process. Refugees will voluntarily repatriate if and when they believe they will receive sufficient protection. Protection, security, more control over one's fate are the key variables in repatriation under conflict. Protection is a perceived political 'space' or opening that provides refugees not only relative physical security, but also material and moral support. The space may be so narrow that only single refugees can return, or it may be understood so broadly as to permit a collective return.

Nonetheless, despite significant protection worries, there is a need to actively promote voluntary repatriation, even under conflict. In an imperfect world that only offers long-term temporary asylum to most refugees, there is a need to assist refugees to go home. In the real world it is inadequate to protest that contemporary repatriation is problematic; confronted with unsatisfactory options one must seek to find the best that is available. Rather than a passive international approach, repatriation should be carefully and actively promoted even before the formal end of hostilities. And repatriation should be seen as a tool for reducing confrontations along tense borders, for expanding or securing zones of peace and stability for returnees, and possibly as an encouragement to talks between the adversaries.

Many of the almost one million refugees who returned home under imperfect conditions in the last few years have stayed at home. Many are in desperate circumstances, but they do not flee again. This is not to suggest that the end justifies the means, that forcing refugees to go home against their will is somehow justified if they are not persecuted or attacked. However, the fact that large numbers of refugees choose to return without international 'protection' tells us something about the efficacy of the protection process and the fact that many are willing to forgo assistance indicates how aid is regarded during this point in a refugee's exile. It is evident from the number of repatriations to date that the end of conflict is not a precondition for repatriation and that suggests there are political possibilities that need to be explored.

References

Aga Khan, Sadruddin (1981) *Study on human rights and massive exoduses*, United Nations Economic and Social Council, Commission on Human Rights, 38th Sess., E/CN.4/1503, 31 December.

Allen, Tim (1993) *Social and economic aspects of mass 'voluntary' return of refugees from Sudan to Uganda between 1986 and 1992*, a report for UNRISD, Geneva, February.

Barry, Deborah (1990) *Nicaragua: evaluation of the impact of UNHCR's assistance program for returnees*, unpublished paper, Managua, 30 June.

Denes, Oto (1990) 'Assistance to refugees, returnees and displaced persons: considerations on policy and appropriate methodology', revised version, UNDP, mimeo, February.

Fagen, Patricia Weiss, and Eldrige, Joseph (1990) 'The Salvadorian repatriations from Honduras', draft case study report to the International Study on Spontaneous Voluntary Repatriation, July.

Gallagher, Dennis and Diller, Janelle M. (1990) 'CIREFCA: At the crossroads between uprooted people and development in Central America', Commission for the Study of International Migration and Cooperative Economic Development, Working Paper No. 27, Washington, DC.

Grahl-Madsen, Atle (1966) *The status of refugees in international law*, I: *Refugee character*, A. W. Sijthoff, Leyden.

Harrell-Bond, Barbara, and Kenyeihamba, G. (1986) 'Returnees and refugees – EEC mission to Uganda', mimeo.

Hartling, Paul (1983) 'Opening Statement' to Meeting of Experts on Refugee Aid and Development, Mont Pelerin, Switzerland, August.

Hendrie, Barbara (1990) 'The Tigrayan refugee repatriation: Sudan to Ethiopia 1985–1987', a study prepared for the Intertect Institute, Dallas.

Keller, Stephen (1975) *Uprooting and social change: the role of refugees in development*, Manohar Book Service, Delhi.

Morse, Bradford (1984) 'Statement by Mr Bradford Morse, Administrator of the United Nations Development Programme to the Second International Conference on Assistance to Refugees in Africa', Geneva, 9 July.

Stein, Barry N. (1981) *Refugees and economic activities in Africa*, a research report submitted to the Agency for International Development (OTR–0000–0–00–1150–00), August.

UN (1984) 'Declaration and Programme of Action of the Second International Conference on Assistance to Refugees in Africa', General Assembly (A/CONF.125/L.1), 10 July.

UNDP (1982) *The future role and structure of UNDP*, Governing Council, 29th Sess., DP/1982/5, 16 April.

—— (1990a) 'Refugees and displaced persons: the present and future role of UNDP', mimeo, final draft for Governing Council, 37th Sess., DP/1990/66.

—— (1990b) 'Refugees, displaced persons, and returnees'. Governing Council Decision 90/22.

UNHCR (1983) *Refugee aid and development*, Executive Committee, 34th Sess., A/AC.96/635, December.

—— (1984) *Report of the 35th Session of the Executive Committee of the High Commissioner Programme*, United Nations, General Assembly, Executive Committee of the High Commissioner's Programme, 35th Sess., A/AC.96/651, 26 October.

—— (1985) *Executive Committee of the High Commissioner's Programme, 36th Session: report of the Sub-Committee of the Whole on international protection*, UNHCR, Geneva.

—— (1989a) *Summary record of the 441st meeting*, United Nations, General Assembly, Executive Committee of the High Commissioner's Programme, 40th Sess., A/AC.96/SR.441, 16 October.

— (1989b) *Summary record of the 444th meeting*, United Nations, General Assembly, Executive Committee of the High Commissioner's Programme, 40th Sess., A/AC.96/SR.444, 10 November.

— (1989c) *UNHCR activities financed by voluntary funds: report for 1988–89 and proposed programmes and budget for 1990*, Part V, *South West Asia, North Africa and the Middle East and Overall Allocations*, United Nations, General Assembly, Executive Committee of the High Commissioner's Programme, 40th Sess., A/AC.96/724 (Part V), 15 August.

— (1990a) *Summary record of the 454th meeting*, United Nations, General Assembly, Executive Committee of the High Commissioner's Programme, 41st Sess., A/AC.96/SR.454, 4 October.

— (1990b) *Summary record of the 456th meeting*, United Nations, General Assembly, Executive Committee of the High Commissioner's Programme, 41st Sess., A/AC.96/SR.456, 5 October.

— (1990c) *Summary record of the 457th meeting*, United Nations, General Assembly, Executive Committee of the High Commissioner's Programme, 41st Sess., A/AC.96/SR.457, 24 October.

— (1990d) *UNHCR activities financed by voluntary funds: report for 1989–90 and proposed programmes and budget for 1991*, Part I, *Africa*, United Nations, General Assembly, Executive Committee of the High Commissioner's Programme, 41st Sess., A/AC.96/751 (Part I), 17 August.

— (1990e) *UNHCR activities financed by voluntary funds: report for 1989–90 and proposed programmes and budget for 1991*, Part V, *South West Asia, North Africa and the Middle East and Overall Allocations*, United Nations, General Assembly, Executive Committee of the High Commissioner's Programme, 41st Sess., A/AC.96/751 (Part V), 15 August.

US Committee for Refugees (1986) *World refugee survey: 1985 in review*, American Council for Nationalities Service, New York.

US General Accounting Office (1990) *United Nations: U.S. participation in the U.N. Development Program*, United States General Accounting Office, Washington, DC, GAO/NSIAD-90-64, February.

US Department of State (1990) *World refugee report*, Bureau for Refugee Programs, Washington, DC, September.

World Bank (1989) *Sub-Saharan Africa: from crisis to sustainable growth*, World Bank, Washington, DC.

4 AMMAR BOUHOUCHE
The Return of Algerian Refugees following Independence in 1962[1]

When the Algerian war of independence began in 1954, it was inconceivable for the majority of people that they would one day be forced to flee their country and live in exile. But in 1958, when each side tried to step up military operations and win the conflict, many civilians found themselves squeezed between the French army and the Front de Libération National (FLN). What made things worse for families settled close to Algeria's international borders was the decision taken by the French army to create 'no-go' areas. People living near the frontiers had to leave their homes if they were within 45 kilometres of the Tunisian or Moroccan border. As a result, refugees began to leave Algeria. By 1962, the number of refugees in Tunisia and Morocco had risen to 300,000. According to the statistics of the Algerian Red Crescent Society, there were 160,000 refugees in Tunisia and 140,000 in Morocco. Of those 300,000, about 50 per cent were children under fifteen years of age, 35 per cent were women, and 15 per cent were men who were mostly too old to join the rebel forces.

At the same time, the French authorities started to expel civilians from areas which had become nationalist strongholds, and in other places they forced the population to stay in fenced camps during the day. By uprooting villagers from their ancestral homes and fields, and placing them in barbed wire encampments where they lived bewildered and listless lives, the French bequeathed independent Algeria a large impoverished and psychologically disturbed mass of people (Gordon, 1966: 64).

Once they were safely across a border, the refugees closely followed the events of the war. They were kept informed by Arabic language radio stations, and in particular by 'The Voice of Algeria', a daily two-hour programme broadcast from Tunis, Tangiers and Cairo. This programme was a platform for the nationalist leadership, and provided news and political education. Eventually it informed people when they could return home.

The refugees began to prepare for repatriation after the Evian Agreements, signed on 18 March 1962, but it was another two months before the process was set underway.

[1] I wish to express particular thanks and gratitude to Mr Sultan Guebaili and Mr Mohamed El-hadi Moussaoui who introduced me to the individuals I interviewed, and who participated in the process of organizing the group discussions in Souk Ahras Derahmma and Souk Ahras from 24 to 26 October 1990. I also would like to thank Dr Kwami Arhin of the University of Ghana and Dr John Rogge of the University of Manitoba in Canada for their critical comments on this paper during the symposium in Harare in March 1991.

4.1 *Among the Algerian refugees there were more than twice as many adult women as men because most of the young men were fighting with the nationalist forces: Algerian refugees in Morocco, 1960 (UNHCR/552/Stanley Wright)*

4.2 *Adequate funds were not made available for the UNHCR to provide transportation, but trucks were allocated by the Algerian Liberation Army: Algerian refugees arriving from Tunisia (UNHCR/no number/S. Wright)*

As late as 15 May it was reported that there was no indication that any efforts had been made to assist in the return, or plans to help them when they reached Algeria (Brace and Brace, 1965: 207). The reason for the delay was that repatriation of refugees depended on decisions taken by the Executive Power of the provisional government, formed jointly by French officials and the FLN.

The Evian Agreements stipulated that:

> Refugees abroad can re-enter Algeria. Committees to be set up in Morocco and Tunisia will facilitate this return. Displaced persons who have been regrouped can come back to their place of abode or normal residence. The Executive Power will take the preliminary social, economic and other measures, destined to ensure the return of those people to normal life.

However, it was also stated that 'the French forces stationed within the frontiers would not withdraw before the proclamation of the results of self-determination' (quoted in Benkhedda, 1986: 76 and 81). Therefore, the refugees could not actually cross the border into Algeria until the interim government authorized them to do so.

The FLN were eager to bring refugees home as soon as possible to ensure their participation in the referendum on national self-determination, but behind the scenes was a conflict between the French government and a secret organization within the army, which was determined to keep Algeria French. Considerable pressures had to be brought to bear in order to force the military's acceptance of the Evian Agreements, and to prevent it supporting the continued resistance of some French settlers.

In the meantime, the UNHCR had become formally committed to help facilitate the repatriation. The organization worked together with the League of the Red Cross and Red Crescent Societies, and seems to have managed to persuade the nationalists to take a more benevolent approach to the returnees' needs. There appears to have been a degree of antipathy among some of those who had fought in the war towards those who had left the country, and initially the Algerian Red Crescent had insisted that the refugees return home without bringing anything with them. This decision was reversed, and returnees were allowed to bring back their belongings. The UNHCR was also able to set up medical teams, and provided 15,000 tents for temporary accommodation. Adequate funds were not made available for transportation, but trucks were allocated by the Algerian Liberation Army, and the majority of returnees crossed the border in these vehicles.

In Morocco the repatriation programme began on 10 May and ended on 25 July 1962. During this time 61,400 people were registered as having received aid from the committee in charge of the refugees. In Tunisia, repatriation started officially on 30 May and continued until 20 July. Around 120,000 persons received assistance. The total number of registered returnees was 200,000. Another 100,000 either remained abroad or returned under their own auspices. Most of those who returned arrived before 3 July, and were able to participate in the referendum. The final result was that, out of six million voters, 5,971,581 voted for independence (Montagnon, 1984: 400).

In 1962, the Algerian government's most urgent need was to re-establish order after the war, and to cope with the serious effects of the mass exodus of French administrators and technicians. The treasury of the newly created Algerian state was empty and the economy was still tied to that of France. Half the labour force was unemployed. With 4.5 million Algerians deemed to be in a state of total poverty, it was only American surplus wheat that kept the population alive over the first months of independence (Horn, 1977: 540). In these circumstance it was not possible to devote substantial resources to the reintegration of refugees.

The returnees were initially taken to reception centres. They were then provided with registration cards and transported to transit centres from where they could be reunited with their families. Very few returnees remained in the transit centres for any length of time, and practically everyone was able to return to his or her home. The majority were warmly welcomed home by their relatives, and were helped in dealing with the hardships of re-establishing their livelihoods.

The war had had tragic consequences for virtually everyone, but the prospect of independence had produced a tremendous sense of optimism about the future, and a spirit of co-operation could make the worst hardships bearable. Any antipathy towards refugees among the nationalist leaders and veterans was not generally reflected at the local level. One informant explained that

> every family had suffered from the loss of many persons who used to cultivate land and raise cattle. The death or disappearance of such persons from the labour market created a vacuum in the field of agriculture, and the people sought the help and assistance of each other. There was no feeling of alienation or gap between the refugees who returned and their compatriots who stayed in Algeria . . . The ones who could not make the adjustment were the children who could not find schools near their homes. While in exile, the children used to find schools in the areas they usually lived, but after their arrival back home, they encountered great difficulties, either because schools were very far away from their homes or because there were no teachers. Many people volunteered to take the children from rural areas to big cities because there were no buses available for the transportation of adults or children (interview with Salah Saadi in Souk Ahras, 25 October 1990).

Some returnees found money waiting for them.

> We got in touch with the people who remained behind and exploited our lands, commerces and took care of our cattle until we came back. When we returned home, we received our share of profits and benefits from our properties during the period of absence (interview with Sultan Guebaili, in Souk Ahras, 26 October 1990).

Other returnees were able to bring money back with them, having run profitable enterprises while in exile. The returnees were additionally helped in mid-1962 by the departure of the French farmers. Many of them left behind harvests of wheat, barley and other crops which became an important source of additional food at a time of shortage.

But no financial aid was provided by the Algerian authorities, and even the highly educated often had no option other than to become farmers in order to secure enough to feed themselves and their children. Many of those without inherited land were allocated plots by the bigger landowners, and they sold surplus crops in the local markets. But incomes were very small, and many were forced to seek supplementary employment by working on commercial farms. Others migrated to the cities as soon as they could (US Government, 1964: 379). As time passed some of those who remained in rural locations gained a reputation for animal husbandry and successfully established themselves as suppliers of cattle, goats and sheep for the meat markets.

Thus, the returnees had to rely on their communities and most received little governmental or international assistance following their arrival. In exile, the refugees had benefitted from assistance provided by the UNHCR, several sympathetic governments and NGOs. But aid stopped as soon as they went home. To some extent this was because the international community took the view that Algeria was an independent state and should be capable of looking after its own citizens. However, the new government also seems to have been reluctant to accept help from Western sources, and many officials had little interest in the returnees' difficulties. In 1962 and 1963 the main concerns of politicians related to power struggles within the administration (Brace and Brace,

4.3 *Food donated by the United States was used to pay labourers for road construction (UNHCR/4493/ S. Wright)*

1965: 214). Several overtures from international organizations wanting to set up projects were ignored, and political instability hindered the implementation of schemes which had been approved.

A government policy which was of benefit to the more educated former refugees, internally displaced people and ex-combatants was an allocation of 10 per cent of jobs to 'victims of war'. In addition some assistance was given to unemployed returnees in the way of permits to open stores, drive taxis and import machinery from abroad, and long-term, low-interest loans were made available to people who could provide employment to others. Some returnees were eventually able to take over the jobs of the 20,000 Algerians who had supported the French in the war and left the country at independence. But for the vast majority the choice was between farming and scraping a meagre living in the towns.

A partial exception to this overall situation was the food for work programme which aimed at providing jobs for 400,000 poor people in rural areas. The labourers were paid with food donated by the United States and did valuable construction work on roads. Interviewed in 1990, one former mayor who organized work of this kind made the following observation:

The aid was a donation and it was supposed to be given to the poor, but we decided to make them do something like building roads instead of remaining idle (interview with Ammar Bouhencher, in Beni Abbas, 25 October 1990).

The economic problems facing Algeria at independence were exacerbated in the following years by conflicts with France and by government policies. On 1 July 1964, France decided to regulate the movement of Algerians into France. This was a breach of the Evian Agreements prompted by Algeria's decision to nationalize the property of French settlers in the country. For the Algerian Government, this represented a major problem, because some two million Algerians depended on the earnings and family allowances remitted by relatives in France (US Government, 1964: 80). Moreover, the financial assistance which France had pledged to Algeria at Evian was withheld, and was used instead to compensate the dispossessed French settlers.

The confiscation of settlers' farms made more land available to returnees and the unemployed, but the state still had few other resources with which to assist them. Nevertheless, the government decided to go ahead with plans for the collectivization of agriculture. A total of 2,300 mechanized state farms were set up, covering more than two million hectares of Algeria's best agricultural land. In theory these enterprises were able to absorb 180,000 permanent and 100,000 seasonal workers, which amounted to about 20 per cent of the agricultural labour force. But inefficient bureaucracy, corruption, mismanagement, price fixing, black marketeering, and lack of training meant that the farms never achieved their potential. The reforms failed to increase production and had little impact on the continued exodus from rural to urban areas. They also had the effect of weakening the social networks which had allowed the returnees to be integrated back into their communities. The peasants were stripped of their ecological and sociological relationships. 'Feeling alienated and isolated, the new rural worker could no longer identify with the land upon which he was working' (Antelis, 1986: 145). The optimism of the rural population at independence was swiftly eradicated.

Fortunately the migration of Algerian workers to France was as much in the interests of their French employers as it was essential to the families who received their repatriated income. Therefore, controls on Algerian entry into France did not, in the long run, lead to the feared ending of labour migration. In 1963, 50,433 individuals left Algeria for France and another 43,802 migrated in 1964 (in 1990 the figure was around 900,000). These workers were given priority in buying land in Algeria and could bring home vehicles and machines without paying customs fees. Other factors also helped the Algerian economic situation to improve. The infrastructure built under French rule – including factories, machines and surfaced roads – had not been destroyed during the war. Arab countries sent some 30,000 teachers and trainers so that Algerians could replace the departed European technicians. As a result, many goods could be produced in the country, reducing the need for imports.

Nevertheless, many returnees never benefitted from these developments. In 1990 I made a trip to the area close to the Tunisian border where many returnees settled in 1962. After three decades of independence, I found a large percentage still living in deplorable conditions. Bullied by a heavy-handed bureaucracy they suffer from lack of water, paved roads, seeds and machines. For these people, the aspirations of homecoming have still to be met.

References

Antelis, John P. (1986) *Algeria: the revolution institutionalized*, Westview Press, Boulder, CO.
Benkhedda, Benyoucef (1986) *Les Accords d'Evian*, Office des Publications Universitaires, Algiers.
Brace, Richard and John Brace (1965) *Algerian voices*, D. Van Nostrand Company, Inc., New York.
Gordon, David C. (1966) *The passing of French Algeria*, Oxford University Press, London.
Horn, Alistaire (1977) *A savage war of peace, Algeria: 1954-1962*, Macmillan, London.
Montagnon, Pierre (1984) *La guerre d'Algérie*, Pygmalion Gérard Wateler, Paris.
US Government (1964) *US Army area handbook for Algeria*, US Government Printing Office, Washington, DC.

5 JOSHUA O. AKOL[1]
A Crisis of Expectations

Returning to Southern Sudan
in the 1970s

Introduction

The North–South conflict in Sudan which lasted from 1955 until 1972 cost the South
an estimated one million lives.[2] This may have been as much as a quarter of its mid-1950s
population. During the war, the countryside of the South became dotted with empty
homesteads, and fields where crops used to be grown or livestock grazed were abandoned.
In some places whole villages disappeared as people were killed or ran away while their
possessions were looted and burned by army units.

The fighting stopped in 1972 as a result of the Addis Ababa Agreement. This was a
negotiated settlement signed in Ethiopia between rep-eresentatives of Nimeiri's military
regime in Khartoum and the Southern Sudan Liberation Movement acting on behalf of
the various 'Anyanya' guerrilla groups operating in the South. Sudan subsequently
experienced one of the largest repatriation operations on the African continent and a decade
of fragile peace. This chapter describes the process of population return, and discusses
problems which had to be overcome by the Repatriation and Resettlement Commission.
It then goes on to look at aspects of development in Southern Sudan during the 1970s and
early 1980s, focussing in particular on ways in which experiences in exile affected particular
populations. The last section of the chapter comments on the ultimate failure to meet the
expectations raised by the Addis Ababa Agreement, and makes some observations about
the current war.

The Repatriation Process

The Organization Stage
The peace agreement between North and South was signed in Addis Ababa on 27 February
1972, and was ratified in March of that year as an organic law and instrument of the state.
Following this agreement, there was an urgent need to create conditions in the South that
would facilitate the return of refugees from neighbouring countries and for the internally

---

[1]With additional material relating to Sudan in the 1980s by Tim Allen drawing on notes provided by Joshua
Akol.
[2]In this chapter, lower case is used for 'southern Sudan' when referring to the geographical area. Upper case
is used when referring to the autonomous region, i.e. the Southern Sudan.

Map 5.1 *Southern Sudan, showing numbers of refugees returning from neighbouring countries in 1972*

displaced persons to return to their homes. However, as local resources were inadequate to meet the needs of returning refugees and displaced populations, the government was dependent upon contributions from the international community. For example, relief voluntary agencies headed by the ACROSS, the Catholic Relief Organization (Caritas), Norwegian Church Aid, Save the Children Fund, German Church Aid, Oxfam, Lutheran World Service, the World Council of Churches, the All African Conference of Churches, the International Committee of the Red Cross, assisted the UNHCR in the provision of shelter, food and medicine (Alier, 1990).

In order to generate, distribute and prioritize all aid and assistance, the government established the Repatriation and Resettlement Commission whose functions included (Government of Sudan, 1972b):

(a) receiving and transporting returnees from neighbouring countries to their original homes.
(b) providing food, medical care and temporary shelter in reception centres and transit camps.
(c) reconstructing social services as well as assistance in the supply of seeds, agricultural hand tools and technical assistance.

The Repatriation and Resettlement Commission was supported by the Special Fund Committee which was created to receive resources from donors and administer financial and technical assistance.

When the Repatriation and Resettlement Commission was established, it was realized that the OAU definition of refugees would deprive certain categories of displacees who needed immediate relief. A modified definition was required in order to meet the specific needs of the refugees and internally displaced persons. Consequently, the Commission broadened the OAU definition to include all persons directly or indirectly affected by the conflict and defined 'refugees' as:

(a) those who had taken refuge in the bush, in towns of the Southern Region and in various parts of northern Sudan;
(b) those who had sought refuge in neighbouring countries where they had come largely under the care of UNHCR and acquired the legal status of refugees;
(c) those who, because of political instability in the Southern Sudan, had fled to neighbouring countries in search of educational opportunities provided by the various agencies for the refugees;
(d) orphaned children and incapacitated persons (Government of Sudan, 1972a).

In this chapter, the term 'refugees', will be used as defined by the Repatriation and Resettlement Commission rather than in its more specific sense as a person who crosses an international border due to fears about personal safety.

The Repatriation of Refugees

Voluntary repatriation of refugees is only likely to take place if conditions in the refugees' country of origin change for the better, and thereby make it conducive for them to return. The conditions in southern Sudan prior to 1972 did not favour such a repatriation. The policies pursued by the governments at that time were too repressive to induce refugees to return to their homes in large numbers. Data show that, prior to the Addis Ababa Agreement, only about 1,000 persons had voluntarily returned to their homes from the bush where they had been in hiding (Government of Southern Sudan, 1974b). However, such numbers are probably misleading, because, first, no accurate registrations were made to determine the number of persons returning, and, second, fear of arrest and interrogation by government forces made many rural and self-employed returnees reluctant to identify themselves as returnees to local authorities. The principal exceptions to this were former government employees who wanted to be reinstated in their old positions.

Following the establishment of the Repatriation and Resettlement Commission in 1972, the repatriation process took on new dimensions. Repatriation branch offices were set up in Ethiopia, Uganda, Zaire and the Central African Republic which became directly responsible for all the refugees wishing to repatriate. The Commission's role included the translation of the text of the Addis Ababa Agreement into various local languages and its explanation to the refugees. The Commission was also charged with the task of winning the refugees' confidence. This was important because people who had returned to Sudan earlier had been persecuted. The refugees wanted guarantees about their safety, and many refugees were reluctant to repatriate immediately in 1972 (Government of Southern Sudan, 1973c).

In 1972, the Commission reported that a total of 219,400 Southern Sudanese refugees lived in neighbouring countries (see Map 5.1). However, their burden was unevenly distributed among the asylum countries. For example, Uganda and Zaire hosted about 70 per cent of the refugees. The remaining 30 per cent were in Ethiopia, Kenya and the Central African Republic.

Apart from such uneven distribution of refugees among host countries, there were also considerable differences in their manner of settlement. The Repatriation and Resettlement Commission's Final Report (Government of Southern Sudan, 1974b) shows that 50.2 per cent of refugees had settled 'spontaneously' among the local population in their respective countries of asylum, while the balance lived in organized rural settlements. The largest group of 'spontaneous' settlers was in Uganda (63 per cent), followed by Zaire (55.2 per cent) and by Ethiopia (42.9 per cent). However, where 'spontaneous' settlements occurred, two factors should be taken into account. In the first place, the ethnic relation between host populations and refugees tended to encourage such settlements. Second, the failure by host governments to take immediate action on the refugees' arrival caused refugees to seek their own solutions through integration with local populations. These differences in the manner of settlement by the refugees in asylum countries had varying effects on their repatriation, the degree of success or failure during exile and the subsequent socio-economic adjustment after return to their home country.

As the repatriation of refugees progressed, the Commission was optimistic that its task would be completed within the prescribed period of 18 months, from May 1972 to October 1973. However, between May and December 1972, only 44,608 (20.3 per cent) refugees were repatriated, most of whom came from Uganda and the Central African Republic. Many refugees remained uncertain about the government's intentions and as a result adopted an attitude of 'wait and see'.

Between January and October 1973, a further 109,106 (49.7 per cent) refugees were repatriated by the Commission, the majority of whom came from Uganda and Zaire. As a large number of refugees (30 per cent) were still outside the country, the life of the Commission was extended up until June 1974. Thus, between October 1973 and June 1974, another 4,578 (2.1 per cent) persons were registered, bringing the total to 158,292 (72.1 per cent) refugees repatriated by the Commission. Of the 61,108 refugees who were not officially repatriated, 13,153 (6 per cent) of them remained in Uganda and Zaire purely for personal or economic reasons. The balance (47,955) remained unaccounted for at the end of the repatriation operation, but it is commonly accepted that they returned independently to their homes, and thus were not registered.

The repatriation and resettlement exercise was executed under very difficult conditions, one of which was the staffing of the Commission. No specific criteria were used in

5.1 *Repatriating refugees arriving from Uganda at the Sudanese border, 1972 (UNHCR/1669/van de Linde)*

recruiting employees. The staff of the Commission were seconded from various government departments, and from the general Southern Sudanese population, where few skills and qualifications existed. Moreover, because the life of the Commission was to be short, little or no training was given and insufficient time existed for them to gain experience on the job.

Poor transportation throughout the South also imposed serious problems. During the civil war, most roads and bridges were either damaged or destroyed, and reconstruction following the war was slow. This reduced the speed with which provisions could be delivered to outlying areas as large sections of the road network remained unserviceable. Poor transportation frequently resulted in supplies reaching rural distribution points very late or in a damaged condition, which in turn led to friction between the Commission's staff and returnees.

In some areas natural forces also imposed themselves, such as in the Upper Nile region where rural roads were open only during the dry season. In the rainy season, river boats had to be used, and their effectiveness was dependent upon the availability of fuel. However, in spite of many problems, the Commission proceeded with its mandate to complete its task by June 1974 and hence must be regarded as an overall success.

5.2 *Poor transportation throughout the South imposed serious problems: relief trucks waiting to cross the Nile ferry at Juba (UNHCR/1785/van de Linde)*

5.3 *One of the infrastructural projects implemented with international assistance after the Addis Ababa Agreement was the building of a new Nile bridge at Juba (UNHCR/4045/van de Linde)*

Factors Influencing the Refugees' Voluntary Repatriation

- *The way refugees had been settled during their exile* was important insofar as the repatriation process was concerned. Unlike 'spontaneously' settled refugees who were widely dispersed and thus not easily grouped together for repatriation, those in organized rural settlement schemes were readily mobilized and thus repatriated with minimal problems. For example, in Uganda where 63.5 per cent of the refugees were self-settled, 13 holding camps had to be set up inside Uganda in order to congregate the refugees for processing (Government of Southern Sudan, 1974b).
- *The first impression of the early returnees of the general situation in the country* was important because it influenced the return of the rest of the refugees from exile. After the civil war, specific measures in favour of the returnees were taken by government to ensure that they were accorded the same rights and privileges enjoyed by the rest of the population. In addition, a special dispensation was made allowing returnees to bring most of their belongings into the country duty free. Although this exemption did not benefit very many of the refugees, it was nevertheless a measure that contributed to the return of some of the more affluent from exile.
- A third important factor influencing the desire to repatriate was *the level of socio-economic development that the refugees had achieved while in exile*. For example, refugees who had become self-sufficient, and perhaps even rich, were reluctant to return to a war-devastated and dis-located economy. It is estimated that over 11,000 refugees remained in Uganda and did not return to Sudan until 1979, following the fall of President Idi Amin. On the other hand, those who were living in conditions of poverty, or those who had developed no economic or psychological attachments to their area of exile, were more readily prepared to return home.

The Resettlement Process

The policy of the Commission was to resettle all returnees with minimal stress and to permit them to resume normal life as soon as possible. On the basis of their previous occupations, experience, qualifications, or physical state, six categories of returnees were identified by the Commission. A brief discussion of each of these groups is undertaken to highlight the main features of government strategy in the rehabilitation and resettlement process.

White-Collar Returnees

This category of returnees consisted of two sub-groups. First, there were the politicians, some of whom had taken part in the Addis Ababa peace negotiations. Many of these politicians were subsequently appointed as ministers in the newly created Regional Government, while others obtained high-ranking positions in the civil service. Second, there were former government officials and employees as well as other returnees who had acquired qualifications or experience while in exile.

This group was absorbed into the various Regional Ministries and Departments. The absorption of former government officials and employees was governed by specific guidelines established by the Central Government in 1970. The main principles of the re-employment policy were stated as follows:

(a) Ministries and Departments should re-instate immediately ex-Southern officials and employees returning from exile, into their former posts where such posts are still vacant, or they should be absorbed into similar posts. But, where a post has been filled or no other vacant similar post exists, the Unit should request creation of a new post stating the standard of the former post quoting in case of officials the post number in the nominal roll in which the returning official was engaged before leaving the country.

(b) Officials and employees not dismissed by Departmental Boards of Discipline were to be re-instated with consideration of period of absence as 'leave without pay'. But re-instatement

5.4 *International assistance played an important role in the initial success of the repatriation programme: unloading relief items at Juba airport, 1972 (UNHCR/1644/van de Linde)*

of officials and employees who were dismissed by Departmental Boards of Discipline should be treated as new appointments and their period of previous service reviewed for continuous service, after full study of causes and circumstances of absence.

(c) Re-instatement of officials and employees should correspond to the same standard of their former posts, the same salary they were receiving before going into exile, and stipulating the same terms of service (Government of Sudan, 1970).

Returnee Students

The overall impact of the war on education in the South was enormous. For almost two decades, most schools were not operational and consequently the majority of children had limited or no education. Only a few school buildings survived the war, and, with the influx of the student backlog that had formed during the civil war period, an enormous pressure was placed upon these limited educational facilities. In most schools, a two-shift system was adopted to alleviate the problem of both lack of space and insufficient teachers.

The Commission recognized that because of the wide range in ages of the potential student population, and the fact that few schools existed, priority for primary school enrolment was given to the older children (eight years and over) who had not had opportunities either inside or outside of Sudan during the civil war. However, although the Commission was genuine in its approach, the enrolment of older boys posed serious problems of discipline in schools. Many of the older returnee students were not prepared psychologically to become peers with much younger children.

A further problem generated by the war was that of language. The returnee students who had been in exile or in 'Anyanya' bush schools had used either French or English as a medium of instruction. On their return, however, they were required to make the transition to Arabic. Attempts were made by the Regional Government to temporarily accommodate this problem by establishing some schools where the medium of instruction remained English.

Unattached Minors and Disabled Persons

The social problems generated by the civil war in Sudan were enormous. In particular, the large number of unattached minors and disabled persons after the war posed a serious problem. While there are no precise data on these groups, estimates show that, in September 1972, 900 unattached minors between the ages of 7 and 17 years were living in the main towns (Betts, 1974). These children had lost their parents or guardians, or had run away from their homes during the civil war. Another estimate in 1975 showed 2,300 unattached minors living in Juba, Wau, Malakal and Aweil. Also, as a result of the war, the number of the physically handicapped in the South was estimated at around 100,000 persons (Government of the Southern Region of Sudan, 1977).

The Regional Government's strategy was to set up a Department of Social Welfare. The policy of the Department was to encourage the children's closest relatives to take responsibility for them. While there are no specific records, it is generally agreed that the Department was successful in this approach. The government also established orphanages and rehabilitation homes for unattached minors whose closest relatives had declined to take care of them.

A second government strategy was to establish institutions such as community centres in the main towns to provide services for the disadvantaged. These centres provided services in, for example, adult education, sewing and typing, to facilitate the integration of disadvantaged people into society.

Petty Traders and Small Businessmen

As part of the resettlement strategy, a programme of loans to petty traders and small businessmen in the South was initiated by the Chairman of the Repatriation and Resettlement Commission to revive small businesses that had been destroyed or dislocated during the civil war. Financial assistance was distributed according to the number of petty traders who applied on the one hand and the extent of damage to their property on the other. However, the programme was not pursued after the first year because of lack of funds.

It is not clear how many returnees benefitted from this programme, although Equatoria Province received 56 per cent of the total disbursement, with Bahr el Ghazal and Upper Nile Provinces sharing the balance equally. Although not documented, there is little doubt that those who benefitted most from the loans were the 'progressive' businessmen who had strong urban connections. It was made conditional that potential loan recipients should have properties and be recommended by persons in government known to loan authorities.

These conditions were met only by those who had strong backing by individuals in the

Regional Government, thus limiting the number of beneficiaries to a small and select group of returnees.

Absorption of the 'Anyanya' Forces

The success of the Addis Ababa Agreement depended very much upon the satisfactory accommodation of Anyanya forces. It was agreed that:

> The People's Armed Forces in the Southern Region shall consist of a national force called the Southern Command composed of 12,000 officers and men, of whom 6,000 shall be citizens from the Region and the other 6,000 from outside the Region (Government of Sudan, 1972a).

The total number of the Anyanya forces was estimated at 25,000 by 1973, of which over 6,000 were absorbed into the national army and about 4,000 into the police and prison service. The balance, estimated at over 14,000 persons, were employed in various government units as follows: 5,353 in Equatoria Province, 4,700 in Bahr el Ghazal Province, and 4,200 in Upper Nile Province (Government of the Southern Region of Sudan, 1973b).

Matters relating to recruitment and integration of the Anyanya forces into the national army were determined by a six-man Joint Technical Military Commission which consisted of three members drawn from the national army and another three from the Anyanya forces. The government recognized that, since the Anyanya forces and the national army had until recently been fighting each other, both needed a period for 'cooling off' before they could accept one another to work together as compatriots.

In this regard, the Joint Military Commission took into account the need for initial separate deployment of troops, until smooth integration of the two forces could be achieved over a five-year period (Alier, 1976).

It is estimated that 15,900 Anyanya applied for absorption into the national army, but only 6,139 (38.6 per cent) were inducted (Beshir, 1975). This was a disappointment to the people who had fought so hard for seventeen years. The selection criteria used by the Joint Military Commission were that the applicant had:

(a) belonged to the Anyanya force;
(b) satisfactory academic qualifications;
(c) passed a medical fitness examination; and
(d) expressed a willingness to continue in the service (Beshir, 1975).

Although the above criteria formed the basis for recruiting Anyanya, the high illiteracy that was prevalent necessitated the use of additional criteria in order to save the Agreement. These included the individual's past performance and rank in the Anyanya force. The criterion of 'belonging to the Anyanya' was not strictly followed because some absorbed into the national army, police and prison service had never been members of Anyanya, but were government officials, employees or students who had joined Anyanya camps in the hope of being recruited. Alier (1990) has pointed out that the recruitment of these groups of people into the forces and demotions of the absorbed forces from ranks held in the Anyanya were sources of bitterness and resentment by the Anyanya forces.

The absorption of Anyanya created a sizeable employment opportunity in the South. However, because many of the ex-guerrillas had not previously experienced the discipline and training associated with the regular army, they had difficulties in coping with their new assignments. The shift to regimentation was, for many, too abrupt, and as a result some were dismissed by their units in the course of integration. Whether or not these dismissals were justified, the Anyanya interpreted such actions as a plot by those elements in the Central Government who were opposed to the Addis Ababa Agreement and absorption of Anyanya forces into the national army.

Rural Returnees

Rural returnees are here defined as subsistence farmers who had been forced to abandon their homes during the civil war. They constituted a substantial majority of the over one million displaced population resettled after the conflict. Conscious of the high expectations which many of the returnees had, the Regional Government outlined a programme for the immediate employment of Anyanya leftovers in Regional Ministries and Departments. The jobs thus created were seen as temporary until other more permanent opportunities could be generated. It was anticipated that industrial employment opportunities such as in a jute factory at Tonj and sugar factories at Mongalla and Melut could have served as additional sources of employment. However, these schemes turned out to be

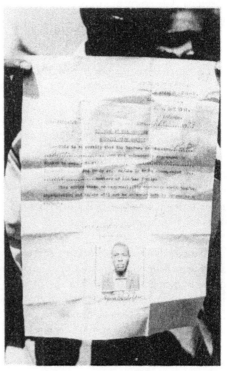

5.5 *A returnee displays his repatriation permit (UNHCR/1770/van de Linde)*

expensive failures, in large part due to poor planning. It did not make economic sense to build factories far away from the larger urban centres where transport facilities were limited and there was no workforce in the immediate vicinity. Consequently, most of the Anyanya leftovers had to be absorbed by the government at great cost.

The employment of largely unskilled manpower had serious implications. The South's resources were too limited to maintain the rising costs of this employment. This was especially the case during the 1973/74 period, when their salaries had to be paid against the special Development Budget given as grants-in-aid by the Central Government to Southern Region. For example, in the Regional Ministry of Agriculture, which had the largest share of the ex-Anyanya, the payment of salaries amounted to 91.7 per cent of the approved Special Development Budget, thus leaving only 8.3 per cent to implement development projects (Government of the Southern Region of Sudan, 1974a).

In addition to the Anyanya leftovers being absorbed in the towns, the totally dislocated socio-economic infrastructure in rural areas following the war created a strong push factor causing rural returnees to migrate to the urban centres in search of services and employment. Consequently, a huge reservoir of redundant employees was created in almost all government departments. Commenting on the seriousness of this problem and the consequent economic crisis in the South, Abel Alier, who was then president of the autonomous Southern Region, stated that:

> Many of our citizens who were in exile or in the bushes of the Region worked hard to till the land and lived by its fruits. All of a sudden citizens are turning their back to the land. Many hours in the day and thousands of hours in the year are lost in pursuit of idleness. Everybody wants a government job. It is not that people want to work for salaries. Our people want to be paid for no work. It is as if Regional Autonomy came so that people may specialise in complaints and search for sinecure jobs in offices. It is as if Regional Autonomy made it a shame to till and live happily on the fruits of one's labour. (Alier, 1975)

In response to this problem, the Regional Government reviewed its position on the question of absorbing people into government employment. After much debate in the Regional Assembly, the Government enforced the lay-offs of those who had been temporarily employed during the 1972 to 1974 period. In order to facilitate and encourage their return to the land, the government provided the laid-off persons with:

(a) advance payment of three months' wages;
(b) seeds for food or cash crops;
(c) agricultural tools and implements;
(d) grain and other food items to feed themselves while waiting for their harvest; and
(e) one year's exemption from taxes, subject to another one year extension (Government of the Southern Region of Sudan, 1974c; Alier, 1990). It is estimated that, of the 25,632 returnees that had been employed using funds from the Special Development Budget, 82.6 per cent were laid off.

Although the government made substantial savings from implementing this policy, it also generated bitterness and resentment among those affected. Interpretation of the policy differed from one group to another. For example, to the ex-Anyanya being laid off meant a breach of the Addis Ababa Agreement, which had promised them the fruits of their struggle. Others rejected the economic explanations given by the government for the lay-offs. They argued that the international community had contributed generously to the South's redevelopment, including the provision of employment for returning populations, yet, through the lay-offs, the government was reneging on its responsibilities and promises.

Alier (1990) has clearly pointed out that the Central Government was not committed to the South's development. Instead of accelerating implementation of the development projects for the returnees, the government in Khartoum concentrated all financial and technical resources on sugar projects in the Central Sudan. The resentment by the absorbed Anyanya forces of the way the Addis Ababa peace settlement was being implemented was indicated as early as 1975, with a mutiny at the Akobo garrison in eastern Upper Nile. The mutineers fled into the bush and called themselves 'Anyanya II'. The incident was one of several which punctuated the period of peace in Sudan. In retrospect it can be viewed as part of a gradual process which eventually led to a return to full-scale war in 1983.

Rural Development in the Southern Region

The rural development strategies adopted by the Regional Government following the Addis Ababa Agreement marked a complete turn-around in agrarian policy. Instead of stressing mechanized farming as was the case in the past, the emphasis shifted to smallholder farmers. Accordingly, rural policy was redefined as intending

> to tap and develop the latent capabilities of the rural people through incentives for production, rewarding employment, and to involve them in affairs of their community and nation.

Development calls for a joint effort of people and government, one in which greater emphasis than hitherto is placed on man, his organization and his institutions (Government of the Southern Region of Sudan, 1973a).

The objective of the new policy was to improve agricultural activities in the South by using existing resources and to make the returnees self-sufficient in food crop production. Schemes introduced under the regional government included the allocation of cash in the form of loans to 'progressive' farmers and the organizing of agricultural fairs. In addition Saturday was declared 'agriculture day' for public and private sector workers during the planting and harvest seasons.

These strategies were not particularly effective, but this probably did not matter because, whatever their initial expectations, most returnees quickly turned to farming as a means of survival. The salaries of the much sought after government jobs were not enough to sustain employees, and sometimes wages went unpaid for months due to lack of funds. At the same time, the sudden arrival of so many people in the South meant that there was a shortage of food, and local market prices were high.

Another important factor in certain locations was experience gained while abroad. In the Equatoria Provinces, the most southern sections of the Southern Sudan, parts of the population had been exposed to the cash crop economies of Zaire and Uganda, and to a wide variety of farming techniques. On their return some families eagerly experimented with imported methods, and tried out a range of new crop varieties (Akol, 1987). Where this occurred it seems to have contributed to increased agricultural productivity and to a general improvement in living conditions.

In 1982, a survey was carried out in Yei, Maridi and Torit districts of Equatoria Province (Akol, 1986) to determine the effects of dislocation on economic activities. In Maridi and Yei over 80 per cent of people interviewed considered themselves relatively better off since the war, and there was no significant difference in this respect between those who had been refugees abroad and those who had been displaced within Sudan. A particularly clear indication of the rising levels of affluence was the commitment to education. In 1977, the Regional Ministry of Finance reported that most of the 300 'private' or 'parents' schools which were built through self-help programmes in the South after the war were located in Yei District. In contrast, over 60 per cent of people interviewed in Torit District who had spent the war in neighbouring countries reported that they had been better off when in exile. Schools in the area were almost exclusively government financed, and tended to be understaffed. Boarding secondary schools frequently had to be closed down for parts of the year due to lack of food for students.

The improvements noted in Yei and Maridi could be linked to a variety of factors. Those who had spent time in Uganda or Zaire had often preserved friendships outside Sudan, and would use these networks to trade illicitly across the borders. Also the arrival of some 200,000 refugees from Uganda following the overthrow of Amin in 1979 meant there was a plentiful supply of cheap farm labour. But, for many farmers, increased incomes appear to have been most closely connected with the adoption of imported crop varieties and a willingness to experiment with crops introduced by the Regional Ministry of Agriculture and international aid agencies, including a new strain of sorghum (Serena DX), coffee, Makula Red groundnuts and pineapples.

In Torit District the levels of adoption of new crop varieties were found to be lower than in Yei and Maridi Districts. This may have been partly because many of those interviewed had not been refugees in Uganda, but had taken refuge in the dense forests of the Imatong mountains. But incomes were no higher among those who had been to Uganda. This group complained that the very high rainfall in the mountainous areas and lack of transport facilities made it difficult to grow and market the crops they had learned to farm.

The 1982 survey was not extended to low-lying areas of Torit District, where conditions are both culturally and geographically similar to the territories south of the border. However, Christopher Terrill researched in the Acholi-speaking parts of the lowlands during 1976–77 (Terrill, 1983), and Tim Allen carried out fieldwork in the same area in 1984 (Allen, 1987).

Terrill's findings bear out the impression that during the 1970s there was a lack of improvement in socio-economic conditions in Torit District. He has argued that the underlying reasons were to do with experiences in exile. He found that families belonging to the chiefly lineages had often not fled to Uganda until fighting became intense near their homes during the second half of the 1960s. In exile they did not become integrated into the local Ugandan economy, but instead remained in camps, waiting to return to Sudan as soon as possible. This was partly the consequence of the Ugandan government policy at the time with respect to refugees, but it may also have been to do with an unwillingness among the Sudanese Acholi to mix with Ugandans, and enter into relationships with patrons who were likely to be of commoner (*lobong*) stock. Once they returned home in 1972, ritually important elders attempted to reassert former controls over social life, and gain access to the best farm land. They tended to be highly conservative and to oppose any agricultural innovations.

Interestingly, Terrill found that at the time of his fieldwork this situation showed signs of changing. Sudanese Acholi of commoner lineages had generally moved to Uganda before the chiefly lineages had done so, mainly as a means of taking advantage of the more dynamic economy in Uganda during the 1950s and early 1960s. They had avoided being treated as a refugee population, and had established their own farms or found salaried employment. Some had worked in the factories or plantations of southern Uganda. Many of them had in effect become Ugandans, and were unwilling to leave the country after the Addis Ababa Agreement. It was the persecution of Acholis under Idi Amin's regime that eventually prompted them to reassert a Sudanese nationality (Amin and his supporters tended to view Acholis as being loyal to the ousted government of Milton Obote).

As a consequence, many of the Sudanese Acholi from commoner clans returned to Sudan several months, or even years, after the bulk of the Acholi repatriated from the official refugee camps. They tended to be better educated, and more commercially orientated. Terrill maintains that these characteristics made them responsive to the activities of Norwegian Church Aid, an international NGO running a large-scale relief programme in Torit District. He suggested that this was having 'dire and unforeseen consequences' for the work of the NGO in that it was leading to an increasingly inequitable distribution of resources. Basically a few 'progressive' commoners were becoming relatively wealthy and the remainder of the population was being economically marginalized (Terrill, 1983).

In the event this feared rapid social stratification did not occur. In 1984, Allen found a relatively even distribution of resources. Elders of the chiefly lineages had generally managed to establish their traditional authority, and also held local positions in the civil administration. Commoner lineages wishing to avoid customary restrictions had moved into previously uncultivated locations and formed new villages, often regulated by the rules of a form of rotating work group which they had introduced from Uganda. Food was generally plentiful, but incomes were very low. If anything they may

5.6 *Rotating farm work groups played an important part in establishing rural communities in the Acholi area of Southern Sudan: a work group drinking local beer after digging a field (Allen)*

have declined for the majority of families since the time of Terrill's research.

Allen makes the following observation about the situation, which is in several respects illustrative of the general situation in Southern Sudan in the early 1980s:

> On returning to Sudan, those refugees who had attained a relatively affluent standard of living in Uganda hoped to retain it. Some began growing cotton . . . and looked to the Regional Government in Juba to establish market channels, and provide amenities like schools and roads. However the administration in Juba was increasingly hamstrung by lack of funds, and acute divisions centred in ethnic factions. It was never in a position to deal with demands placed upon it . . . Pressure was placed on foreign aid organizations to step in where the State could not, but until 1978 the agency operating in Acholi (area) . . . was orientated towards relief and resettlement, not long-term development. The resources were simply not available to provide the wide range of basic facilities needed, and once markets across the border dried up due to the oppression of the Ugandan Acholi under Idi Amin, there was no incentive to continue production of crops for sale (Allen, 1987: 74).

Inadequate state services, limited markets and ineffective or inappropriate international aid was a problem in much of the Southern Sudan during the 1970s and the situation deteriorated further in the 1980s. The economic development of Yei and Maridi and some other districts of Equatoria to the west of the Nile was in fact always the exception rather than the rule, and closely connected with location. The border trade with Zaire became particularly lucrative, and infrastructure continued to be improved as a consequence of the activities of international aid agencies working among the Ugandan refugees.

Elsewhere in the South the expectations of people following the Addis Ababa Agreement were not met. Indeed, for most of the population things were much bleaker than they were in Torit District. In Upper Nile and Bahr el Ghazal, there was little in the way of grassroots development programmes, while large amounts of money were invested in schemes, such as the Jonglei Canal, which were of no obvious benefit to the local population. In Juba, the scarcity of funds exacerbated ethnic antagonisms within the Regional Assembly, and increasingly incapacitated administration. Meanwhile, in Khartoum Nimeiri's regime shifted away from the politics of compromise and moved towards Islamic fundamentalism.

Conclusion: The Failure of Compromise

The relatively successful integration of displaced people following the Addis Ababa Agreement proved short-lived. War broke out again in 1983. In May, the garrisons at Bor, Pibor, and Pochalla mutinied and withdrew towards the Ethiopian border with all their weapons and military hardware. Several other mutinies followed, and by July the soldiers had joined forces with various 'Anyanya II' groups and began operations as the Sudan People's Liberation Army (SPLA). The consequences for Sudan have been disastrous (Amnesty International, 1989; Africa Watch, 1990; Allen, Mawson, Keen and Hutchinson, 1991). The numbers of people who have died as a direct or indirect consequence of the fighting have been much higher than before, and larger populations have been displaced, some of them being forced to live in appalling circumstances.

The reasons for this failure of compromise in Sudan are complex (Johnson, 1988; Allen, 1989; Alier, 1990; Badal, 1988), and there is no space to review them in detail here. But it is worth emphasizing that the attempts made by the regime in Khartoum to change regional boundaries in areas where mineral and oil deposits had been found and the efforts to introduce Islamic law in the South were only part of the problem.

There were basic flaws in the Addis Ababa Agreement in that it relied too heavily on the maintenance of trust between those with political power. The regional administration in Juba remained dependent on the central governments for funds, which were never provided in full. During the eighteen-month transition period in 1972/73, only 40 per cent of the special development budget was made available, and in 1974/75 this dropped to a mere 5 per cent. Long-standing divisions between southern leaders opened up and were exploited by Khartoum. One faction was played off against the other, and by the early 1980s antagonisms within the South were as fierce as antipathy to the North. In particular a conflict emerged between a group with its rural support in the agriculturally productive parts of Equatoria and politicians from the other southern provinces.

Many of the representatives of Bahr el Ghazal and Upper Nile were from pastoralist communities who recognized a common Dinka identity. Taken together these Dinka 'tribes' formed by far the biggest ethnic group in Southern Sudan. The first president of the Southern Region and one of the architects of the Addis Ababa Agreement was Abel Alier, who was also a Dinka. Although Dinkas did not form a united political faction, and many of those who had senior positions in Juba tried to be even-handed in their approach to government, members of other ethnic groups complained of Dinka domination. Some Equatorians, particularly from Juba area itself and from Yei, Maridi and Yambio districts, asserted that they were being held back from progress.

In 1979, the ranks of this discontented Equatorian group were swelled by the return of Sudanese who had been sympathetic to Amin's regime in Uganda. Most of these people were from ethnic groups of western Equatoria. Some of them had become relatively highly educated in exile, and expected to be given senior level jobs. But such positions were already filled, sometimes by Dinkas or individuals from other ethnic groups in Bahr el Ghazal and Upper Nile. For this reason, many of the new returnees supported a call for the Southern Region to be split up, and for the establishing of a separate Equatoria Region.

The dividing up of the South was opposed by the majority of other southerners, including most of the Dinka. In 1981 southern constituencies returned a two to one anti-divisionist majority to the national assembly. But those wishing to weaken the southern lobby in Khartoum continued to exploit the issue by supporting the Equatorian faction. It was against this background that the army mutinies occurred in May 1983. In the following month Nimeiri unilaterally decreed the division of the South into three regions, each with very limited powers. It was not until September that Islamic law was introduced.

It was partly because of these conflicts within the South that the SPLA adopted a nationalist rather than seccessionalist political position. The organization aimed at gaining or possibly sharing power in Khartoum, not the recreation of an autonomous South. During the present war there has been bitter fighting between 'southerners', as well as between 'southerners' and 'northerners'. In some areas Nimeiri's administration and its successors in Khartoum have waged war by proxy, arming selected southern ethnic groups to fight the SPLA. Populations in parts of Equatoria have viewed with fear guerrilla successes against government forces, and the SPLA occupation of territories bordering Uganda have been experienced as a kind of Dinka invasion. Thousands have consequently fled into exile.

In several respects the present tragedy has unfolded because of the way in which the reintegration of the displaced southern Sudanese occurred in the 1970s. It is as much the result of a failed peace as it is a resurgence of long-standing historical divisions between the North and the South. This is a fact which has both added to the awfulness of what has happened and made a resolution of Sudan's current plight all the more intractable.

References

Africa Watch (1990) *Denying the 'honor of living': Sudan, a human rights disaster*, New York, Washington, London.
Akol, J. O. (1986) 'Refugee migration and repatriation: case-studies of some affected rural communities in Southern Sudan', Ph.D. thesis, University of Manitoba, Winnipeg.
— (1987) 'Southern Sudanese refugees: their repatriation and resettlement after the Addis Ababa Agreement', in John R. Rogge (ed.) *Refugees: a Third World dilemma*, Rowman and Littlefield, Totowa, NJ.
Alier, A. (1975) Statement to the People's Regional Assembly, Juba, 6 May.
— (1976) Speech to the People's Regional Assembly on the process of integration, Juba, 12 May.
— (1990) *Southern Sudan: too many agreements dishonoured*, Ithaca Press, Exeter.
Allen, T. (1987) 'Kwete and Kweri: Acholi farm work groups in Southern Sudan', *Manchester Papers on Development*, Vol. 3, No. 2, July: 60–92.
— (1989) 'Full circle?: an overview of Sudan's "Southern problem" since independence', *Northeast African Studies*, Vol. 11, No. 2: 41–66.
Allen, T., A. Mawson, D. Keen and S. Hutchinson (1991) 'War, famine and flight in Sudan', *Disasters*, Vol. 15, No. 2: 133–71.

Amnesty International (1989) *Sudan: human rights violations in the context of civil war*, London, December.

Badal, R. K. (1988) 'The Addis Ababa Agreement ten years after: an assessment', in Mom K. N. Arou and B. Yongo-Bure (eds) *North–South relations in the Sudan since the Addis Ababa Agreement*, Institute of African and Asian Studies, Khartoum.

Beshir, M. O. (1975) *The Southern Sudan: from conflict to peace*, Hurst, London.

Betts, T. (1974) *The Southern Sudan: ceasefire and after*, The Africa Publications Trust, London.

Government of Sudan (1970) Ministry of Finance, Establishment Branch Circular No. 12/70, Khartoum, 6 May.

— (1972a) The Addis Ababa Agreement on the Problem of Southern Sudan, Khartoum, 12 March.

— (1972b) *Projects for relief and reconstruction in the Southern Region*, Government Printing Press, Khartoum.

— (1973) Ministry of Foreign Affairs Circular No. MFA/EO/36.3.2, Khartoum, 16 July.

Government of Southern Region of Sudan (1973a) Regional Ministry of Agriculture, *A new outlook in agricultural, forestry and animal wealth in the Southern Region*, Juba, November.

— (1973b) The High Executive Council, *Peace and progress, 1972–73: a report*, Regional Ministry of Culture and Information, Juba.

— (1973c) *Repatriation and Resettlement Commission's interim report on first phase of repatriation, relief and rehabilitation*, Juba.

— (1974a) The High Executive Council, *Progress report for the period April 1972–October 1973*, Juba, January.

— (1974b) *Repatriation and Resettlement Commission's final report*, May 1972–April 1974, Juba.

— (1974c) Regional Ministry of Public Service and Administrative Reform, *An ad hoc summary report on the number of absorbed ex-Anyanya who were employed against the special funds*, April 1972–April 1974, Juba.

— (1977) Regional Ministry of Health and Social Welfare, 'Progress report for the period April 1972–March 1977', Juba.

Johnson, D. H. (1988) *The Southern Sudan*, The Minority Rights Group Report, No. 78.

Terrill, C. F. (1983) 'The creation of the Acholi minority of the Southern Sudan: their dispersal as refugees, repatriation and resettlement', paper presented at the IGU Commission on Population Geography Symposium on the problems and consequences of refugee migration in the developing world, Hecla Island, Manitoba, 29 August–1 September.

6

J.B. KABERA & C. MUYANJA
Homecoming in the Luwero Triangle

Experiences of the Displaced Population
of Central Uganda following
the National Resistance Army Victory in 1986

Introduction

Uganda had enjoyed relative peace, security, economic stability and development in the later years of Protectorate rule and the first years of independence. But this began to change in the mid-1960s when Milton Obote imposed an executive presidency on the country. The situation deteriorated further under Idi Amin during the 1970s and in the period following the Tanzanian invasion of 1979. In 1980, Obote returned to power, ostensibly as the result of a democratic election, but in fact due to the support of the Uganda National Liberation Army (UNLA) which had entered the country together with Tanzanian troops. The elections appear to have been rigged, and disaffected groups commenced guerrilla activities. Intense fighting took place in the region to the north of Kampala, including Mubende, Mpigi, Mukono and Luwero districts. This has become known as the Luwero Triangle. It was the area of operations for the disciplined and effective National Resistance Army (NRA). Led by Yoweri Museveni, this emerged as the most important force opposing the second Obote regime.

The Luwero Triangle

In the southern parts of the Luwero Triangle, there is much luxuriant natural vegetation. The soils are fertile and the rainfall is high. There are many low-lying swampy valleys which drain eventually into the Kafu and Katonga rivers and Lake Kyoga. The favourable conditions allow for cultivation of various perennial and annual crops. These provided subsistence food for the guerrillas. The forests also afforded excellent cover.

Fighting started slowly and was played down by the government. In 1983 the UNLA were mobilized in an operation against 'armed dissident groups'. Initially the war was concentrated in locations flanking the Bombo–Luwero–Nakasongora road, and some sections of the Triangle remained relatively unaffected throughout the conflict. But, out of a total population of 1,500,000 people (according to the 1980 census), there were 150,000 persons registered as receiving relief from aid agencies in 1983, and about 750,000 were thought to have become displaced. By 1984 it has been estimated that insecurity had spread to about half of the three districts in the Triangle, a total of 22,000 square kilometres (Johnston, 1985).

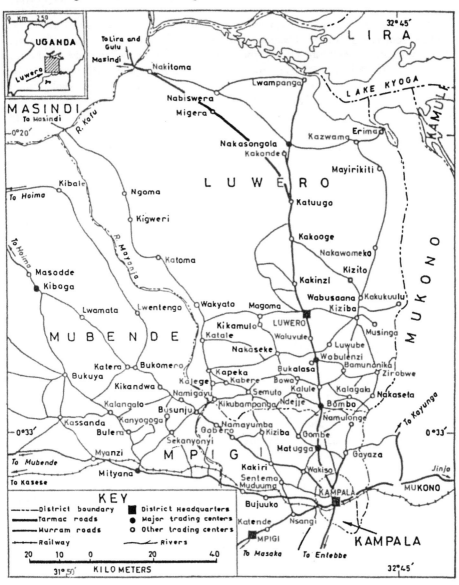

Map 6.1 *Luwero Triangle*

Obote seems to have been determined to hold on to power at all costs, and the UNLA soldiers, too, saw the threat of being overthrown as a danger to their means of survival. There was also a significant ethnic aspect which reinforced their distrust of the local population. The NRA was largely made up of people from parts of the country where the populations speak Bantu languages closely related to the languages spoken in the Luwero Triangle. Obote and most of the UNLA soldiers came from northern parts of the country, where the main languages are of the Nilotic Lwo group. As the war dragged on, a large section of the UNLA become dissatisfied with Obote, and in 1985 they ousted him in favour of Tito Okello, an army officer. He too came from the north, and was equally unacceptable to the mass of southerners. Peace negotiations took place in Nairobi, but the war continued with unrelenting ferocity.

The strategies adopted by the UNLA were extremely brutal. The large number of killings was revealed by the hundreds of skeletons found after the war ended. In addition to those who died in the fighting, appalling atrocities were perpetrated on civilians, mainly by the UNLA. Under Obote, functionaries of his political party, the Uganda People's Congress (UPC), were also involved. In places known to be infiltrated by the guerrillas, the population either fled or was forced into makeshift internment camps, adjacent to temporary military posts. At these camps, rape was common, in some cases involving young girls before puberty and mothers in front of their own children. Women were also forcibly 'married' to soldiers and some were taken north by the defeated UNLA in 1986. Other acts included the disembowelling of pregnant women, theft, maiming, torture and mass killings (Righter, 1983). It was common for several people to be thrown down a pit and murdered with a grenade. Destruction to property was often total. In several places all buildings were demolished by artillery fire or grenades. Iron sheets and window frames were systematically looted. Trading centres like Kapeka, Nakaseke and Kalasa were completely ruined.

Often there was no advance warning when the UNLA clashed with the NRA. Individuals could be caught in cross-fire and fled without their property. If there was advance information, people would hide their belongings or try to sell them off cheaply. They would depart, leaving their houses unlocked in the (usually vain) hope that this would discourage the army from destroying them. Pastoralists lost their herds or gave the animals to the NRA on the promise that they would be compensated when the war was over.

Most people had never ventured far away from the vicinity of their home villages, and some seem to have left without any clear idea of a destination. Customary roots could be cut, and ways of life fundamentally changed: pastoralists became farmers, farmers became small-scale traders, young men joined the NRA. Many ended up with relatives, were welcomed by families living on the fringes of the Triangle, or shifted from place to place, trying to keep away from both sides until hostilities ceased. Others settled in the small towns, like Wobulenzi, Bombo and Luwero, which could be relatively free from insecurity, and some moved further away to bigger towns outside the region, like Jinja, Masaka and Masindi, where they would try to find work. A few remained close to their homes. They would hide in the forests during the day only to reappear at night to tend their fields. But this was a risky strategy, and many were killed in UNLA raids. Inevitably there were also those who collaborated with the UNLA. The UNLA would provide protection from NRA attacks and the peasants might provide the army with local intelligence. There were even those who would take advantage of the conflict. Individuals with grudges against a neighbour might accuse him or her of being a spy and would encourage the destruction of possessions and perhaps assist in killings.

Sometimes families were split up, and some have never been reunited, particularly in cases where a child cannot recall where he or she came from. An extreme case was that of Robert Mugabi Mayanja, who was left behind in the forest by his parents. It is said that he was cared for by monkeys. He is presently being looked after at the Naguru Children Adoption Centre. He could not speak and could only walk on all fours, like a monkey. Now he has managed to walk on his legs and is beginning to speak, but it is feared that his brain is permanently retarded.

In the later stages of the war the government and the NRA set up refugee camps. Unlike camps for international refugees which are located away from conflict zones, these were right inside the Luwero Triangle. They consisted of temporary dwellings made of local materials like banana leaves, grass and branches. Civilians could be screened at these camps, and movement outside was restricted or prohibited altogether.

Those run by the UNLA were more like prisons, and people lived in atrocious conditions with little food and restricted access to drinking water. They were in effect large versions of the internment camps which the UNLA had been setting up next to their military outposts. Obote had persistently denied the existence of these camps (Obote, 1983), but had come under international pressure to recognize that there was a serious problem in the Luwero Triangle. The government responded by establishing refugee camps, and allowing several aid agencies to provide them with a small amount of basic relief. International NGOs, like the International Committee of the Red Cross (ICRC), which worked together with the Uganda Red Cross, provided some medical care and a few commodities like soap, salt and sugar. Unfortunately most of those who were settled at these camps ended up being murdered by the UNLA before they finally retreated from the Triangle.

In the camps under NRA control, inmates were encouraged to organize themselves for various tasks, including defence, procurement of food and water, politicization and education. Activities were regulated by elected committees, known as 'Resistance Councils' (RCs), which became institutionalized as part of the administration of the whole country following the NRA take-over.

Some of the aid agencies working within the Triangle tried to assist in locations infiltrated or controlled by the NRA, but, when caught doing so by the UNLA, they risked being thrown out of the country if they were expatriates, or being beaten and possibly killed if they were Ugandans. Local church groups found it hard to assist because their properties were looted by the UNLA and they were treated as collaborators with the guerrillas. The international agencies complained about the government atrocities, but they were ignored by the regime and seem not to have been believed by the international community as a whole. The full scale of the horrors only became apparent in 1986.

Returning Home

The initial call for displaced people to return to their homes occurred in 1985, following the fall of Obote. However, few people had much faith in the Okello administration, and it was not until the NRA take-over that the return and rehabilitation process began.

Gradually the word spread that the Triangle was safe, and people started going back to their old farms. Most returned on foot because roads had been destroyed or bus fares were too expensive. They could be seen pushing heavily laden bicycles and wheelbarrows along the dirt paths. Families which were still intact tended to return in stages. The family head and perhaps the eldest son ventured first, and, once a shelter had been erected, other

family members would return to help
clear the field of bush cover. Children
of school age often remained with relatives away from the devastated locations,
because former school buildings had been
destroyed. Displaced people who had
managed to establish themselves in business
enterprises while they were away often
stayed in their new homes until they had
raised funds to re-establish their former
dwellings. Several have become absentee
landlords or property owners. They prefer
to collect rents or allow relatives to use
their premises.

As soon as it came to power, the
National Resistance Movement (NRM)
government set about facilitating the
reintegration of the displaced people. Both
internal and international assistance was
sought. Provision of relief and the general
rehabilitation of Luwero Triangle was
vested in the office of the Prime Minister as
the central co-ordinating authority of relief
assistance from various governmental and
non-governmental organizations, assisted
by the Ministry of Relief and Social Rehabilitation. Each district team was responsible for co-ordinating distribution of
emergency relief and rehabilitation. These
district teams work together with the RCs.

6.1 *Gradually the word spread that the Triangle
was safe, and people started going back to their old
farms (Oxfam/UGA/BM/1/Ben Male)*

The crucial task during the initial period of reintegration was the provision of emergency
relief (food and some implements such as pangas, hoes and jerry cans) and the drilling of
boreholes. The distribution of dry rations (comprising maize and beans) was characterized
by irregularities. Some returnees complained of insufficient attention to their needs. In
some cases, where devastation was only slight, the returnees were not offered emergency
relief. The official policy, perhaps, was that these areas were not so adversely affected as
the others. However, many such areas also needed emergency relief, although there had
not been massive destruction of infrastructure, because the population was forced out of
farm work for long spells.

In the initial stages of reintegration, relief and emergency rehabilitation were provided
in haste. The donor organizations, local and foreign, rushed in to provide assistance,
but apparently there was no concrete and co-ordinated plan. The returnees were not
adequately organized to handle relief or rehabilitation in their areas. This explains the
numerous complaints raised by some returnees that emergency relief was not reaching
them or that boreholes were not rationally sited. Complaints were voiced about the
inefficiency and the corruption of the Ministry of Relief and Social Rehabilitation, as
well as of RC executives. It was known that relief commodities had been sold off in
Kampala. Those who were caught red-handed were reprimanded, but, in the absence of
hard evidence, most embezzlers were never prosecuted.

To a degree, this situation improved with time. Several development organizations became more effectively operational, including the churches, MUZAMAT (a Muslim relief organization), FAO (Food and Agriculture Organization of the United Nations), UNICEF (United Nations Children's Fund), German Emergency Doctors, Oxfam and Action Aid. Grants from the European Community were used by the government to supply some commodities and transport facilities, and the United States Agency for International Development (USAID) helped with a general rural economic recovery programme. The NRM government did what it could to support self-reliance. The Uganda Commercial Bank started a 'rural farmers scheme', which offered soft loans to farmers irrespective of sex. The herds of those pastoralists who had handed their animals to the NRA during the war were partly restocked. Poll tax was waived in 1986 and again in 1987, and school fees were exempted for a period. Also the new RC system has now given villagers a voice in local administration, which means that at least their complaints are heard.

Nevertheless, the inadequacies of the relief effort in 1986 and 1987 meant that the returned population had to manage as best as it could on its own. Five years of war had plunged many into a state of extreme poverty. When they first arrived back at what remained of their compounds and farms, they survived on crops which were growing wild in the bush, or were helped by relatives living in less devastated places. There was a great deal of borrowing of items such as water containers, cooking utensils, tools and cuttings or seeds of fast yielding crops. Communal work groups were organized (locally known as *bulungi-bwasi*) to do essential tasks like clear roads and tracks, erect schools and protect springs.

One of the crucial problems facing people was locating relatives. Various methods were used to identify infants and children. The elderly and mature people would examine the physical appearance of the displaced children and correlate them to particular families they happened to know (the feet, birth marks, resemblance of parents or relatives, stature, build, and other facial features). For the slightly older children, the task was simpler; they could try to describe their former villages and probably mention village names or names of their parents/benefactors, sisters, etc. They were able to narrate specific incidents and social workers and adults used this information to start the search for their relatives and parents, if they happened to be alive. Sometimes tracing back one's relatives was sheer luck. During conversations in camps or migration groups, many were able to find that they were related or that they fled from similar geographical regions, villages or counties. Various NGOs, including ICRC and UWESO (Uganda Women's Efforts to Save Orphans), played a significant role, driving from village to village trying to trace the relations. The media (especially the radio service and newspapers) were also used. However, for some unfortunate children, it has not been possible to reunite with relatives. They are still kept in foster homes, such as Naluvule Islamic Foster Home near Luwero and Naguru Children's Home in Kampala.

Another source of worry for many was access to land. Often the former owner had died and it was unclear who should inherit. Moreover, many of the people who had formerly earned salaries or herded animals had now turned to farming, so there was more competition for plots in some places. Few individuals had registered rights to land, so a relationship with the previous owner generally had to be established. Conflicts could be bitter. They were generally resolved by the local RCs but often resulted in long-term grudges which could make village life difficult.

Many old ways and values have been abandoned. Children – some as young as eight years old – who joined the NRA, have grown up in a completely different way to their parents.

6.2 *There was a very limited amount of assistance provided to the displaced people of the Triangle following the NRA take-over: distributing relief items, 1986 (Oxfam/UGA/BM/1/Ben Male)*

Others have spent several years in urban locations, where they were exposed to cinemas, video shows, discothèques and, of course, to AIDS. Older people complain that religious beliefs have been set aside and that theft and rape are now common.

Attempts have been made to resist such tendencies, including the setting-up of clubs known as *Munno Mukabi*, a term which can be translated as 'a friend in need'. These organizations render assistance to members and engage in community work. All members are supposed to subscribe by paying a fixed fee each year. Some of this money is used to purchase commodities like saucepans and plates in bulk for distribution to members. When a bereavement occurs, members contribute food from their own gardens for the funeral ceremony as a way of reducing the expense, which could be a large proportion of a family's annual expenditure before the war.

Other new developments have included the involvement of women in petty trade and even wholesaling. This has partly been due to the numbers of families in which all the adult males have been killed, forcing women to find additional sources of income. Other new skills have also been learned in exile. There have been marked improvements in carpentry and building work, and better techniques of poultry farming and fruit growing have been introduced. Maize cultivation has been widely adopted (formerly the crop had hardly been grown in the region but people who had received relief rations had become used to it). Beer brewing using sorghum, millet and bananas has become more common, and women can be seen selling beer at local markets. Trading networks between villages have intensified, and travelling by bicycle over quite long distances has become a normal practice. This has all been the consequence of exposure to ideas from outside the local area.

Conclusion

The Luwero Triangle was devastated during the war between the UNLA and the NRA, and the organized relief efforts which followed the NRA take-over in 1986 were slow to be effective. The people of Luwero have survived due to their own efforts. The Triangle is now self-sufficient in food and animal products like milk and meat. There is even a surplus of some crops, notably maize, which make their way to markets in Kampala and elsewhere. But huge problems remain. Quite apart from the immediate practical difficulties mentioned here, there is the task of coming to terms with what has happened spiritually and mentally. Some people will surely never recover from their terrible experiences.

Refugees who flee across international borders may suffer terribly, but at least they are often safe. Those who do not live near such a border may be unable to escape. They are forced to stay in their own country and witness or experience torture and death. Clearly the international community should turn its attention to such abused populations, and try to afford them whatever assistance is possible. Their needs when they are able to re-establish their homes are just as acute as those who repatriate from abroad.

References

Johnston, A. (1985) 'The Luwero Triangle: emergency operations in Luwero, Mubende, Mpigi districts' in Dodge C. and P. Wiebe (eds) *Crisis in Uganda*, Pergamon Press, Oxford: 97–106.
Obote, A.M. (1983) 'No internment camps in Uganda', *Uganda Times*, 9 July.
Righter, R. (1983) 'Massacre in the camps of death', *Sunday Times*, London, 5 June.

6.3 *Coming to terms with the psychological and social effects of what happened in the Luwero Triangle will take a long time. Some scars will never heal (Oxfam/UGA/JM/15–27A/28/Jenny Matthews)*

7

STELLA TANDAI MAKANYA
The Desire to Return

Effects of Experiences in Exile on Refugees
Repatriating to Zimbabwe in the Early 1980s

Introduction

The prospect of mass voluntary repatriation of refugees to their countries of origin is
something which has only received prominence in recent years. Cuny and Stein (1990)
describe it as the 'most desirable' durable solution but hasten to give a pessimistic
evaluation of its prospects. It is, however, worth noting that this 'most desirable' solution
is a response to the emergence of large refugee populations in the developing world.
Refugees that were created by the Second World War or by the inter-Baltic state
conflicts were quickly absorbed into a prosperous and industrially expanding Europe
whose doors were opened widely for them to enter and stay. In comparison, refugee
populations in the present-day developing countries are hosted by some of the world's
poorest countries and are often confined to squalid camps, in remote border areas and
with little opportunity to fend for themselves. They, therefore, end up depending on
handouts from the international refugee aid regime which treats them as objects rather
than subjects of aid.

Zolberg, Suhrke and Aguayo (1989) estimate that, since the late 1940s, upheavals in the
developing world have caused more than 40 million refugees (although the actual numbers
needing protection and assistance at any one time are considerably smaller). While some
refugee-creating situations get resolved, new ones are constantly being created. Zolberg
et al. observe that

> somewhat like passengers of a bus whose total represents the temporary excess of those who get
> on at previous stops over those who get off . . . [the population of the displaced in developing
> countries] has some refugees who get off easily whereas others linger on for so long (p. 229).

A comparison between the circumstances of those refugee populations that 'get off
easily' and those who 'stay on for so long' may lead to an understanding of the reasons
why some situations lend themselves to solution while others do not. Zolberg *et al.* argue,
however, that this can be explained mostly by looking at 'why they got on to the bus to
start with'.

The movement of various refugee populations in developing countries has been studied
and documented, from the flows occasioned by the creation of Israel in the late 1940s,
to the Korean and Vietnamese conflicts of the 1950s, the Cuban exodus of 1959, the
decolonization of Algeria 1954–63, the independence of Zaire and Rwanda in the 1960s,

and massive flows in Africa and Asia in the 1970s. The list is long and all these present different lessons. Nevertheless, the desire for a greater understanding of the nature of upheavals that cause refugees and the search for durable solutions continue to present major challenges to the social sciences.

Kibreab (1990), trying to find a common denominator for the situations that prompt large numbers of people in Africa to leave their homes in search of international protection, concluded that no single cause could be generalized to the whole continent. He listed, however, six major categories of causes of displacement in Africa, namely, wars of national liberation; South Africa's destabilization policies; the denial of the right to self-determination for groups or states annexed to others by former colonial powers; tyranny of some political leaders; religious persecution; and forcible relocation and villagization. However, large categories such as those listed often disguise the unique features of each of the refugee-creating situations.

Just as the immediate causes and consequences of an exodus may be diverse and complex, any research into the social, cultural and economic responses to forced uprooting of large populations must identify the historical contexts and the socio-political processes that generate these refugees. The historical background of refugee populations often determines the refugees' perceptions of themselves and the extent to which they can resist or submit to being dominated by the aid regime. Through an understanding of this historical background, one can even attempt to predict outcomes and plan for solutions.

While the exodus from Zimbabwe during the liberation war may be labelled as any other 'escape from violence', it had a combination of characteristics which made it quite different from many other refugee exoduses in Africa, and which resulted in a unique experience. This chapter examines the refugee experience of Zimbabweans who sought asylum in the neighbouring states. It analyses the historical circumstances that caused the refugees to leave their country and the circumstances that motivated their return, arguing that the bitterness of the pre-flight experiences of Zimbabweans made it inevitable for many of those who fled to return to their homes as soon as the conditions that sent them away had changed. It further illustrates how the discipline and political conciousness that were inculcated in the refugee camps determined the refugees' attitudes towards repatriation. The chapter argues that the high level of political control which the parties that were waging the liberation war had over the refugee camps, and the low level of direct interference by international aid agencies in organizing the activities of refugees in the countries of asylum, made it possible for a strong liberation ideology to be inculcated into the refugee population. This factor, coupled with the limited social and economic assimilation into the economies of the host countries, made it easier for the collective decision to return home to be made once the political situation that caused the exodus had changed.

In this discussion, the terms 'refuge' and 'exile' are used interchangeably. While it is recognized that the term 'exile' has no legal definition in international refugee law and that it has the historical connotation of political banishment, the term is preferred to describe those Zimbabweans who left their homes for neighbouring countries, because of the political nature of both the decision to flee and the choice in the direction of flight. By using the term 'exile' the chapter is, therefore, trying to make the distinction between the refugee who is 'helpless' and the one who is determined to liberate himself/herself.

---

* The reader may find it helpful to refer to the chronology of events in Zimbabwe on p. 164.

Causes of Mass Exodus

The flight from Zimbabwe started as a trickle soon after the Unilateral Declaration of Independence (UDI) in 1965 and reached its peak in the period between 1977 and 1978. In the early days of the exodus, the people who left Rhodesia were mainly young men who had been recruited to go and train so that a liberation war could be waged. In later years, the exodus included peasants, students, workers and even children. At the height of the war in 1979, it was estimated that 90 per cent of refugees in the camps in Mozambique were below the age of 25.*

There were several long-term causes of discontent among black Zimbabweans that fuelled the mass exodus. These included discrimination in land distribution; poor social services, especially the very limited educational opportunities; low wages and poor working conditions; and the clamp-down on trade union activities.

Discontent with the distribution of land was one of the main grievances against the settler regime for the black people of Zimbabwe. This resulted in the land question becoming the main rallying point in the nationalist debate. The Tribal Trust Lands (TTLs) were estimated to have a maximum carrying capacity of 275,000 families, but in 1977 there were already 675,000 families living in these infertile and predominantly semi-arid lands that are unsuitable for intensive agriculture (Riddell, 1979). Yet, at that same time, the best arable land that is well-watered was in the hands of about 7,000 white farmers. The Zimbabweans who had traditionally lived in these well-watered areas had been forcibly moved to make way for the newcomers. For an agricultural people such as Zimbabweans are, the land policy of the colonial regimes was most dehumanizing and was thus one of the people's major grievances. Lack of suitable agricultural land meant that larger numbers of peasants had to survive by selling their labour at extremely low wages.

Limited educational opportunities were, perhaps, the second major grievance of the black people of Rhodesia against the settler government. Many of the freedom fighters of the sixties and early seventies left the country because they had been denied opportunities for further education. The lack of opportunity to be educated was glaring. For example, there was a decline in the absolute numbers of school places from about 713,000 in 1968 to 703,000 in 1970 and yet the annual population growth rate was more than 2.5 per cent (Rhodesian Government, 1970). Of the 113,941 pupils who began their first year in school in 1960, only 37,673 (about one-third) completed primary education and only 6,754 (about one-sixth of those who completed primary education) obtained places for secondary education (Murphree, 1975). This very high drop-out rate in the educational system was not accidental but was well calculated. The government's attitude towards the education of blacks was summed up by the Rhodesian Minister of Education in a statement to Parliament in 1966 when he stated that 'for the great majority of Africans, there is no purpose in education other than literacy' (Martin and Johnson, 1981: 59).

Education for whites, by comparison, was compulsory for all children under the age of sixteen and the government support levels per white child in school were 36 times those at which African children were supported.

The discrimination in educational opportunities for blacks inevitably led to a third cause of major discontent among Africans in Rhodesia, that of labour conditions and job opportunities. In a country where education provided the only channel for mobility from being a labourer to being a skilled worker, lack of educational opportunities meant that most Africans were condemned to remain at the lowest rung of the labour ladder.

Discriminatory labour practices were first institutionalized through the Master and Servant Act of 1901 and were reinforced by the Industrial Conciliation Act of 1959, through its many amendments in 1964, 1967 and 1971. The Master and Servant Act prohibited Africans employed in domestic service, in agriculture and in mining from being called workers and from joining trade unions, and yet these were the sectors that employed the largest proportion of black workers as cheap labour. The Industrial Conciliation Act, as amended several times, gave the government unparalleled power to control the activities of unions.

While such control was intended to make it difficult for the unions of black workers to fight for their rights and develop a class consciousness, there emerged powerful labour organizations which produced many of the generation of political leaders who led the fight for Zimbabwe's independence. Out of the activities of the early labour unions, political parties were born which started advocating, among other things, majority rule, higher wages, better education and better working conditions for the workers.

In addition to these long-term causes of discontent which fuelled the flight into exile in the years to follow, there were other more immediate factors which triggered off the mass exodus of Zimbabweans into neighbouring countries. These included the repressive apparatus of government that tried to stop political activities among the Africans; the Rhodesian government's response to the insurgence of freedom fighters in the northeastern border of the country; a change in tactics of the guerrilla war from aiming at engaging the enemy forces to focussing on mobilization of the masses as a first step; and the geo-political changes that occurred in the sub-region especially the independence of Mozambique in 1975.

After UDI, the government of Rhodesia engaged in brutal suppression of political activities of Africans. The main political parties had been banned, Zimbawe African People's Union (ZAPU) in 1962 and Zimbabwe African National Union (ZANU) in 1964. These parties then decided to establish headquarters in Zambia and in Tanzania, from where they planned the launching of the liberation struggle. After the beginning of the decisive phase of the liberation war that was marked by the attack on Altena farm in the northeast of the country on 20 December 1972, recruitment to join the struggle gained momentum. In those early days of the war, men and women were encouraged to join the war due to their admiration of the courage shown by the early guerrillas in challenging the enemy who in the past had seemed invincible. The desire to join the war was also prompted by the teachings of the freedom fighters which highlighted the repression of political activities, and the disadvantage and exploitation under which the people were living.

The actual departure from home was, however, in most instances precipitated by police brutality and threats of arrest once one had been suspected of 'subversive' political activities. The police force, which was predominantly black, was used by the settler government as a major instrument for its repressive measures and was subsequently deployed in the war zones on counter-insurgency duties.

The response of the Rhodesian regime to guerrilla insurgence in the country was another one of the major causes of mass exodus. From 1973 onwards, the government passed a series of even more repressive legislation than had been hitherto experienced, to deal with the black population that was being accused of supporting the guerrilla war. In the war zones, schools, clinics and even churches were closed. The police and the district commissioners were empowered to impose collective fines on communities who were aiding 'terrorists' or failed to report their presence. An example is cited by Ranger (1985) in which a rural community in Weya Tribal Trust Land was fined Z$35,000 in March 1977 after being accused of 'holding meetings' and 'willingly' carrying out instructions given by the 'terrorists' to steal cattle from the neighbouring white commercial farmers.

Thousands of villagers were forced to leave their homes to go into 'protected villages' (PVs or 'keeps' as they were popularly known). These were small, fenced and guarded camps where peasants of an area that was considered to have a high level of guerrilla activity were concentrated so that they would not come into contact with the freedom fighters. They were guarded by a special unit of the security forces called the Guard Force. The inmates of these PVs had their freedom of movement severely restricted. For example, the gates would only be opened for a few hours of the day when the villagers were allowed to leave the camp to work on their fields, gather firewood, go to look at the damage, if any, to their homes and carry out a host of other tasks that were necessary. 'No-go' areas were created outside the PVs and legislation was passed making it lawful for the security forces to destroy property left behind by villagers which was thought to be useful to the guerrillas. This meant the destruction of all the property that the rural people could not take with them when they escaped the violence of the war, including cattle, houses and any household implements and utensils.

The Indemnity and Compensation Act, passed in 1975 and backdated to December 1972, was designed to condone any acts of destruction and brutality perpetrated by the security forces upon civilians in the conduct of the war. The Catholic Commission for Justice and Peace noted in 1976 that acts of torture were often committed

> with the aim of extracting information about the movements of insurgents, or of compelling the population to co-operate with the authorities, or punishing villagers suspected of having assisted [the guerrillas]. (Martin and Johnson, 1981: 168)

The Indemnity and Compensation Act barred any court action for any of the acts committed in pursuit of the war including wanton killing, torture of innocent people or destruction of property. Villagers could be detained for up to 60 days by the police without being accused of any offence. In 1974, over 12,000 rural people in the north-eastern border areas had been arrested for activities associated with assisting the freedom fighters.

In addition, the villagers who had been forced into the PVs were exposed to considerable violence and personal abuse at the hands of the security forces. For example, in October 1979, a white soldier was sentenced to 14 years' imprisonment on various charges of rape and assault against the residents of the PV under his command. According to the magistrate who tried the case

> the charges made horrifying and gruesome reading, and showed that the people were subjected to savage and brutal onslaughts where little or no regard was paid to age, sex or the condition of those attacked. (A report in *The Sunday Times* of 21 October 1979 quoted in IDAF, 1980: 14)

It was an absolute rarity, to say the least, for cases such as the one cited above ever to come to court. The fact that this one did can be interpreted to mean that such cases were so widespread that leaving them unattended was proving to be an embarrassment for the Rhodesian government.

By committing repressive acts such as the ones cited above and many more, the Rhodesian government had put an end to the hope of ever winning the allegiance of black Zimbabweans. At that same time, when the settler regime was resorting to violence, the guerrillas were going through a process of mobilizing the masses to give more support to the liberation war. The freedom fighters took the instances of violence and repression as further examples and reasons for pursuing the war. The peasants did not need much persuasion to follow the teachings of the fighters. They saw in these teachings a hope to regain their land and in the guerrillas a chance to hit back in any significant way for the violence perpetrated against them. As was noted by Ranger (1985), peasant consciousness was fully adequate to sustain the horrors of a guerrilla war by the 1970s. Through songs and lectures at the meetings in the night (the *pungwes*), the rural people were convinced that it was essential for them to take up arms against the oppressive regime.

The response of the Zimbabweans to the violence and repression of the settler regime and the mobilization of the guerrillas was not surprising. As Ranger observed, the peasants did not merely provide food, shelter and information to the guerrillas, they also actively supported the war and one type of action taken was to go into the neighbouring countries to join the fight.

After the independence of Mozambique in 1975, the trickle of recruits of the earlier years turned into a flood. The length of the border between Zimbabwe and Mozambique increased the number of routes available to leave the country. Unlike the Zambian border where one had to cross the huge Zambezi river, the Mozambique border was quite porous. Added to the 640 kilometres of the Botswana border, the area for the Rhodesian forces to patrol in order to stop the crossings was considerably increased and their ability to stop the flow out of the country was greatly reduced. Martin and Johnson (1981: 205) quote a Rhodesia Broadcasting Corporation report, starting that 'in September and October 1975, recruits were crossing into Mozambique at the rate of 1,000 a week'. A UNHCR source quoted by Zolberg *et al.* (1989) stated that, by the end of 1975, there were an estimated 14,500 Zimbabweans in refugee camps in Mozambique.

For many Zimbabweans, therefore, the decision to leave home was a rational and conscious one. In many cases it was also an individual one. The causes were clear and their intention was not ambiguous at all. Young people, at most times, left their homes without telling any members of their families where they had gone because they knew that the families would be harassed by the police if there was any suspicion that a member had gone to join the struggle. In the border areas, whole families went to escape the violence of the forces trying to stop them from supporting a cause which was their own. Entire student bodies of schools crossed the borders into Mozambique or Botswana, and, as in the case of the Tangwena people, villages or groups of villages went across the border *en masse* to give support to the liberation war.

Such movements as these call into question the distinction that is often made between voluntary and involuntary migration of refugee populations. While the movements may have been determined by the socio-political situation which existed, they were considered by the migrants themselves to be necessary in order for them to achieve certain aims. There was, in a way, some limited measure of choice especially in the selection of destination and timing of the movements. The exodus could even be considered to be voluntary in so far as it gave the oppressed Zimbabweans a chance to achieve self-determination. There is no doubt that there was bitterness and even pain on leaving home, but the feeling of the Zimbabweans was that this was a sacrifice worth making.

How Long Did the Refugees Expect to be Away from Home?

As has been shown above, there was little doubt in the minds of the people who left Rhodesia as to why they fled and where they were going. At the height of the war and after the independence of Mozambique, with little exception, those in the ZAPU area of influence went to Botswana and then on to Zambia, and those in the ZANU zone of activity went to Mozambique. In 1979 there were an estimated 25,000 refugees in Botswana, 45,000 in Zambia and 150,000 in Mozambique, according to a UNHCR source quoted in Zolberg *et al.* (1989: 84). These large numbers of people could not be trained and absorbed into the liberation war as quickly as they came. Moreover, up to 50 per cent of them were children under the age of fifteen (McLaughlin, 1979). The creation of refugee camps in the neighbouring countries was, therefore, a necessity.

Although the refugee camps provided both the Zimbabwe African National Liberation Army (ZANLA) – the military wing of ZANU – and the Zimbabwe People's Revolutionary Army (ZIPRA) – the military wing of ZAPU – with readily available sources for the recruitment of trainees, there was a clear distinction, by both ZANU and ZAPU, between the refugee camps and the training camps and rear bases for the fighters. This distinction was necessary for several reasons including security, logistics and administrative efficiency. For those refugees who were old enough, fit and keen to fight, the only available option was to go into the refugee camps and await their turn to be recruited into a training unit. The wait could be long; for some it was months and for others years. A large majority of the people who left Zimbabwe to join the struggle never got to train or to fight before the war ended.

When these Zimbabweans left their homes, for whatever reason, be it to join the war, to escape from violence or to join other family members who had already left, they had no idea how long they were going to stay away. Although there was no doubt about the eventuality of returning home, there was no way of knowing how long it would take. Leaving home was, therefore, a sign of a commitment to a cause, a desire and a determination to struggle as long as was necessary.

In fact, because of the levels of oppression at home, it was difficult if not impossible for someone to decide to go back home after escaping into a neighbouring country. Except for the populations who lived in the extreme border areas who could cross the border back and forth (such as Chief Tangwena and his people), it was inconceivable to return until the situation in Rhodesia changed. Moreover, in Rhodesia, the very idea of going to join the struggle was an offence punishable by death. The people who had fled, therefore, had no option but to stay there until Zimbabwe was free; moreover, this was part of the ideology of the struggle.

As this ideology was taken by the exiled group, their resolve to fight and only to return to a free Zimbabwe, even if it meant spending all their lives in exile, was strengthened. A collective identity was, therefore, created in exile and it would last as long as the war lasted. If ever a decision to return home before Zimbabwe was free was contemplated, it would have been interpreted as a betrayal of the struggle by fellow refugees and would have meant death at the hands of the Rhodesian regime at home.

There is no attempt to romanticize life outside Zimbabwe and especially in the refugee camps in neighbouring countries. As will be shown later, there was much suffering as a result of too little assistance from the international aid community, coupled with the very limited capacity of the poor host countries to sustain such large numbers of asylum seekers. The major source of the suffering for the refugees, however, came from the cross-border attacks by the Rhodesian regime's forces. On 9 August 1976, an attack on the Nyadzonia refugee camp in Mozambique killed more than 1,000 Zimbabwean refugees. Even the soldiers who took part in the Nyadzonia massacre knew that the camp was inhabited by thousands of unarmed refugees. In fact when the enemy forces arrived with their disguised appearance, many refugees ran towards them, thinking that they were comrades who had come to select the next group of recruits to go for training. As expressed by one of the participants in the massacre, the intention of the Rhodesian regime was:

7.1 *Nyadzonia after bombing by the Rhodesian airforce (UNHCR/6108/Vieira de Mello)*

7.2 *Distribution of food rations to Zimbabwean refugees in Mozambique. Some of the women seen in this picture suffer from leg paralysis attributed to the psychological shock of the raid on Nyadzonia camp (UNHCR/7079/Vieira de Mello)*

to wipe them out while they were unarmed and before they are trained rather than wait for the possibility of them being trained and sent back armed into Rhodesia (Martin and Johnson, 1981: 241).

Another major attack on refugees in Mozambique by the Rhodesian forces took place at Chimoio in 1977. For several days commencing on 23 November, the enemy forces roamed the bushes and used helicopters, destroying a whole residential complex that included schools, clinics and administrative offices, killing as many unarmed refugees as they could find. On that same mission, they also attacked two other refugee camps at Tembwe. Similar raids were also made on refugee camps in Zambia on 18 and 21 October 1978 and in July 1979. In the attack on Mkushi camp in October 1978, the people who were killed by the Rhodesian forces were predominantly women since this was a camp for women and girls who were undergoing training in skills such as typing and administration. The J. Moyo camp that was also attacked in Zambia was exclusively a boys' school.

Despite the insecurity and the lack of protection in the refugee camps, the refugees stayed in the neighbouring countries until the war of liberation had ended. Those that survived the massacres left to settle in other camps. Their suffering was to be later translated into heroism. Those who had died perished for a worthy cause and were buried in mass graves in the camps.

There had been several attempts at negotiated settlements to the Zimbabwean independence issue before 1979. When the Lancaster House Conference that brought about independence started in September 1979, refugees could not have predicted that their stay was about to come to an end. In fact, the exodus from Zimbabwe continued even during the Conference.

It can, therefore, be concluded that the refugees who left Rhodesia due to persecution, war, discrimination or lack of opportunities had demonstrated to the whole world their dissatisfaction with the situation at home. They could not be seen to return to the same situation from which they escaped without seriously weakening the cause for which they had already suffered. They, therefore, had a moral duty to continue the struggle. Furthermore, none of those who had escaped could be persuaded to go back home before the political situation had changed.

Under What Circumstances Did They Expect to Return?

The oppressive machinery of the settler regime may have prevented the return of the Zimbabwean refugees, but there was no doubt in their minds about the inevitability of eventual repatriation. They believed in this so much that it became one of the reasons to justify their suffering while in exile. It was one of the main aims of the liberation ideology to keep this hope of going home alive and to rekindle it even when times were difficult. The need to become the core of conscientized people to spearhead the transformation of Zimbabwe was stressed in political teachings by the liberation movements.

Part of the liberation ideology was to clarify why the war was being fought and what it was expected to achieve. The education given in the refugee camps was intended to answer these questions. The focus of the teachings was to show how the people had been dispossessed of their birth-right and had been denied basic human rights by the system of government in Rhodesia.

This was done through the tracing and reinterpretation of their history. The main grievances of the people were again stressed and the reasons for the sacrifices made were reiterated. As has already been mentioned, the issue of the land was the main rallying point.

Zimbabweans, therefore, expected to go back to a country where they would be accorded the right to use the land of their fore-fathers without being discriminated against because of the colour of their skin, where there would be free political activity and where the government would be composed of true representatives of the majority, where educational opportunities would be equally open to all and jobs would be allocated according to merit and not skin colour. Above all, Zimbabwean refugees expected to return to a situation where there was no war and they trusted the leaders of the liberation movements to make the judgement of when war would no longer be necessary.

Factors Influencing Refugee Attitudes Towards Repatriation While in Exile

While one may be driven from home by circumstances that make home an unworthy place to live, exile still has to be explained to oneself in such a way as to make it a justifiable option. Family ties are broken, property is lost, one's means of survival are abandoned, and the whole social and cultural fabric is threatened with disintegration. For the Zimbabwean refugees, a justifiable explanation for leaving home was not difficult to find. The need to fight the system was a just cause. What was necessary, however, was to maintain the spirit of the struggle and sustain it 'until final victory'.

There were several factors that influenced the refugees' attitudes towards repatriation whilst they were in exile. These included the political education given in the camps, the type of communities in which refugees lived while in exile, the level of control enjoyed by the political parties and liberation movements and the low levels of integration between the Zimbabweans and the host communities.

The refugee communities that were formed in exile were very useful in maintaining a Zimbabwean identity, resisting cultural disintegration and establishing community values. As part of a strategy to ensure the suvival of that identity, it became necessary to establish closed communities where dependence on each other was stressed. For example, the camps in Mozambique were organized communally, with centralized sources of food supply, common cooking facilities and collective food production. In Zambia, camp inhabitants were separated according to age and sex, and facilities were also supplied from centralized sources. The closed communities became so closely knit that a new bond was established among them and they felt an increased responsibility towards each other. As De Wolf (1981: 5) expressed it, '. . . they had become mother and father, brother and sister to each other in situations where their very lives depended on this solidarity'.

One of the main consequences of the control of political parties over refugee camps was that aid agencies were not allowed a free rein in the camps. While this might have had other repercussions, it also had a significant effect on the refugees' attitudes towards repatriation. The issue of assistance will be discussed in the next section.

Levels of Material Assistance Provided
The level of control secured by the political parties over the administration of the camps and the distribution of assistance was one of the main reasons why these parties managed to maintain the refugee population as an integrated whole and were able to co-ordinate their response to repatriation. Experiences related from other refugee situations where the

international aid regime has had a free rein are fraught with instances of manipulation of refugee populations and frustration of their aspirations, competition among the agencies, use of aid to refugees as a political tool and an expansion of the foreign policies of the agencies' countries of origin, and a general creation of dependency which can be counterproductive for these populations' future.

International assistance to Zimbabwean refugees in Botswana, Mozambique and Zambia was very minimal. At the height of the war in 1979, there were an estimated 200,000 Zimbabwean refugees in the three countries. For example, in the five camps that were run with the assistance of the UNHCR in Mozambique, there were acute food shortages and the supplies were erratic. The food provided was mainly starch in the form of maize meal. Water for drinking, bathing and washing was obtained from nearby rivers, was untreated and was an obvious health hazard.

In each of these camps there was a small clinic that was run by trained personnel, but there were hardly any medicines or medical equipment. Malaria was an obvious major health problem, but there were no medicines either for prevention or for treatment. At the Doroi refugee camp, for example, there was an outbreak of cholera in 1978. Although medical supplies were airlifted to the camp by the Lutheran World Federation after the outbreak had been reported, they came too late for some people and there were many fatalities.

Sister Janice McLaughlin, in a report of a fact-finding mission to the camps in Mozambique on behalf of the Zimbabwe Project in June 1978, assessed that, although several international agencies were assisting, the levels of assistance were far below those required for the maintenance and care of the estimated 150,000 refugees in the camps. She also reported that she had been informed by UNHCR that the amount of clothing and blankets that had been received for the year was enough to cater for only one-tenth of the refugee population.

In terms of availability of assistance, the situation in Zambia was not as acute as that in Mozambique. For a start, ZAPU had to cater for a considerably smaller number of refugees than the ZANU camps in Mozambique. In March 1979, there were an estimated 45,000 refugees in the camps in Zambia, although the UNHCR gave a lower figure of 22,000 (Acton, 1979). In her report of a Zimbabwe Project fact-finding mission to Zambia in July 1979, Judith Acton noted that the lack of agreement between ZAPU and UNHCR on the numbers of refugees meant that assistance provided by the latter was for only half the population of refugees that the former was catering for. Although ZAPU also got assistance from other agencies such as, for example, the LWF in the form of a field hospital and some medical supplies, there were reports of food shortages, inadequate clothing and insufficient housing for the new arrivals and the school children who had to move to a new camp after the attack by the Rhodesian forces in 1978. ZAPU also had the problem of the transportation of refugees and recruits for whom it was responsible from Botswana to Zambia. The donor community and aid agencies did not see the logic of paying for the airlifting of refugees from Botswana to Zambia, yet ZAPU insisted that this was necessary. The situation in Botswana has not been covered in this chapter, but the difficulties there included the increased insecurity due to the country's proximity to South Africa, and the resultant attitude of its government towards granting protection to asylum seekers who had direct connections to liberation movements. In the light of this, the ZAPU desire to remove vulnerable refugees from there gains a new meaning.

Assistance to refugees by the international aid regime had the usual features of paternalism which the Zimbabweans had loathed at home. Rarely were the requests made by

7.3 *UNHCR and several other aid agencies wanted a clear distinction to be made between those training or intending to train for the liberation war and those who were 'genuine civilian refugees': emergency supplies being airlifted to Mozambique for Zimbabwean refugees in 1977 (UNHCR/7198/Y. Muller)*

the representatives of the refugees met. Decisions were often made by the agencies on what the needs of the refugees were and the expectation was that donations would be accepted without questioning. For example, the categorization of exiles into political refugees, freedom fighters and civilians fleeing from war, conflict and other forms of persecution was quite unrealistic. In many cases, the three groups were one and the same.

UNHCR and several other aid agencies, however, wanted a clear distinction to be made between those training or intending to train for the liberation war and those who were 'genuine civilian refugees'. In both Mozambique and Zambia there were some refugee camps that UNHCR refused to assist on the pretext that these were guerrilla camps. Zolberg *et al.* (1989: 85) noted that in 1978 UNHCR temporarily stopped assisting ZAPU affiliated camps in Zambia because they judged that the party was not making a clear enough distinction between liberation forces and civilian refugees. In Mozambique, however, the demands by UNHCR for the clear distinction between assistance to 'civilian refugees' to the exclusion of the trained fighters were often frustrated by Nucleo de Apoio aos Refugiados en Moçambique (Nucleo). This was the government's refugee relief co-ordinating body which worked closely with ZANU in administering the refugee camps and all assistance to refugees had to be channelled through this agency. Nucleo did not recognize the distinction and therefore made it difficult for UNHCR or any other agency that was assisting refugees to strictly adhere to that requirement. There were, however, camps in Mozambique which did not receive UNHCR aid and were run exclusively by ZANU and Nucleo. In addition, UNHCR's levels of assistance were far below those required to support the large number of refugees in Mozambique. This was probably because it had a much lower estimate of those considered to be the 'genuine' refugees.

Although requirements for such distinctions are often imposed on refugee populations, it is doubtful whether they have any legal basis in international refugee law. For example, there is no indication found in either the 1951 Geneva Convention or the OAU Convention of 1969 for making any distinction between the refugee who has been granted status but who later decides to undergo military training in order to liberate his/her country from an oppressive government, and the civilian refugee. Except where the host government withdraws refugee status as a result of such training, UNHCR would have no legal justification for withholding assistance on the pretext that a refugee has received military training. Such demands, therefore, raise questions about UNHCR's ability to provide protection and assistance to refugees while allowing them freedom to determine their own destiny. This is a clear example of the paternalism of the refugee aid regime.

Further examples of the paternalism of aid agencies were cited by Father Nigel Johnson in the final report of his stay in a refugee camp in Zambia:

> A representative from an aid agency would arrive for a day to assess the needs [of refugees] over the next three months. He would discuss all the needs with the administrator of the camp, take notes and return to Lusaka. Discussion would be held within the agency in Lusaka, telexes sent to the agency headquarters and decisions taken on which things would be provided. Sometime over the next three months, various of the requested supplies would suddenly appear at the camp; the camp administrator not knowing what to expect or when to expect it. The agency representative comes expecting grateful thanks for what he has given to the camp, only to be greeted with 'When will the new electric generator be coming, that's what we have been waiting for for the past three months.' And the reply 'They decided in Europe 10 weeks ago that you did not really need it' is accepted with an expressionless resignation. (Johnson, 1980: 2)

From his experiences, Father Johnson concluded that many of the agencies that visited the camps were more interested in taking photographs of the worst sites and the most rugged refugees than in appreciating the efforts by the refugees to become self-reliant. He, however, warned that the expressionless faces of refugees were not expressing fear and helplessness but resentment of the photographer who had no real interest in the person whose picture he was taking.

Some agencies blamed the inadequacy of international assistance to the refugees in camps in both Mozambique and Zambia on the relatively underdeveloped economies of these countries. For example, some agencies that came to assist refugees found that they could not get the goods that the camps required within the host countries and these had to be imported, thus incurring huge transport costs which greatly increased the cost of the assistance programme, and ended up providing far fewer goods.

While such claims might have had some credence, there was, however, also the need to recognize how the countries that hosted the large numbers of Zimbabwean refugees had suffered, first due to the influx of large numbers of people into fragile economies, and second due to the attacks by the Rhodesian forces which often destroyed infrastructure such as bridges, school and clinics. In the case of Mozambique, the refugees started coming

in large numbers when the country was only just emerging from its own ten-year liberation war. It has been shown in other refugee populations that such pressure on an economy
would inevitably lead to strained relationships between the refugees and the host community. Mozambicans, however, gave Zimbabweans unparalleled support even in their
poverty. Sister Janice noted in her report that the people of Mozambique, in addition to
providing all the land that the Zimbabweans needed to grow food, also contributed one
day's pay per month to the solidarity fund to assist the war effort.

Despite all the attempts at paternalism and instances of withdrawal of conditional aid,
the political parties continued to control the camps and to run them in a manner that was
in agreement with the aims of the struggle. There was a strong belief in self-reliance in
the ideology of the liberation war which made it essential for aid agencies to take heed
of the needs articulated by the refugee community when these agencies went on their
'needs' assessment trips. The communal lifestyle and the policy of self-reliance were
intended to inculcate into these communities the values that the liberation war cherished.
As Sister Janice noted after her visit to the camps in Mozambique in 1979:

> The spirit of determination, enthusiasm and self-reliance in the camps overshadows the poverty,
> fear and lack of facilities and supplies. Instead of feeling sorry for the refugees, I went away
> with a feeling of respect and admiration for them and the new life they were living . . .
> It was obvious that self-reliance was not just a slogan, but [was] the motivating spirit of
> the camps. I was struck, for example, that most needs were stated in terms of raw materials rather
> than finished goods: requests for wool and knitting needles rather than sweaters, cloth and
> thread rather than clothes and farm tools and seeds rather than imported foods. (McLaughlin,
> 1979: 8–9)

General experiences of refugee assistance that have been observed in Africa, however, tend
not to recognize such a desire for refugees to control their lives, and there is a tendency
to 'impose aid', with any questioning being regarded as ingratitude (Harrell-Bond, 1986).
The experiences of Zimbabweans in relation to control over aid, therefore, provide useful
lessons for both aid agencies and refugee populations.

Information about Changes in the Political Situation at Home

Life in refugee camps revolved around getting and disseminating information. Considering
the insecurity in the camps which were subject to numerous attacks from the Rhodesian
forces, one could not afford to keep uninformed of the recent developments, especially
on the situation at home. Information in the camps was disseminated in a number of
ways. The party was the main source of information on political matters. Since the political parties leading the liberation movement were involved in the administration of
the refugee camps, it was easy to provide the necessary information through the party
channels.

Secondly many refugees kept themselves informed through listening to the radio.
The 'Voice of Zimbabwe' programmes beamed from the radio stations of the frontline states were used to inform of the atrocities committed by the enemy and to poli-
ticize the masses of Zimbabwe. It was quite usual to find refugees clustered around the
few radios that could be found in the camps, listening to the news on the most recent
developments.

Sister Janice McLaughlin, during her visit to Matenje camp in Tete where there was
a large educational complex, noted that:

> the level of awareness in the camps was exceptionally high. The kind of questions I was asked
> revealed a knowledge of international politics that is far beyond that of most young people in
> the United States or Europe. The students know what is happening in their own country as

well as the relationships of other nations with the liberation movements and with the internal regime. (p. 9)

The third way of disseminating information was 'the grapevine'. The insecurity of the camps coupled with the spirit of responsibility for each other meant that, once one person got information that was vital for survival such as that on the situation at home, every effort would be made to disseminate it to as many people as possible. The lives of the refugees depended on that and they could not afford to be complacent. And, with such a high level of awareness and vigilance, the refugees in the camps followed the events leading to the Lancaster Conference and the developments that were taking place there with keen interest. When the formal agreements were signed and a cease-fire date was fixed, in addition to the word from the camp administration, messages were beamed on the Voice of Zimbabwe channels. News of the departure of the guerrilla commanders for Salisbury also spread very quickly. The refugees could not help being overjoyed at possibilities that the war had come to an end and that they could go home.

The Process of Returning Home

The decision to go home was a collective one for the refugees in the camps in the neighbouring countries. Just as they had survived as a community, so did they decide to leave. For many of the refugees in the neighbouring countries, however, the decision was taken as an act of faith, hope and great determination; faith in the judgement of the leadership of the liberation movements that negotiated at the Lancaster House Conference, hope that there would be a dismantling of the repressive machinery that had caused the people to rise and take up arms and that there would be a lasting peace, and determination to make a new start.

The need to go home as promptly as possible was brought about by several factors, the major one being the desire to participate in the pre-independence general elections scheduled for 27, 28 and 29 February 1980. The Lancaster House agreement had stated that repatriation of refugees would be carried out as quickly as possible especially for the adults in order to enable them to take part in the elections. At the request of the British government, UNHCR was asked to facilitate the repatriation exercise and the HCR, therefore, set up an office in Salisbury early in January 1980 for that purpose.

UNHCR has three preconditions that have to be fulfilled if it is to take part in the organized repatriation of refugees. First, the repatriation must be voluntary, secondly, there must be an agreement between the host country and the country of origin 'on the modalities of the movement and the conditions of the reception', and thirdly, the returnees should be allowed to go back to their former homes and villages (Cuny and Stein, 1990). In line with these requirements, an agreement was signed between UNHCR and the Department of Social Affairs (representing the government of the country of origin) and Christian Care (a voluntary organization) for the implementation of the repatriation programme. In the camps in Mozambique, UNHCR worked with Nucleo and ZANU to organize the transportation of refugees to the reception centres in Zimbabwe, while in Zambia the logistics of the departure were organized together with ZAPU, the Zambian Refugee Council and other aid agencies that had assisted in the camps.

The plan of operation was that there would be six reception centres inside Zimbabwe scattered near the border areas of the three countries that hosted Zimbabwean refugees. These centres would fall under the authority of the Department of Social Affairs. At each

of the centres there would be representatives of UNHCR and Christian Care (as representing the heads of denominations of the various churches). Immigration and customs
formalities were to be dealt with by the officials of the Ministry of Home Affairs. It had
also been planned that, once the refugees had arrived at the reception centres, transportation would then be provided by the Department of Social Affairs either to the refugees'
own homes or to transit centres further inland. The transit centres were to be supervised
by the churches that were being represented by Christian Care, while the UNHCR
would provide the funds for the assistance programme to returnees through Christian
Care.

The implementation of the plan outlined above was, however, fraught with problems.
For example, according to a report prepared by the Catholic Institute for International
Relations (CIIR) in consultation with the Catholic Commission for Justice and Peace
(CCJP), the first group to be repatriated under the UNHCR programme arrived at the
Tegwani Mission reception centre near the border with Botswana on 21 January 1980. The
group, numbering 1,000, was from the Selibe-Pikwe camp in Botswana. It consisted of
young males only. A description of the experience of that group clearly demonstrates some
of the problems that were to be faced by most of the refugees who would be repatriated
through this programme:

> On arrival [of the refugees at the reception centre] there were, apart from an army of news-
> paper reporters, a strong presence of armed District Assistants [DAs]. Only five customs and
> immigration officials were present. [Although] it had been agreed by all parties concerned that
> a reception centre could process about 1,000 refugees a day, on this particular day only 200 were
> processed. No refugees were, therefore, sent the next day. When the other 1,000 arrived on the
> third day, the local authorities declared that no more could come as there was a water problem.
> The programme was, therefore, to be temporarily suspended. When another convoy arrived
> on the fourth day, the Rhodesian authorities impounded the lorries and made it clear that any
> further arrivals would not be welcome (CIIR, 1980: 23).

In the instance described, the Rhodesian authorities seemed to be the ones with the overall
power to dictate the pace of the repatriation exercise. One could also conclude that the
refugees were returning to a situation that had not greatly changed from that which they
had fled. However, the determination to return home, the hope that there would be a
peaceful future and especially the desire to take part in the elections made the refugees
courageous enough to face the repressive machinery again. De Wolf (1981), writing on
her experiences at a reception centre near the Mozambique border, observed that, because
in the initial stages of the repatriaton exercise the government was in the hands of the
same government that had opposed the liberation war, the refugees were treated with the
same resentment and suspicion as the guerrillas that were in the assembly points. She noted
that the reception of the returnees was very unfriendly and sometimes even violent.

The Rhodesian authorities were not eager to facilitate the speedy return of the refugees
before the elections and were working as much as they could to delay or hamper this goal.
De Wolf observed that the ages of some of the returnees were falsified in the documents
that were issued by immigration officials in an attempt to make the returnees ineligible
to vote in the February elections. There were often suspicions that these refugees were
liberation fighters who were avoiding the assembly points. Some refugees were arrested
and tortured by the police. Buses that brought refugees from the reception centres to
the transit centres were often rudely stopped by police and searched. The chairman of
Christian Care at that time, Father Edward Rogers, described the reception centres as
looking more like army camps than welcome-home centres for refugees. Describing the
centre at Tegwani, Father Rogers observed:

The centre was fenced by a high and heavy security fence. At the gate, there were policemen, with four district assistants who had FN rifles and one with a machine gun, whilst inside armed district assistants were very much in evidence (CIIR, 1980).

Father Rogers commented that he had been made to believe that these centres would be under the Department of Social Affairs and that the Home Affairs personnel would be limited to customs and immigration officials only. But the reality was very different. The Rhodesian authorities were keen to demonstrate that they were still in control of the country and this caused a lot of discomfort to the returning refugees.

According to the initially agreed UNHCR plan, the returnees were supposed to stay at the reception centres for no longer than a day, upon which they would be taken to a transit centre and to their homes. The slow processing of returnees at reception centres often meant that they remained there for longer periods. The facilities at some of these centres were very inadequate and none of the centres were intended to keep large numbers of people for long periods. The delays meant that there was a lot of discomfort for many, especially mothers with young children who had to live in the open, without shelter from the rain and other elements.

The questioning that took place at these reception centres was also cause for concern for the returnees. It took place in the presence of armed men and some of the questions asked were totally irrelevant for the purpose of repatriation and were quite embarrassing and irritating for the returnees. For example, questions were asked about what occupation they had in the countries from which they had fled, the name of their previous employer in Rhodesia, the reasons for leaving Rhodesia and what political party they supported.

With all the above-mentioned problems being confronted by those who were being repatriated through the formal channels, the deliberate delaying tactics and the hostility of the Rhodesian authorities, it was clear that the agencies that had been asked to oversee the repatriation exercise had virtually no control over the events and the physical safety of the returnees could not be guaranteed. Such a situation left the refugees who were in the neighbouring countries awaiting their turn to be transported very impatient. When it became clear that the Rhodesian authorities wanted to frustrate the returnees and interfere with their participation in the forthcoming elections, many decided to take the same initiative that they had taken when they fled from the country instead of waiting for the official repatriation. Of the estimated 200,000 refugees in the neighbouring countries, only about 30,000 were repatriated through the formal channel in time for the elections (Ehrenpreis, 1983: 29) and a total of about 50,000 were repatriated by the close of the exercise in 1981. The majority of the refugees, about 150,000, therefore returned to their homes outside the official repatriation programme.

Even with such initiatives having been taken, the home-coming of those who opted to 'spontaneously' repatriate themselves was not without its own problems. The police and the security forces harrassed and even detained those who crossed the borders without going through the designated reception centres. A news article in *The Guardian* of 19 January 1990 reported that about 900 refugees from Botswana who entered Zimbabwe one day before the formal repatriation exercise started were arrested and detained for questioning at a Bulawayo prison. It was later claimed by the Rhodesian officials that 35 of them were found to have been trained ZIPRA combatants (IDAF, 1980: 15).

Those who had managed not to be detected by the police while crossing the borders were confronted by the security forces and especially by Muzorewa's auxiliaries who were freely roamimg the countryside terrorizing the rural people. Although the auxiliaries were designated as an extension of the security forces, activities that they engaged in, such as undisguised election campaigning for Muzorewa's party, the United African National Council (UANC), left people wondering why they had not been confined to barracks in the same way as the other political armies. The auxiliaries had, instead, moved into the areas where the liberation armies had operated before, harassing the villagers and especially the returnees.

The return of the refugees to their homes was further complicated by the continued existence of the 'protected villages'. The details of the dismantling of the PVs had not been discussed at Lancaster House and the Rhodesian regime was not in a hurry to dismantle them. It was unclear, therefore, whether the returnees were expected to join their families, relatives and neighbours in these 'keeps' or whether they should go to their original homes that had virtually been destroyed by the Rhodesian forces. As has already been indicated in this chapter, the inmates of the PVs lived under armed guard and were exposed to considerable violence and abuse by the security forces. Even after the cease-fire, there were reports of continued violence against the inhabitants of the PVs (IDAF, 1980: 14).

Police harassment was a major disappointment to the returnees. Considering that the Lancaster House agreement had mentioned the police as the authority that would oversee the security of voters in the forthcoming elections, many organizations that were concerned about the fate of the returnees were very worried about the role of the police, who had found it difficult to be impartial in view of the role they had assumed in the war.

Due to the disruptions to life and the congestion that was expected to occur during the initial repatriation process, it had been agreed at Lancaster House that schools in the three countries of asylum would continue to operate in these countries until more adequate preparations had been made for them. Schools in the camps in Mozambique and Zambia were repatriated in July and August 1980, but, even at that time, no arrangements had been made for their reception. De Wolf (1981) observed:

> At the Old Umtali transit centre they [the school children] spent four months waiting to be resettled, continuing their classes with the same volunteer teachers they had been with in Mozambique. They borrowed black boards, chalk and footballs from the neighbouring schools and held their classes outdoors as they had been accustomed to doing all along, sharing a small handful of tattered text books among them and faithfully copying notes . . . into their exercise books.

While these children waited, they could not help comparing themselves to those who were in established schools and noticing the difference. Even by the end of the year, 1980, these children were still overcrowded in run-down buildings of schools that had been abandoned in the war.

It was, however, worth noting that the treatment given to the returnees was not very different from that given to the combatants who were in the assembly points and the leadership of the liberation movements who had come into the country to campaign for the elections. Although the leadership of ZANU and ZAPU commanded a lot of respect and support among the masses of Zimbabwe, as was shown by the election results, they were treated by the transitional government as villains. It was as if there was an unspoken yet very tangible fear in the British administration that, if ZANU won the elections, it would be a disaster. There was blatantly preferential treatment given to Muzorewa, especially in the scheduling of campaign rallies and in coverage by local media.

Adam Curle (1980), in a confidential report to CIIR, pointed out several incidents that showed the bias of the transitional government. For example, he noted that the scheduling of election campaigning rallies was determined by its convenience to the UANC's campaign; that the Rhodesian security forces were being used as the law-enforcing agents against ZANLA and ZIPRA combatants yet they had been fighting on opposite sides; that the press still referred to the combatants as 'terrorists' and the alleged cease-fire violations by the guerrillas were given greater prominence than those of the Rhodesian forces; and that the remarkable success of the cease-fire effort on the part of the liberation movements (with over 21,000 guerrillas in assembly points) was being minimized. He warned of the possible nasty outcomes of the behaviour of the transitional government:

> Are the British trying to place PF [Patriotic Front] forces into a position in which they are helpless, goad them into breaking the cease fire so they can be eliminated from the elections? . . . If the British are trying to influence the outcome of the elections instead of conducting them freely and fairly, they would be running a great economic and diplomatic risk as well as the perils of renewed war. (Curle, 1980: 3)

Although the fears expressed above were very real at that time, they proved to be unfounded. This could be attributed partly to the discipline and statesmanship that was displayed by the PF leadership who took the trials of the transitional period as an extension of the war that they had waged for the past 15 years. The same spirit had been adopted by the returnees who dealt with the problems of that period as requiring the same sacrifices as those they had been required to make all along in the struggle for the country.

Conclusion

This chapter has tried to describe the experiences of refugees in neighbouring countries and to follow the events of the early days of a repatriation exercise that has been hailed as one of the most 'successful' in the history of African refugees.

There is little doubt that a large number of refugees did return to Zimbabwe from the neighbouring countries, and it has been argued that this became possible due to a combination of several factors that were quite unique. First, conditions that caused the exodus of Zimbabweans were overtly political. Thus, the nature of the decision to flee and the direction of the flight was tantamount to making a political statement. Second, the role of the liberation movements in welcoming, educating and caring for the refugees increased political consciousness. The allegiance of the exiled Zimbabweans to the political parties enabled these parties to wield a great deal of control and thereby limit the influence of the international refugee aid regime. Third, because of the Lancaster House agreement, the political situation in Zimbabwe held real prospects for change. This combination of factors rarely exists among refugee populations in Africa today and claims that the Zimbabwean repatriation was a carefully thought through and professionally implemented operation need to be treated with caution. If it was a success story, then it needs to be asked: 'a success for whom?'. It clearly had a great deal more to do with the discipline and determination of the refugees themselves than the competence of those who sought to assist them.

But such a guarded conclusion should not be interpreted to mean that lessons cannot be derived from the Zimbabwean experience. Several lessons actually spring to mind. First, people, no matter how poor, have the capacity and power to change their situation and turn their experience into a success. Examples of 'successful' repatriations in Africa have been experienced by Tigrayans for instance, who 'repatriated' themselves against the wishes of the international refugee aid regime and without external assistance, but have not been hailed as successes just because they were not supported by the UNHCR (Cuny and Stein, 1990: 298). Second, a lesson can be learnt on the effects of overt politicization

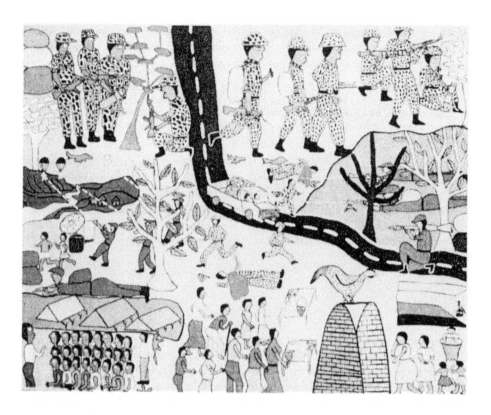

7.4 *A painting by Abishell Risinamhodzi depicting the war of independence, the announcement of the cease-fire in a refugee camp, the repatriation, the elections of 1980, and the birth of Zimbabwe (Weya Communal Training Centre, PO Box 61, Macheke, Zimbabwe)*

of refugee populations and the extent to which this can give meaning to their suffering thereby creating an ideology which instils discipline and determination, which brings about lack of dependency and enables refugees to contribute to the solution of their own problems. In recent years, there have been several attempts by the refugee aid regime to depoliticize the problems of refugees, electing to focus on famine in Ethiopia rather than the self-determination of the Tigrayans and the Eritreans, and on hunger in Mozambique rather than South African destabilization. Such foci are unlikely to inform the search for durable solutions to the problems of refugees.

References

Acton, J. (1979) 'Confidential report on a visit to Lusaka', Zimbabwe Project, 30 June–6 July 1979.

CIIR (1980), 'Rhodesia: some notes on the current situation', a report prepared by CIIR, London, in consultation with the Catholic Commission for Justice and Peace in Rhodesia, 1 February.

Cuny, F. and B. Stein (1990) 'Prospects for and promotion of spontaneous repatriation', in Loescher, G. and L. Monahan (eds) *Refugees in international relations*, Oxford University Press, New York.

Curle, A. (1980) 'The situation in Rhodesia', a confidential report written for CIIR, 16 January.

De Wolf, S. (1981) 'The resettlement and rehabilitation of refugees in the Umtali area', an address given at the University of Michigan, December.

Ehrenpreis, P. (1983) *From Rhodesia back to Zimbabwe: all my hopes were to go home one day*, Refugee Stories, SIDA.

Harrell-Bond, B. (1986) *Imposing aid: emergency assistance to refugees*, Oxford University Press, Oxford.

IDAF (International Defence and Aid Fund for Southern Africa) (1980) 'Political repression in Rhodesia', Briefing Notes, February.

Johnson, Nigel, S.J. (1980) Final report of the attachment to a refugee camp in Zambia, August.

Kibreab, G. (1990) 'State of the art review of refugee studies in Africa', a paper presented at the International Seminar on Refugees in Africa: Improving Relief Assistance and the Search for Durable Solutions, Arusha, Tanzania, 30 July–3 August.

McLaughlin, Sr Janice (1979) 'Needs of Zimbabwean refugees', a confidential report of a fact-finding trip to Mozambique for the Zimbabwe Project, 15 August–23 September.

Martin, D. and P. Johnson (1981) *The struggle for Zimbabwe: the Chimurenga war*, Faber and Faber, London.

Murphree, M. W. (1975) *Education, race and employment in Rhodesia*, Artea Publishers Salisbury.

Ranger, T. (1985) *Peasant consciousness and the guerrilla war*, Zimbabwe Publishing House, Harare, and James Currey, London.

Rhodesian Government (1970), *Rhodesian digest of statistics*, Government Printers, Harare.

Riddell, R., (1979), Prospects for Land Reform in Zimbabwe, Rural Africana, Nos. 4/5 (Spring/Fall), 17–32.

Zolberg, A., A. Suhrke and S. Aguayo (1989) *Escape from violence: conflict and refugee crisis in the developing world*, Oxford University Press, New York.

8

JEREMY JACKSON
Repatriation & Reconstruction
in Zimbabwe during the 1980s

Introduction

Ten Years On: the Benefits of Hindsight
It is now ten years since a programme of assisted repatriation (1980–81) brought a large proportion of Zimbabwean refugees 'home'. A considerable measure of 'spontaneous' or 'self-repatriation' combined with the formal repatriation. Moreover, a massive and resource-intensive parallel programme for rural rehabilitation helped the vast majority who were internally displaced persons. As part of this integrated approach, observers soon judged the repatriation exercise a success. Arguably the right proportions of humanitarian help for repatriation and reintegration combined well with development support for rural rehabilitation. The whole exercise would not have been possible without the backing of extensive international finance and material support. Within one complete season a spectacular agricultural sector performance rewarded the largely rural population and their programmes. The immediate post-war prospects for the rural masses looked promising.

However, given the benefit of hindsight, it is apparent that the decade of the 1980s has seen the reproduction of the peasantry as the poorest sector of the economy. Recurrent drought relief and social welfare programmes signal the presence of a chronic structural rural poverty. A long-term assessment of the repatriation needs to be more measured. However, our knowledge of the nature and dynamics of rural poverty remains partial and limited. For example, it is possible to argue that rural poverty is expanding and deepening. However, we are unable to say to what degree or whether ex-refugees are more than proportionally represented in the cohorts of Zimbabwe's rural poor. The early assessments of the success of the programme also took place before the failed political integration of Zimbabwe's Ndebele minority began to smoulder. By 1983 reconstruction in Matabeleland had turned into 'dissidence', civil unrest and government crack-downs. A smaller, but post-independence, wave of refugees left Matabeleland. Here too a longer-term assessment of 'successful' political integration needs to be more measured.[1]

Contexts & Definitions
Between 1960 and 1990 the number of refugees in the Southern African region has expanded from a few thousand to over 1.2 million persons. One person in 50 is a refugee

[1] The nine countries of Southern Africa are Angola, Botswana, Lesotho, Malawi, Mozambique, Namibia, Zambia, Zimbabwe and South Africa.

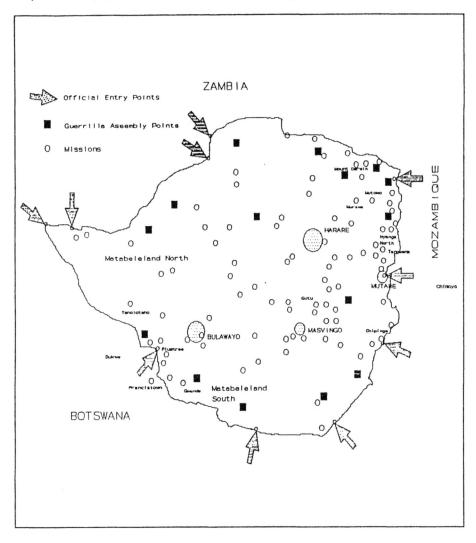

Map 8.1 *Zimbabwe: distribution of official entry points, guerrilla assembly points and rural mission stations*

8.1 *Refugees returning to Zimbabwe from Mozambique in time to participate in the 1980s elections (UNHCR/10147/E. Birrer)*

and 1 person in 20 is internally displaced.[2] Most of the sub-continent's refugees come from rural areas with minimal infrastructure, services, and administration. People and the administration are easily disrupted. The recent civil unrest and regional destabilization rests on the shaky foundations of wars of decolonization, drought and poor economic development. As opposed to *select* 'persecuted' groups or people, *mass movements* of displaced persons into exile or local internal displacement suggest the wider collapse of the provincial economic base and services. Civil unrest is central to the process. There are, however, three critical contributory contexts.

First, refugees are largely rural, and rural poverty is endemic. Exiles and displaced persons assess the costs of flight versus the need to protect their assets and livelihood. The levels of poverty found in the region's modern rural slums temper decisions.

Second, internally displaced persons and refugees emerge from a wider context. This is the social reproduction of a legacy of Southern African labour reserves designed to assure a 'supply' of labour. Local, regional and even illegal international migration has long been

[2] Cover story, *Southern African Economist*, February/March 1989.

part of rural economic strategy. Water-tight definitions of 'legitimate' refugees or displaced persons begin to blur.

Third is the context for help and support. Narrowly conceived strategies for refugees or for the repatriation of exiles, in isolation from rehabilitation programmes for the internally displaced and wider development strategies for the rural poor, are likely to have limited effects. They may fail or generate a wave of second-round problems. In this sense rural refugees in Southern Africa are part of a necessarily broader challenge – development strategies for an inherently mobile rural poor.

The repatriation of Zimbabwean refugees from Mozambique, Zambia and Botswana at the end of the liberation war fits a classic model of repatriation. Helped by the Office of the United Nations High Commissioner for Refugees (UNHCR), refugees returned to their country of origin after cessation of conflict. However, the repatriation depended critically on refugees' own informal networks, and on channels created independently of the UN effort. Together these alternative structures dealt with more returnees than did the UN system. Many refugees chose not to use formal channels.

The UNHCR worked with two local implementing partners, Christian Care and the Ministry of Labour and Social Welfare. Working under difficult and repressive circumstances the Christian Care umbrella organization had gained experience in providing help before and during the war. This organization's network of intelligence and support was a critical feature affecting the success of the repatriation.

The Christian Care heads of denominations had also worked with the underfunded wings of central and municipal government's 'Social Welfare' departments. Those displaced by the war had mostly flocked into the towns. The development of urban site and service schemes, during the war, led on to the independently financed programme for an estimated 0.75–1.0 million internally displaced persons following the cessation of hostilities. The numerically dominant internally war-displaced simply fell outside of the UNHCR mandate in 1980.

Christian Care's network of mission stations in the countryside played a central role in the formal UNHCR repatriations. Church representatives took on several responsibilities. They welcomed, counselled and briefed people on conditions in the country before organizing their onward dispatch and transport back to their homes and communities. There was rapid decentralization from the transit and urban centres to the missions. Later missions acted as local service and support satellites for the food aid and other rehabilitation assistance. The same network of rural centres serviced the internally displaced.

In Phase I, the UNHCR officially repatriated 35,133 refugees. During the same period a large number repatriated themselves. Estimates suggest that the Christian Care network may have supported as many as 60,000 'self-repatriated' refugees who simply used the support network for the internally displaced. Phase II started in April, two months after the elections. It was slower and better planned and focussed on the young, including whole schools with teachers and equipment, the ill and war victims. At the end of Phase II approximately 70,000 refugees were officially repatriated out of the estimated 150,000–200,000 in exile. Phase III involved the handing over to government and development organizations, and the emphasis changed to rehabilitation.

Two concurrent analytical themes have guided the interpretation which follows. The first is a tentative framework for the examination of refugees and the rural poor in a broader development context. The approach defines major structural limits to rural economic integration. It examines Zimbabwe's demographic transition, historical trends in the food balance, non-farm economic links and the limited effect of post-independence state intervention aimed at alleviating rural poverty.

Aggregate statistics on Zimbabwe's Communal Areas (CA)[3] suggest that 'peasant' incomes are in reality made up of as much as a 60 per cent non-farm share. Moreover, the 40 per cent agricultural income is inherently much more variable and erratic. The local residence but external non-farm economic orientation makes the distinction between 'international labour migrants', 'economic refugees' and 'political refugees' difficult and somewhat arbitrary. Migrants with just a little political and social insecurity at 'home' might have to opt to become refugees. Both refugees and migrants are economically snared in the local and regional context of expanding unemployment. The same lack of distinction applies to 'local' rural–rural labour migrants and their later emergence as 'internally displaced' persons, 'squatters' or 'urban destitute'. These separate categories are largely a feature of the reproduction of rural poverty and hence migrant labour in Southern Africa.

The continuity (if not a deepening) of rural poverty in many areas provides a context that challenges the notion of repatriation as a durable solution. Political and economic factors motivate refugees. Pockets of resistance to 'voluntary' repatriation, following the removal of political and security risks through reconciliation and peace, are rooted in both political uncertainty and the harsh and unacceptable economic realities of attempting rural economic reintegration.

The second analytical theme simply recognizes the logical sequence of examining cause and effect of events. The approach therefore examined the links between the pre-flight period; the flight into exile/internal displacement; the survival experience; and the repatriation/resettlement and subsequent reintegration. From a policy perspective the approach therefore examined the step-by-step links between ad hoc relief and long-term aid for development.

Refugees & the Rural Poor: an Analytical Framework

Structural Limits to Rural Economic Reintegration

Mass voluntary rural repatriation would in many situations appear to be much better than being in exile. Socially and in terms of subjective reintegration 'going home', and all that it implies for feelings of well-being, is a universal human experience. Unfortunately, however, the wars or civil unrest that spawned refugees are more often than not closely rooted in economic problems, especially those of rural poverty. These structural conditions persist intact, following repatriation. Indeed, conditions may well be worse. The first stage in the longer-term development for economic reintegration is reconstruction and rehabilitation.

Reportage of 'successful' repatriation tends to be based on restricted or limited criteria such as the media coverage of the 'social' and 'emotional' high spots of coming home. A hidden, but much more exacting, agenda lurks behind these images of 'success' – the assumption of practicable economic reintegration. The bottom line for returnees dumped back out into rural areas is a vague and tenuous 'self-help' development path out of rural poverty.

---

[3] The term Communal Areas (CA) refers to both Tribal Trust Lands and Communal Lands. Under colonial rule land in the colony was divided between the settlers, natives and the Crown. The original areas designated as Native Reserves were subsequently defined as the Tribal Trust Lands (TTLs) in the 1960s and 1970s. Since independence in 1980 the TTLs have been renamed as Communal Lands.

A Continuity of Rural Poverty

Analysis of Zimbabwe's inherited structural legacy of 'native labour reserves' and its peripheral 'peasant' agriculture over the past three decades dramatically confirms that the peasantry remains the poorest sub-sector within the economy.

In relation to a dominant and historic role as *the* source of wage labour for the rest of the economy, differing analytical approaches – concerning different periods of history – have led to some apparently contradictory images of the economic 'health' of peasant agriculture. At the extremes this has encompassed accounts of early 'high' levels of participation in commodity markets followed by the 'destruction' and the complete 'proletarianization' of peasants into the 'Labour Reserves'. In its extreme form this would imply millions of hectares of dormitory suburbs in which agriculture had simply disappeared! This is an image incompatible with the hindsight of the peasant agriculture's depressed and inadequately slow growth in the 1950s to 1970s on the 'African' side of Apartheid-style settler agricultural policies. More recently, images of a modernizing, dynamic and successful 'small-farm sector' have emerged in the 1980s. The analysis below is less optimistic about the potential for a modernizing and successful small-farm path out of rural poverty. The reality involves forms of rural social differentiation and deepening rural poverty.

The Demographic Transition & the Employment Balance

Scrutiny of the relative growth rates of the population, the labour force, formal wage employment and urbanization defines the peasant sector's default and expanding role as a 'rural sponge' mopping up the 'residual' population on the fringes of the formal economy. This shows (with some important qualifications, notably the massive improvements in the provision of rural social services – health, education and welfare) a broader structural reproduction of the 'labour reserves'. Arguably the post-independence resettlement schemes are a variant part of this expanded reproduction of rural poverty. Thus while the national employment balance is ever increasingly violated it is in the peasant (and to a lesser extent resettlement) sectors that its effects are most felt. An expanding urban informal sector accompanies the crisis in the employment balance.

The Food Balance in the Rural Areas

Zimbabwe's national aggregate food balance has always looked impressive in juxtaposition to her Sub-Saharan neighbours. The contributions to marketed produce has include clear evidence of a growing share of marketed food 'surpluses' from the peasant sector since independence. The state has managed impressive, if on occasions not 'excessive', national food stocks.[4]

A disaggregated analysis (even at the level of broadly aggregated sub-sectors of agriculture – the 'peasants' versus the 'commercial' estates) presents a much less glamorous picture of the adequacy of peasant subsistence through direct production or through effective purchasing power as derived from income generated in the commodity markets. This raises questions about the adequacy of the incomes and subsistence provision of the rural poor at a time of high inflation and wider economic stagnation.

Furthermore an account of the net surplus coming out of the sector (i.e. marketing minus reverse flows in the form of social welfare, drought relief, public works, remittance transfers and market transactions) suggests that a very large proportion of the expanding

---

[4] Agricultural trading losses associated with national stockpiles in excess of needs are linked to the budget deficit. They are therefore a target for reduction under the economic structural adjustment plans.

rural population remains highly vulnerable, its food and income insecure. In 1982, 1983, and 1984, 34 per cent (305,000–315,000 people) of Matabeleland's rural population were recipients of drought relief. In 1991–92 low producer prices, inappropriate policies and poor planning, combined with the worst drought in decades, have left 13 million people across the Southern African region in need of food relief. In Zimbabwe two million people are expected to be on regular drought relief before the next harvest. The regional and national food security situation has deteriorated rapidly in the early 1990s.

Non-farm Economic Links

For many of the workers in the formal wage economy, economic strategy encompasses a continuing strategic split stance between positions in formal sector jobs (or as self-employed) and farming as 'migrant managers'.[5] The rationale underlying this position is the long-term significant difference between real aggregate average earnings for formal wage labour outside of agriculture versus aggregate average returns to labour in peasant agriculture. Aggregated analysis suggests that this statement holds at least for the past 30 years – even for lowest paid formal sector positions and probably for a much longer period for those workers who penetrated the transport, communications and manufacturing sectors where wages grew at an average rate of 10 per cent between 1954 and 1962.

Short periods of quite rapid growth in formal wage openings, in relation to the growth rates in the population in the age groups 15–64 years (the potential labour force), define formal wage opportunities as structurally restricted. This has become particularly acute during the last 15 years – the evidence shows that since 1975 there has been virtually no aggregate growth in formal wage employment. Total unemployment has grown rapidly from 240,000 in 1979 to a projected estimate of 1,000,000 for 1990. Over this period there has been a maintenance of the gap in real earnings between 'urban' and 'rural'. This restricted or differentiated pattern of access to formal wage employment (past and present) defines a select group. Within this elite the levels of remuneration vary significantly in relation to their positions in the wage-skills hierarchy.

An economic straddling of farming and wage earnings by migrant labour has undoubtedly contributed to a 'tidal wave' of surplus accumulation and expansion of the forces of production outside of the peasant sector. A much less impressive reverse 'trickle' of remittances accompanies the migrant and more recently 'stabilized' wage-labour relation. Set against the broad flows of surplus out of the labour reserves, superior non-farm incomes provide the basis for an incremental long-term remittance-led shift in the economic stance of rural households. It differentiates those 'with' and 'without' off-farm formal wage incomes. Particularly it conditions a strategic lower risk-adverse stance towards the erratic rain-fed agricultural enterprises of the semi-arid tropics. It also contributes to a progressive differentiation in the levels of productive assets for both agriculture and other local non-farm economic activities.

The structurally limited access to formal wage incomes has also been highly gender specific. Women's share of formal wage employment has been very low, maintaining a 16.5 per cent share of total employees over the 10-year period 1975–85. There is, therefore, nationally a high degree of domestication of women's labour.

---

[5] This has emerged from a recruitment system of short-term contracting of labour out of the reserves in the 1920–50 period with the low skills requirements of earlier labour-intensive forms of employment. Over time acquired skills have stabilized the labour force in some sectors. However, in the boom–bust reality of some important sectors (such as the building industry) workers continue to move in and out of short periods of employment. Contracts are taken up as and when available.

Within the peasant sector and the historical confines of customary law there is a much more profound dimension to the status of women and property relations. Besides the load of the domestic economy in the wider process of social reproduction – and notwithstanding the high degree of female or joint decision-making within 'male enterprises' – female labour remains subordinated (through customary law, marriage, community structures and norms) to patriarchal control of access to productive resources and assets.

The weight of social disruption caused by 70 years of male labour migration, besides a rural guerrilla war, has eroded the economic position of many women. The property relations implicit in customary marriage need to be set within the context of the resource crisis of the Communal Lands.

The result is a significant group of poor rural women, defined by their restricted access to productive rural resources (such as cattle and land), their restriction to labouring in the domestic economy and peasant agriculture and by highly restricted possibilities for entry into some of the minimum-wage niches of the formal wage sector. In this light gender emerges as a pervasive dimension of rural social differentiation.

State Intervention & Rural Development
The post-independence modernization and development of the peasant sector were through a form of state-regulated market administration. Commodity prices were set at high levels, in the early 1980s, aimed at improving the incomes of small-scale producers. It was also to serve as a mechanism of rehabilitating the war-torn countryside. Zimbabwe's large rain-fed semi-arid agricultural production systems are subject to an inherent erratic large variation in volumes of production both in the commercial farms and even more so in the ecologically marginal peasant sector. Given the system of administered prices in the marketing and trading of these commodities and related processed staple foods, government has had to budget subsidies to agriculture and industry in order to meet the obligations of the legislated state monopoly and retail price controls. Concurrent with adjustments (cuts in subsidies and increases in administered prices for consumers), food subsidies in the 1980s have amounted to between 1.7 and 2.6 per cent of gross domestic product (GDP) and have accounted for 15–20 per cent of a sustained budget deficit of more than 10 per cent.

Other developments have included the expansion of agricultural services, the improvement of rural infrastructure and a rural resettlement programme.

Rural Social Differentiation & Deepening Rural Poverty
In spite of the massive rural development drive and resettlement programme the default consequence has been a process of selective commoditization within the peasantry. There are three broad mutually reinforcing dimensions to this mechanism. The first refers to the regionally specific variations in innate agro-ecological potential. The second refers to significant variations in endowments at the level of producers. The third is the pattern of access to the credit services targetted at the peasant sector.

As little as 18 out of 170 communal lands account for the vast bulk of maize marketing (Amin, 1989). Equally at the level of producers the variations in levels and combinations of endowments eliminate a very large proportion of producers from any serious participation in commodity markets. This holds true even in some of the better-potential peasant areas. The expansion of factor inputs through the provision of government-backed credit for the peasant sector is within a wider restriction of government credit expansion. Following severe droughts and significant defaults of loans, tight credit supply is highly selective, delivered to only the most creditworthy, asset-rich, and proven surplus-producing top

10 per cent of the peasantry. By definition they are in the better-potential areas. Over-whelming evidence from a large number of detailed rural economy studies confirms that, *sub-regionally*, only a small proportion of the peasantry accounts for a vast proportion of the gross production and marketed surpluses in any locality.

The apparent post-independence 'expansion' of peasant commodity production has to be made within an understanding of the country's wider demographic transition. Growth in relation to historic levels of production is a rather inadequate measure. Growth in rela-tion to necessary expansion *within* the sector is more realistic. The growth in the peasant's agricultural sector share of GDP, from 4–5 per cent in the 1960s and 1970s to 10 per cent for some years in the 1980s, yields a static rural *per capita* provision. Compared with the catastrophes elsewhere, perhaps this is good performance. However, given the phenomena of selective commoditization outlined above, the implications for a disaggregated analysis are the expansion and deepening of rural poverty.

Quite logically the transformations outlined above have been accompanied, in the post-independence period, by substantial, and historically new, patterns of provincial-wide recurrent rural income transfers, in the form of both government and NGO-based drought relief, public works and social welfare programmes for the rural destitute. These 'relief' measures are both necessary and welcome especially in Matabeleland. However they appear to be inherently limited in their ability to bring about any major shift in the structural context that is so massively reproducing rural poverty. As such they supply a bottom line or safety net of maintenance (if that) of the status quo! There is thus a critical development issue here – the efficacy of these strategies. Do they arrive as a series of unrelated piecemeal measures with little prospect for effecting long-term change, or are they part of a broader and more 'credible' development strategy?

The Post-Lancaster House Repatriation

Zimbabwe's 1980 Post-Lancaster House Experience
As a durable solution to the problems of the vast majority of the exiled Zimbabweans the repatriation was a success. As an exercise in the collaboration and co-ordination of interna-tional and local organizations in the effective channelling of humanitarian and developmen-tal assistance it was also a success. (International assistance recognized, promoted and built on the local potential for a high degree of self-help through a tripartite agreement.) The Zimbabwe programme broadened the concept of 'refugee' to include the internally dis-placed.[6] Thus the Zimbabwe practice of parallel assistance programmes in 1980 preceded what has subsequently become the mainstream 'integrated' strategy[7] articulated in the Oslo 1988 refugee conference. Despite the vast numbers involved, the implementation and administration of the programme maintained an extraordinarily humane face. It *listened* to individuals, politely asked questions and in particular inquired from the refugees what

---

[6] Reporting to the press in May 1981 at the end of the programme, UNHCR officials stated the term 'refugee' was stretched past its usual definition of someone who had fled into exile. About a million people, who had left their homes because of the war but stayed in the country, were brought into the programme (*Sunday Mail*, 24 May 1981). However, the programme to assist internally displaced people was supported by church funding only. The UNHCR did not provide aid for this programme as they argued that the programme was not in their mandate. Christian Care National Office co-ordinated most of the ecumenical funding (Ziswa, 1989).
[7] i.e. the focus on refugees, returnees and internally displaced persons; the linking of humanitarian assistance for refugees and displaced persons with recovery and development assistance of host countries or countries of origin.

assistance *they thought* they might usefully need. People were being assisted *in their own* repatriation. It successfully linked individuals to communities through a massive intelligence network. A very rapid social and economic reintegration was achieved.

In late 1979, the news of the Lancaster House constitutional settlement and timetable towards the elections prompted an immediate appeal in January 1980 for US $22 million by the UNHCR for the first phase of a programme then labelled 'repatriation of refugees'. The formal repatriation began in January 1980 – a very short time in advance of the February 1980 elections. In April 1980 there was a further UNHCR appeal for US $110 million for the second phase plus an amount of US $30 million for food.[8] However, within 16 months of starting out (i.e. by April 1981) the UNHCR had begun to wind up its affairs in Zimbabwe.

The UNHCR, at the top of a broadly co-ordinated programme (including the important parallel and independently financed programmes for the internally displaced run by the Heads of Denominations (HOD) Christian Care Refugee Committee within the structure of Christian Care), had in the end provided assistance for resettlement and relief for an estimated 1.25 million Zimbabweans. The UNHCR formally repatriated 70,000 persons, and, depending on which figures one uses for estimates of people outside the country in the early 1980s, anything in the range 70,000–140,000 persons were self-repatriated. Project documents drawn up between the UNHCR and its implementing partners, the Heads of Denominations Christian Care office and the Ministry of Labour and Social Welfare, budgeted on there being 215,000 returnees, of which 60,000 would return through facilities provided by the churches. Thus right at the beginning it was anticipated that there would be a significant self-repatriation; many people would cross back the way they went – through the bush.

Contradictory figures suggest that there could have been between 750,000 and 1.0 million internally displaced persons. The quality of the statistics in any war situation is likely to be highly unreliable and subject to the politics of both under-estimation and over-estimation. The distinction between those Zimbabweans 'formally' repatriated and the others, whether they be self-repatriated or internally displaced, both before and after the programme, was clear. What is not clear is the extent to which the poor/inaccurate estimates of total exiles likely to be self-repatriated became blurred in the implementation for assistance to the internally displaced, i.e. to what extent were the resources spread into a flexible, responsive and highly desirable support for the self-repatriated but administratively defined 'internally displaced'? Christian Care, local church and ecumenical church finance supplemented the UNHCR funding. A special appeal was made through the World Council of Churches (WCC) for it was the opinion of these groups that UNHCR support would not be enough, being based on low repatriation figures and the non-accounting of internally displaced people or the needs to rehabilitate destroyed infrastructure necessary to house returnees.

Thus the parallel repatriation and assisted internal resettlement were backed up by provision of shelter and equipment, a logistically awesome food distribution programme – running at US $2.0 million per month, medical care, various relief needs, transport and cash grants. Concurrently there was a further parallel development assistance programme (in which 70,000 seed–fertilizer–tool packs were distributed), supported by a massive agricultural extension drive manned by 1,500 agricultural staff. In the 1980–81 agricultural season the rains were good and, almost miraculously, a busy agricultural season, as

[8] UNHCR (1981).

facilitated by all these parallel initiatives, was followed by a bumper harvest. By June 1981 all of the UNHCR services relating to Zimbabwean returnees were phased out.

It is worth noting that the HOD Christian Care Refugee Committee had already begun in early 1981 to develop and implement a 'reconstruction programme', co-ordinated through the Zimbabwe Christian Council (ZCC). It focussed on the reconstruction of missions and facilities[9] and continued to provide assistance to individuals who had lost their homes. The Christian Care umbrella provided the intelligence and support for other sectoral initiatives such as the child supplementary feeding programme. By November 1982 the ZCC Reconstruction Committee shifted its emphasis from a relief to a development assistance programme.[10]

Commenting at the time, the then Head of the UNHCR Delegation in Zimbabwe, Mr D. Chefeke, stated,

> . . . the programme would not have been so successful were it not for the people themselves. I think that the results indicate that Zimbabweans are extremely hard-working and strong willed. This victory is theirs.

Within Africa at that time, the problems of refugees *in exile* dominated the scene. Documenting and learning from a policy analysis of a successful and well-administered repatriation were not a priority. Given the context at the time repatriation as a strategic option was low on the list of priorities, although ultimately an ideal. People were too busy to take time out to evaluate, digest and learn from the experience. The experience has therefore remained surprisingly thinly documented.[11] Yet policy issues surrounding possible, proposed and ongoing repatriations have now taken on greater significance.

The Pre-flight Situation & the Importance of the Churches in the Tribal Trust Lands (TTLs)

The struggle for Zimbabwe[12] has been well documented. The extent to which it was a struggle between the churches and the settler state has not been as widely recognized as it should.[13] Many Christian mission stations were established long before pioneer columns arrived. These communities, isolated in deep rural locations, had a culture of their own. Starting emphatically with the Land Apportionment Act[14] in the early 1930s, the settlers proceeded with a relentless implementation of racial and discriminatory policies. By the 1960s the state had begun to meet with strong opposition from the people and the churches.

The settlers, however, simply responded with even more oppressive legislation. The

---

[9] The infrastructure of the mainstream churches in Zimbabwe's countryside had in the pre-independence era provided in the region of 80 per cent of the schooling and 95 per cent of the rural health services. Reconstruction of this capacity was strategic and clearly part of a wider rural reconstruction effort.

[10] Ziswa (1989) notes, '. . . movement from relief to development has not been an easy process. [It] required transformation of staff perspectives, rethinking strategies, learning new or identifying new skills or personnel needs, redesigning programmes, hiring specialized staff, re-orientating church leadership committees, and even evaluation or consultation to determine new directions and assistance from those who have skills and experience in similar processes in order to keep staff and programme focused . . .'

[11] Apart from a short write-up by Rodgers (1982), Ziswa (1989), Gwazemba (1984) and De Wolf (1981), this very impressive and well-executed programme has not been documented.

[12] For a good account see Martin and Johnson (1981) and Frederikse (1982) *None but ourselves*.

[13] To understand much of the basis of the successful repatriation, reconstruction and reintegration of the returnees and internally displaced in the 1980–81 period it is vital to appreciate the pivotal role of the 'Christian Care' organization and its activities.

[14] The act apportioned a very large section of the best land to the settlers and segregated access to land on a racial basis.

infamous Law and Order Maintenance Act of 1960 was a turning point. Broad powers of search, arrest, detention and restriction were given to the Minister of Law and Order. A prolonged state of emergency followed the Unilateral Declaration of Independence (UDI) in 1965. Many people opposing these changes were simply detained, restricted, imprisoned or put into rural detention centres. There was, by the late 1960s, a significant number of political activists in exile. Within the country there was now a significant number of political prisoners, detainees, displaced persons and destitute families.

There were both public and church-based responses to the detentions, restrictions and the resulting destitution of their families. The network of churches linking the rural and urban-based churches was soon to channel reports of the situation in Rhodesia to the international community. They appealed directly for funds for humanitarian assistance for detainees and their families. The plea received the support of international church and human rights organizations. Following the UDI there was a direct state attack on the church-based humanitarian programme and the expatriate staff of these programmes were progressively deported. The response from the church within the country was then to set up an indigenous hierarchy to take over these operations. For some period of time the government took over the support of destitute families of detainees. The 1966 Welfare Act eliminated the Christian Council and its committee from being eligible as a welfare organization. The Council then drew up a new constitution and formed a new organization to handle the welfare programmes under the co-ordinating committee. It was called Christian Care. Shortly afterwards, by 1968, Christian Care had become the sole source of assistance for these destitute families.

Christian Care developed its operations under three committees: (a) the Relief Committee, which initially dealt with assistance for detainees and their families; (b) the Prison Education Committee provided for educational and vocational activities for detainees; and (c) through its Emergency Relief Committee it also had a high profile of humanitarian assistance in the rural areas including drought relief, water supplies and health services. In the latter stages of the war it had penetrated right into the protected villages with its assistance programmes.

As a welfare organization Christian Care was thus close to many of the future political leaders. Its track record of assistance before and during the war under a broad humanitarian Zimbabwean Christian approach had given it much experience in flexibly responding to historically specific needs and situations and in the operation of assistance programmes guided by special committees, under what were often difficult and repressive circumstances. This experience and credibility equipped it well as an organization that the people could trust in the post-war transition.[15]

Impacts on the Rural Population – War Atrocities, Curfews & Protected Villages (PVs)
Between 1968 and 1972 the conflict moved into a combined political and armed struggle. Some of the first and important engagements between rural guerrillas and the Smith regime took place in the early 1970s. As before, the regime responded with a massive counter-offensive, this time in the context of a rural guerrilla war. By 1975 a report

---

[15] Gwazemba (1984: 32) notes, with reference to Christian Care's role in the repatriation of 1980–81, that most of the nationalists coming back heading the refugees had been in prison or detention prior to their departure to neighbouring countries to wage the war of liberation. Many had, therefore, been exposed to the services provided by Christian Care. This was either for themselves or their families while in prison or detention.

compiled by the Catholic Institute for International Relations (CIIR) made public its findings on 'The man in the middle: torture, resettlement and eviction' (CCJP, 1975). (Eleven months earlier there had been 'An appeal to conscience', by eleven church leaders.) They were concerned that, while the public had been made fully aware of the assaults by insurgents,

> . . . they are not aware of the frequency and seriousness of assaults committed by some members of the security forces and the effects these are having upon the civilian population in the tribal areas, caught as they are between two contending forces.

As one victim had expressed it,

> If we report to the police, the terrorists kill us. If we do not report, the police torture us. Even if we do report to the police, we are beaten all the same and accused of trying to lead the soldiers into a trap. We just do not know what to do.

The resettlement of people inside 'protected villages' (PVs) began in the latter half of 1973 on the Zambezi valley floor. By mid-1974 the entire population of Chiweshe Tribal Trust Land, just 65 km north of Salisbury, were to be moved into 21 PVs. Within a month 43,000 to 47,000 people had been moved from their homes. Other Tribal Trust Lands were soon to follow the same fate. In Madziwa TTL 13,500 were moved into 10 PVs. By late 1979 it was estimated that 600,000 had been forcefully relocated into PVs. The impact on the agriculture and livelihood was direct. The sanitation and water supply conditions within the PVs were often appalling and initially people were living without any shelter. There was severe social disruption and obstruction of education for the masses of children affected.

Outside of the PVs, a system of dawn-to-dusk curfews was progressively enforced over large parts of the country. In emergencies 22-hour curfews were enforced. The four years of war between 1974 and 1978 saw a rapid escalation of engagements, the failure to establish further PVs in some areas and the de facto definition of liberated zones. This was particularly so in the remote areas, which were difficult to patrol or administer. While there had been a progressive build-up in the numbers of people going out of the country to train or contribute to the armed struggle, it would seem that there was a breaking point and a quite sudden and significant pouring out of the rural civilian population into the neighbouring countries in the years of 1977 and 1978. A large proportion moved out of the border areas. The escape into urban exile, i.e. internal displacement, involved many more and was spread out over a longer period.

Patterns of Flight into Exile & Internal Displacement
The preceding account of aspects of the pre-flight situation and impacts of the political and military struggle being waged from both within and outside the country has begun to outline some of the patterns of flight into either exile or internal displacement.

Building on the experiences of labour migration and as a consequence of the limited educational opportunities for Blacks in colonial Rhodesia, the first exiles were drawn from those educated male black elites who almost inevitably found themselves spearheading a political struggle against the settler state. Later, as the conflict moved into both a political and military struggle, this pattern was to repeat itself, drawing albeit a much younger, but relatively better-educated and largely male group of recruits into the political and military wings of the parties in exile. Clearly this process exacerbated the pre-existing situation whereby, through labour migration of males, a large proportion of the rural areas were made up of the 'residual' women and children.

As the war progressed into the mid-1970s, and contacts with both sides occurred, another round of men, this time the older male local authorities and officials of Zimbabwe's rural patriarchy, were walking the knife edge of the interrogations described in the report of the Catholic Commission for Justice and Peace (1975). They included headmen, *kraal* heads, headmasters of schools, and any local officials responsible for manning government services in the rural areas. Consequently, and dependent upon locality and circumstances, the latter stages of the war involved mass movements of predominantly women and children as they were forced into either PVs, internal displacement or into exile.

Personal history 1 – Involuntary Flight into Exile

At 59 years old Ben Matasva returned to Sabvure ward in the Nyamaropa area of Nyanga North in 1977. This was after 23 years of employment as a shopkeeper's assistant in Bulawayo. His family at that time consisted of himself, his wife, his resident mother and 5 children. Five months after his return, and following the presence of both Zimbabwe African National Liberation Army (ZANLA) guerrillas and Rhodesian security forces in their ward on 'follow-up operations', a small group of guerrillas called the community to a dawn meeting at the business centre. Three 'sellouts' – a storekeeper, Mr Muzonsa, and his son and one other person – were executed by the guerrillas in front of the assembled community on the morning of 17 June 1977.

Ben Matasva was then immediately conscripted into a group of 52 villagers, mainly women, girls and children too young to be separated from their mothers, to carry all the stock from Mr Muzonsa's shop to Mozambique. Their forced porterage/flight into exile was not planned nor was it voluntary. Shortly after entering Mozambique, most of the goods were sold by the guerrillas and the group was channelled towards Chimoio over 100 kilometres away. Shortly after their arrival in Chimoio they entered a refugee camp at Doroi. After 32 months of separation from his family Ben became part of the formal Phase I February 1980 repatriation to the Toronto Reception Centre outside Mutare. Ben returned to Sabvure to find his family and home intact.

An important distinction appears to exist between these loose groupings of types of exiles. While the early political exiles and the later recruits went into exile as a consequence of political persecution and were clearly highly motivated and often better-educated, their exile was more or less planned. The other group of older men and dominant 'residual' women and children that emerged as a consequence of the escalation of the war often had to flee without any preparation. For the headmen, *kraal* heads, local government officials, there was no time to think. People simply had to flee, in the night or whenever. Families were suddenly split, husbands from wives and children from their parents. Mobilization/abduction of large numbers of school children across the borders had by this stage become a feature of the war.[16] While for some of those who remained behind, either in the PVs, liberated areas or in internal displacement, news trickled back of the whereabouts of their family, others had to wait years and some until the repatriation in 1980–81 before any news of the whereabouts, fate and/or health of their kin was known.

The internally displaced persons outnumbered the exiles 3:1. For some of these people links with the wider urban and other formal wage sectors (agriculture and mining) formed the basis of a path into exile, especially into the urban areas. There was a fair amount of rural–rural migration to other safer and less volatile Tribal Trust Lands and onto the

---

[16] Southall (1980), quoting UNHCR figures, outlined the situation as it affected the exiles: '. . . there were 150,000 Zimbabwean refugees in Mozambique (including 30,000 children), 40,000–45,000 in Zambia (including 20,000 children) and 26,000 in Botswana (including 6,000 children) . . .'

workers' compounds of commercial and state farms as well as some mines. However, the sheer scale of this movement generated problems. Firstly, the pre-existing and often minimal services and infrastructure simply could not cope with the situation – an unprecedented influx of people. Some estimates suggest that by late 1979 the population of Salisbury/Harare had doubled. Secondly, the breadth of the social and economic links with the urban areas was perhaps not as wide as many assumed. People with family members or relatives with either jobs and/or housing employed an extended family network to the limit. They were, however, only a fraction of the internally displaced, quite how many is difficult to assess. Many internally displaced persons could only find their way into the swelling 'squatter camps', garbage dumps and quarries of the towns, and were severely socially and economically dislocated. There they had to face a hostile government and survived predominantly on church and local NGO assistance.

Survival in Internal Displacement & Exile – the Beginnings of an Integrated Approach

In the late 1970s (in what was then Rhodesia) the word 'refugee' was used to denote both the formal refugee and the internally displaced person. In fact the coverage of the fate of the formal refugees was minimal. While the numbers of internally displaced people progressively swelled to 750,000 between 1974 and 1979 they moved into a very hostile environment. It was only during the short transitional Muzorewa government of national unity in 1979 that the administration began to give any official recognition to the phenomena of *war-displaced* persons. This came about eventually after a strong conflict between local (municipal) and central government over the crisis management of the urban homeless. For the four years 1976–79 the vast brunt of the organizational and material assistance for the internally displaced was church- and NGO-based. Christian Care was part of a co-ordinating umbrella organization formed to better facilitate this assistance. It was quite understandable that Christian Care, in the immediate post-elections/independence phase, recognized the importance of, and went ahead with developing, a parallel programme of assistance for rural resettlement of the internally displaced.

The Consequence of the Lack of a Government Response

Although the monolithic inhumane face of the state was beginning to crack, it seemed quite understandable that it was virtually impossible for international organizations to give assistance to the government at the time. This was so despite the fact that there were many progressive people within the system fighting for change. They included people such as the staff involved in municipal social welfare work and services, and the 'Native affairs' sub-committee of the city council. The consequence of the lack of government (and international) support was to increase the demands on the local non-governmental organizations in the cities and towns. Initial ad hoc responses from a wide range of bodies (church groups, individual appeals, individual and company donations, etc.) gave rise to a potential overlap of efforts and opportunities for aid racketeers. A co-ordinating umbrella organization, including Christian Care, was formed. This strengthened network was later to provide the intelligence, administrative and implementation capacity through which the international assistance for projects and programmes for returnees, internally displaced and the reconstruction and development programmes were so successfully channelled.

The Institutional Response & Assistance for the Internally Displaced

The nature of the internally displaced – predominantly women and their children and older men – and the features of the urban situations into which they headed[17] were to determine many of the problems they were to face, and condition much of the assistance they subsequently required.

Over and above the likely trauma and stress of flight from their homes, the internally displaced were to face big problems as they poured into the towns. Both the university and the International Committee of the Red Cross (ICRC) were carrying out research into the so-called 'squatter problem'. They were trying to get some global sense of its scale and dynamics. The Council Health and Environmental Committee were very concerned about the situation. The Chitungwiza Urban Council, which was then described as a peri-urban African township, was unable with its financial resources to do much about the squatter problem other than maintain its existing 'Zengeza 4' transit camp. In fact the problem was so fast growing and soon so enormous that it was beyond the resources of the city itself. Harare-Musika rapidly became an open squatter camp with scores of refugees arriving from the war-torn areas every day.

Thousands of women and children were without any shelter. They cooked, ate, slept and gave birth to children in the open. The City Health Dispensary Infant Welfare section was struggling to cope with a grave public health hazard. Children were malnourished,[18] there were scabies and measles and they faced problems of unimmunized new arrivals every day. Ablution and toilet facilities were non-existent or defied description. Others were living on the municipal dump – later to be known as 'Trash City'. The dry seasons turned to the rainy seasons and the war-displaced struggled to keep dry and free of disease. Many suddenly found themselves socially too close to refugee camp prostitution and drunken male violence. They were desperately poor or destitute.

This scenario was not atypical of the situation in nearly every major urban centre in the country. Government continued to decline to comment on the issues of the war-displaced. Community services within the council were powerless to do much in the absence of specific information and/or plans by the government to deal with the problem.

For many in these camps, what they had managed to build since their flight was all they had. Their future still looked very bleak, for their rural homes and property had been destroyed and many or all of their cattle confiscated or killed. Understandably some of the elderly men in the camps could not see themselves going back to start all over again. What little they owned had taken a long time to acquire. Others, however, were convinced that they would return to rebuild their lives.[19]

For those working with the internally displaced over several years, the initial ideas of a possible compensation for war losses or assisted relocation back home through resettlement and a rural reconstruction programme were beginning to emerge as a real possibility. What was needed was an end to the war and a durable political settlement.

---

[17] Historically, the settler colonial towns had kept people out, through various forms of influx controls. What little infrastructure and services had been set up for the predominantly male labour migrants were not easily expanded or stretched to assist women and children.

[18] People, along with the guerrillas, were being starved out of the liberated areas. The Catholic Commission for Justice and Peace reported on a briefing given by N. Shamuyarira and D. Mutasa to the Rhodesia Group of the British Council of Churches.

[19] In an interview reported in *The Herald*, Mr Albert Kambarami (45 years) who used to run a small business at Murewa was now without his shop or home and penniless at the Seke camp. He was quoted as saying, 'There is nothing to go back to but home is home and will always be better than whatever I can get here. I have no idea how I am going to start off again, but somehow I am convinced I will manage.' Nyarota, G. (1978/9).

The assistance started in an ad hoc way through public appeals. Funds, food and material support were channelled through a number of NGOs. They included the YMCA, the Salisbury Council of Social Service, the Emergency Relief Committee of Christian Care, the Rhodesia National Council for the Welfare of Children, Anglican church groups, the Red Cross, the Adult Literacy Organization, a 'special' appeal and various refugee shelter funds. Towards the end of 1979, a national co-ordinating group, organized by the Council of Social Service, was set up to streamline all volunteer resettlement and rehabilitation programmes in Zimbabwe-Rhodesia. The organization was to serve as a clearing house for information relating to the activities and ideas of the voluntary and non-government bodies. The mood had changed and there was a clear indication of a transition phase between war and peace. The organization set up nine key sub-committees. They encompassed: agriculture, employment, housing, medical services, refugees, training and education, vocational guidance, youth and the war-handicapped. The aim was to be able to dovetail ideas and projects.

The initial emergency relief assistance developed into ongoing programmes. It encompassed the supplementary feeding of children, which subsequently became incorporated into day-care centres, play groups or schools.[20] Play centre courses for mothers were established along with other adult literacy programmes. Displaced teachers were assisted in their efforts to provide children with some continuity in their education in make-shift classrooms. People were assisted in moving location. Plastic sheeting was distributed to improve the quality of shacks and shanty settlements. The emphasis was on assisted self-help initiatives. Slowly, and totally inadequately, the councils were drawn into providing site-and-service schemes for a few hundreds of the tens of thousands desperate for assistance. By November 1979 (and just three months before the Patriotic Front government was elected) the then Ministry of Manpower, Social Affairs, Youth and Rehabilitation had begun to indicate a 'top priority' plan for war refugees' resettlement. It was the beginning of the back-to-the-land approach. It emphasized how it would aid people to again become proud, independent and productive members of Zimbabwe-Rhodesia. Many of the country folk who had suffered for years in the urban camps were orientating towards their eventual return home. There were many push factors from the predicaments in the shanty towns that made the return to the rural areas an attractive option. For example as few as 150,000 out of the estimated 750,000 (20 per cent) had managed to work their way into the networks of city hawking and other informal or self-employment.

The experience of struggling to assist the internally displaced in the cities and towns had another spin-off effect. Frustrated professionals and progressives within the municipal and other government social service departments were looking forward to being able to do something *with the support* of a new government and administration. They had also been part of a considerable debate about the issues and in the process many important personal and professional links between the NGO and government social service departments had been established. It is not surprising therefore that the two local implementing partners recruited for the UNHCR-supervised[21] and priority programme for the repatriation of refugees outside the country, were Christian Care and the Ministry of Labour and Social Welfare. Within Christian Care, a special HOD Christian Care

---

[20] Administrators of refugee children literacy projects had initially been confronted by children collapsing only to discover that some of the children had not eaten for two days!

[21] On 15 January 1980 the UNHCR formally requested the churches to participate in the repatriation programme.

Refugee Committee was established and it set up an office which was bombed shortly afterwards.[22]

The Transition to Independence & a Substantial Growth in Bilateral Assistance

The priority programme for the repatriation for refugees had a powerful political dimension. It was written into the Lancaster House agreement that refugees of voting age should be brought back into the country to participate in the first genuine majority rule election. Response to appeals for funds for assistance for the transition to independence came from the EEC, Germany, the Netherlands, the USA and Nigeria. This was the start of a period of expanding bilateral assistance.

The Planning of the Repatriation & Resettlement Programmes

How many refugees fled Zimbabwe for neighbouring territories and how many came back will probably never be known with any exactitude. Equally, the precise situation in the protected villages and the numbers of the internally displaced will have to remain at best 'estimates'. To varying degrees both the Zimbabwe African National Union (ZANU) and the Zimbabwe African People's Union (ZAPU) wanted some of their supporters and combatants outside the country to be able to participate in the elections. (For the minority ZAPU supporters this was more important. ZANU confidently held the majority in many parts of the country and strategically kept combatants out of the country.) Some exaggeration would have been prudent in negotiating for resources to facilitate their repatriation. The remnants of the Smith regime and the Muzorewa government were to propagandize and play down the numbers. They went on to frustrate and deliberately slow down the repatriation.

However, the disparity between the numbers of those officially repatriated by the UNHCR programme and the original estimates cannot be explained by these pressures alone. The degree of self-repatriation is another possible explanation. This may have occurred from the ranks of refugees who were outside the official camps. The extent of self-repatriation from official camps during Phase I was small.[23] Self-repatriation was the likely reaction and response of a fair number of the adult exiles to the presence of the Rhodesian security forces and their aggressive screening processes and deliberate slow-down of the procedures at the entry points. (Under Phase I of the repatriation plan as many as possible of the adults of voting age were to be repatriated such that they could participate in the election and formation of a new government. While accompanied by UNHCR staff, returnees had to face the Rhodesian authorities and military at the official crossing points.) The Christian Care organization felt that it had not achieved an adequate presence at all crossing points during the early days of the repatriations.[24]

Personal history 2 - Self-repatriation

Shortly after the June 1977 executions of 'sellouts' at Sabvure in Nyanga North, the headman, Mr Matasva, had to rapidly plan his family's exile. Soldiers of the Rhodesian security forces were looking for him. As headman they wanted to question him about the incident at the store. Leaving his lifestyle as builder–farmer behind, he left with his whole family, leaving his 6 cattle and homestead and tools and other equipment with his brother.

[22] The bombing took place at the Presbyterian Church Centre, Jameson Avenue (now Samora Machel Avenue). The office was forced to evacuate and took a low profile in the Salvation Army headquarters (Ziswa, 1989).
[23] Personal communication from N. Morris of UNHCR, December 1989.
[24] Ziswa, personal communication, 1989.

He and his family kept together throughout their exile and, although they ended up in Chimoio, they refused to fall under the refugee camp administration. As a result they received less assistance. Based on information obtained from Frelimo soldiers he organized his own repatriation. To finance the family's journey they sold clothes and took a bus from Chimoio to Katadika and then crossed the border on foot via Nypanga and returned to Sabvure. They came back via the route of their exile to vote in the February 1980 independence elections.

On their return Mr Matasva's brother was able to give them immediate assistance and supplied his family with maize. By 1989, he considered his family to be 'well settled'. He maintains his status as headman. Since his return, agriculture has been more important as his source of livelihood. In 1988–89 he produced 20 bags of maize, 10 bales of cotton and 10 bags of sunflowers.

Refugees returning from Mozambique and Zambia seemed to provide especial opportunity for harassment. The Rhodesian authorities impounded lorries and embarked upon a thorough administrative obstruction with the explicit aim of deterring potential voters from returning before the elections. The impact of this 'screening' of the civilian population for 'terrorists' was to slow down the rate of the whole repatriation process. News of the elections following the Lancaster House agreements had reached people in exile quite some time before news of any possible assisted repatriation. Plans to vote probably preceded plans to be repatriated. Those wishing to vote simply *had* to get back within a matter of weeks. By mid-February, less than two weeks before the elections, the UNHCR had to make an official complaint about the rate of repatriation. Southall (1980) argues, therefore, that large numbers of the refugees deliberately circumvented or ignored the official procedures, particularly during the early 'cease-fire' period when guerrillas both inside and outside the country were converging on the assembly points designated under the Lancaster House settlement. It is quite likely that there was a large but unseen flux of people before any official repatriation had started. Many observers, however, doubted that it could have been as many as 100,000 people.

Quite how, to what extent and when this movement took place remains unclear. Security forces were there *in force*, and as per the Lancaster House agreement combatants outside the country had to stay out. Moreover, ZANU (PF)[25] strategically did not want to have (nor did it need to have) all its combatants back in the country. Judging from the mood portrayed in the press, the importance of participating in the elections was paramount and the feeling was that *every* vote would count and everybody who could possibly vote should be there for the elections. ZANU (PF), however, clearly had a confident majority in many parts of the country. Based on projections of the 1968 population census the Commonwealth observers overseeing the elections claimed to have estimated the electorate with a high degree of accuracy for the different districts across the country. The ZANU (PF) victory was based on an estimated 90 per cent poll! A very high proportion of the total adult population must have been back in the country by the last week of February 1980. Of the 34,000–36,000 Phase I returnees something in the region of 20,000–25,000 were estimated to be of voting age (*Le Monde*, 29 February 1980). As a proportion of the total electorate of 2.8 million their influence was marginal. While virtually all of the refugees from Botswana were repatriated in advance of the elections, only a small fraction of the then high estimates of exiles in Mozambique were officially repatriated before the election.

If the estimates for the numbers in exile were in any way credible, the above account would give support to the assumption that there was a significant degree of self-

[25] ZANU and ZAPU formed a 'Patriotic Front' in the late 1970s – hence the 'PF'.

repatriation. The actual numbers will remain unknown and may well be a consequence of poor and/or exaggerated figures on the total number of exiles. Our understanding of the formal repatriation is much more substantiated. Its specific programmes supported by a parallel approach for the internally displaced and broad-based rural reconstruction strategy certainly aided the self-repatriated.

The first phase of the formal repatriation exercise began with the signing of the tripartite agreement between the UNHCR, Christian Care and the Ministry of Labour and Social Welfare on 15–20 January 1980. The elections were held on 26 February! What was achieved in the 35 days of the Phase I repatriation was astounding. Budgets were drawn up for shelter and equipment, food, medical care, various relief needs, transport, cash grants and administration. The three-phase programme was conceptualized. All effort was then focussed onto Phase I. A network of reception, urban, transit and mission centres was established.[26]

Repatriation started from Botswana on 21 January and lasted until 24 February (two days before the elections). During the Phase I pre-election repatriation the UNHCR officially repatriated a total of 35,133 refugees: 10,935 from Mozambique, 4,290 from Zambia and 19,908 from Botswana. Quite how many were able to simply walk across the borders from neighbouring countries during this period, is impossible to assess.

After a month to 6 weeks of further preparation Phase II of the repatriation started – on 23 April 1980 in Mozambique and 12 May in Zambia. It was slower, better planned, involved much more consultation with the government and lasted until early July 1980. It focussed on the young (including whole schools as entities including teachers and their equipment), many ill persons and war victims. A special camp for war-disabled was created at Ntabaziduna and was manned by the Presbyterian Church with support from the Christian Care Office and was given strong backing by the government.

At the start of Phase II the UNHCR had dramatically lowered its estimates of refugees remaining outside the country, to between 50,000 and 60,000 – a figure of 100,000 refugees below the original estimates. It will always remain a guess, but perhaps as many as 40,000–60,000 were self-repatriated and the remaining difference was attributable to an overestimate, in the region of 40,000. The number officially repatriated from Mozambique, as against the original estimated numbers of refugees, was very low. A Christian Care Refugees Committee note, 'Information on refugees' dated 8 July 1980, mentions that 13,000 self-repatriated refugees were reported to have walked from Mozambique into the Chipinge and Zambezi areas. Unofficial repatriations that were eventually later registered at the reception centres, for those from Botswana, amounted to as much as 8.5 per cent of the total. As many as 1,265 Tangwena people in the eastern border were repatriated to the Garezi as a group, but not through the formal channels (Gwazemba, 1984: 37-9).

---

[26] *Reception centres* were to be established at or near the border entry points (including some in the cities for those who might be flown in). This would be the first place where a refugee would go and be given medical check-ups, food, overnight boarding, assistance in the tracing of relatives by the ICRC and registration by the Ministry of Home Affairs. Given the network of mission stations in the countryside, representatives of churches took on the responsibility for welcoming, counselling and briefing people on the situation in the country (or back home), before organizing their onward dispatch and transport to the nearest transit or mission centre. *Transit centres* were necessary for those whose homes were not accessible directly from the reception centres. People could stay for up to five days in a transit centre. They were rapidly decentralized into the *mission centres* to avoid congestion. The mission centres remained as service and support satellites for the food aid (which lasted for approximately a year) and other rehabilitation assistance. For many whose homes were destroyed these mission centres provided a critical base from which they could survive while reconstructing their homes.

8.2 *Seeds, fertilizer and agricultural tools being supplied to returnees in 1981 (UNHCR/11064/ E. Birrer)*

These illustrations suggest that unregistered repatriations could have been as large as is suggested above.

Phase III of the repatriation saw a significant emphasis on transfer of implementation capacity into the hands of the government. The accent of this phase was on assisted rehabilitation of the returnees. For the UNHCR it was a staging post between a repatriation programme and the later transfer of responsibilities for development assistance to the United Nations Development Programme (UNDP), which had not yet set up an office in Harare. Although Phase III was only signed in June 1980, the government had established 19 district welfare offices by July and these had taken over some of the structures and the programmes of the ICRC. The massive initial food aid programme was ongoing and the Department of Social Services was responsible for 31,000 recipients and Christian Care was dealing with another 55,000. This food provision was to be maintained until the next harvest. Between July and September 70,000 agricultural packages targetted at the formally repatriated refugees had been distributed.

A parallel rural reconstruction programme for the displaced and others distributed a further 300,000 seed packs. The agricultural rehabilitation programme encompassed winter vegetables, summer crops, agricultural tools, tillage aid, rehabilitation of irrigation works and training courses. It is estimated that the extension training drives reached 250,000 families. Not far short of half of all of the country's estimated 800,000 rural families had been supplied with agricultural inputs in advance of the 1980–81 agricultural season.

The Cease-fire, Violation Issues & Information on Life Back Home

Prior to any repatriation or internal resettlement of the displaced the planned cease-fire had to be implemented. It was a difficult transition to manage. No matter how charged, tense and fragile, it was vital that it should succeed.

Between 28 December 1979 and 4 January 1980 *all* Patriotic Front forces were to go to assembly points (and associated rendezvous positions) with all their arms and equipment. The public was advised to avoid these areas and the routes between them, so as not to hamper the movements of the PF forces and the monitoring force. By what subsequently became the first deadline (4 January 1980) 12,000 PF had grouped at the 16 assembly points. In the days and weeks that followed the guerrilla military command was to warn PF forces outside the assembly places to come forward or face the consequences. Lord Soames made a personal 'final call' broadcast to Patriotic Front forces still in the bush to go to the Commonwealth Monitoring Force assembly points. Both the British and the Rhodesian security forces accepted that the exercise was in danger of turning into a 'numbers game'; however, there was a lot of concern about the number of PF forces not yet in the assembly points. It was recognized that the arrival of the first 12,000 PF men in by the first deadline represented 'a real effort by the PF to abide by the cease-fire agreement'. However, the British and the Rhodesian military intelligence were talking about 16,000 to 17,000 men inside Rhodesia. The PF assessment of 31,000 men was considered to be a great exaggeration.[27] Progressively more guerrillas did come into the points.

In an operation (beginning in February 1981) to remove all weapons from the assembly points, the figure of 22,000 former guerrillas is used. The operation took three months to complete. Thus for a period of over 17 months a fully armed guerrilla army of 22,000 men remained in 16 camps. Given the circumstances, cease-fire violations and lawlessness were minimal. Clearly the operation was not without its problems. By August–September the 1,000-strong Libyan-trained ZANLA forces at assembly point 'X-ray' had begun to run a parallel administration and had virtually taken over the Mutoko centre. The police had withdrawn into their fortified camp and the guerrillas had taken over control of the approaches to the town. The issues went beyond those between the administration and the guerrillas to include the local populace. People who had fled the area but were returning were ideologically screened by the ZANLA. There were complaints of the sexual abuse of women, including minors, and other incidents of violent crime. Kangaroo courts and trials were taking place. Rex Nhongo, the Zimbabwe guerrilla commander, visited Mutoko and took action to defuse the tension in the area.

Concurrently with the plans to disarm the former guerrillas a series of national amnesties for arms, ammunition and all other military equipment and uniforms miraculously mopped up an enormous number of weapons and military apparel in both the countryside and cities. (The later discovery of large ZAPU arms caches was part of a major breakdown between sections of the Patriotic Front.) In general there had been a successful return to peace. Many of the internally displaced in the cities and towns had begun in March 1980 (directly after the election) to return to their home areas to take stock of their losses and assets and to assess the general security situation in their home areas before deciding to return home.

---

[27] It was later asserted by the Zimbabwean government that a total 35,763 ex-combatants had been demobilized over the period 5 October 1981 to June 1983.

The bus services to Murewa, Mutoko, Mount Darwin and Gutu were suddenly under enormous pressure, as the internally displaced returned home to 'see how the land lies'.

Planning the Movement of Three-quarters of a Million People
During the build-up to the elections the country began to organize itself for a 'refugee trek'. The refugees awaiting repatriation in Botswana, Mozambique and Zambia were considered only the smallest part of this problem. Figures suggested that there were 750,000 'displaced persons' and an additional 225,000 still in the 149 protected villages. The rural, urban and mission transit centres established by the Christian Care committee as part of the UNHCR programme were used by the internally displaced persons. Many were given assistance. The money for that aid came from church organizations. The numbers of rural transit and mission centres were expanded. In many of the areas where help was most needed the missions had been forced to close down. Re-establishing and manning these missions was a priority. These mission stations were the key to the resettlement in many of the worst war-affected areas. The UNHCR budget of US$1.2 million included the costs of supporting the 'external refugees' at these mission stations. The estimate of the costs of the programme for the displaced persons was US$5.0 million.

Critically, peace and the establishment of the new majority government had come at the end of the 1979–80 agricultural season. As far as the rain-fed agriculture was concerned there would be very little to do for another six months. Hence the food aid programme was essential if people were to go home and become more broadly involved in their own rural reconstruction. Nonetheless in areas where sufficient water was available a total of 70,000 winter vegetable production packs were distributed.[28]

By March 1981 the immediate post-war recovery programmes were simply described as 'assistance for refugees and displaced persons'. They had provided transport for refugees and displaced persons to their home areas, aid in rebuilding their homes, assistance in the form of inputs for crops, provision of emergency food until the first crop was harvested, and social services.

For the formally repatriated exiles it is possible to differentiate four broad areas of assistance. The first was the temporary/in-transit assistance (registration, transport to transit centres, information exchange in transit centres, provision of clothes, food, blankets and health care). The second was assistance to help in their longer-term integration and rehabilitation. This included the sustained food aid, support for reconstruction of housing and the grants of inputs for their agriculture. Third, for the school children who were exiled there was a strong effort to support and achieve continuity of schooling; during this first year 14,000 refugee school children were supported in boarding schools. Fourth, special programmes were devised and developed for the war victims and disabled. Apart from the special centres that were established to examine and evaluate the needs of war casualties, special funds were allocated for social services, and legislation was enacted to provide disability pensions and other benefits for war-wounded people and their dependants.

Within the social services plans for a special programme for the 35,000 former combatants were in process. The initial aim was to integrate as many as possible into the national defence forces and to employ as many as possible in productive activities through an extended demobilization over a number of years. The combatants in the expanded national defence forces were to move into the rural reconstruction and agricultural production plans of the early 1980s.

---

[28] Each pack contained sufficient inputs to permit a family to reap about 1 kilogram of vegetables per day, six weeks after planting, and the harvest was estimated to be spread over six months.

Of all the combined assistance programmes for refugees and displaced persons the most demanding activity was the provision of emergency food supplies. By the beginning of what would be the normal pre-rains hungry season, the food aid required had expanded from 450,000 to 600,000 persons per month – a monthly cost of about US$3 million. The turn-around time for the food aid in kind was slow – 15,000 tons of maize shipped by donors had not been received by Zimbabwe. The massive emphasis on food production proved to be strategic; without the 1980–81 bumper harvest the country could have been facing chronic food shortages and food insecurity. The agricultural success within the first year of the post-war recovery programmes was a good start. However, following many years of war, it was quite clear that a massive rural reconstruction was needed.

Reintegration: a Wider Look at the Impacts of the War
The movements of people into exile or displacement are, more often than not, indications of the wider collapse of the infrastructure, services and administration in the war-torn rural areas. These impacts were particularly severe in the TTLs. Schools, clinics, water supplies[29] and roads were destroyed. In particular community health and the veterinary services (especially dipping) broke down. Diseases like malaria, measles and bilharzia began to spread. Food production had declined or collapsed. Supplies from surplus areas were hampered by the state of, and/or lack of, roads and the lack of transport. There were severe malnutrition and other manifestations of nutritional deficiencies, especially among the very young children. On the cattle front, it is estimated that 1 million cattle died – one-third of the peasant herd.

Highlights of the Reconstruction Programmes
The rehabilitation programmes lasted for a very short period of time and were to be followed by a much more substantial reconstruction initiative. Between June and December 1981 a Z$28 million rehabilitation scheme had been implemented. The scheme was backed by Britain, the United States, Australia, the Netherlands, Sweden and Denmark. This assistance had several important features and effects. First, the aid came in as foreign exchange. Second, the programme generated a significant amount of employment inside Zimbabwe. Third, the assistance schemes combined short-term relief and long-term developmental programmes. As it turned out a good rainy season yielded a substantial harvest of food and cash crops. Fourth was the scale of the programme: approximately one million people were put back on the land. Fifth, the donors who backed the projects were impressed with the efficiency and honesty of use of the assistance. Within a year visiting economists, agronomists, congressmen and aid officials evaluated the scheme positively.

March 1981 saw the launching of a major reconstruction programme. The principal components focussed on schools, roads and bridges, vehicles and plant and water supplies. It was, however, very broadly based and in addition plans for cattle, training, health services, rural businesses, forestry, irrigation, conservation, the clearing of mine-fields laid down during the war, government buildings, tools and expendable stores, water transport, air transport and communications were included. A full evaluation of the impacts of all these separate sectoral and other more specific projects and programmes is well beyond the scope of this chapter. Together they were to facilitate a major transformation of the economy. However, some highlights of the more important programmes are worth mentioning.

---

[29] Some water sources and fruit trees were poisoned and were to pose serious problems for people wanting to reintegrate (Ziswa, personal communication).

As far as the roads were concerned it was not so much the spinal link roads but the minor ones servicing the rural areas that had been most adversely affected. Approximately 14,000 kilometres of these grade roads were targetted for maintenance or upgrading. This reconstruction was carried out rapidly and provided the all-important access for other equipment, supplies, buses, staff and workers necessary for other projects. Strategically the system of roads was re-established through minimal repairs in order to make them passable as soon as was possible. Substantive reconstruction or upgrading was left for a later phase.

Reconstruction of the rural water supplies was critical for both the human populations and the cattle. Emphasis was again focussed on the restoration of as much of the existing capacity as possible though in many ways it would remain totally inadequate. Given the central importance of the cattle in the peasant economy, cattle dips, disease control and veterinary inspection, fencing, aerial spraying and marketing facilities and services were all targetted for reconstruction.

Because of the war, some 2,000 of the 2,500 primary schools had been damaged or needed major repair. Hundreds of thousands of school children could only receive a minimal schooling in the open air during the dry weather. The reconstruction of government schools operated very much on the basis of community self-help with government assistance. Where schools had been completely destroyed, pre-fabricated and open-sided classrooms were established. The schools would later have to be completed with help from the parents. Many of the secondary schools had closed down and reopened on a limited basis. Major assistance was required for the secondary schools.

Between one-quarter and one-third of the small rural businesses collapsed during the war. Through special loans in conjunction with credits from the wholesalers many of these traders were able to re-establish themselves.

Impacts on Reintegration

The longer-term reintegration of exiles and the internally displaced was greatly assisted by the reconstruction programmes that were to follow in the next three years. Support for peasant agriculture was to expand and continue. Social services, especially education and health, improved visibly in a short period of time. The sustained food aid and the child supplementary feeding programme in 1980 provided a good rehearsal for the subsequent drought relief programmes that had to be launched to cope with the potentially devastating three years of successive drought which followed the 1980–81 bumper harvest (fortunately the national stocks amounted to two-and-a-half years of food supply). The government embarked upon an impressive 21-month demobilization programme[30] combined with two years of support for monthly stipends for the ex-combatants.

Failed Political Integration of the Ndebele Minority 1983–88

Two Repatriations to Matabeleland

This part of the chapter presents an account and analysis of two repatriations of refugees to Matabeleland – 'home' for Zimbabwe's Ndebele-speaking minority who account for

---

[30] This involved demobilization; employment in the national army, police and various ministries; further education; support in the establishment of co-operatives and the establishment of an employment creation fund.

8.3 *Some 2,000 primary schools had been damaged or needed major repair (UNHCR/11070/ E. Birrer)*

15 per cent of the country's 9 million inhabitants.[31] These two flights of exiles from Matabeleland and their later 'successful' repatriations are related. The first was a consequence of the Ndebele contributions to the wider nationalist struggle for independence and the war of liberation in the 1970s. The second came about as a result of the open political rift that emerged between ZANU and ZAPU two years after the 1980 elections following the establishment of political independence and majority rule. Both reflect on the contexts outlined above.

The first repatriation refers to the 'Matabeleland part' of the wider national 1980–81 post-Lancaster House programme, reviewed above. The Ndebele-speaking exiles were just a portion of the national programme. As part of the constitutional and political transition to independence, this exercise involved 70,000 formally (UNHCR) repatriated refugees from Zambia, Mozambique and Botswana (UNHCR, 1981).

The second repatriation refers to the post-ZANU/ZAPU 'Unity Accord' which took place seven years later in 1988 after six years of what outwardly appeared to be ethnically-based conflict in Matabeleland. The rural unrest and the (ZANU) government's crackdown on the (ZAPU) 'dissident problem' in Matabeleland resulted in the death of 1,500–3,000[32] civilians, hundreds of arrests and the torture and disappearance of many 'suspects' or sympathizers. These events triggered outside concern at the growing 'facts' of atrocities associated with Zimbabwe's human rights violations. The 'near civil war' generated an immense social and economic impact compounded by devastating droughts and an economic context of stagnation and decay in the 1980s. One feature was the consequent exile of 4,000–5,000 registered refugees in Botswana.

In 1987 there was an amnesty for dissidents and, following the 'Unity Accord' between the two parties, both the political and security threat to the civilian population was largely removed. (This was despite the very low public turnout of 150 dissidents – ranging from ideologues to criminal elements.) In relation to the first 1980 homecoming this later repatriation from Botswana was much smaller. Something in the order of 4,000 exiles were formally repatriated with help from the UNHCR. The euphoria, motivation and willingness of the returnees in the earlier repatriation exercise contrasts with the mood of the second group of returnees. There was scepticism about the political accord and pessimism about their future economic prospects. Among these exiles there was thus much resistance to the proposed 'voluntary' repatriation. Nevertheless, the governments of Botswana and Zimbabwe could maintain that the 'political' basis of their status was now no longer valid. Based on initial UNHCR expectations, as many as 1,000–1,500 Dukwe camp-based refugees appear to have 'avoided' formal repatriation.

Many (interacting) elements affect reintegration. Economic opportunities are pivotal in the process. There are, however, serious structural (and local) limits to rural economic reintegration. Rural returnees must fit into a much more onerous long-term task of development, which, in the 1980s, generated a few 'winners' and many 'losers'. The default path of development in the 1980s has defined an overall expansion of rural poverty.

---

[31] The analysis is based on 47 guided interviews with returnees in Matabeleland North and South in April 1990 (22 returnees from the recent 1987–88 repatriation from Dukwe and 25 from the 1979–80 post-Lancaster House transition to independence). The research included interviews with key informants and examination of press reports and secondary sources. The structural limits interpretation has emerged from a research concern to understand and locate micro-level processes within historically specific constraints affecting rural mobility.

[32] Collet Nkala reports in Parade, October 1990, using a figure of as many as 3,000 civilians killed. Villagers in Tsholotsho and other parts of Matabeleland are currently challenging an apparent death certificate ruling whereby officers issuing certificates say they were instructed not to mention anything concerning the Fifth Brigade.

Beyond going back 'home' to 'family' this is the 'hidden' agenda for returnees in rural repatriation.

Personal history 3 – Struggling to Economically Reintegrate
The respondent fled from Matabeleland South in 1984 following severe beating by Zimbabwean soldiers. His family left all their property with relatives at short notice. They had no notion of official refugee status in advance of their departure. They simply left. After receiving two weeks' medical treatment for his injuries in Francistown he and his wife and six children were forwarded to Dukwe refugee camp. While receiving assistance he also became involved in fishing and agriculture. He brought eight bags of maize back from Botswana when repatriated.

While the family was able to get reasonable assistance in transit during their repatriation in 1988, they found their homestead destroyed and they had lost their livestock. They were promised assistance for the first six months of their reintegration. It turned out to be four months. The family has since expanded to include 8 children and this burden is now combined with a chronic chest condition. He is unable to do strenuous work. Without livestock and the strength to farm fully his main sources of income are food-for-work and collecting fuel wood for others. While he received training and experience in gill-net fishing in Dukwe he has been frustrated in his attempt to get a fishing licence from the Zimbabwean authorities. They have insisted that he must be part of a co-operative before he can get a licence to fish.

In addition to his health and insecure livelihood he has other problems with the authorities. Because his wife does not have a birth certificate he faces a residual difficulty of getting birth certificates for his children.[33]

Historical Background to Matabeleland
There are deep and long historical roots to politicized ethnicity in Zimbabwean polity. In the pre-colonial period the Ndebele peoples occupied and conquered part of the Shona country and for some time established relations of domination over people who became a lower 'caste' within Ndebele society.

Struggles against colonial Rhodesia began with what is now called the 'First Chimurenga'. It involved separate Shona and Ndebele rebellions shortly after the imposition of British South Africa Company (BSAC) rule in the 1890s. These two regionally separate uprisings were punitively crushed by the settlers with military help from South Africa and the British. Issues of 'native politics' appear to have then remained substantially suppressed under the 'might' and 'right' of the settlers during the first 30–40 years of colonial rule.

In Matabeleland, this suppressed nationalist sentiment would resurface in the 1940s and extend into the 1960s as a complex mix

> . . . of Ndebele rural protest – of ethnic nationalism and 'traditional' leadership, of migrant worker organization, of large cattle-owner indignation, of small peasant fears of total immiseration' (Ranger, 1985: 123).

There were similar sentiments and frustrations among the Mashona peoples.

The Emergence of Separate Nationalist Movements
Based on earlier political developments and organizations, the 1960s saw the formation of the two dominant nationalist political parties – now forming the current ruling Unity Accord coalition. (The parties are closely, but by no means exclusively, associated with the country's two dominant ethnic groups.)

---

[33] All interviews in Matabeleland were anonymous.

In Matabeleland, ZAPU was founded in 1961 and was banned in the same year. In 1963, ZANU emerged as a separate political party (from ZAPU) based on differences in strategy for nationalist movement – though, in addition, ZANU has long been linked to the Mashona majority. ZANU, too, was banned by the settler state in 1964 and as from 1965 both ZAPU and ZANU operated from bases in exile until the signing of the Lancaster House constitution in 1979. In exile ZANU and ZAPU developed separate political and military strategies and guerrilla armies. For a brief period (1976–79) the two parties formed a 'Patriotic Front' (PF).

Thus, during the struggle for national independence these two dominant political and military wings of the nationalist struggle were loosely 'unified' in the 'Second Chimurenga', their struggle against the common enemy – white minority rule and the Rhodesian settler state. They had differing political and military strategies, regional and ethnic foundations.

The ZAPU Zimbabwe People's Revolutionary Army (ZIPRA) offensive, largely on the western front of the Ndebele homelands, would place a large part of Matabeleland North and South under curfew and martial law by 1977. The scale of the terrain – 140,000 square kilometres – and its nature, a scrub savanna combined with vast wilderness areas, and a low population density and minimal infrastructure were ideal for guerrilla tactics. ZAPU would soon strain the military and other resources of the settler state in Matabeleland. By 1979, except for Bulawayo and surrounding European commercial farms (and a few other towns), the entire area was under martial law. (NB. ZANU and its military wing the Zimbabwe African National Liberation Army (ZANLA) concentrated on the north and northeastern Zambezi Valley and the entire eastern front of the country and were equally successful in their campaigns.) The joint initiatives of the nationalist movements culminated in the 1979 Lancaster House constitutional settlement for a transition to majority rule.

Disaffection & Dissidence

Following the February 1980 independence election results, where ZANU gained 57 out of the 80 'B Role' seats and ZAPU 20 of the remaining 23, relations between ZANU and ZAPU soured. Dr Joshua Nkomo's refusal of the presidency offered to him by Mugabe in 1980 set an intransigent tone to the Ndebele minority's disaffection with the outcome of the elections (despite this more than proportionate representation of Ndebele interests in the new government in 1980). This would deteriorate into an open rift between ZANU (PF) and ZAPU by February 1982.

The critical issue of developing an 'integrated and united' new Zimbabwe National Army out of the three former separate armies partially broke down. While broadly a success, about 3,000 former ZIPRA guerrillas deserted with their weapons. From the outset it was already clear that 'integration' was ultimately part of a demobilization programme which some felt concentrated on ZIPRA combatants. The result, along with the discovery of massive arms caches on ZAPU farms (violating national amnesties aimed at mopping up all arms and military equipment), was the rapid re-emergence of rural civil strife. This was because of both acts of dissidence and the response of government which set about 'dealing' with the so-called 'problem' in western Zimbabwe.

In 1983 the government reacted to the 'dissidents' and Ndebele disaffection by sending in the Fifth Brigade – a North Korean-trained unit formed from the ranks of loyal ZANLA guerrillas. This solution proved to be catastrophic. Between late 1982 and March 1983 harrowing tales of massacre, rape, looting and torture emerged. Rural clinics were filled with patients suffering from broken arms and legs, bruised kidneys and bayonet wounds.

Initial denial of the atrocities was replaced by a special commission of enquiry into alleged atrocities. The results have never been made public.[34]

Government revised the strategy and the brigade was withdrawn. (The period 1983–84 remains known as the 'Gukurahundi', the name given to the brigade, which describes a type of violent tropical rain-storm that marks the end of the dry season by sweeping the accumulated litter from the land.) The political, economic and social effects of the 'Gukurahundi' on the civilian populations of parts of Matabeleland resulted in a second (but post-independence) wave of refugees who largely moved to Botswana and South Africa. The blame was largely put on the tactics and methods of the security forces. Dissidents were also responsible for many deaths, atrocities and destruction of property. An aura of fear and insecurity gripped the community. Abductions of leaders in Ndebele society took place at night. For a time during the height of the conflict the problems of 'security' resulted in an 'inevitable' deprivation of the areas from central government resources including emergency drought relief. The net effect was that parts of the administrative system and rural economy became paralysed.

Figures from the National Health Information System (which has been operational since 1987) show that the two Matabelelands have the worst figures for malnutrition in the country. For each of four age categories in each province the levels of under-nutrition are higher than the national average (National Health Information System, 1987, 1988 and 1989). This, however, cannot be attributed solely to the civil unrest and disruption of people's lives; it is also due to the inherent erratic and low agro-ecological potential for cropping in these regions.

Elements of politicized ethnicity have thus been pervasive in Zimbabwe's pre- and post-independence polity. It has been closely associated with an intolerant political culture and violent struggles against clear 'enemies'. In 1983 dissidents became the new enemy. The 'near civil war' between ZANU and ZAPU lasted six years until an amnesty and the signing of the Unity Accord.

Continuities & Discontinuities in the 1980 & 1988 Repatriations to Matabeleland
An account has been given above of the pre-flight context, the patterns of flight into exile and internal displacement and the 1980 post-war repatriation, and reconstruction and reintegration of refugees in Zimbabwe in 1980. The analysis which follows builds on this earlier exploratory account and takes a comparative look at the two repatriations in Matabeleland in the light of the structural context outlined above.

It is important, first, to summarize the main features that emerged from the 1980 repatriation.

The impact of the war of liberation generated refugees and internally displaced persons in the ratio 1:3. There were many more internally displaced persons than refugees. Their plight and circumstances were disturbing, living in protected villages, forced into rural migrations or urban exile in swollen shanty towns. They were more visible than refugees proper. The hostile settler government did not respond to the enormous urban influx which it labelled as 'squatters' and there were no assistance programmes or recognition of these people as being 'war-displaced'. This lack of state response launched a large compensatory private/church/NGO response. The broad umbrella organization which emerged in the 1970s played a leading role in the repatriation programme but also

---

[34] The Lawyers Committee for Human Rights (1986) remains the most accessible account of the conflict in Matabeleland 1983–86.

championed the cause of the internally displaced. Through their initiatives the 'repatriation' programme became an integrated programme of assisted 'internal resettlement' as well. The resources were thus allocated proportionally between these equally affected groups. Arguably the returning refugees were able to piggy-back onto the impressive programmes set up to help the internally displaced.

Civil Unrest & the Internally Displaced, 1983–88

Accounts of the urban destitute in the city of Bulawayo and surrounding towns and some of the rural squatters in Matabeleland hint at the scale and circumstances of the internally displaced as generated by the post-independence conflict. The full realities remain very thinly documented. In contrast to the 1980 'internal resettlement' programmes for the war-displaced, there were no special programmes or resources specifically allocated to the plight of the Ndebele internally displaced in 1987–88. The existing programmes of government and NGO operations were to suffice. The extent to which 'failed' economic reintegration of some of the 1987–88 returnees links with elements of failed economic reintegration of the assumed more numerous internally displaced is difficult to assess. Based on past patterns of flight there may have been 12,000–15,000 internally displaced associated with the 1982–87 conflict. The two repatriations were differently organized. In the 1980 repatriation there was a tripartite arrangement between UNHCR, a powerful church and NGO umbrella organization and two departments of the new government in transition. The second 1987–88 repatriation simply involved the UNHCR, and the governments of Zimbabwe and Botswana. NGOs appear to have had a minimal role.

Regional & Historically Different Structural Constraints

The repatriation of returnees at independence was within a euphoria of attainment of political independence and the expectations that radical transformations in the economic sphere *would* take place. With the hindsight of the last decade it is now clear that the post-independence Matabeleland repatriations have elements of both success and failure. There were major achievements in the initial social and economic help in 1980–81 and this transition seemed broadly successful. However, within a couple of years the reintegration of the Ndebele in Zimbabwean post-independence polity broke down. Economic rehabilitation and reintegration were partial. In the latter (1987–88) group of rural returnees, prospects for economic reintegration were more limited than in 1980.

Because of, first, the civil unrest 1983–87, second, a low profile with agrarian reforms – a relative 'go-slow' on resettlement programmes – and, third, the selective nature of the modernization of peasant agriculture, a large number of the region's 'producers' are operating at or below subsistence level. The human and economic costs have been vast. In relation to a range of household coping strategies many have long exhausted their productive assets and are now on the fringes of destitution. Given the stagnant aggregate per capita income and wholly inadequate growth in employment over the post-independence decade, the scope for opting out of the rural economy into employment elsewhere is highly restricted. The long-standing recourse to international labour migration as instructed by the original design of the native labour reserves remains an option. Many Ndebele speak Tswana and can easily converse in the urban and regional Zulu/Ndebele-speaking communities within Botswana and South Africa. Informal (but highly-organized and efficient) nexuses for labour recruitment aid people to get into Botswana and South Africa.

The broader regional ecological constraint on the rural economy of Matabeleland is important to understand. It has frustrated hopes for the emancipation from rural poverty.

The war in the 1970s resulted in the loss of one million head of cattle in the peasant sector. Losses totalled one-third of the herd. In Matabeleland where cattle, as a component of agricultural incomes, are economically more important, we surmise that economic effects of these losses were disproportionally felt in the region. Moreover, by the time the 1981–82 agricultural season had proved itself to be well into a severe drought, the herd had simply degenerated. At the time the government, through the Cold Storage Commission (CSC), introduced a cattle rescue programme to save nearly 1.5 million animals. By June 1982 the plan was failing, falling far short of its intended capacity initially because of a 'poor response at the communal sale pens'. However it seemed that large numbers of cattle were turned away as 'rejects' unlikely to survive a move to places of grazing. Commercial speculators were therefore able to offer worried communal farmers 'the price of a skin' for their animals.

Later (by April 1982) the CSC changed its policy, buying all cattle on offer. However, there was no guaranteed price. The anticipation that 'thousands of cattle will die' came to pass. By September the press would report that the 'smell of death is everywhere' as the strangle-hold of drought tightened its grip on the Communal Areas. By October 50,000 communal land cattle in Matabeleland had already died. Another 10,000 would die within the following three weeks. The general expectation of the cattle relief operation was that the aggregated effects of sales, movements and deaths of cattle would halve the Matabeleland herd. A disproportionate share of the deaths took place within the Communal Areas. In the end the commercial ranchers were the main beneficiaries of the cattle rescue scheme. Budgets for the 1982 programme were for 1.45 million head for the Matabeleland, Victoria and Midlands areas. The Communal Areas participation in the scheme was in all likelihood a small fraction of this.

The drought in 1981–82, disastrous as it was, turned out to be just the first signs of the 'El Nino' which would adversely affect the weather patterns in the southern hemisphere for three years. Between March 1982 and October 1984 there would be 30 months of drought and water shortages.

The loss of cattle as productive assets within the peasant farming system and rural economy is illustrative of a much wider economic cost. In the 1970s the cattle losses were primarily war related and there was by no means a complete rehabilitation of the herd losses during the reconstruction programmes in the first 18 months of independence. Draught power shortages for the arable agriculture were limiting the potential of the farming system. Although there had been some mention of a cattle finance scheme to help reconstruct the herd nothing subsequently happened.

In combination with severe droughts the civil unrest in the mid-1980s has simply worsened this constraint. By the late 1980s there were chronic shortages of animals. At the time of writing in the early 1990s, the scale, timing and likely success of the arable option, should the rainy seasons prove to be supportive, remain restricted.

Violence made the provision of veterinary, agricultural and other services and emergency relief such as improved community water supplies difficult. This applied to both the late 1970s and mid-1980s. For the former the minimal provisions broke down and for the latter the much more expanded 'development' programmes and initiatives were frustrated. Both periods perpetuated and worsened rural poverty.

Patterns of Flight
There are close parallels to the patterns of the two flights into exile. The roles of men who fight in wars and the nature of the patriarchal rural social structure play a large part. Building on a long-standing system of male labour migration, increasingly politicized men

spearheaded the nationalist struggle, followed by many young male recruits into the political and military wings of the parties in exile. Schools as prominent rural institutions were the focus of mobilizations/abductions in border areas and increasingly large numbers of school children would swell the ranks of the exiles. The guerrilla war 'back home' – among the residual women, young children and elderly men – would at stages of the conflict trigger mass movements predominantly of women and children into exile. They followed the men at a later stage in the conflict but did not necessarily go to the same places. This took the form of rural–rural migrations across borders in remote areas or movement as displaced persons into urban areas.

In both periods the reason why there were flights of refugees was the civil unrest as triggered by the political context. People were simply caught up in harassments, beatings, rape and the cross-fire of a guerrilla war and the later 'dissident problem'. There are some obvious differences between the two.

In the mid-1980s, the mass flights of women and small children into exile appear not to have taken place to the same extent. Urban internal displacement and rural squatting absorbed the majority. The realities of the internally displaced in the mid-1982–87 period were much less visible. The comparative health statistics for Harare and Bulawayo suggest this was the case. The urban health services in Bulawayo city dealt with an influx of rural health problems (NHIS, 1987). In addition, because of the localized nature of the disturbances the numbers of refugees did not rise to anywhere near the pre-1980 level. The targets in the anti-dissident campaign were young men and some fled from fear of persecution or from further harassment while a few 'ideologues' may well have gone into exile as recruits into dissidence/civil defence militia.

This domestic picture is broadly reflected in the statistics on the exiles. When the repatriations were promoted in 1987–88 the camp at Dukwe in Botswana had a gross sex imbalance of 2,500 men to 450 women. A remarkably high percentage of the female inmates of the camp were pregnant or had a baby. (The possibility of a choice of contraception did not seem to exist in Dukwe.) The corollary of this sex ratio 'back home' is that rural poverty is partially associated with female-headed households, a portion of whom tend to have no access to remittance income, have no livestock and are experiencing the erosion of their marginal incomes by price inflation of necessary inputs to the rural economy. The social fragmentation is also closely associated with family breakdown, abandonment of rural wives, children and economic breakdown. What acts as a coping strategy is socially and economically very unstable.

Blurred Definitions

The Matabeleland experience of returnees highlights the difficulty of distinguishing between 'refugees' and 'displaced persons' and 'regional migrants' whether they be local or foreign. There are those who manage to wear several hats – that of a refugee and an economic migrant. Being in 'exile' but economically independent removes the need to be more formally defined as a refugee – though at times of great hardship it might be prudent to register and take up residence in a camp. Thus learning about survival strategies of officially repatriated refugees (in camps) limits one to the specifics of this broadly less mobile group. The exiles in the Zambian, Mozambican and Botswanan camps in the 1970s were at one end of a continuum while the many thousands of graduates outside the country and camps and internationally much more widely dispersed were at the other end. Almost exclusively these latter exiles have not been rurally reintegrated. Strategically they preferred to exploit the labour migration option – even internationally.

Personal history 4 – Failed Economic Reintegration: 'The Only Solution Left will be to Go to South Africa'

At 22 years old the respondent fled Matabeleland South with his parents in 1977. He had hoped to get military training and fight for the nationalist struggle. He was, however, not selected and remained in Botswana until he was repatriated in 1980. He then attempted to gain employment in Bulawayo but after a long period of frustration failed and returned to assist his parents on their farm. He carves wood independently as an additional source of income. He acquired no skills while in exile and at the age of 33 years he feels the need to be employed in order to provide support for his wife and two young children currently living as an extended family on his parents' farm. The only solution left for him now would be to go to South Africa.

Regional 'Push' & 'Pull' Factors

Notably between 1982 and 1989 Botswana ran the most ambitious famine management programme in Africa. First, the strategy aimed at maintaining income and limiting the erosion of assets. It therefore set out to transfer income to households facing destitution. Second, the strategy placed the rural economy in an optimal position to take advantage of good rains as and if they came. Third, there was protection of the assets of cattle and land. The instruments of the strategy included: food aid and distribution – including supplementary feeding programmes; labour-based relief – the 'Pula for work programme'; water relief and development; and agricultural relief. Some of Zimbabwe's exiles integrated into these public works programmes. Respondents from Dukwe noted this under the 'skills/experience' acquired while in exile.

Lessons from the Matabeleland Repatriations

The Matabeleland provinces experienced two periods of refugee exodus and repatriation. While the post-independence repatriation is held up as broadly a 'success' story, the later political rift between ZANU and ZAPU is evidence of 'failed' political reintegration for the Ndebele minority in 1982–87. Partly because they are rare occurrences, and partly for political reasons, evaluations of repatriations are sometimes massaged into 'model' events. The evaluation of the 'success' of the 1980 repatriation was made on the basis of a very limited (if any) medium-term appraisal of economic reintegration. The assessment took place before such an appraisal was possible. The same applies to the 1987–88 repatriation. The image of Zimbabwe's broadly based peasant agricultural success story in the early 1980s would hide the realities of the clear default path of selective commoditization and the expansion of poverty within the sector over the decade. There are therefore elements of failed economic reintegration for both repatriations, although it seems clear that there was a proportionally greater degree of economic failure for the latter group of returnees, due to the historically specific economic context into which they were repatriated. What are the other continuities and discontinuities that can be established for the two repatriations?

The numbers involved in the two exercises were significantly different. The first repatriation involved 70,000 refugees (nationally) while the second involved approximately 4,000. The country of exile for the latter group was exclusively Botswana while the former group of returnees came from both Zambia and Botswana. The differences in numbers were also reflected in the range of agencies and support services involved. In 1980 the UNHCR in co-ordination with the governments of Zambia, Botswana, Zimbabwe and NGOs outside and inside Zimbabwe played a major role in respective repatriations, rehabilitation and reintegration. This encompassed the provision of transport, from host country ultimately to their homes, and food supplies to see returnees through at least to the end of the next agricultural harvest. Steps were taken to ensure that returnees would have a good start in the next agricultural season by the provision of seed packs, chemicals and agricultural hand tools. Other rehabilitation relief materials and services were provided in addition to the much bigger parallel programmes of support for the internally displaced from the same communities or areas. By 1981 it was possible for the UNHCR to withdraw most of its staff from the repatriation exercise. The bumper harvest of the 1980–81 season added to the sense of success and satisfaction at the rehabilitation and reintegration.

In the second repatriation there was little NGO activity. The UNHCR's involvement was limited to the movement of the refugees from Dukwe to the Zimbabwean border – thereafter they became the responsibility of the Government of Zimbabwe through its Department of Social Welfare. The level of back-up services characteristic of the 1980 repatriation was not provided. Transport of refugees to their homes and food for the journey were supplied. Once the returnees had reached their homes no other form of assistance was provided. Only a minority, who while in Botswana had demanded an audience with Joshua Nkomo, as leader of ZAPU, received Z$50 each (Z$100 for family heads) for four months, though it had originally been promised for six months. Those who had more or less been forcibly rounded up and returned to Zimbabwe did not receive any additional form of assistance other than their repatriation.

The contrast between the responses of the refugees to the two separate proposals for repatriation is illuminating. It was reported that in 1979 when the Botswana refugees were told that Dr Joshua Nkomo was now in Zimbabwe and that everyone should go back and vote for ZAPU there was a roar of joy. However, when in 1987 the refugees in Dukwe were told that Nkomo was now in power and they should go home, they refused and asked Nkomo himself to come and address them. When he arrived he faced a difficult situation. The refugees demanded concrete economic and political reassurances, i.e. more than simply being asked to come back with their needed skills and participate in Zimbabwe's development.

No doubt there were those who longed to be back in Zimbabwe, to re-establish and continue with their 'normal' lives. However, there were those who knew that with or without peace they had very little to gain by returning to Zimbabwe. The decision to move away from one's home to seek refuge is influenced by a series of factors; among them security is important, but also other factors including the perceived losses and gains in terms of earning a livelihood are present. Likewise such considerations are made before one decides to repatriate 'voluntarily'. The hopes and aspirations for a new Zimbabwean social order in 1979–80 seem to have been absent in 1987. Those with the least to lose escape into refuge – hence the large number of youths who formed a significant part of the refugee population and also the 'problem' of trying to encouraging them to go back to Zimbabwe.

A lesson which could have been learnt was the importance of a necessary cluster of back-up services as provided in the 1980 repatriation by the NGOs, church organizations and the UNHCR. In the post-Unity Accord repatriation the government played the major role in the repatriation and (if any) rehabilitation and reintegration exercise. As a result, not much was done to ensure that the returnees found a basis for restarting their lives. The argument was that the exiles were simply going back to rejoin their families. However, the majority of these families are located in the very rural areas bound by the structural problems outlined above. The repatriation was a matter of releasing people into an area and society least equipped to cater for their needs. Given that many returnees had mixed feelings about repatriation it is not difficult to understand why some have again crossed the border, this time to become part of the labour migration process to Botswana and South Africa.

If civil unrest and lack of peace were the sole driving forces pushing people into exile, voluntary repatriation ought to follow automatically from removal of these forces or at least be easy to promote. The Matabeleland experience has made us question this type of narrow political interpretation of circumstances surrounding exiles and returnees. Refugees are spawned from within a wider historically structured rural economic context. Economic push and pull factors are major determinants of population movements locally and/or internationally. Civil unrest has certainly suddenly swelled the numbers. Large parts of the rural economy are part of a depressing contemporary dynamic – that is their role as a rural sponge mopping up an expanding population of rural slum dwellers on the periphery of the formal economy. Arguably structural adjustment programmes, notwithstanding their integration with expanded rural development initiatives and impressive land and agrarian reform proposals, may perpetuate this role. This will be the economic context spawning future exiles – given a little rural unrest or disaffection – and, apart from issues of re-establishing peace, sets the economic context and challenges of 'successful' rehabilitation and reintegration of returnees.

Conclusion

There are major structural economic constraints facing people in 'mass voluntary rural repatriations'. The situation is by no means unique to Zimbabwe and hence the issues raised may well have a broader relevance to the wider plight of refugees and possible future repatriations in the region.

The hidden agenda of 'successful' repatriation is fundamentally that of meaningful economic reintegration. In a decade of post-independence 'transformation' in Zimbabwe this has proved very difficult to realize. This is broadly as a consequence of the historical structuring of rural poverty and as a consequence of the contemporary reproduction of poverty as the default 'development' path for vulnerable groups in the rural economy. In the all too familiar rural economic context where agriculture is highly risky, insecure and provides less than basic needs in many circumstances, non-farm sources of incomes have become a critical component of economic survival. Yet village-level crafts, artisanal and other small rural enterprises as a local economic option appear to be frustrated by the weight of poverty and the resultant ineffective demand. Moreover, in the context of recession, there has been a structural narrowing of wage employment opportunities in the formal economy. Repatriations in combination with limited rehabilitation programmes in acutely depressed rural areas on the periphery of a wider economic stagnation run the danger of failing to even rehabilitate the *status quo ante*.

The pockets of resistance to 'voluntary' repatriation, following the apparent removal of the political and security risks through reconciliation and peace, are rooted in both political uncertainty and the harsh and unacceptable economic realities of attempting rural economic reintegration. The distinction between 'political' and 'economic' refugees and migrant labour progressively becomes more and more blurred, particularly in the light of the historical economic structuring of Southern Africa on the basis of local and internationally promoted labour migrations.

While there are many initiatives promoting regional economic co-operation (outside of the issues of refugees which nonetheless demand resources), the regional liberalization of labour and the prospect of future labour migrations do not appear to be on the agenda.

8.4 *After a decade of independence, agrarian poverty remains a serious problem in Zimbabwe (UNHCR/no number or photographer)*

Are there potentials for 'development' or dangers in aiding the perpetuation of the exploitation of immigrant labour? The suggestion that for example Zimbabwe might (a) assist the repatriation of the Mozambican exiles currently in the country and (b) aid their economic reintegration *in Mozambique* by openly allowing them the right to return *to Zimbabwe* as local economic migrants/seasonal workers, I fear, would simply be viewed as heretical! Repatriation is the 'permanent solution': they *must* go home and *stay* home! This, however, is not what they have been doing in the immediate past and it is not coincidental that two of Zimbabwe's camps for refugees have 'grown up' adjacent to major irrigation schemes where there are opportunities for thousands of seasonal, contract or piece workers. Until relatively recently agriculture has absorbed the largest share of 'formal' wage employment albeit at very low wages. The historically dominant labour migrations have in fact been rural–rural movements.

Rural migrations tend to be viewed as the last stage or expression of social and economic collapse of an area. Many are surely the consequence of crises and in their own right pose major problems. This is not universally or necessarily so. They can be part of a pattern of local rural–rural migration from areas of seasonally differing labour bottlenecks, or as a response to severe droughts. Arguably returnees (perhaps more so than others?) might well need to fit into such rural labour markets. Yet, while some Mozambican peasants openly market their crops 'across' the border to Zimbabwean parastatal bodies, that *labour* should be marketed across international borders seems to be another matter.

By their actions many rural poor are questioning why they should be linked exclusively to local public works if other more lucrative possibilities exist. This appears to have happened in Matabeleland South, particularly as young people are moving out.

The Botswana famine-avoidance programmes appear to have been remarkably successful in restricting the amount of what implicitly seemed would be 'disruptive' internal migration. This, however, has been on the basis of levels of resource flows that were unsustainable in Zimbabwe. Regionally Botswana's national programmes thus appear to have acted as a wider catchment for refugees/migrants, including those from Matabeleland, Zimbabwe.

The overwhelming impression of economic adversity comes out in the interviews. Unemployment supplemented by the food-for-work opportunities (while much appreciated) falls far short of meeting anything like the basic needs of a family. It is not the economic basis of an accumulation for rehabilitating critical productive assets or for securing some savings that might motivate a slightly less risk-averse stance towards agriculture or for diversifying into other economic activities. Thus some children drop out of school. They are simply unable to 'further' their education because of the barrier of school fees. The reason is not 'because our crops did not do so well this year' but 'both my parents are *unemployed*'. The comparison demonstrated that those surviving on local agriculture (with minimal productive assets) and local relief/maintenance appeared markedly more miserable than those with regional non-farm economic links. The latter group certainly explode the lingering colonial myth about the 'full-time' farmer as being inherently better off. Agriculture, at its best, for a large number of 'peasant farmers' is a supplement to what must necessarily be a more diversified range of income sources.

Examining refugees within a wider development context alerts us to the dangers of looking at them in isolation. They are very much analogous to the highly visible 'tip of the iceberg'. Just below the water-line there is a wider band of legal/illegal immigrants and exiles. A little deeper down many more numerous internally displaced persons 'back home' are exploring strategies of 'domestic' refuge. All are spawned from a much more awesome development challenge – the depressed, drought-prone rural periphery carrying a disproportionate share of the results of a wider economic stagnation.

Figure 8.1 *Brief chronology of events in Zimbabwe*

1890–1923	British South Africa Company (BSAC) rule in Rhodesia.
1897–1898	Ndebele and Mashona opposition to company rule. Rebellions are overcome when the BSAC gains assistance from both South Africa and the British.
1920	Order-in-council apportions land in the colony: 23 per cent 'Reserves', 32 per cent for European settlement and 45 per cent Crown land for future development.
1931	The Land Apportionment Act.
1945–1960	The 'Second Occupation of Mashonaland' marks the immigration of approximately two-thirds of Rhodesia's white population.
1951	The Native Land Husbandry Act.
1957	The formation of the Southern Rhodesian African National Congress (SRANC).
1958	SRANC is banned.
1960	Zimbabwe African People's Union (ZAPU) emerges and is formed from the banned SRANC.
1960	Emergence of Zimbabwe African National Union (ZANU) under Reverend Ndabaningi Sithole.
1962	Settler state bans ZAPU and ZANU.
1963	First stage of revolutionary nationalism when ZANU adopts a policy of confrontation.
1972–1979	Contraction of the UDI economy in the wake of growing escalation of the war and international sanctions and isolation.
1977–1979	A large number of rural civilians flee the war-torn countryside for neighbouring countries – Botswana, Mozambique and Zambia.
1976–1979	ZANU and ZAPU form a loose coalition called the 'Patriotic Front'.
1979	Lancaster House all-party constitutional conference forces the resignation of the Muzorewa government.
1980	Phase I UNHCR-assisted repatriation.
1980	ZANU-PF wins the general election to decide the first government of independent Zimbabwe. Nkomo (ZAPU-PF) turns down Mugabe's offer of the presidency.
1980–1981	Phase II and Phase III UNHCR repatriations.
1983–1987	Early post-war reconstruction in Matabeleland turns into 'dissidence' and civil unrest.
1987	Unity Accord is signed between ZANU and ZAPU.
1988–1989	The second repatriation of refugees to Matabeleland.

Selected References

Agricultural Rural Development Authority (ARDA) (1982), 'Communal area development report No. 3, South Matabeleland: South Gwanda baseline survey': 50, plus annexures.

Amin, N. (1989) 'Peasant differentiation and food security in Zimbabwe: emerging contradictions', paper presented at Farming Systems Research Symposium, 9–12 October, Fayetteville, Arkansas.

Asrat D. *et al.* (1989), *Children on the front line: the impact of apartheid, destabilization and warfare on children in Southern and South Africa*, UNICEF, New York: 126.

Bush, R. & L. Cliffe (1984) 'Agrarian policy in migrant labour societies: reform or transformation in Zimbabwe?', *ROAPE*, 29: 77–94.

Catholic Commission for Justice and Peace (CCJP) (1975) 'The man in the middle: torture, resettlement and eviction', Catholic Institute for International Relations (CIIR), London.

Cleghorn, W.B. (1986) 'Report on the condition of grazing in the Tribal Trust Lands', *Rhodesia Agricultural Journal*, 63: 57–67.

Cliffe, L. (1986) *Policy options for agrarian reform in Zimbabwe: a technical appraisal*, FAO (draft), Rome: 138.

Correspondents (1989) 'Cover story', *Southern African Economist*, February/March: 5–15.

Davies, R. and D. Saunders (1987) 'Stabilization policies and the effect on child health in Zimbabwe', *Review of African Political Economy*, 38: 3–23.

De Wolf, S. (1981) 'The resettlement and rehabilitation of refugees in the Umtali Area', *Issues*, Vol. 11, Nos 3/4, Fall/Winter: 27–30.

Dube, G. (1988) 'Former refugees are happier at home', *The Chronicle*, 22 July.

Frederikse, Julie (1982) *None but ourselves*, Zimbabwe Publishing House, Harare, and James Currey, London: 386.

Green, R.H. (1985) 'Parameters, permutations and political economy: Zimbabwe 1973/83, 1986/96', paper 20, Conference on Economic Policies and Planning under Crisis Conditions in Developing Countries, Department of Economics, University of Zimbabwe, Harare, 2–5 September: 58.

Gwazemba, F.S.D. (1984) 'The role of non-governmental organizations in the provision of refugee relief in Zimbabwe: A case study of the Christian Care Refugee Relief Programme – 1979–1983', University of Zimbabwe, Bachelor of Social Work Dissertation: 59.

Hay, R.W. (1988) 'Famine incomes and employment: has Botswana anything to teach Africa?' *World Development*, Vol. 16, No. 9: 1113–25.

Hocke, J. (1988) 'New consensus on Southern Africa', *Refugees*, 57: 8–9.

Hodges, T. (1984) 'Africa's refugee crisis', *Africa Report*, January–February: 4–10.

Jackson J. (1989) 'Refugees, repatriation, reconstruction and reintegration: an exploratory account of the "success" of Zimbabwe's post-Lancaster House repatriation', seminar presentation at UNRISD, Geneva, September.

Jackson, J. and P. Collier (1988) 'Incomes, poverty and food security in the communal lands of Zimbabwe', Rural and Urban Planning Occasional Paper 11, Department of Rural and Urban Planning, University of Zimbabwe.

Jayne, T.S. *et al.* (1990) 'Grain market reliability, access and growth in low potential areas of Zimbabwe: implications for national and regional supply coordination in the SADCC region', in M. Rukuni, G. Mudimu, and T.S. Jayne (eds) *Food security issues in the SADCC region*, University of Zimbabwe, UZ/MSU food security research in Southern Africa Project: 113–27.

Kadhani, X.M. (1986) 'The economy: issues, problems and prospects', in I. Mandaza (ed.), *Zimbabwe: the political economy of transition 1980–86*, CODESRIA, Dakar, Senegal: 99–122.

Knox, M. (1989) 'After six years of bloodshed, peace comes to Matabeleland', *Weekly Mail*, 3–9 February.

Lawyers Committee for Human Rights (1986) *Zimbabwe wages of war: a report on human rights*, New York: 171.

Mandaza, I. (1985) 'The state and politics in the post-white settler colonial situation', in I. Mandaza (ed.) *Zimbabwe: the political economy of transition 1980–86*, CODESRIA, Dakar, Senegal: 21–74.

Martin, D. and P. Johnson (1981) *The struggle for Zimbabwe: the Chimurenga war*, Zimbabwe Publishing House, Harare.

Ministry of Economic Planning and Development (1981) 'Post-war recovery programmes', Zimcord, Harare, Government Printers: 25–33.

National Health Information System (NHIS) (1987, 1988, 1989) 'Annual Reports' (Extracts provided by MOH) Harare.

Nyarota, G. (1978/9) 'Future still bleak for the refugees', *The Herald*, press cutting, no day.

— (1987) 'Refugees in Dukwe coming home', *The Chronicle*, 28 November.

Ranger, T. (1985) '*Peasant consciousness and guerrilla war in Zimbabwe*', Zimbabwe Publishing House, Harare, and James Currey, London.

Rodgers, E.W. (1982) 'Christian Care National Office 1981/82 Annual Report', Catholic Services and Development in Zimbabwe.

Saith, A. (1990) 'Development strategies and the rural poor', *Journal of Peasant Studies*, Vol. 17, No. 2, January: 171–243.

Sandford, S. T. (1982) *Livestock in the Communal Areas of Zimbabwe*, report for the Ministry of Lands, Resettlement and Rural Development.

Sithole, M. (1986) 'The general elections 1979–1985', in Mandaza *op. cit.*: 75–98.

Southall, R. J. (1980) 'Resettling the refugees', *Africa Report*, November/December: 48–52.

The Chronicle (1983) 'Dukwe camp scandal: many dying, say former refugees', 3 January.

The Chronicle (1985) 'Refugees return', 12 December.

The Chronicle (1988) 'Dukwe refugees return', 16 April.

The Chronicle (1988) 'Refugees anger Nkomo: come home, says Nkomo', 19 May.

The Chronicle (1988) 'Dukwe not just an ordinary refugee camp', 23 May.

The Chronicle (1988) 'Dukwe refugees delay', 4 June.

The Chronicle (1988) '254 from Dukwe arrive in Plumtree', 15 June.

The Chronicle (1988) '370 returning from Dukwe', 31 June.

UNHCR (1981) 'Office of the United Nations High Commissioner for Refugees: UNHCR assistance activities in Zimbabwe', HCR/155/12/81 GE.81-02624, Geneva.

UNICEF (1984) *Situation analysis of women and children in Zimbabwe*, UNICEF, New York, and Government of Zimbabwe, Harare.

Utete, C. M. B. (1979) *The road to Zimbabwe: the political economy of settler colonialism, national liberation and foreign intervention*, University Press of America, Washington DC: 170.

Waniwa I. (1988), 'Help pledge for returnees – 300 more ex-Dukwe refugees arrive', *The Chronicle*, 29 June.

Wiseman H. and A. M. Taylor (1981) *From Rhodesia to Zimbabwe – the politics of transition*, Pergamon Press, Oxford: 168.

Wuyts, M. (1989) 'Food and employment balances: an analytical framework', *Population and development teaching texts Module 1.*, Institute of Social Studies, The Hague: 54.

Ziswa, V. T. (1989) 'Zimbabwe churches' experience in the returnee, resettlement, rehabilitation and reconstruction programme', Ecumenical Co-ordination Office for Emergencies in Southern Africa, Harare, mimeo: 15.

9

K.B. WILSON with J. NUNES[1]
Repatriation to Mozambique

Refugee Initiative & Agency Planning
in Milange District 1988–1991

Introduction

This chapter explores the significance of how and why formal programmes of refugee repatriation are conceived by governments and agencies with little reference to – or understanding of – the pattern of refugees' own flight and return movements. It focusses upon the experience over the last decade of the people of Milange, an important district of northern Mozambique on the Malawi border, and addresses a whole series of paradoxes apparently typical of such situations. These include the dramatic failure of official repatriation programmes to be implemented whilst tens of thousands of refugees manage to self-repatriate; the fact that the largest flight movements are usually associated or soon followed by the greatest repatriation flows despite the continuation of the war; and that, whilst assistance programmes usually do little to help the people directly, they nevertheless can have dramatic and unexpected negative and/or positive effects upon their strategies. The chapter also demonstrates how the nature of the war and of asylum at the micro-social level have caused social groups to pursue contrasting strategies of flight and return.

The argument of the chapter is developed as follows. First there is a brief introduction to the war in Mozambique and the general issues of repatriation during conflict, and a presentation of the methods by which refugee and agency strategies were investigated. Subsequent to a short introduction to Milange and the course of the war in the district the chapter then presents four perspectives on the situation. The first presents a chronology of flight and return movements demonstrating how the strategies of different social groupings interacted with the unfolding of the war and the asylum situation. The second re-examines social dimensions to these migration strategies. Next an account is presented of the rehabilitation of Milange town following its recapture from the Renamo rebels in 1988 and the significance of this for repatriation is evaluated. Finally, the chapter turns to the repatriation planning and programmes of the major agencies demonstrating the limited and often counter-intuitive relationship between these and refugees' own strategies of return and rebuilding of livelihoods.

By focussing on the complexity of the example of a single district, our aim is to draw attention to the significance of a likely diversity of local social determinants of repatriation

---

[1] The authors wish to acknowledge the considerable support given by UNRISD and the editors of this volume during the lengthy and difficult production of this chapter. See p. 236 for a glossary of acronyms.

in each area of the country, rather than to argue that the particular patterns in Milange are either typical or especially important in themselves. In fact the conclusion that such local variations are important is only underlined by evidence that the experience of the war has been markedly different elsewhere in the country, even in the same province. And it should be noted that Mozambique has 128 districts in its 10 diverse provinces.

The Mozambican Context

Mozambique has one of the best resource bases in Africa, yet it is now one of the poorest countries of the world, with a shattered infrastructure. This tragedy reflects a combination of particularly distorted economic exploitation under the Portuguese, over-ambitious state-centred post-independence programmes by the Frelimo Government, and especially an enormous programme of destabilization led by the Rhodesians and then the South Africans (Hanlon, 1984). The rebel force 'Renamo', initially constructed as a mercenary force by the Rhodesians to undermine its socialist neighbour, eventually managed – after substantial military and other aid – to control enormous areas of the country and to virtually self-sustain its operations through a parasitic tribute and looting economy (Hall, 1990; Vines, 1991). Meanwhile Renamo's destruction of the economy had forced the government into one of the highest debt service ratios in the world, and into dependence upon international aid which in recent years has comprised more than three-quarters of the GDP.[2] In a complex and ambiguous manner this international aid has served both to disintegrate further the state and its institutional frameworks and also to enable its continued survival. The dependence on aid also served both to force through a radical structural adjustment package from 1987, and to make its implementation more 'effective'. These wide political-economic changes have shifted the engine of economic initiative to the private sector in general and international capital in particular, and have undermined the central role of the state in securing access to services and resources. The interaction of these far-reaching political and economic reforms by Frelimo, in a situation of global political changes, means that since the late 1980s Renamo has received declining support from South African and far-Right sources. This and a general collapse of the rural economy of the country under war and drought have provided the context for negotiation of a political settlement of the war in Rome, with church and other international mediation.

By 1991 the war in Mozambique had generated almost two million refugees in the neighbouring countries, about half of whom are in Malawi. There were a further 1.9 million officially 'internally displaced' within the country living in camps around the Frelimo garrisons.[3] The government also designated between one and two million people as 'affected' by the war and therefore in need of some emergency assistance, although not resident in garrisoned camps. In addition there were in 1991 probably more than a million rural people dwelling in new shanty-camps around cities where they are uncounted. (On the basis of rural–urban equity it has been decided they should receive no special assistance, though the emergency programme maintains food availability in commercial markets for urban populations.) Research also indicates that there are large 'displaced' populations in areas outside of the control of the government, and that in many but not all Renamo-controlled zones people are living a highly precarious existence. Most of the fifteen million

---

[2] According to World Bank figures, per capita income fell during the 1980s from US$200 (already one of the lowest in the world) to just US$100 (despite this aid), while national debt trebled to become more than four times the GNP. Meanwhile at the official exchange rate the metical was worth in early 1991 only one-twentieth of its 1986 value (*Financial Times*, 1991).

[3] The number of those 'internally displaced' in this manner is possibly closer to three million, since the 1.9 million figure was negotiated as part of the aid programme as an achievable target.

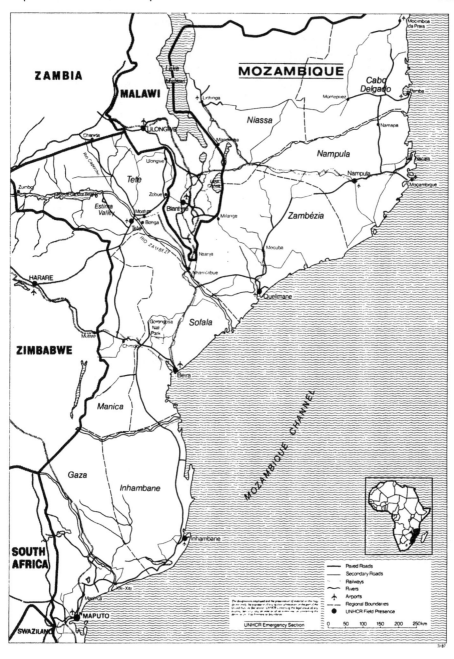

Map 9.1 *Mozambique*

rural Mozambicans are no longer living in their home areas, and indeed many have been displaced several times during the course of the war.

Mozambican governmental capacity for assistance to the internally displaced and affected populations, and for generally handling the emergency grew considerably from the mid-1980s, under the overall co-ordination of the Comissão Executive Nacional de Emergência (CENE) (CENE/DPCCN, 1988). The Departamento de Prevenção e Combate as Calamidades Naturais (government relief agency) (DPCCN), created in 1980 and initially responsible for handling natural disasters, grew substantially. The day-to-day management of DPCCN and other groups' activities have been overseen since mid-1987 by CENE which is chaired by the Minister of Co-operation and supported full-time by the Vice-Minister. The Mozambican Government always emphasized a developmental response to the emergency (CENE/DPCCN, 1988), and, together with the World Food Programme and various bilaterals, it was the United Nations Development Programme (UNDP) that became the most significant institutional partner to CENE. Meanwhile, national development programmes had essentially been replaced by the local version of the Structural Adjustment Programme, Programa de Reabilitação Economica (PRE) (later PRES when the term 'social' was added to 'economic'), and national economic policy was therefore pursued in co-ordination with the World Bank and the International Monetary Fund. Many observers have noted that the IMF and World Bank have made little change to their standard programmes to take account of the war and emergency situation.

Nucleo de Apoio aos Refugiados e Movimentos de Libertação (government agency responsible for refugees and returnees) (NARML), originally responsible for liberation movements in Mozambique and other refugees with asylum in Mozambique, continued its UNHCR link by taking on responsibility for the Mozambican refugees outside of the country and their repatriation. NARML has maintained its links with the Ministry of the Interior, but also has some co-ordination role within CENE and steady progress was being made to rationalize DPCCN and NARML programmes for what were often mixed populations (internally displaced persons and returnees) in the same locations.

'Provincial Commissions for the Emergency' (CPEs) were established in the mid- to late 1980s – though with some unevenness – in the ten provinces and these co-ordinated not only the emergency bodies themselves, but also their interactions with the line ministries such as agriculture, health, education, construction and water. In the most war-affected provinces the CPEs quickly came to handle the most significant activities in the rural districts, and also controlled the bulk of resources available (derived largely from aid). Throughout this period of institutional change during the worst years of the emergency, the rapidly changing and often contradictory demands of the various donors and myriad of NGOs often appeared as much of a challenge as it did a support (Hanlon, 1991), not least because different agencies and donors made alliances with different government institutions. Nevertheless, aid became the backbone of the economy, and the 'emergency' the principal focus of government. One of the further challenges generated by the broadly successful construction of the emergency institutional structures will be how authority, experience and resources can be returned to the line ministries and local government, co-ordinated by the re-emergent planning department in the context of peace.

Official repatriation programmes in Mozambique have arisen from a variety of contexts. The forced return (*refoulement*) of those Mozambicans who manage to enter South Africa (despite the electric fence), but are not settled in those 'Homelands' that accept them, is a major challenge for the Mozambican Government. The returnees are handed over at the border. Their home areas are usually distant and often unsafe, and considerable assistance is therefore required in holding-centres and settlements. Returns of Mozambicans from interrupted labour contracts in East Germany and from schooling in Cuba, as well as forced

9.1 *Destitute old man from western Zambezia in a Malawi refugee camp, June 1989 (K. Wilson)*

9.2 *Food relief flight in western Zambezia, November 1991 (K. Wilson)*

repatriations from another neighbouring country have also provided institutional challenges in recent years.

Following the launch of an appeal for a 'Special Programme of Limited Assistance to Mozambican Returnees' in March 1987 at the request of the United Nations-Secretary General (UNHCR-Geneva, 1990), a Tripartite Agreement was signed between the Malawian and Mozambican Governments and the UNHCR in December 1988, and a series of meetings were held. As will be discussed in more detail below, official repatriation planning has been dominated by the Malawi returnee issue since this date. Yet official figures suggest that only about 5–10 per cent of returnees from Malawi in recent years have utilized the official procedures (*Noticias*, 1990). During 1991 the authorities recognized that refugees self-repatriated because the procedures did not address returnees' specific needs and because official programmes lacked adequate donor funding; however, they proved unable to address these shortcomings.

Repatriation during Conflict: New Research Propositions & New Dilemmas
This examination of repatriation in Mozambique can be usefully contextualized within the findings of the study of 'spontaneous voluntary repatriation' during conflict co-ordinated by Cuny and Stein that is reported on elsewhere in this volume (see Chapter 3). Just as has occurred in Mozambique in recent years, Stein and Cuny found that over 90 per cent of refugees repatriating since 1975 had done so without a formal end to the conflict that created them, and essentially without official repatriation planning and support. Thus refugees' own strategies were clearly central to the process, and they were not simply 'beneficiaries' of UNHCR, governmental or other agency initiatives. Stein and Cuny also found that their initial conception of the nature of the problem was wrong in other ways that can be applied to Mozambique. First, these return movements were not 'spontaneous' but in fact highly organized and planned but by the refugees themselves on an individual or collective basis. Second, the movements were not 'voluntary' in any simple sense of the word, because they generally represented struggles by refugees to improve their situation by taking on the problems 'at home' because the situation in exile was one of 'no hope' in the long term. Third, most of the movements were not necessarily 'repatriation' because they did not always imply some kind of re-establishment of the bond between state and refugee. In some cases the refugees had never felt that the bond with their country and government had been broken; their return was seen as maintaining and not re-creating it. In other situations the state was often a marginal element in what people conceived of as their community (it never was a 'patria'), and neither refuge nor return had thus changed the situation. Indeed, as in the rest of the world, many if not most of the returnees to Mozambique actually went back into areas not controlled by the government.

There are also parallels in this study between the patterns of factors that influence refugees' decisions about return movements in the examples studied by Cuny and Stein and those observed in this Mozambique case study. Refugees' concerns for security, control over their lives, the desire to construct a possible and meaningful future, and the flow of information and ideas are all indeed key. Moments precipitating return also occur within the same framework as Cuny and Stein propose. Each flight event in Milange was followed by 'ricochet' return movements of populations unnecessarily displaced by short-term processes or crises. This study also found 'relocation-stimulated' repatriations of people who did not want to be moved into camps further from the border. Return movements were also generated by what Cuny and Stein call 'community and alienation' processes, whereby people who no longer identify with – or are no longer identified as belonging by – the camp community returned to Mozambique. Finally, we also found in this case study what they call 'major return' movements, where large groups of people repatriate so as to maintain their social networks with other returnees. This Mozambican case study further emphasizes, however, the impact of the heterogeneous nature of the refugee population on the patterns of return movement: different sectors of the population move at the same or different times for different reasons. It also provides further detail on the complexity of how socio-political spaces in the conflict open through space and time for particular categories of returnees to reinsert themselves despite the war continuing at a macro-level. Another important goal for this chapter is exploring whether the manner in which the state and agencies intervene actually influences the nature and size of these 'windows' for refugee repatriation.

Dilemmas concerning the role of outsiders in situations of repatriation under conflict need to be aired, which are raised by the Milange study – as well as the other case studies in this book and those in the programme of Cuny and Stein. If so many refugees are busy organizing their own return even when the conflict continues, does this not mean that we should accept the current agenda of the donors and UNHCR that refugees should be encouraged to go home since this is the best 'solution'; after all the UNHCR is referring to 1992 as the 'year of voluntary repatriation'? Do refugees really require asylum if they can so successfully self-return; would not more be achieved in the long term if efforts were shifted to improving the context for return than just helping people in exile; is this not obviously part of the new Western agenda of African 'democratization' and attention to human rights 'standards' through aid conditionality? In a country like Mozambique where refugees are officially stated not to be fleeing the government, is it not logical for donors as well as governments to transfer resources and population from the relief context in the neighbouring countries to rehabilitation and development at home? Is assistance to return movements not an ideal candidate for current proposals within the UN system for a new co-ordination of relief in emergencies?

Critique of such questions concerning the apparently matched refugee and donor agendas can be derived through two processes. The first is the decision as to whether we seek to address the 'refugee problem' (the political and institutional challenge that the continued presence of refugee populations poses for governments and international agencies), or refugees' 'problems' (the difficulties and struggles of refugees to construct a better and more meaningful present and future life). If our commitment is to working for or with the refugees – and hence we see repatriation not as by definition always the desired outcome and ultimate objective – then we have a clarified framework within which to assess the desirability and appropriateness of different kinds of interventions in asylum and repatriaion. Second, a detailed consideration of the refugee self-return process suggests that it occurs successfully largely because refugees themselves are able to discover and quietly negotiate their own reinsertion into the home country as and when opportunities arise: thus by definition large external programmes will prove little capable of identifying and exploiting such opportunities. In fact, not only are the policy instruments available to such programmes usually too blunt to open spaces for returnee reintegration, it is just as likely that the launching of such a high-profile programme would damage existing return opportunities. This chapter indicates, however, that in practice elements of international returnee assistance in Mozambique have actually played quite a useful role, even if it has been in ways not initially conceived by the policy makers. This suggests amongst other things the ambiguities of interventions in complex, unstable and little understood situations. Third, consideration of the dilemmas of refugees and returnees – as well as those of the people who stayed in the war zone – suggests that what is significant to them is control of their own lives and not some kind of 'durable solution' (defined as place of residence) conceived and implemented by international forces.

A number of analysts have expressed themselves highly disturbed by the very discussion of refugee self-repatriation initiatives of the kind described in this chapter, since they believe that they will be a pretext for officials to deny persecution or danger in the countries of origin. Evidence that thousands of refugees have self-returned into war zones is considered threatening not only to the honouring of pleas for asylum and protection by other refugees who have not returned, but also threatening to the claims of researchers and advocates of the profound nature of their 'persecution' and exposure to violence in the country of origin. One problem with these criticisms is that they reveal how the international humanitarian norms – as articulated by both intellectuals and bureaucracies – require of refugees certain kinds of behaviour in their 'contract'. Except for running away from the country of origin, refugees are to be passive victims in the face of cruel authorities or militaries. They must accept that certain international legal and institutional instruments should deliver them protection and construct their future whilst they remain in exile consciously not involving themselves in affairs at home. Yet the very point of the new wave of detailed empirical research on repatriation – just as was the principal discovery of previous work on assistance – is that refugees do not accept the legitimacy and authority of the frameworks provided for them, except insofar as it is considered useful in their own scheme of things. Refugees like other people struggle to preserve some autonomy. Anyway, the humanitarian regime simply does not deliver sufficient 'protection' or 'durable solution' for refugees to rely on it.

It is therefore inevitable that refugees actively set about carving out their own protection strategies and their own futures, which often involve decisions to self-repatriate at one stage or another. People may decide that returning to face and seek to transform persecutory or violent authorities is the best way to create a meaningful future, and they have a right to do this just as much as they have a right to run away and be provided with asylum. They may return because they decide that their rights to land and community membership can only be secured at an acceptable cost to their safety. An international humanitarian system guided towards helping refugees on their own terms would thus have to handle the ambiguities between securing and granting refugees power/rights on the one hand, and recognizing on the other that they already have power/rights that they will use in pursuit of their own agendas, and which will ultimately subvert the very international humanitarian programmes which allegedly seek to provide them that space.

Methods & Sources

The methods and sources for this chapter are tailored to the objective of documenting the forces shaping refugee movements and their attitudes towards exile and return, in relation to the policy and planning procedures of the responsible governments, United Nations agencies and non-governmental organizations. It has been essential to obtain access to official and refugee/returnee thinking and knowledge of activities through the rapidly changing situation over the last ten years, requiring of the researchers both intense fieldwork and the use of documentary sources.

The refugee and returnee perspective has been obtained mostly from fieldwork undertaken with several other researchers, notably Florence Shumba. Ken Wilson's early field studies with refugees from Milange in Malawi and Zambia focussed mostly upon their livelihood situation in exile and only limited information was obtained about their reasons for flight and attitudes towards returning home (see Wilson et al., 1989; Black et al., 1990; these studies were funded by World Food Programme and the Economic and Social Research Council). The conceptions of the future of one section of the refugees from Milange (the Jehovah's Witnesses in Zambia) have since been investigated (Wilson, 1991a, funded by Oxfam-UK and World Vision of Britain), and KBW has undertaken two field studies in Milange (March–April 1991 and October–November 1991) with funds from the Nuffield Foundation, Christian Aid, Save the Children Fund (UK) and UNDP-Mozambique.

The Milange field studies examined, amongst other things, the causes and significances of both flight and the return movements, and the relief and rehabilitation situation. To access people's own perceptions numerous 'life story' interviews were undertaken, with a careful and slow progression (in a relaxed atmosphere) through the sequence of life events and migrations that the informant had experienced, allowing them to indicate the dominant forces and motivations for their different actions and attitudes. Mother-tongue translation, mostly through the local research assistant, Alexandre Jaze, was used throughout. The views of local officials in government and agencies about the nature and causes of past and present movements were also useful in understanding what the people were saying and experiencing, as were written field reports by these officials. Direct observation of the situation in the field also proved extremely useful. The combination of documentary sources with interview material enhances the credibility of both sources, and provides some controls for bias. (Margaret Hall and Alex Vines deserve special credit for provision of useful news reports.)

Understandings of the programmes of government and agencies were obtained through a combination of interviews with managerial and field staff, the use of internal and public agency and government documentation, and, direct observation of officials at work. Information on institutional perceptions and programmes is somewhat uneven between agencies and through time because of the high mobility of officials, the paucity of documentation, as well as the fact that many discussions and documents are confidential, and in fact the attentions of researchers receive variable welcome. This chapter – like several others in this volume – nevertheless indicates the value of relief agency archives as a source for social investigation in Africa, particularly of a historical orientation, though of course with the same caveats as are applied to other sources like the records of mission and colonial officers. Greater use should be made of these sources for students of recent changes in Africa, and efforts initiated for their preservation in local research institutions.

The particular contribution of Jovito Nunes to this chapter combined insight on contextual issues in the Mozambique experience, and the possibility for extrapolation of field research on the social consequences of displacement in Mocuba of central Zambezia. The Swedish International Development Authority (SIDA/ASDI) and Oxfam funded Nunes's research.

Wilson, together with other researchers, has also undertaken field studies on repatriation to northern Tete (in Zambia in September 1991 and in Angonia and Maravia in Tete Province in December 1991), funded by Oxfam and World Vision, but the material from these studies that focuses on refugee and returnee attitudes and not institutional questions will be little drawn upon in this chapter (see Wilson, 1991a and 1991b).

The writing of this chapter has been constrained by our desire to positively influence the policies of governments and agencies towards refugees and repatriation. This means that a fuller and more objective analysis, particularly of the nature of institutional planning and assistance, will have to await the end of the current refugee situation in the area.

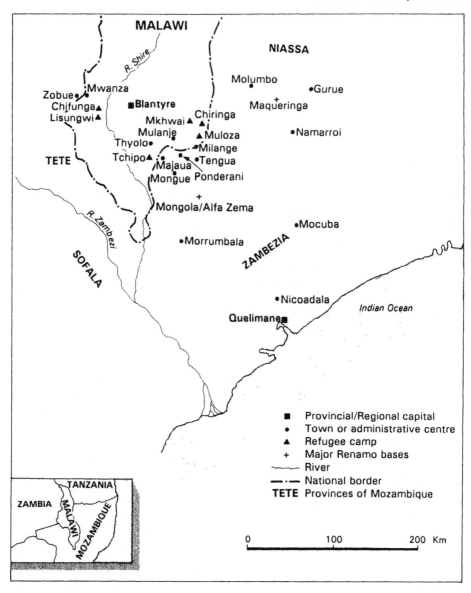

Map 9.2 *Location of towns and refugee camps in Zambezia and Malawi*

The Milange Case Study

Background to Milange

Milange is an important district of about 10,000 km^2 in western Zambezia in north-central Mozambique bordering with the Mulanje district of southern Malawi. The bulk of the district is of medium altitude with fertile soils and good rainfall. By Mozambican standards Milange has long been highly populated and economically developed. The district has about 300,000 indigenes giving it a density of 30 persons/km^2,[4] indicative of close settlement, but no overall marked land shortage. The population speak a variety of Elomwe and Echuabo affiliated dialects, the most important being Marendje (Wilson, A.D., 1961; NELIMO, 1989). Little has been written on these matrilineal peoples, except a pamphlet on their history from a Malawian standpoint by Boeder (1984). Under the Portuguese, Milange became a centre of tea estates, commercial farming by immigrant 'colonos', and also peasant production (Vail and White, 1980). Milange had some roads, an important Catholic Mission at Tengua, and in more recent years some health and education services.

Due to more favourable economic conditions than in the interior districts many people from Namarroi, Ile and other areas came to settle temporarily or permanently in the district, which also provided a launching pad for flight to Malawi when and if Portuguese taxation or labour demands increased. Milange was thus comparatively calm, and a net population-receiving area during the colonial period, whilst forced labour and harsh administration meant that in the province as a whole there was extensive migration including into southern Malawi, continuing the demographic instability that pre-dated formal Portuguese authority in the region (Boeder, 1984; Chivilumbo, 1974; Vail and White, 1980; Vaughan, 1981; White, 1987). Likewise as Malawi became progressively more crowded (principally through Mozambican immigration), Milange has experienced reverse migrations from Malawi into the border areas in search of extensive quality land, whenever conditions have been conducive.

Migration within Zambezia and across the border has, therefore, become a central feature of Lomwe society over the past 150 years, and Boeder (1984: 17) has written of earlier refugee flows to Malawi that 'often a month or two was spent preparing for the journey', with such preparation including a special medicine, *chidima*, that protected the migrants from danger on the way, adding that Lomwe often headed for Mulanje in Malawi, because the mountain there conjured the image of Namuli, the mountain which Lomwe envisage as their cultural centre and point of origin as a people (see also Wilson, A.D., 1961). Historically the capacity of the peasants to migrate across the border has meant some constraint in Milange on the imposition of harsh economic and political policies; Renamo behaviour has been similarly constrained. Migration across the Malawi border has also intertwined historically with economic interdependence between the two countries, and for many years even goods destined for the rest of Mozambique have often had to pass through Malawi (ION, 1989: 229; interviews with Ministry of Commerce). During the 1980s the Milange economy has become virtually dependent on its Malawian linkages.

---

[4] Official population statistics in the district and provincial headquarters actually vary from something over 100,000 to as many as 350,000.

The War in Milange

This section briefly outlines the history of the war in Milange, and with the aid of a chronology (Figure 9.1) provides for a periodization that can help to characterize the different flight and return movements.

The war of independence (1964–74) had relatively little impact on Milange district, except in terms of its mobilization of the elites. It became a 'liberated zone' in 1974 during Frelimo's second offensive in the Zambezia province, essentially through a truce with local Portuguese forces, the mid-1960s offensive having earlier collapsed with the arrest of many Frelimo activists. The area has, however, been a centre for anti-Frelimo guerrilla movements since Mozambique's independence in 1975, and it is clear that these represent a variety of different forces including the remnants of groups fighting for a separatist northern Mozambique since before independence (Fauvet, 1984; Vines, 1991), as well as peasant groupings opposing state rural development programmes, externally sponsored destabilization forces, and the continuation of a long tradition of banditry in the region. Some of the groups described by local residents and officials at different times in the 1975–82 period were those of Sagwati, Wocha Weka, Maramara, Nharene, Involiwa, Partido Revolucionario de Moçambique (PRM); and several of these movements also carried the label 'Africa Livre'.

In August 1982 Renamo expanded its operations north of the Zambezi and absorbed surviving members of the original bandit groups (Hall, 1990). This marked the beginning of the period when Frelimo's external enemies sponsored Renamo to undertake major infrastructural damage in this key district of one of the country's richest provinces. Renamo, however, actually limited its initial attacks and concentrated on building its logistical and administrative system in the rural areas. Early expansion was somewhat uneven, but most areas were occupied during the 1982–84 period. Rural Milange thus became administered by the reappointed 'traditional' chiefs (whom Frelimo had formally deposed at independence), using 'madjuba' militias, and operating under fairly close Renamo control. Renamo's changing national strategies and shifts in external support meant large expansions in Renamo activity in 1984, from which time Frelimo control was restricted to the administrative centres, which by August 1985 in Milange district comprised only Majaua, Mongoe, Molumbo and Ponderani, in addition to Zalimba and Tengua near to Milange town. In early 1986 Renamo sent in further forces, taking first the border

Figure 9.1 *Brief chronology of the war in Milange district*

1975	Mozambique independence.
1975–82	Numerous small guerrilla and bandit groups operate in Milange. Renamo is created and heavily supported by Rhodesia and then South Africa, but is yet to operate in northern Mozambique.
August 1982	Renamo arrives in Zambezia, incorporating and suppressing local guerrilla movements.
1982–84	Renamo builds its administrative machinery at local level, starting in more peripheral areas.
1984–86	Renamo control expands steadily with the taking of administrative posts; Renamo establishes its tribute economy.
September 1986	Fall of Milange town as part of collapse of Frelimo power in Zambezia.
1986–88	Renamo becomes sole authoriy in Milange district, military situation stabilizes, Renamo administration reaches its greatest potential.
June 1988	Frelimo retake Milange town in joint ground and aerial assault.
1988–89	Frelimo defends its limited positions in Milange; Renamo is secure in its own areas. Renamo tribute system intensifies and is increasingly resented.
1990–91	Frelimo expands the area under its control taking new centres, with the support of the Naparama peasant militia; groundswell peasant sympathy reverts to Frelimo.

town of Majaua in January, and then, after an initial failed assault on Milange town, steadily isolating and enclosing it until it ultimately fell to the rebels on 29 September 1986. These years of Renamo expansion saw the systematic looting of almost the entire infrastructure and capital goods of the district, largely for sale in neighbouring Malawi, generating funds for the logistical support of Renamo's war effort and perhaps earning revenue for its external backers. There is evidence that certain exiled business-men specifically ensured the destruction of their former enterprises. The extensive commercial–industrial complex of Majaua, for example, was blown up by a foreign explosives expert after occupation by Renamo.

The almost complete control of Zambezia province achieved by Renamo at the end of 1986 proved militarily unsustainable, and during 1987 and 1988 a newly invigorated government force drove Renamo out of all the district capitals. The reasons for these changing fortunes in the war are complex. They include failures by Renamo to establish a coherent and legitimate administration, leading to the mutiny of Renamo soldiers, the pursual of private agendas by many chiefs and Renamo officials, and popular opposition from a disgruntled peasantry who resented the levels of tribute and the absence of com-merce and hence consumer goods. Frelimo military success also resulted from better training and logistical support of the army, and the arrival of effective contingents of Zimbabwean and Tanzanian forces, and effective use of air power. Milange was the last major centre in Zambezia to fall to the government, being retaken in June 1988 by a joint aerial and ground assault by the commandos. The rise – or probably more accurately the re-emergence – of a second guerrilla organization, União Nacional Moçambicana (military faction now a registered political party) (UNAMO), and its fighting against Renamo in Milange and other parts of Zambezia, is also a complex and little understood element to the changing fortunes of the war at this time.

During the years of Renamo occupation, Milange (and the neighbouring district of Morrumbala) became an important logistical centre and backstop for Renamo in its key Zambezia zone, as well as a nationally important access point to the outside world. Alongside a rudimentary administrative system with schools and clinics, Renamo con-structed a highly organized system of tribute and forced labour for the extraction of food and for porterage. Elaborate but not continuous violence was used by Renamo to maintain its control of the population (Wilson, 1992a), together with occasional bursts of weakly structured political mobilization. Since the recapture of Milange town in 1988, there has been a gradual expansion of the area under government control (it held in mid-1991 four of the more important centres – Majaua, Molumbo, Ponderani and Tengua). Nevertheless, Renamo maintained control of large parts of the rural areas of the district, moving its national headquarters temporarily to the provincial base in the Metolola mountains in the south of the district in late 1990. Milange and the Zambezi valley districts were the only important areas of northern Mozambique where Renamo was not to lose substantial ground against government forces during 1990–91, largely because Frelimo's then allies – the Naparama peasant movement led by the 'warrior-priest' Manuel Antonio – never played a major role in the area, although a unit was formed in Milange in mid-1991 (Wilson, 1992a). In recent years living conditions in Renamo-held areas are reported to have declined dramatically due to increasingly heavy Renamo extraction of resources from a declining resource base, and Frelimo's growing ability to raid the Renamo-controlled zones. Attempts by Renamo to reinvigorate morale in late 1991 by attacking Frelimo posi-tions were successful only in Majaua.

9.3 *Overconcentrated settlement of Muloza refugee camp, Mulanje district, Malawi, May 1989*
(K. Wilson)

The Movements of People: Refugees, Internally Displaced & Returnees

Introduction

The brief overview of the war allows us to proceed to identifying the various 'vintages' of refugees and internally displaced populations generated by the conflict in Milange. The concept of 'vintages' has been adapted from the theoretical work of Frank Kunz (1973, 1981), who examined the way in which institutional forces shaped flight and reception in interaction with refugees' motivational factors. Studies of refugee populations have found that Kunz's theories give inadequate attention to the capacity of refugees' own strategies and complex ideologies to subvert the effects of these wider forces, but nevertheless the concept remains useful for appreciating the differentiation of refugee populations, as will be demonstrated below. This Milange study also elaborates a further critique of Kunz's theory as applied to the kinds of contexts existing in Mozambique: since individuals and social groups maintain their social networks across the boundaries of the vintages, and even into the refugee-producing zones, this undermines the social processes generating discreteness of each group. The result is further flexibility and social (and hence physical) mobility. The opportunities to return home existing for different vintages of refugees at different times can be conceptualized in terms of windows of socio-political opportunity that open and close – with varying magnitude for different people – as the nature of the war changes through time and space. Where refugees detect these opportunities, they can choose whether or not to return. These opportunities often – but not necessarily – comprise of relative freedom from conflict or persecution. More importantly people identify them as 'windows' on the grounds that they are situations providing opportunity to work towards a more desirable future. As will be demonstrated, not all such returns prove to be sustainable.

So as to provide a framework for the discussion, a brief chronology of the main movements is provided in Figure 9.2, and a graph of the estimated size of the various population fractions is provided in Figure 9.3.

Redistribution within Milange as Renamo Power Expands

The effects of the early bandit and guerrilla groups in the 1975–82 period on population distribution were fairly limited. These effects included the intensification and then ending of the government's villagization plan in Mongoe *posto*, and slowing down of the programme elsewhere. Furthermore, some government officials, Frelimo affiliates and businessfolk were obliged to relocate themselves into the larger centres for safety, although many reported having slept in the forest at night during these years to avoid being caught in sporadic attacks. With the arrival of the major rebel group, Renamo, in the area, however, the situation changed dramatically. Teachers, health workers, government officials, party secretaries, co-operative officials, businessfolk, and indeed all categories of the population associated with the state became targets. Whilst the numbers of such people being killed and/or mutilated were considerably lower than in some other areas of the country, they were obliged to congregate in the larger administrative centres from the early 1980s in the worst-affected areas. As these centres fell to Renamo, the Frelimo affiliates gradually moved into the more important places of government authority, though they could be sent back again if government forces temporarily recaptured an area. A few of these elite officials defected to Renamo during this period, and obtained positions in its hierarchy, but the overall effect of the war was to concentrate such people by late 1986 in the encircled Milange town.

Interviews with both peasants and officials in 1991 indicated that many peasants also sought the protection of the government in the towns during the mid-1980s. Whilst there was no international aid or specific government budget for assistance at this time, state companies (e.g. in Majaua) and the party (e.g. in Milange town) did provide some minimal relief. Yet as Renamo power increased most of the peasants decided to return to the Renamo-controlled zones. The main reasons for this included: the collapse of the economy in the Frelimo-held towns due to isolation and other factors, inadequate relief supplies, and the belief that Frelimo authority was doomed and so staying risked a dangerous labelling as a 'Frelimo supporter'. In order to manage this relocation to rural areas, the returnees had to convince Renamo and/or its agents that they had been, for example, temporarily residing elsewhere or in Malawi, and were not coming in from Frelimo-held areas, as they would otherwise be at risk of being considered a spy. Losing their grip on the situation, government forces further alienated many peasant in the war zone by treating all as *de facto* Renamo supporters and abusing them.

This 1982–86 period also saw the relocation of the population within the rural areas between areas controlled by the different militaries, just as had happened in the *posto* Derre area of Morrumbala in the same period, though in Derre the strong support of certain chiefs for Frelimo complicated matters substantially (Wilson, 1992a). Informants referred specifically to the process of 'rambela', as the local relocation in relation to security. The

Figure 9.2 *Brief chronology of population movements in Milange district*

1975–76	Tens of thousands of Jehovah's Witnesses relocated into a re-education camp north of Milange town (Carico).
Late 1970s	Government seeks unsuccessfully to villagize, especially south of Milange town (Mongoe).
1975–82	Minor dislocations of populations, especially of officials and businessmen, due to small guerrilla and bandit groups.
1982–86	Relocation of peasantry within rural areas depending on local security situation; Renamo steadily gaining control of population.
	Frelimo officials and affiliates restricted to increasingly important administrative centres as Renamo power expands.
	Small number of people take refuge on individual basis in Malawi.
1985–86	About half the Jehovah's Witness population of Carico organizes escape from Renamo to Tete and Zambia across Malawi, to other areas of Zambezia, and to the Chiringa refugee camp in Malawi.
September 1986	Government-affiliated population of Milange town flees to Malawi and accommodated in Muloza. Many government soldiers and officials repatriated via Tete (Mozambique).
1986–88	Self-repatriation to Renamo-held areas from Malawi. Low rates of outmigration from Renamo-controlled zones in Mozambique.
	Part of Muloza and Chiringa population (especially officials and Jehovah's Witnesses) assisted to return to Tete and accommodated in Benga or transferred to Maputo and elsewhere.
June 1988	Frelimo aerial assault leads to massive panic movement to Malawi, most of whom self-settle there and return home within a week or two to Renamo-controlled areas. Many Renamo affiliates and people from vicinity of Milange remain in Malawi, the majority being transferred to new refugee camp at Mkhwai in Malawi.
1988–89	Rehabilitation of Milange by government, international agencies and local businessmen begins.
	Frelimo begins low-level recuperation of peasant population around Milange town.
	Steady repatriation from Malawi camps and self-settled communities in Malawi to the Frelimo garrison in Milange.
	Repatriation from Malawi to Renamo-controlled areas now less than number fleeing Renamo's administration.
	Official repatriations of bulk of remaining Milange populations from Tete to Milange and Quelimane.
	New arrivals in Malawi sent to camps in far-distant Mwanza: increase in self-settlement in Malawi as a result.
April 1989	First meeting of the Tripartite Commission for the Repatriation of Mozambican Refugees in Malawi (agreed in December 1988); national repatriation planning launched.
1990–91	Substantial self-repatriation from Malawi to Frelimo-held area of Milange.
	Frelimo and (from mid-1991) Naparama recuperate substantial peasant populations from an enlarging secure zone, and establish new population centres in Majaua, Tengua and Aleixo.
	Substantial numbers leave increasingly harsh situation in Renamo-controlled areas to become refugees in Malawi.

river Lualua, for example, became the political boundary for some time in the early 1980s. Renamo regularly raided across the river into the Frelimo-controlled zone from the southwest, and over a couple of years large numbers of peasants moved across the river to the quieter areas under Renamo control, where Renamo were also distributing some of the goods looted from government-held areas. Although it is well-known that Frelimo had a weak social base in Zambezia for historical reasons (Vail and White, 1980; White, 1985: 329), and certain chiefs did actively facilitate Renamo's expansion, the main reason for the rapid increase in the population controlled by Renamo at this time was the relative military–economic weakness of the state rather than the political

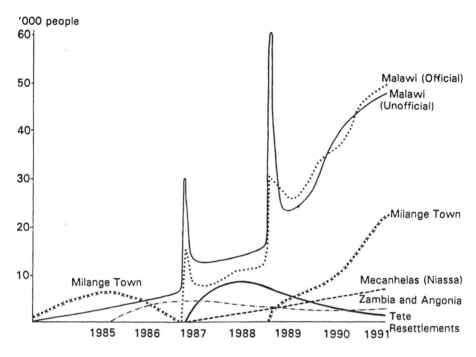

Figure 9.3 *Changes in displaced and refugee populations in Milange district*

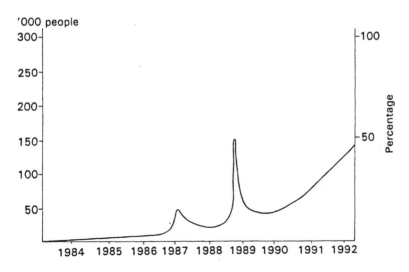

Figure 9.4 *Proportion of population of Milange displaced outside of Renamo areas*
Sources: official figures and local estimates

inclinations of the peasantry. Thus, at this time there were also peasant migrations occurring into those remaining areas that were little controlled by either Frelimo or Renamo.

One final important process of peasant relocation in the early 1980s occurred between areas under the control of Renamo. Renamo uprooted large numbers of people from one area and then resettled them under a chosen chief in another distant zone. Although they were initially captives, they quite quickly became 'ordinary' civilians in the new areas, contributing to production and labour much in the manner of local people, although with greater clientage to their new chief than the original residents. The numbers of people relocated in central Milange were not very large in contrast to other areas, though they include, for example, a group of Makua speakers brought in to Nanhende. Since the main reason for such movements of population was to provide a client population in strategic locations, this suggests that Renamo found the existing distribution of populations adequate in Milange. The main population relocations in the region were around the northern border of Milange in the vicinity of the Maqueringa base in Namarroi, and on the southern border of Milange with Morrumbala, around the Alfa-Zema and Mongola strongholds. Here Renamo relocated thousands of people to build up populations around their mountain bases. The existence of these internal movements, some of which have become somewhat stabilized, further complicates post-peace return movements.

Early Flight from Milange
Considerable numbers of people decided to leave the rural areas of Milange for Malawi in the early 1980s to escape the gathering war. Those included many 'Malawians' – often actually of earlier Mozambican descent – who had come to Mozambique after independence in search of land. These return movements have not been officially discussed by governments or relief agencies for a variety of institutional reasons. Most of the individuals concerned simply activated existing family networks and integrated or reintegrated into Malawian society in the same manner that Mozambican migrants had always done. It is unclear whether the extent to which the general increase in emigration from Mozambique into Mulanje district of Malawi, reported during a visit by one of us to the border area in 1985, was a function of a collapse of the rural economy in this part of Mozambique versus these more directly security-related movements. Indeed, many existing labour migrants probably found themselves made into refugees as the war situation worsened at home, since returnee labour migrants (and their goods) were a special target of Renamo looting and killing. Up until mid-1986 Malawi was not officially recognizing the refugee influx, and was trying to cope with it as it had earlier waves of Mozambican migration, whereby the immigrants were simply treated as Malawians. Where populations crossed the border in large numbers after attacks, as they did, for example, in the case of the 500 refugees with the fall in Majaua in January 1986, those who wished to return to Milange town were simply quietly assisted by the Malawi police after a few days in a makeshift camp at Chinyama. Though the rights of these early migrants were generally well respected by Malawian officials and the general populace, there were a few cases reported where people classified as illegal immigrants were allegedly taken to the Frelimo-controlled border post, or forcibly recruited into Renamo.

Milange district also contained a re-education camp of 22,000 Jehovah's Witnesses most of whom were originally from Malawi and southern Mozambique. Renamo counted upon gaining the support of such religions groups who had been persecuted by Frelimo in the early years of independence. Between 1984 and late 1986 it set about seeking to persuade – and later to force – the Witnesses to support the war effort. Despite Renamo offering to make concessions and negotiate, having failed to intimidate the Witnesses through brutal murders, beatings and rapes, the Witnesses refused to concede their pacifist and non-political stance, but migrated within the area, and into other parts of Mozambique, Malawi and Zambia, as will be described in Chapter 10.

At this early stage in the war most people in rural Milange concentrated on seeking to accommodate themselves to the new social order of chiefly authority and Renamo tribute. Though migration has always been a peasant tool of resistance to over-exacting administration in Zambezia, it is a method of last resort with high costs to the migrants. People therefore believed it was better to stay put if at all possible. Reluctance to flee for Malawi grew with the increasing economic decline and land hunger there during the 1980s. Furthermore, the fact that Milange was a border district enabled people to cope better with Renamo's destruction of the commercial infrastructure, since they could continue to sell their surpluses and acquire consumer goods in the border markets. Peasant concern to achieve affiliations appropriate to their long-term survival rather than short-term welfare will emerge as a recurrent theme in the Milange case study. To have run away prematurely from Renamo in the early 1980s might have permanently excluded them from their homes and resource base were Renamo to have gained state power.

Milange town has long been an important centre for Zambezia's multi-ethnic mercantilist elite. None of these traders chose to abandon Milange faced by Renamo's inexorable advance. Furthermore, whilst a number emigrated to Malawi following independence, right across Zambezia few such people defected to Renamo, despite the constraints (admittedly uneven and variable) that Frelimo placed on private accumulation. In fact the business community played a key role in trying to maintain the morale and supplies in the town, though of course many also took advantage of the peculiar business environment created by the war. The main reason for their reluctance to flee was that in the Zambezia context they were socially constructed as *patroes* achieving their standing through intricate networks of power and patronage in defined geographical areas: flight from 'their' places would mean (and did later mean) a catastrophic loss of status. It was very hard to open a new business elsewhere because of the constricting nature of the *patrao* system together with Frelimo's state planning of the economy, and the dire commercial situation at the time. Second, whatever their difficulties in relation to government, they realized early on that Renamo was in practice even more hostile to their interests because it identified them with 'privilege', 'civilization' and 'acculturation'.

Movements After the Fall of Milange Town to Renamo, 1986

With the fall of Milange town to Renamo in September 1986, the three army battalions and the bulk of the population of the town and its surrounding tea estates fled the five kilometres to Malawi. Here the refugees clustered on the swampy football field of a tea company at Muloza, and transformed themselves into the refugee camp locally called 'ground'. The local Gambula Catholic Mission quickly supplied some minimal relief, as did a number of local Malawians, and, according to the refugees involved, the Malawi security came in and staged a generally highly professional operation (in an extremely charged atmosphere) to sort out the soldiers from the refugees through individual interviews. (At this stage the UNHCR had not been invited into Malawi, and the Malawi Government had not signed any of the international legal instruments that grant refugees protection.) Despite this the authorities provided such good protection that, with the help of sympathetic local Malawians, the security police even dealt with some local people who sought to steal the refugees' remaining property. The Frelimo troops were taken by the

Malawi military to Blantyre and imprisoned in poor conditions for several days, whilst the Mozambican Ambassador negotiated their return to Tete, via Zobue (see also Finnegan, 1992: 156). After some confusion and delay in Tete, not least because of the death in a mysterious air crash of Mozambique's President Machel in October, the soldiers were returned by air to Quelimane (with those members of their families still present). A fair number of government soldiers chose instead to desert in Milange; and hide their identity during the screening process.

Renamo managed to capture a large number of Milange residents and imprisoned many of them in the extensive 'Club' recreation complex, in bad conditions with minimal food. Here they were subject to extended political speeches and allocated domestic and looting tasks. Although the Renamo soldiers attempted to be vigilant, they were insufficient to control such a large number of people over such a large area, and small groups continually escaped to Malawi on such pretexts as the collection of firewood. A number of Milange residents came forward to identify former Frelimo agents described as harsh and arrogant, and also 'crooked' businessmen, and these were imprisoned in the Customs building prior to deportation to the provincial base. Amongst the religious organizations the only group that faced problems was the Jehovah's Witnesses, because they totally refused to co-operate. An informant saw a number of them subsequently being marched away as slave porters. Several of the amnestied Renamo soldiers interviewed by Minter (1989) stated that they had been captured and forcibly recruited in this attack on Milange.

Members of Milange's trading elite who had sought refuge in Malawi at this time generally proved capable of rapidly returning to Mozambique. For example, one of Milange's traders of Portuguese descent explained how he had fled to Malawi during the attack of 29 September 1986, but had stayed only twenty days in Malawi before he was flown back to Tete with the assistance of some people of Portuguese origin who were resident in Malawi. In Tete the trader was able to pursuade other 'big people' to fly him over to the capital of Zambezia, Quelimane. After two years of 'hardship' in Quelimane he was able to return again to the now recaptured Milange (by private plane) and start to rehabilitate his business.

Other elite refugees from the fall of Milange returned to other government-controlled areas of Mozambique by road. Whilst some of these first Muloza refugees claimed to have been taken by road to Tete as little as one month after their arrival, it was as much as six months after taking refuge that the more substantial movement occurred of '7 lorry-loads [of] top civil servants, technicians and soldiers' wives [who were taken] to Tete' (Cisternino, 1987: 13). This population of salaried government staff had only been held outside of the country as 'refugees' for this long because of diplomatic and possibly logistical problems for their return (for the slow thawing of Mozambique–Malawi relations see Hedges, 1989). They saw the return not as 'repatriation' but as maintaining their unbroken link with country and government. In fact many petty officials and other refugees chose to arrange their own transport to Tete because the official movement 'was not well organized and had insufficient transport and inappropriate arrangements', as one put it, and was targetted at 'senior party members', another complained. Self-repatriation to Tete also occurred at this time from the Lower Shire camps, according to an example provided by Finnegan (1992: 145–6). However, according to a Malawian official and a local church source, the Malawi Government was later suspicious about the fate of several of the people repatriated by the Mozambican Government to Tete, and so such arrangements were allegedly stopped on these grounds. Indeed, it was precisely to avoid the real or imagined threat of enforced organized repatriation that some refugees during this period were said by others to have self-settled outside of the Muloza camp. Some refugees, such as a radio-operator, told us in 1989 that they lived in the camp in poverty, glad not to be obliged to repatriate because of the continuing war situation. Deserting soldiers were a significant group amongst those not wishing to repatriate, though we interviewed one who had later self-repatriated to Milange when it was back under government control, confirming as his reason for desertion not a hostility to Frelimo but a lack of confidence in Frelimo's capacity to win the war without major losses.

Despite the departure of many *comerciantes*, troops and officials from the Malawi camps, a significant section of this early vintage remained in Malawi, comprising rural Frelimo officials, tea workers and local people from the Milange town area, and some Jehovah's Witnesses. Muloza camp held around 10,000 people during Renamo's occupation of Milange (1986–88). Most of the Witnesses, however, dwelled in a second camp, Chiringa, on the northern border of the district opposite their re-education camp of Carico, the history of which is provided in the next chapter in this volume.

It is significant that the bulk of the people driven from Milange in this first stage of the war were those least integrated into its rural social fabric; indeed, many did not even come from Milange originally. Cisternino (1987: 13) refers to the 'tea plantation workers, brought to Milange more or less compulsorily', and states of

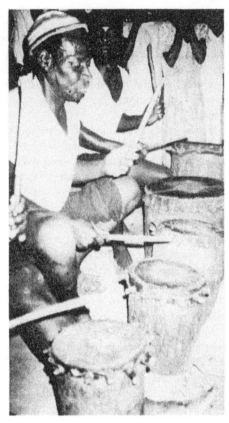

9.4 *Spirit possession ceremony, Muloza camp, Mulanje district, Malawi, May 1989 (K. Wilson)*

Muloza camp that 'in fact those showing ties with the local population are fewer than in any other district [of Malawi]'. (Actually these plantation migrants have generally been 'voluntary' insofar as that concept can be applied to a political-economic context such as that of Mozambique.) The 'alienness' of this refugee vintage meant that they suffered a double disadvantage. In addition to lacking the social networks to protect them in Mozambique and integrate them into the new Renamo order, they also rarely had relatives and other contacts in Malawi who could assist and protect them in exile. This was, indeed, one of the reasons why they were obliged to remain in the refugee camp at Muloza; Cisternino (1987: 12) noted that because of the poor conditions at the camp 'all those who have acquaintances or relations in the villages pass the night there. One sees them when food or something else is distributed'. Of those refugees in this group who were originally from Milange, most had been closely involved with Frelimo from as long back as the early 1960s. They had built their lives on an alliance with a modernizing state, a strategy which had distanced them from local people and the kinds of 'traditional' powers that Renamo sought to strengthen. For them to have shifted allegiance during the course of the war was impossible: they were banished with their Frelimo patron with the fall of Milange. Naturally, this kind of selective migration process has a bearing on repatriation and reintegration, since, among other issues, many of these people prefer to return to their areas of origin and not Milange, and/or see their 'reintegration' as dependent upon the return of a Frelimo state, and not on rebuilding their links with the peasants who remained behind.

It was mainly from amongst the minority of truly local peasants in the refugee population of late 1986, who had been obliged to flee only because of their proximity to the district capital, that a spontaneous repatriation flow started soon after Renamo secured its hold of Milange. The return movement was so large that the refugee population in Muloza fell from around 15,000 at the end of September 1986 to 8,700 in the middle of 1987 (Cisternino, 1987: 12), though some of this reduction was the result of refugees leaving the camp to find employment in other areas of Malawi like Thyolo, or through the repatriation to government-held areas of Mozambique via Tete described above. In fact these official figures greatly underestimate the number of returnees at this time, since those people who had never officially reported as refugees, but had stayed in Malawi in local villages with relatives proved even more likely to return to Mozambique than those from the camp. According to several people interviewed in Milange some years later, most of those who left for Malawi in September 1986 actually returned to try to grow crops back in Mozambique during the October to April rainy season; they said they considered this better than trying to survive on food aid and local wage labour. To achieve this return they actively sought an accommodation with Renamo rule, presenting themselves to the new chiefs. Indeed, in the face of recruitment campaigns in the camps even a number of Mozambican officials, teachers and health workers decided to defect to Renamo in 1986–87, at a stage when Frelimo forces were restricted to Mocuba and Quelimane cities on the other side of the province. There is also evidence that a number of Malawians, who were widely alleged to have assisted with the looting of the town after its fall, also came and opened farms in the Renamo-held areas at this time.

This return movement of population into the Renamo-held areas in 1986–87 was not to last. It was reported that by mid-1987 'harrassment and siesure [sic] of crops by Renamo' were 'now forcing some back [to Muloza] again' (Cisternino, 1987: 12), illustrating the effects of the harsh regime that Renamo had established in the area. It is possible that the returnee group was treated particularly roughly because of their earlier flight, and because they were located close to the town and border where Renamo's needs were perhaps especially great. Indeed, for several months people resident near Milange town were obliged to work as 'labourers' on the looting of the town, though this exempted them from Renamo's agricultural taxes. Some informants denied that returnees at this time faced particular problems: one of the chiefs involved argued to us that Renamo would have no grounds for 'demanding of such local people why they had returned'. Yet there was undoubtably a return into exile of some of the repatriates and by mid-1988 the refugee population had increased again to around 12,000, suggesting that perhaps several thousand had given up trying to reinsert themselves into the new order in the district. However, calculating precise numbers of people involved in such a repatriation and return to exile is made more complex by the existence of other new arrivals who, having remained in Renamo-controlled areas to assess the situation, had decided later to abandon Mozambique. What is clear, though, is both that the initial group of refugees became a vintage 'labelled' as Frelimo supporters in contradistinction to those who remained in Mozambique with Renamo, and yet many refugees managed to negotiate themselves out of identification with this vintage and go back to Renamo-controlled areas of Mozambique, in the belief that this represented their most secure future.

In the years after the fall of Milange there is evidence that Renamo was seeking the organized repatriation of refugees in Malawi to their own areas. One of Renamo's principal agents in Malawi, a missionary code-named 'Joseph', reported on negotiations with the Malawi Government and proposed talks with the ICRC, in a radio message to Dhlakama on 20 May 1988. The message has been reported as follows:

> The Malawi Government would be pleased to help move Mozambican refugees in their country to areas occupied by Renamo within Mozambique, such as Milange District in the central province of Zambezia, then occupied by Renamo; 'we shall ask the International Red Cross to contact the Malawian Government so as to finalise the plans', 'Joseph's' message adds.

Such proposals are distinct from the attempts in 1988 by the Malawi Government to create a peace zone in distant northern Angonia (Finnegan, 1992: 160–1), ideas that were taken up again by the ICRC some years later, because in the case of Milange, Renamo was to administer the returnee area itself. Note also that Renamo was apparently hoping for the return of people to the areas it controlled who were not its supporters. Through this programme Renamo also appears to have been seeking to strengthen its relationships with external institutions. Without supporting documentary evidence it is unclear how far such negotiations actually reached, and what was really the position of the Malawi Government. Anyway only two weeks after this message was relayed Milange fell to an enormous Frelimo assault.

Movements After the Retaking of Milange by Frelimo, 1988

The government's retaking of Milange town in June 1988 was achieved through the combination of a large ground force that came overland from Quelimane, together with a substantial aerial assault. The ground force fought its way through Derre, Liciro, Tengua and Aleixo before arriving in Milange, and all along its route local peasants from these places were 'recuperated' in some numbers. ('Recuperation' is a term used since independence by Frelimo in such contexts as re-education of 'social undesirables', and has come to be used in recent years for peasants collected by force in Renamo-controlled areas and brought to the government garrisons.) The bulk of these recuperants were settled in Milange town, but others were collected in a return movement to Quelimane of a smaller body of troops, and later settled in Nicoadala (near to the coast) with other internally displaced populations.

The aerial assault of Milange in June 1988 created panic throughout the central zone of the district, even in areas far distant from the town itself. This was despite the fact that there was no bombing of villages, though this has occurred in other parts of the region at other times. Likewise the only accounts of punitive actions against civilians in the Renamo-held areas by ground troops were in areas en route like Liciro which were far from the battle zone.[5] Participants' accounts describe the almost instant scattering of the whole population and full-scale flight towards Malawi. In addition to the cross-border movements, contemporary reports also describe large movements 'towards the interior of Zambezia Province' during the month after Frelimo's successful assault (WFP, 1988a). It is thus possible that as many as 100,000 people were displaced at this time. We interviewed

---

[5] Seventeen of the eighteen women recuperated from Liciro now living in the Nicoadala settlement are widows. Only a soldier involved at the time – now demobilized – had the courage to explain why in an interview in November 1991.

only one person then resident in central Milange district who had not tried to run during the attack: an old man who simply waited for Frelimo to secure the town. (A few fleeing Milange residents were also rounded up by the returning Frelimo soldiers.)

Field interviews demonstrate that few of this new wave of refugees actually presented themselves to the authorities in Malawi. Despite this, the fighting in June 1988 still led to an immediate surge in official registration (Christian Service Committee, 1988) of the order of 16,000–18,000 new arrivals (Smith, 1990: 78; Zieroth, 1988: 4 and 6). Most new arrivals never registered as refugees and sought temporary accommodation with relatives or friends, and, as soon as was possible, returned to their homes which were still mostly in Renamo-held areas of Mozambique, after having sent scouts to check on the situation. Even amongst the officially registered group, the population in this new influx had declined to around 14,000 by the end of the year (MSF-F, 1988), because of repatriation. Once more there is evidence of high mobility of refugees in and out of formal registration as they sought socio-political solutions to the problem of exile. Health officials complained of Muloza that the population was 'moving a lot [into Malawian villages and was] . . . difficult to control', adding more generally of southern Malawi at the time that 'the mobility of the people' is because they 'go back to Mozambique or to another part of Malawi to look for their scattered family members' (MSF-F, 1988: 26).

Although some of the newly arrived refugees in mid-1988 were saying that Frelimo had told them to 'run to Malawi until we can assure you that Milange will be protected on a permanent basis' (Smith, 1990: 78), this did not prevent this vintage from being labelled 'Renamo supporters'. But such a label was much too simplistic. Many had left because they simply did not know how the Frelimo forces would treat civilians they found in the war zones. Finnegan interviewed a small group from this vintage several months after their arrival in Malawi, and recorded their regret that they had fled en masse with their chiefs, leaving only a few chiefs and people to remain with Frelimo.

According to those refugees, those who had remained 'had not been punished. They [the chiefs who had stayed] were now working with Frelimo, trying to lure the people who were living in the hills with Renamo back to Milange' (Finnegan, 1992: 159). In regard to whether those who had lived with Renamo were its supporters, a refugee we interviewed in Muloza in mid-1989 stated that he himself had decided to remain under Renamo control from 1986 to 1988 due to 'rumours [that were] circulating that the war would soon end' (in which case those who had fled would be branded as 'Frelimo supporters'), but that 'later [i.e. with government forces retaking the town] I realised that I might die for things I didn't understand, and so I came to Malawi'. Thus by seeking not to become refugees so as to avoid being labelled as enemies and outsiders, such people ended up with a 'Renamo' label, which meant among other things problems with returning to a Frelimo-controlled Mozambique.

With the new influx into Malawi in mid-1988 there were tensions in the crowded Muloza camp between those who left Milange when it fell to Renamo in 1986, and those who had just arrived with Frelimo's recapture of it. Life in exile usually generates a strong sense of community identity and hatred towards a common enemy. In the case of Muloza, with its strong Frelimo leadership (Kalemba et al., 1988; field observations, 1989), anybody who remained under Renamo rule was deemed a collaborator by that refugee vintage, and was not welcome among them. This contributed to why so many of the newly arrived refugees in June 1988 chose to live unregistered in the villages around Muloza under their Mozambican chiefs, unwilling to come into the camp (source: interview with health official). The existing overcrowding in Muloza was nevertheless significantly worsened by those new refugees who did present themselves to the authorities (the population increased from 10,500 to 14,500 by September 1988 (MSF-F, 1988), despite some relocations to the Chiringa camp). Given the threat of violence in the camp between Frelimo and Renamo affiliates, and Malawi's national security concerns, most of these new arrivals were relocated in a new camp (Mkhwai) much farther from the border (Smith, 1990: 79; MSF-F, 1988: 54; other sources). The international agencies sensitively assisted with this necessary relocation, though the reasons for it could not be publicly discussed.[6] The files of a relief agency contain notes from a briefing by UNHCR Malawi Office in 1989, for example, that observe 'the 6,000 at Mkhwai arriving after liberation were bandits or their sympathisers and can't go to Muloza for this reason'.

The new Mkhwai camp had a population of around 7,000 by the end of 1988 (MSF-F, 1988). The refugees in Mkhwai were mostly from the villages in the immediate vicinity of Milange town, and, uniquely, the camp was organized spatially with people settled in sections named after their home villages and under the chiefs who had been in power in the Renamo-held areas. Interviews with former residents confirm that the camp also contained many of Renamo's officials and other leaders from the recaptured areas of Mozambique. This has led, not surprisingly, to tension with the Mozambique Government. It is interesting that the camp population subsequently chose to depose their 'Renamo' leaders (this will be returned to below).

The Mkhwai camp faced numerous environmental problems. An international aid official who visited it some months after it opened even called it a 'hell-hole'. Mulanje is an extremely crowded district with large areas of tea estates and it was difficult for the Malawi Government to find suitable land for the camp. Transfers to Mkhwai even had to be halted in August because of the conditions. Indeed, it was subsequently even difficult to keep people from fleeing the site:

> due to the difficulties faced by the refugees (lack of firewood, food, area mosquito-ridden, curative structure insufficient) people have been leaving this camp since October (MSF-F, 1988: 64).

A cholera outbreak later accentuated this out migration process, but new arrivals brought the population to around 8,000 by the end of 1989 (MSF-F, 1989). Since refugee survival in this part of Malawi is greatly eased by access to Mozambique (for fuel, building resources, food, etc.), the Renamo label and the distance from the border were also a problem for its inhabitants. It appears that some refugees decided to repatriate when faced with the prospect of life in Mkhwai.

In contrast to the difficult situation for the newly created refugees, the return of Frelimo forces to Milange provided welcome opportunities to the earlier vintage in Muloza. As one recalled some years later:

> Two days after watching the battle, we saw new clean-looking soldiers at the border-post, who told us that we could now come back in, since they were Frelimo soldiers, adding 'your town is liberated'. Those with courage went back in to see the place, and took the news to the refugees in Muloza, who were looking for a safe place to stay.

Following Frelimo's recapture of Milange, there was considerable discussion between the international agencies and the Mozambique Government concerning organized repatriation, although, as described below, this official return never actually occurred. Meanwhile some refugees repatriated themselves, following exploratory visits to the recaptured town. One of the very first to return came because he was a political activist who

---

[6] The Malawian representative at the UNRISD conference where the first draft of this chapter was presented stated that overcrowding in Muloza was the only reason for the creation of Mkhwai.

stated that his intention was to 'mobilise the people with Frelimo politics'. This individual indicates how refugees make decisions to repatriate into areas of instability and danger because they hope to struggle to improve those conditions. They are not mere 'victims' avoiding persecution and danger. Another returnee Frelimo party secretary, interviewed by a journalist a few months after the government's return, stated that the size of the returnee group was small because of insufficient food supply in Milange (Finnegan, 1992: 155). As will be demonstrated below, however, most of the refugees decided to wait before returning for more complex reasons than food supply. The articulation of the reason 'the lack of food' was probably simply an example of how refugees and returnees have to construct their reasons for doing things in terms of assistance issues when communicating to agencies and outsiders. Indeed, it is one of the many ironies that one of the main reasons that people did not now return was because they could feel more secure in exile given the presence of friendly forces at the Milange garrison. This made possible retreat in the face of any potential threats to their well-being or security. Sometimes a greater ease of return can actually mean refugees have a reduced need to return.

In addition to these small early movements of returnees back to Frelimo-held Mozambique, a group of internally displaced people accumulated in Milange town. The size of this population was estimated as 1,500 in the first days, increasing to 2,800 by 8 August 1988 (WFP, 1988a and 1988b; Christian Council of Malawi, 1988: 25). This group was 'displaced from operational zones', and the number was increasing because the Mozambican army 'continue to clear the surrounding countryside' (Christian Council of Malawi, 1988: 25), though it also included some individuals who stayed in their homes adjacent to the town throughout and others who fled to the government forces voluntarily. Conditions were fragile in the early days and urgent supplies of food, clothing, cooking utensils, and medicines were recommended in July by the World Food Programme mission (WFP, 1988a). The expansion of this relief into a major programme of rehabilitation will be analysed in a subsequent section.

Population Movements between 1989 & 1991

During 1989 and 1990 the number of refugees in the Malawi border district of Mulanje continued to escalate, the official figure reaching about 47,000 by April 1990 (UNHCR-Blantyre, 1990), before stabilizing. Overall, the return of government forces to Milange, and their increasingly strong military position, far from reducing the refugee influx, ironically actually increased the levels of flight. By late 1990 official monthly influxes into Malawi across the Milange border were reaching the order of 500–2,000 persons. The reasons for this were extremely complex. The bulk of this new population was leaving Renamo-controlled territory within Milange district, although around 5,000 came from Renamo zones in the interior of Zambézia Province, especially in Namarroi district (UNHCR-Blantyre, 1990), where a similar expansion of Frelimo power was occurring. Movements out of Renamo areas following Frelimo expansion reflected in part the increase in coercion that Renamo used to sustain the control and logistics for its war effort. However, interviews suggest that people were also leaving because they no longer saw Renamo as the likely long-term authority in their home areas. They did not see a reason to continue to suffer when Renamo was not going to be there to stay. Finally there is evidence for the occurrence of waves of displacement, with people primarily moving out of those zones beginning to form the boundary between Renamo and Frelimo forces. These areas, which would later become completely uninhabited, as can be seen from the air, are clearly the most dangerous places to dwell, partly because of the activities of

9.5 *One of Milange's tourist cafés reopens, November 1991 (K. Wilson)*

9.6 *Reconstruction of business complex wrecked during Renamo occupation, October 1991 (K. Wilson)*

independent bandit groups. As the government-controlled zone expanded, the occupants of the moving boundary region were divided between those who came into the government garrison under Frelimo escort, those who moved further into the Renamo-held interior, and a growing proportion who left of their own volition for Malawi. Many of these emigrants to Malawi actually used it as a staging post for a safer movement to government-held areas of Milange since directly crossing the Renamo–Frelimo boundary was considered dangerous.

Refugees were also leaving Renamo-controlled areas of southern Milange district for Thyolo in Malawi in large numbers during 1989. The main reasons for this flight were given in a contemporary Malawian church agency report as Renamo violence against civilians, the collapse of institutions in Renamo-held zones, and the increasing harshness – even famine – in the Renamo-held zone (ZOA Refugee Care, 1990). These refugees were not registered with the relief programme and received no formal assistance at this time, although ZOA sought to extend health care and other services to them alongside local Malawians. One newspaper report from late 1989 declared:

> In the absence of a refugee camp in Thyolo district, the Mozambican refugees live with their relatives and aquaintances [sic] with who [sic] they share food and accommodation in the villages . . . [and] some of the tea estates in the district (*Daily Times*, 1989a).

A second refugee vintage from this area was the massive movement of 20,000 or so refugees out of the Majaua area following the recapture of this border centre by government troops in August 1990. The bulk of this group was established in a border camp at Tchipo in Thyolo district, though some were transferred to Mwanza (see below). Like the groups who left Milange in June 1988 this movement reflected the wholesale transfer of people with their chiefs once Renamo, their military patron, had been ousted. There is some evidence that more violence was used against civilians by Frelimo in this attack than in most of the earlier operations in Milange. The Frelimo garrison in Majaua subsequently recuperated around 500 local peasants, but did not attract returnees from Malawi or voluntary settlers from the Renamo-controlled areas. Majaua fell again to Renamo in November 1991. During the battle the civilians fled to Malawi and a number may have since returned to Renamo-held areas with some of the Tchipo refugees, although data are lacking, except to note that the net population of refugees in Thyolo continued to increase into 1992. The government garrison from Majaua arrived in Milange via Malawi the following day. Contemporary agency reports suggest that the inhabitants of other localities taken by Frelimo in mid-1990 (Tengua, Ponderane and Mbessa) also went en masse to Malawi (SCF-UK, 1990a). Mbessa, unlike the other two localities, continued to be a centre for instability and population relocation at least until late 1991.

The extreme overcrowding of the camps in Mulanje district, and the difficulties with identifying new camp sites in the area, meant that the Malawi Government decided in late 1989 that it could accommodate no more refugees in the district (the DC of Mulanje, Mr Kawonga, declared in October 1989 that Mulosa, then holding 30,000, 'could hold no more refugees' and Mkhwai, then with 9,300, 'could only take an additional 700; *Daily Times*, 1989b). New arrivals since 1989 in Mulanje (and also the southern Nsanje district) were to be transferred across the country to Chifunga (and later to another new camp, Lisangwi) in Mwanza district. Chifunga is a Shire valley camp that was then holding a small population from the province of Tete, and in a relatively little populated area. Refugees stated to us in 1989 that they were reluctant to transfer across the country on the grounds that it would separate them from their compatriots, and make self-repatriation more difficult (in terms of information and logistics), and this reluctance apparently delayed the implementation of the proposals. Despite initial delays, however, around 7,000 new refugees were indeed sent to Chifunga in the first year of the programme (MSF-F, 1989). Officially the move is voluntary. However, according to refugees – and the officials involved on the ground – only very special cases such as in family reunion are allowed to remain in Mulanje; furthermore, refugees often 'escape' from vehicles during the move or return to Mulanje under their own steam afterwards. Many refugees report that they decide not to register as refugees in Malawi to prevent relocation. Some people chose to live in the camps without declaring themselves, sharing the limited aid of relatives and seeking local employment at very low rates of pay. Rumours during 1990 that Malawi would open camps in the north for new arrivals in the southern region proved unfounded.

It has become increasingly difficult to estimate the size of the Milange district refugee population in Malawi not only because of the diversity of camps that they are located in, but more importantly because the proportion of the population that has self-settled appears to be increasing and is very difficult to estimate. It appears that in Malawi, like elsewhere in Africa, many of the refugees prefer to stay with local people and meet their own needs (where they can obtain access to land and/or work) rather than to live in a camp dependent upon aid. For most returnees we interviewed the decision to accept aid in Malawi was presented as the result of constraint or failure, and not the taking of an 'opportunity'; little had we realized this when we were working on refugee livelihood strategies in Malawi itself (Wilson et al., 1989). (There is some evidence, however, that an attitude of reliance on aid may emerge with time in the camps.) If the accounts of Milange residents who have lived in Malawi are taken at face value, then by 1991 there may have been as many self-settled refugees from Milange in Malawi as there are officially registered (that is, perhaps as many as 50,000) though not all of these would be currently resident in Mulanje district. Viewed through this perspective, self-settlement, which has generally been understood to reflect the desire to maintain control over one's life in exile (Hansen, 1979) and to meet livelihood requirements more effectively, can now be seen also as a long-term strategy for better controlling the social networks that can enable reintegration after peace.

Having discussed the changing nature and level of refugee migration from rural Milange district into Malawi, we will now discuss the changing size and nature of the population in Milange town, and the other Frelimo centres in this district of Mozambique.

During 1989 there was a good deal of self-organized repatriation to Milange town, which was just 5 kilometres across the border from the Muloza camp, as well as a certain amount of recuperation of people by government forces from around the town. During 1989 the population increased from 5,000 in mid-February (SCF-UK, 1989a) to 7,350 in mid-July (UNSCERO, 1989) and over 10,000 by December (CCM, 1989). (These figures do not include the sizeable garrison and the families of the soldiers, or the officials and other residents of the town.) One Mozambican who had taken refuge in Malawi said about his repatriation at this time: 'I see people who returned just a few months ago, and are already they are producing food. The security seems good enough now and it is time to come back so that we can prepare our fields' (Maier, 1989). However, the bulk of the refugee population in the adjacent Malawi camps declined to return, mainly because of a continued sense of insecurity and the memories of the terror of the taking of the town in 1986 (field visit, 1989; Maier, 1989). A journalist was told in Muloza that the refugees were monitoring the situation at home and that 'sometimes we receive information from people who leave the camp clandestinely, go home and see that the war situation has improved' (Mozambiquefile, 1989a). In fact the border crossing was extremely busy as hundreds of refugees crossed every day for trade and with Mozambican firewood. Thus people could easily determine that there was a marked improvement in Milange, but many refugees also believed that Renamo could retake the town at any time; indeed, during our field visit in May 1989 people stated that Renamo were only waiting for it to be properly resupplied. This was another of the reasons why many refugees continued to live in Muloza camp but relied on land and other resources from Mozambique during the day.

In addition to the steady process of self-repatriation in 1989–91, UNHCR/NARML were also bringing several hundred official repatriates to Milange in 1989, but back from Tete by bus, where they had been repatriated two years earlier (see above for a description of this repatriation and an examination of the policy involved). Although official repatriation programmes from Tete and elsewhere were halted from 31 December 1989 due to insufficient funding (UNDRO, 1990), UNHCR/NARML still managed to bring around 600 more returnees from Benga in Tete in October 1990. There was also some return of populations from the settlements in Nicoadala near Quelimane during 1990, but apparently mostly on an informal basis. Many people remained in coastal Zambezia, frustrated by the lack of available transport, including recently demobilized soldiers from the district who had been fighting in eastern and central Zambezia following their flight from Milange in 1986. (Individuals with contacts with the relief programme would take opportunities of space on the flight aid programme funded by SCF-UK to link the districts, or find other means to travel.)

During 1990 the army generally increased its 'recuperation' of peasants from Renamo-held areas in Zambezia as its capacity to raid beyond the district garrisons increased, and in its attempt to undermine Renamo's tribute economy. Although recuperation was not on a large scale in Milange compared to certain other districts in the province, several thousand people were forcibly relocated into Milange during 1990. For example, a situation report from the town in January 1990 observed that there were 'about twenty new arrivals per day mostly brought in from villages to prevent Renamo getting food. Only a few are returnees' (CCM, 1990a). Self-repatriation from Malawi did also continue at this time, however, especially once the dry season had set in, which is the time when building and land preparation are easiest. Conflicts between returnees allocated land around the town and the original owners still in exile began to be exacerbated, but the common situation in Angonia district on Malawi's western border whereby refugees often returned to settle as soon as their land came up for allocation to other returnees did not develop (Wilson, 1991b). Instead, the absent refugees merely spread rumours of revenge once they returned with a future-victorious Renamo. The population of government-held Milange officially reached 14,318 in mid-1990 (DPCCN, 1990; *Noticias*, 1990), and by the end of the year was around 20,000 (CPE figures). During 1990 the number of elite traders returning to Milange had also increased.

The population of Milange town increased more slowly during the first half of 1991, but had reached 23,900 by late August (SCF-UK, 1991). According to a field visit at that time 'refugees returning from Malawi normally subsequently return again to Malawi due to the absence of food at times, and the conditions of accommodation. It is two months since there was any food in the DPCCN warehouse' (SCF-UK, 1991). A senior DPCCN delegation in September 1991 recorded that there were similar numbers of recently returned refugees and locally recuperated peasants (c. 2,500 each), and that food for the town had arrived in August (DPCCN, 1991). In the closing months of 1991 there appeared to be an increase both in returnees from Malawi (most of whom had been self-settled there but others came from each of the camps) and in the numbers of people being recuperated by the Naparama popular militia and Frelimo military around Milange and the other centres. In November 1991, *Posto* Molumbo, which is in the extreme north and supplied from neighbouring Gurue district was said to have 6,000 people, and the nearby centres of Aleixo, Tengua and Majaua had 180, 685 and 522 respectively. New official figures for Milange are not available for this period. In 1991 the local DPCCN office estimated that two-thirds of Milange's total population were repatriates and one-third recuperated in origin.

The temporary closing of the Mulanje–Milange border by Malawi in December 1991 (MIO, 1992) provided a threat to the welfare of the population in Milange town, and, to a lesser extent, to the continuing repatriation process. The Malawi Government argued that cross-border operations were responsible for the banditry in Mulanje district that other observers have alleged involves Malawians, but perhaps with weaponry obtained from the Mozambican combatants (*Africa Confidential*, 1991). Fortunately, a meeting of the joint Defence and Security Commission on 7 January 1992 handled the concerns and reopened the border post (MIO, 1992).

One of the persistent social problems in Milange town during recent years has been the number of individuals in the town who wished or needed to travel to other centres to reunite with their families or continue their lives. Amongst those we interviewed have been a refugee school boy returning from Malawi to move on to secondary schooling but needing air transport to Quelimane, a southern Mozambican who had now divorced the Malawian she had married before the war and was seeking a route home, and two young men from Marromeu who had escaped from Renamo after kidnap and could not get home to their families. Whilst the government administration was doing what it could, the transport available (the flight aid programme) has simply been insufficient, and was wound down during 1991.

Flight out of the northern part of northern Milange district due, it appears, to Renamo coercive and violent administration, has tended to take people not to Malawi but to a relatively secure garrison at Mecanhelas in Niassa Province. According to official figures there were around 5,000 internally displaced persons from Milange district at this centre in mid-1990 (DPCCN, 1990: 8). It is unclear whether the number has continued to rise, and no information is available to us on their situation.

The Social Construction of Migration
The manner in which the war and migration have shaped – and been shaped by – social dynamics is a major theme of our research projects. It is the intention in this chapter merely to reflect upon some of the more critical aspects of this for understanding the issues connected to cross-border and repatriation movements.

Gender, Lineage & Migration
An interesting feature of the refugee movement in this area has been the apparent bias towards the movement of men relative to their proportion of the population as a whole. Some of the explanations advanced for this are that men are especially vulnerable to one or both of the military forces (the problem with this view is that it ignores the issue of rape); and that women are more valuable to Renamo than men (especially for agriculture), so that women's departure is more restricted (this view was most strongly articulated by priests familiar with Sena society and not Milange where both men and women do agricultural work). More likely than either of these reasons, however, is the fact that, in this kind of matrilineal society in which men move to their wives' villages on marriage, women have much more to lose through migration than men in terms of property, rights, and social relationships. Therefore, they remain in their homes in the face of much greater forces. Similar patterns have been observed in famines and periods of warfare in this area

in the past (Mandala, 1990; Vaughan, 1987). Furthermore, although the demographic evidence is uncertain, it appears that the gender bias is different among the patrilineal populations of the Zambezi Valley of this part of central Mozambique. In a process of repatriation women will be much more anxious to return to their areas of origin than will men, for similar reasons. It should be noted, however, that, in past migration movements across this border, research has shown that over time 'Lomwe' women have proven remarkably capable of reconstructing social systems that protect their relatively secure role in this society (White, 1987); research amongst matrilineal Tonga displaced further up the Zambezi Valley by the Kariba dam also indicates some ability by women to claw back their rights and position in society despite the devastating effect that relocation had particularly on their land holdings (Colson, 1971, 1980; Reynolds, 1991: 38–40). In-depth interviews with both men and women in Milange suggest that strong forces exist to re-establish elements of matrilineal organization but that emergent social relations will reflect the unpredictable socio-political processes during the construction of peace.

Using the Country of Asylum Merely for Transit

The options available for people living in the war zone in Milange include that of flight to safer areas of Mozambique, as well as that of becoming refugees in Malawi, or trying to enter the recaptured Milange town (which meant crossing the Renamo/ Frelimo frontier). It is significant that many of the flight routes brought people temporarily into Malawi due to its better transport services and greater security for travel. This use of the asylum country contradicts the assumptions behind refugee protection and assistance instruments, since these Mozambicans entering Malawi in flight had no intention of staying there, but were merely using Malawi to access to more secure areas of Mozambique. For example, Jehovah's Witnesses fleeing areas of northern Milange where they were being particularly heavily taxed by Renamo, used the Malawi railway line from Luchenza to Tengani to get more easily into a Renamo-controlled chiefdom in Morrumbala (Chirombe) where conditions were better. Indeed, the bulk of the movement of Jehovah's Witnesses from Milange in 1985–86 involved using Malawi as a transit point through which to reach Tete Province, and ultimately Zambia, and this is discussed in the subsequent chapter. (Similar processes have occurred on the other borders; one of the Mozambicans interviewed in Zambia had been working in Mutarara and had only been able to rejoin his family in northwestern Tete, when Mutarara became embroiled in the war by travelling through Malawi and Zambia.) Interviews in Milange in late 1991 also indicated that the Malawian border markets served as gateways for people and information to flow between the Renamo- and Frelimo-held areas of Milange district.

Sometimes bureaucratic processes of labelling people as refugees can mean that people are obliged to do things defined as illegal, even though they achieve solutions desirable for themselves, governments and the relief agencies concerned. For example, during late 1988 and early 1989 many refugees fleeing north from Milange to Mecanhelas (Niassa Province, Mozambique) discovered that it was possible to use the Chiringa refugee camp in Malawi as a staging post on the journey, picking up food and other supplies from the aid agencies there. However, to do this they found that they had to pretend that they had arrived to stay permanently in the camp. On receipt of supplies, and after resting, they then moved on and reached safer areas of Mozambique further to the north. When this was discovered by the Chiringa camp administration, a rule was laid down to require people to permanently settle (build a dwelling) in the camp before receiving any assistance.[7] In April 1989, after this cutting off of the supplies en route, a relief worker came across 64 families who had escaped from Renamo control, fleeing northwards from Milange district into Frelimo-held areas of Mecanhelas district in Niassa Province. Presumably unable to get through to Milange town, they had used secret paths identified by a guide that they had chosen to send ahead to scout out the route. The journey was so long and hazardous because they had been unable to enter Malawi since they 'lacked money' (Malawi currency), which, under the circumstances, was now necessary to survive the journey on that route. Mecanhelas district continued to receive displaced people from Milange right up to mid-1990 (DPCCN, 1990: 8).

Integrating & Alienating Forces in Exile in Malawi

Considering the political forces operating on and within Malawian society, Malawi Government officials have provided Mozambican refugees with a high level of protection in Mulanje. Only a few security incidents have been reported by international observers and researchers (published incidents in Mulanje include those reported by Cisternino, 1987: 13; and Minter, 1989: 43). The continued presence of the world's third largest refugee population (one million) in Malawi is clear evidence that the refugees highly value the asylum that they have been provided. Likewise, the Malawi Government has not yet ceased to honour asylum despite the enormous costs to the country, and the inadequate levels of donor assistance. Yet Mozambicans typically state that they find exile an unpleasant experience, and this generates a sense of alienation and acts to strongly propel repatriation.

Historically, and up until 1986, Malawi had steadfastly refused to classify Mozambican immigrants as refugees to be held separate from local people against their will, in a situation where most southern Malawians have Mozambican origins. Not only did the state accept their presence, Malawians welcomed and assisted them, demanding of wider Malawian society that their need for asylum be met under some kind of 'common law'. Since 1986, however, the situation has changed dramatically. The sheer size of the influx during that year, and the subsequent arrival of an aid machinery geared to the separation and targetting of refugees with hand-outs, has meant that in recent years being 'a refugee' has become as important an element of identity as was being 'a brother/sister' (as Malawians refer to Mozambicans).

The concerns of national security and the administrative control needed for 'aid' (amongst other factors) have meant that refugees have generally found themselves living in camps and governed as powerless recipients. The opportunity for self-settlement in Malawian villages has been constrained, not least because Malawi is a densely populated country that has faced considerable economic problems in the late 1980s. The power and frequent superiority complexes of expatriates and Malawian relief workers and officials have fuelled Mozambican resentment, particularly amongst the refugee elite. Minimal refugee participation and lack of information disbursement have encouraged amongst the refugees a greatly exaggerated view of how much corruption and incompetence there are amongst the people who administer their assistance. Repression of refugees making accusations of foul play, whether such accusations were correct or not, has increased a sense of alienation, and has also indirectly encouraged greater corruption and abuse of power by local officials. Whenever we were alone with refugees in Mulanje and other areas of Malawi, and despite the fact that such issues were not the subject of our research, we

---

[7] Information collected on field visit to Chiringa, May 1989. More senior officials disputed that this policy existed, but in ways that were inconsistent and not convincing.

received a barrage of bitter criticism, often followed with statements like 'it is better to go home to die than be humiliated like this', and examples of individuals who had done just that. It is thus of no surprise that the Mozambique Information Agency quotes refugees in Mulanje camps saying 'that conditions in the Malawian camps were "very difficult" and that the Mozambican Government "should come and fetch us home" '. 'We have no land to cultivate', one woman said. 'The owners here [local Malawians] humiliate us. Relations with the camp authorities are bad' (*Mozambiquefile*, 1989a.) This general atmosphere, unfortunately common in refugee camps, does disguise, of course, the extent to which refugees vary in their attitudes to the authorities.

The engagement between Malawians and their hosts in the Mulanje camps is more complex, however, than one simply of power relations engendered by the assistance programme. Two of the main vintages of refugees from Milange belonged to groups with which there had been a history of hostility in Malawi: the Frelimo officials and the Jehovah's Witnesses. Whilst the accounts above and in the next chapter suggest a remarkable capacity of the Malawian Government to give primacy to humanitarian concerns in dealing with these groups in Mulanje district, this historical legacy remains. (One relief worker, for example, reported that, in contrast to the government officials, the attitudes of many local party officials in Mulanje had been negative to the Frelimo refugees and their rights.) It is perhaps ironic that one consequence of the marked improvement in Malawi–Mozambique relations in the late 1980s and the desire of the Malawian authorities to make the camps peaceful was that quite apart from Malawian secret police some refugees complain about the presence of Frelimo agents in the camps which makes them feel insecure; the 'disturbing presence of Mozambican intelligence people' was actually reported to a visitor as far back as 1987 (Cisternino, 1987: 15).

Processes of integration into Malawian society have often been facilitated by existing kinship relations or social networks with former immigrants. In fact, as noted in the section on background, it is more appropriate to see the border as central to the community than as a boundary dividing the people. Access to 'Malawian' social networks was common and enabled people to obtain some assistance, irregular employment, or a place to stay. Simply finding a better residence site was an extremely valuable resource (Cisternino, 1987: 12). In some cases refugees established new friendships with Malawians on the basis, mostly, of economic interaction, such as the mixed group of women we came across in Muloza in 1989 who had set up an informal needlework co-operative, under the guidance of a highly skilled Malawian woman. Within the camps there were also relations of patronage between prominent refugees and Malawian officials and local leaders, as well as friendships between refugees and their hosts. In general it would appear that, whilst these relationships between refugees and host in camps may influence the timing and mode of repatriation, they are unlikely to fundamentally affect its course. Links with local Malawians may be just as likely to accelerate repatriation through increasing people's resources and knowledge, as they are to retard it through entrapping people in social obligations. Self-settled refugees with good links in Malawi were dominating return to Milange during 1991.

Wider economic factors have played an integrating role for some Mozambicans, though the great shortage of arable land and relatively low demand for refugee labour on the tea estates have meant this has been limited compared to previous periods of Mozambican immigration into the district. As discussed above, Mozambican immigrant labour has long been of major importance on these tea estates, and in the past included both seasonal and short-term contracts as well as permanent immigration into Malawi. However, declining working conditions in Malawi were leading to net out-migration back to Mozambique in the early 1980s (Cisternino, 1987: 13), until the economic collapse of Milange, and the effect of war in the mid-1980s, which increased labour supply to Malawi once more (author's journal notes, Mulanje–Milange border, 1985). Nevertheless, tea estates provided food and relief to refugees fleeing the fall of Milange to Renamo in 1986, and the estates even publicly expressed the hope that they might absorb many of the Mozambicans into their labour force. In 1989 the Malawi Government had not entirely resolved its official attitude to whether refugees could be employed on the estates. One official statement, made in an international forum, was that employment was permitted. However, tea estate owners were being privately warned not to on grounds of security and competition with local Malawi labourers (field notes and interviews, 1989–90). Visits to tea estates, and discussion with refugees, indicated that many Mozambicans had obtained work through 'Malawianization' by purchase of Malawi Congress Party cards and poll tax certificates (Wilson *et al.*, 1989: 84). Mozambicans had particularly migrated to the estates at Thyolo, where there was a relative labour shortage compared to the border district of Mulanje (field notes and aid agency sources). Though it might have been predicted that such people are likely to respond to repatriation initiatives more slowly than those who have remained in the border camps, it has been demonstrated that some of the first people to return to Mozambique were those then working in Malawi who were offered work on the reopened Mozambican tea estates.

In addition to work on the tea estates, there has also been a fair amount of employment on local tea smallholdings, but this tended to provide piece-meal resources for survival rather than a truly integrating force, just as has been the *ganyu* domestic piecework for Malawian peasants (Wilson *et al.*, 1989: 84–92). In Mulanje refugees have negatively affected the natural resource base, such as fuel wood availability, and labour markets for poor Malawians, but the effects are neither so large nor so negative as to have led to large-scale social and economic conflict. This is partly because since the reoccupation of Milange by government forces in mid-1988 the refugees in Muloza have relied as much on resources gathered across the border in Mozambique as they have on those obtained locally in Malawi (Wilson *et al.*, 1989). They even sell such resources – especially firewood – to local Mala-wians at low prices. Since 1989, furthermore, limited initiatives to improve health care and other services in Muloza have also provided some benefits to the local population and helped to assuage tensions.

The construction of refugee communities in the Malawi camps has occurred both at formal and informal levels. Each camp has had its own type of official leadership with cer-tain (though limited) powers, which they use to establish their authority. In the small camp of Chiringa, prominent Jehovah's Witnesses were selected by the local Malawian authorities, but of course operated without explicit reference to their religious convictions. In Muloza, prominent Frelimo party people were granted leadership positions by the Malawi Government, whilst in Mkhwai the Renamo adherents were settled in their former villages under the same chiefly authorities they had been administered by under Renamo. In each of these camps the designated authorities faced problems of a divided con-stituency. In Chiringa, the proportion of non-Witness refugees increased over time, but the established Witnesses have continued to dominate the camp. In Muloza large popula-tions of Witness, pro-Renamo and neutral refugees have lived in the camp, especially since 1988, and yet had to live under a Frelimo refugee leadership. During our interviews of the camp leadership in May 1989 we were struck by their authoritarian manner, and former residents of the camp report that conflict had been a major feature of community life.

In the Mkhwai camp that was established in 1988 for the influx of people subsequent to Frelimo's recapture of Milange, the population was originally relatively homogeneous.

The fact that whole communities had relocated might have been expected to make community integration easy. But as early as January 1989 Mkhwai was being identified as having some of the worst health problems, including increasing mortality among under-fives. According to health staff this reflected not only the swampy ground and malarial exposure but the fact that 'there is a feeling of lack of natural leadership amongst the refugees despite organisational efforts implemented' (UNHCR Health Sector, 1989: 3). Indeed, as noted later by a consultant, 'a great deal of community conflict characterised this particular camp' reflecting 'a general wish to be free of' the chiefly leadership of Renamo and a subsequent replacing of 'most of them with elected leaders' (Tolfree, 1991: 59). This desire to replace the 'traditionalist' leadership may have its roots in the period shortly after flight as people then realized that it had been the decision to stick with the Renamo leadership that had obliged them to flee and settle in the refugee camp, whilst they would have been better off to have defected to Frelimo (see the interviews in Mkhwai in September 1988 reported in Finnegan, 1992: 158–9). Certainly Frelimo's increasingly strong position in Milange since 1988 must have suggested to them that the old Renamo leaders would play a less important role in the future, let alone lead the rapid and triumphal return to Milange that Renamo promised. It is also clear that the desire of people to identify with a partisan leadership reflects their wish to maintain their membership of a particular community and the access to resources that this ensured, but that where such leadership appears unable to deliver they are prepared to overthrow them. Indeed, by 1991 there were refugees from Mkhwai returning to Frelimo-held Milange town, without seeming to entirely compromise their social relationships in Mkhwai.

Informal community structures in the camps also provided powerful networks of support and concern. Interviews with individual returnees suggested that the decision to return was often part of a wider realignment within a family or network between people in the Malawi camps and even the Renamo-held areas of Mozambique, and the desire to secure a foothold in Frelimo-held Milange. Indeed, even the very movements of people between the camps, self-settled areas and Milange town are usually facilitated by accommodation and other support with relatives or associates in the different places. Some decisions are consciously made collectively, particularly in the emergent churches in the camps. One church, for example, had extensive deliberations before deciding that their pastor should repatriate, but that church elders should continue to reside on both sides of the border. Such networks are taken seriously by the refugees not only because people want to belong and live in a manner which ascribes social value and purpose to their lives, but because important material assistance can be mobilized through this. Vulnerable categories in the population, in particular, find it essential to 'belong' to such religious and other social groups in order both to receive ongoing support (which is usually at a low level), and particularly to provide back-up in the case of contingencies. They will certainly move together with these networks and not before. To date, the main impact of these associational factors has been to focus repatriation on the construction of social bridgeheads in Milange, but once security improves they are likely to propel repatriation not only more effectively but also significantly faster.

According to returnees from Malawi to Milange arriving in 1991 there are socio-political factors relating to this construction of community reducing the desire to return. They state that the refugees in Muloza are divided into factions supporting Renamo and Frelimo respectively, and those who support neither. Leading Frelimo- and Renamo-supporting refugees clearly remain in the camps at least partly to press their political cause against one another. More significant, however, is that Renamo-supporting refugees are threatening the other refugees that if they return to Milange they will be severely dealt with if and when Renamo retakes the town. It is also widely reported by returnees that certain Malawians inform refugees that if they choose to return to Mozambique now, and then fighting breaks out again, they will not be given a second period of asylum. Whether any Malawians do indeed say this, and, if so, which people do and why, cannot be reported with any certainty. Once again, however, these returnee accounts indicate how people are making decisions on surprisingly long-term criteria, rather than current conditions or aid disbursement. A good number of refugees in the border camps are maintaining their options open: they use land and other resources in Mozambique, but they maintain their residence in Malawi. Interviewees also report, however, that after five years on aid some refugees have come to rely on aid disbursement in the Malawian camps as a supplement to their own efforts, and that this is resulting in their reluctance to pursue self-reliance. Whilst claims of 'dependency' tend to be exaggerated, it remains to be seen whether there will be a significant social or motivational legacy of prolonged food distribution. What is ironical, however, is that many of the people involved are the Frelimo affiliates: modernizers and progressives who hope for a continuation of their alliance with a re-emergent strong and resource-distributing state that now looks extremely unlikely in the new Mozambique.

The Rehabilitation of Milange Town, 1988–91

Introduction
Milange had been well-known before the war as a beautiful and wealthy town drawing income from the tea estates, a healthy peasant cash crop sector, and a tourist and border trade. A shocking scene of devastation due to Renamo looting and Frelimo aerial bombing greeted the delegations of government and agency workers who came after its recapture from Renamo in mid-1988. Nevertheless, by late 1991 astonishing progress had been made in the town; yet this economic strength resulted not so much from the competent government administration and a reasonably effective provision of rehabilitation assistance by the agencies: it was actually rooted in the revival of commerce. Thus it is ironic that the agencies had initially conceived only state-led (and 'community' and 'service') rehabilitation, though the realities of contemporary Mozambique (which they themselves had contributed to creating) located the engine of rehabilitation in private commerce. Indeed, in late 1991 it was the leading businessmen who stepped in to provide the military with the logistics they believed would stave off the Renamo offensive. The purpose of this section is briefly to describe the processes by which Milange town was brought back to life, and how these processes interact with the reintegration of returnees.

The physical isolation of Milange from the rest of government-controlled Mozambique has meant that the good relations on the Malawi border were critical both for effective relief and for commercial activity (SCF-UK, 1990d: 2). Frelimo's Milange commander took a consciously conciliatory stance, seeking to overcome poor official relations (Fauvet, 1988). Mozambique did request the return of looted property in part on the basis of 'information on the whereabouts of livestock, machinery and other looted goods' supplied by the Muloza refugees (Fauvet, 1988), but subsequently there was talk only of co-operation.

The Role of International Agencies & Government Programmes
Prior to embarking upon analysis of the nature and impact of international agency and government rehabilitation programmes in Milange, it is appropriate to briefly review the objectives of and constraints upon these bodies.

As elsewhere in Zambezia the Mozambique Government was seeking to combine securing Milange town militarily with the re-establishing of civilian structures and services which Renamo had sought to destroy systematically – even ritualistically (see Wilson, 1992a). For the much praised military administrator for civilian affairs in Milange, Captain Raimundo Kantumbianga, 'priorities for government [were] described as (a) securing area and (b) consolidation of civil administration in all aspects' (WFP, 1988a). With the arrival of the dynamic civilian administrator, Sr Manso, in early 1989 the government's capacity to achieve this consolidation and return to normality on all fronts was further enhanced. Like other garrison communities, Milange was a highly disciplined and ordered society, but the atmosphere was different from a refugee camp.

For the relief agencies, the objectives of the rehabilitation of the town combined providing direct relief with service provision to the population, and preparing the area for repatriation. In common with government, however, the agencies construed improving of the morale of the population and local government as essential in countering Renamo's anti-civilization mission, and for bringing the population physically back under the control of the government and for winning the war. How central this was viewed is indicated by the telexed report of the follow-up to the first United Nations/Mozambique Government mission after its reoccupation by Frelimo. The delegates 'believe psychological aspects very important', and so 'if centre secure then rebuilding/land clearance' would be important to 'provide activity/sense of purpose' and 'construction tools/materials/cement etc. therefore needed' for such reconstruction (WFP, 1988b). In July 1990 another UN mission to Milange emphasized the need to make government capable of achieving its objectives in terms of morale: 'there was evidence of a momentum in Milange to rebuild social services. Immediate continued support is important to maintaining this process' (UNSCERO, 1989).

After 1987–88 the province of Zambezia experienced an enormous influx of aid and international agencies alongside and in the wake of its military advances against the almost total Renamo occupation of late 1986. In addition to the demands placed on government by the war and the need to re-establish itself in the reoccupied zones, government experienced at this time a major redistribution of activities and resources into the new Emergency Programme involving independently operating Western non-governmental agencies. In fact, the government did build up an emergency co-ordinating structure that rapidly rationalized management and secured the involvement of each relevant government department. It was only in Milange that the 'Provincial Commission for the Emergency' (CPE) played a weak role, because of the cross-border nature of most operations there, although in practice Milange followed a model of rehabilitation developed by the CPE and SCF in the earlier programmes in Mopeia and Morrumbala. In Zambezia each district was handled by a single aid agency in an attempt to minimize institutional conflict and duplication.

SCF-UK became the main agency working in Milange, and their stated objectives were to 'support provincial government and district-based administrations in rebuilding and recuperating certain towns in Zambezia using local labour and materials wherever possible' (SCF-UK, 1990d). SCF-UK field staff for Zambezia have been acutely aware of the challenges posed by the commitment to rehabilitation and development by working with government rather than directly implementing programmes themselves. Alistair Hallam, for example, referring to experience in Milange and several other districts in 1989 and 1990 explained on the one hand that there was a need for more consultation with the communities involved to make activities pursued 'less a reflection of local government or SCF' views, whilst on the other hand noting that SCF and the other agencies were using their spheres of interest and energies to facilitate an unfortunate distancing of the provincial government from the situation on the ground (SCF-UK, 1990d). Hallam has more recently noted that the dependence on formal state initiatives reflected in part the fact that SCF 'appreciated that we knew almost nothing about the society in rural Mozambique, and certainly not enough about the dynamics of the refugee process' and were working in difficult conditions to visit garrison towns in a military zone where participative and exploratory social development initiatives were inconceivable. Thus SCF 'felt that we had to support the government's initiatives – this led to an over-emphasis on bricks and mortar (school rooms, health posts) rather than training and supply of more basic materials' (personal communication, 1992). His successor, Steven Thomas (1992), has further explored the complex impact on governmental capacity occasioned by the work of his agency (exploring, amongst other things, how it influenced the relative strengths of different ministries versus local government, and the roles of district versus provincial authorities), in part in response to important work by Egan (1991) amongst others on the institutionally damaging effects of large aid programmes and parallel structures.[8]

Achieving co-ordination between the different relief agencies in their programmes in Milange proved challenging. Ultimately it was fairly successful amongst the agencies, largely due to good personal relations, although the government tended to be relegated to a diplomatic position in this process. Not only were two different United Nations agencies involved (UNHCR and WFP), there were two non-governmental agencies (SCF-UK and the Christian Council of Malawi [CCM]).[9] Furthermore, the WFP and CCM operated straight from Malawi, whilst the UNHCR was run from Maputo and Tete, and SCF-UK from Quelimane in Zambezia.

Each agency secured a different legitimacy and co-ordinating relationship with the Mozambican Government, which further complicated matters. The CCM worked with its Southern African regional Protestant church body, which is based in Harare (Zimbabwe), and was legitimated at the request of Mozambique Christian Council in Maputo. In practice, however, even the Christian Council of Mozambique's Zambezia emergency programme remained virtually unaware (until a recent mission) of the Milange activities run from Malawi although they are 'technically under Quelimane' (Colvin, 1992: 10). In fact the CCM actually became involved in Milange because the Malawi-based WFP field officer (who had previously worked for the World Council of Churches) had asked them for assistance with the milling of food aid maize being sent from Malawi, and the CCM later visited the district and became aware of its wider needs (T. Colvin, personal communication). In its activities in Milange, the WFP tended to co-ordinate with the Mozambique Embassy in Malawi and in practice, in a more vague and not always easy way, through its office in Maputo; WFP understood that it had been nominated by the Mozambican Government to co-ordinate all aid agencies' deliveries to Mozambique from Malawi. WFP-Malawi's cross-border programme was increasingly brought under the control of WFP-Maputo, and, though more clearly co-ordinated, its effectiveness in delivery declined. UNHCR for its part worked with the weak government unit NARML and with the distant Maputo authorities, whilst SCF-UK was answerable to the provincial authorities in Zambezia, whose commission for the emergency (CPE) naturally believed itself to be the sole rightful co-ordinator of emergency activities in the province.

These contrasting conceptions of co-ordination and responsibility of the agencies working in Milange constrained systematic planning and implementation. Thus as early as

---

[8] Hanlon (1991) provides an important overview of the destructive effects of aid on Mozambican institutions, though its dogmatic and rhetorical content requires several cautions (Wilson, 1991c).
[9] Confusion – at least my own – was perhaps increased by the fact that the CCM annual reports cover most rehabilitation activities in Milange; it was only fieldwork that could establish which were actually its own.

August 1988, the WFP was worried about duplication with SCF-UK which it had heard was applying for British Government funding (WFP, 1988b), whilst SCF-UK was meanwhile attempting to deal with 'duplication in food supply planning' with UNHCR and the church agencies. In October 1988, WFP managed to avert the importation of seed by both SCF-UK and the CCM, and to co-ordinate the number of hoes each brought, but was concerned that UNHCR Tete had visited Milange without reporting its intended activities (WFP, 1988c). From this date on co-ordination improved in terms of general relief provision, but in Milange it was nevertheless reported 'there are too many organizations operating' and that 'they get played off against one another by the population', leading to a decision by SCF, for example, not to involve themselves in new craft associations (SCF-UK, 1990a). The outstanding problem for co-ordination came in 1990–91 to be the issue of planning for repatriation, where SCF-UK, CCM and UNHCR each came with very different perspectives and plans in the 1989–91 period.

During the first weeks after the reoccupation of Milange the welfare situation of the displaced people was really precarious. Whilst during Renamo occupation 'local maize cultivation [had been] kept alive' though it had 'evidently . . . suffered heavily due to population movements', the 1,500 internally displaced were in a 'visibly distressed condition' holed up in the district capital, and required immediate food relief together with clothing and cooking utensils (WFP, 1988a). People sheltered in the destroyed buildings. The extent of health problems is illustrated by the fact 500 adults and 300 children were serviced in the first week of services though the 'absence of adequate medical supply and competent medical personnel [was] very discernible' (WFP, 1988a). Initial relief was supplied by the WFP and the CCM in a cross-border operation from Malawi (CCM, 1988; WFP, 1988a). Milling was a recurrent problem, recognized at an early stage by each of the agencies involved (WFP, 1988b; CCM, 1988; SCF-UK, 1988), but continually re-emerging over the next few years. Whenever whole grain rather than flour was provided and when the mill in Milange was not operating, large quantities of grain had to be traded into Malawi to pay for milling costs there (Wilson et al., 1989; UNSCERO, 1989; CCM, 1990b; Finnegan, 1992: 153).

To enable reconstruction to begin in Milange, SCF-UK arranged for the cement and other building materials to be delivered through collaboration with its Malawi office, although a whole series of technical and logistical problems meant that these did not arrive until the end of September 1988, and even then were incomplete (SCF-UK, 1988). Both SCF-UK and CCM provided agricultural equipment and seeds during late 1988. There were recurrent food shortages in Milange, for example in October 1988, and even World Vision from Tete had to step in at one point (CCM, 1988: 25; SCF-UK, 1989a). The airstrip was not usable until SCF-UK was finally able to get a grader in from Malawi in December 1988, until which time Milange had been cut off from everywhere except Malawi; extensive delays had occurred because (among other things) the Mozambique Consulate hoped that a private contractor would do the work, but in fact only the Malawi Government was willing to operate across the border (SCF-UK, 1988 and 1989c). The displaced population in the town began to increase more rapidly during the rains from November onwards, when the aid provided became somewhat more regularized (CCM, 1988: 31–4).

The infrastructural and institutional rehabilitation of Milange town gathered momentum during 1989 and 1990, during which period the population quadrupled. A system of food relief was required and the DPCCN, working with NARML distributed 10.5 kg of maize per month per capita, and sometimes tins of fish and/or 1 kg beans, $\frac{1}{2}$ litre of oil and 1 kg sugar. Some disbursements of blankets, clothing, domestic items, and so forth have also been made. Clothing, tinned fish and maize grain were extensively traded into Malawi for general consumer goods, since these represented the only capital goods Mozambicans had available to meet their various other needs (field notes from Muloza, May 1989). Shortages in both food and non-food items were recurrent (e.g. UNSCERO, 1989; field observations, 1991). The lack of salt was often cause for particular complaint (SCF-UK, 1989e). Reliance on overland transport from Malawi or Tete (via Malawi) greatly eased supply because of the lack of need to rely on expensive air lifts, but it did expose Milange to such problems as the closure of the Tete corridor due to Renamo attacks in early 1991 following the withdrawal of the Zimbabwean forces as part of the limited cease-fire agreements.

Over time the administration sought to target relief at the 'recent arrivals' and others defined as being particularly in need as opposed to the relatively self-sufficient. The capacity of DPCCN to manage such targetting was, however, limited. Judging by the crowds of people continually pressing their entitlement claims around the DPCCN office, bargaining power and tenacity appear to have played a critical role in disbursements. Temporary accommodation was provided by the administration for the recent arrivals whilst they built their homes in the *bairros* (villages) to which they were allocated, and those categories in the population less able to build new homes, like the disabled, were allowed to stay longer, or in a few cases even permanently. In practice, however, some returnees from Malawi first built their homes in a preferred *bairro* whilst still dwelling in the Malawian camp, and then presented themselves to the authorities, so as to obviate the need to dwell in these temporary accommodation centres. Officially there were no resources targetted to longer term 'vulnerable categories' in the population, such as the isolated elderly and disabled, although the locally based churches and lineage networks tended to provide some minimal assistance in terms of labour and material needs. During 1991, and to a lesser extent at earlier times, the level of leakage of relief goods began to constrain the capacity of the system to meet the beneficiaries' needs. Patterns of leakage were complex, however, and included mechanisms that effectively subsidized the civilian administration in ways that enabled government staff to meet their basic needs in a context where salaries – when they were received – were simply insufficient for survival. Even the most senior administrative figure was earning just 110,000 MT per month (£25) and most government and service workers were paid half or less than this.

It was SCF-UK, with its £200,000 grant from the British Government, that played the key role in supporting the government's rehabilitation activities in Milange. Working with the Ministry of Construction and Water, SCF-UK has rehabilitated the town's excellent gravity-fed piped water system, and constructed wells in areas that the system could not reach (SCF-UK, 1990c; interviews with officials). SCF-UK inputs also enabled the establishment of a functional health post during 1989, and progress with the warehouses and schools (SCF-UK, 1989c: 5; Maier, 1989), the building work for which has been undertaken with the Ministry of Construction and Water.[10] By March 1990 the school population was 1,311, but was waiting for materials from Tete (SCF-UK, 1990f). Compared to the 163 primary schools in the district in 1985, Milange had just seven in the government-controlled area in 1991; there was a new secondary school (there had been another secondary school before the war), but it was not operating. There was also a basic programme to try to address the needs of 'traumatized' children. In 1991 the education

---

[10] The Ministry of Construction and Water representative in Milange reported that a shift in February 1991 from direct SCF-UK employment of workers, but under Ministry supervision, to direct contracts with the Ministry to get the work done had led to a great increase in speed and efficiency.

department struggled on minimal recurrent budgets, and in the face of a national strike for better salaries. During 1990, the CCM provided some school supplies and sports and recreation facilities (CCM, 1990b). During 1990 an electricity generator was provided to the large and extensively damaged district hospital at which large sums were spent on a partial rehabilitation. MSF-France have assisted the health clinic in Milange in a cross-border operation by their Malawi progamme, but SCF-UK has been reluctant to intervene over such things as failures in supplies of drugs and bandages where they consider that this would undermine the responsibility of the provincial Ministry of Health (SCF-UK, 1990a). The Ministry of Health is under-resourced but fairly active in such areas as maternity, prevention programmes, and sexually transmitted diseases, and the health situation is stable.

In order to combine stimulation of the local economy with the provision of relief goods and the rehabilitation of the town, SCF essentially created and then sponsored co-operative groups of tinsmiths producing pots and buckets, and tailors making clothes, items that were then distributed to new arrivals (SCF-UK, 1989c and 1989d; Hallam and Thomas, 1992). SCF-UK even entered into correspondence with WFP-Malawi in Blantyre (copied to the CCM) in June 1990 that the international agencies should buy from the tinsmiths' associations in Milange, rather than just distribute factory-produced items, though WFP-Blantyre replied regretting that they did not make such local purchases. When in late 1989 SCF-UK attempted to make the tailors self-sufficient by withdrawing the automatic purchase for relief distribution, they found that they could not compete with the commercial supplies available due to the Malawi border, and the scheme failed in contrast to those in the isolated garrison towns of the interior (SCF-UK, 1989e). The CCM was also involved in support of activities such as brick-making and carpentry, but in a smaller way (CCM, 1989, 1990b; SCF-UK, 1990a). In 1990 SCF-UK resolved that the associations had served their purpose and decided that, though they might buy goods from existing associations, they would not start any new ones (SCF-UK, 1990a); it appears that CCM had similar realizations. Subsequently the agency workers involved criticized attempts to convert the associations into independent businesses on the grounds that the programme had never addressed the organizational constraints on these associations (Hallam and Thomas, 1992). Hallam and Thomas, who administered the programme, subsequently argued that the 'directive' approach they adopted because of the war also contributed to a lack of commitment to the associations among members. Indeed, by 1991 it was individuals and self-organized small groups who dominated local production in most of the craft activities. Yet the associations had been a useful intervention in the 1988–90 period as a way of stimulating production and securing income transfer, it was not necessary that they be 'sustainable' to be useful.

The agricultural support programme (of seeds and tools) had begun in a limited way in 1988, but there was apparently little success with the 5,000 people assisted because of late and inadequate supply of inputs, though the 1989–90 season was more successful (SCF-UK, 1990b and 1990f). According to a reporter who visited Milange during the land preparatory period in this second season after reoccupation, the returnees were not expecting timely delivery of inputs, but were nevertheless preparing the land as well as they could, despite some delays in land allocation (Maier, 1989).[11] The 1990–91 season continued to witness increasing agricultural activity, particularly in the informal opening of

---

[11] SCF-UK suspects that it may have given too much emphasis to the provision of hoes and other agricultural inputs, because, even though they continued to arrive late (February in 1991), people had nearly always been able to manage without (S. Thomas, personal communication).

land on the mountain to the north of the town, where it provoked considerable concern about soil erosion and threat to the town's water supplies. The areas of land available for farming remained too small to enable Milange to become self-sufficient: only 1,250 hectares were then being officially provided for a population of 11,000 people (SCF-UK, 1990f). (Even if people were privately farming as much land again as they were officially given, the total available was only about a quarter of that needed for subsistence.) As the agricultural programme has progressed various lessons have been relearnt (as they continually have to be in Mozambique), such as the preference for local maize varieties over the soft hybrids imported from Zimbabwe and the very particular hoe-type preferences (interviews of Ministry of Agriculture and SCF-UK). The provision of seeds and tools proved by far the largest programme financially, and, being broadly successful, it has not only enabled people to meet part of their food needs, but also facilitated peasant demand for consumer goods, and so stimulated the development of commerce.

The Importance of Commerce

Somewhat to the surprise of international relief officials (WFP, 1988a), Empresa Moçambicana da Cha (the state tea company) (EMOCHA) moved very quickly to seek to rehabilitate Milange's tea estates, whose factories had been looted and fields become overgrown during Renamo's occupation. By December 1988 the necessary machinery had been brought in from Malawi for the rehabilitation, and relief agencies were requested to provide shelter for the 'up to 500 labourers [they] must entice . . . back from Malawi'; a request declined on the grounds of their mandates (CCM, 1988: 34–5). This process of selective repatriation of former workers was being discussed only unofficially in Malawi at the time (Wilson *et al.*, 1989), though, by February 1989, EMOCHA had already employed 150 workers (SCF-UK, 1989f) and by late 1991 the figure was 406, although money for salaries was not available (field notes). Officials and skilled workers returned to their former jobs, but seasonal labour was recruited on an open franchise. Estate clearance was fairly advanced by May 1989, and provided enormous benefits not only to refugees in Malawi who were allowed to cross the border to collect around 50 tons of tea bush off-cuts per day for use and sale as firewood (Wilson *et al.*, 1989: 159), but also to returnees to Milange who could use the firewood trade to capitalize the reconstruction of their homes and farms.

The re-establishment of EMOCHA was understood by both government and later the agencies as central to rehabilitation and development, because, among other things, local employment would 'create a market' because 'currently the *deslocados* [displaced people] have no purchasing power' (SCF-UK, 1989f).[12] Furthermore, EMOCHA provided numerous services within the town including transport and radio. SCF-UK thus even provided some technical assistance to EMOCHA in 1989 and 1990, including some agricultural equipment, paint, sanitary goods, a tractor, grader and trailer (internal memos). By June 1990, EMOCHA was contemplating opening a tea factory and a sawmill (SCF-UK, 1990a), as part of a three-phased rehabilitation, starting with 600 of the 1,678 hectares (scheduled to open in March 1991), but, without multinational investment dependent on cheaper more reliable access to ports for export, this did not come to fruition.

AGRICOM is the parastatal body charged with the purchase of agricultural products and the sale of basic consumer goods to the peasantry. Despite being wound down nationally as part of the shift to the 'free market', AGRICOM has played an important

---

[12] Incidentally SCF-UK found problems with the strength of EMOCHA in late 1990 when it found that its carpenters were better paid than those on the SCF-UK programmes.

role in reinvigorating livelihoods in the districts. It has also provided opportunities for local aid agency purchases, particularly useful in isolated garrisons. AGRICOM returned to Milange soon after reoccupation, but its commercial activities began to take off in 1989. AGRICOM purchased over 60 tons of maize in both the 1989–90 and 1990–91 seasons, as well as increasing quantities of butter beans, cassava, garlic, rice, pigeon peas, beans and chick peas, with its working capital of 30 million meticals (c. £10,000). Due to AGRICOM's lack of transport, the plan had been to resell this production to private traders, but in fact the bulk of the food was bought by the military. The overhead on crop sales is below 30 per cent, which is much less than the private traders. AGRICOM has also played an important role in the smaller garrisons.

Private capital and trading came back strongly in Zambezia in the late 1980s. The commercial elite had never been completely destroyed either under the supposedly Marxist policies of the first decade of independence, or by the ferocity of Renamo's assault on privilege and trade in the mid-1980s. In addition to the new opportunities for business provided by 'structural adjustment' and 'free market' policies from 1987, various aid programmes provided them with opportunities to re-establish their capital. First and foremost, Quelimane city became host to a number of very substantial international agencies at this time who injected millions of US dollars. Second, several agencies in Mozambique, particularly USAID, undertook projects specifically to provide capital, vehicles and other assistance to entrepreneurs. Third, the Mozambique National Bank was encouraged to make substantial loans for private commerce. These opportunities tied in well with the return of governmental control to the district centres within which the Zambezian *patroes* have always found their strength. Sufficient money was already being made in Zambezia by 1991 to reduce the dependence on these essentially fragile external inputs.

Between January and June 1990 the number of shops in Milange increased from two (CCM, 1990a) to eleven (SCF-UK, 1990a), and by late 1991 there were two dozen traders with authorization from the Governor of Zambezia to trade in Milange, and one with local authorization, though only half of those actually resided in Milange (interview, Ministry of Commerce). Many of these traders had been among the 110 that were licensed prior to the war, though the bulk of those of Asian descent had come in from Tete and Quelimane. In 1991 Asian traders were already the most powerful, one of them monopolizing wholesaling, and they faced rising resentment.[13] Access to capital and cash-flow problems, worsened by the failure of the bank to open in the town, were major constraints on business.

Supplies of goods for Milange come very long distances from Beira (via Zimbabwe, Tete and Malawi), Tete (via Malawi) or direct from Malawi itself. Clothing and basic consumer goods (e.g. cooking utensils, cigarettes and soap) were the principal items sold, as well as fish, salt, biscuits and cooking oil, although by late 1991 it was even possible to buy a television in Milange. In 1991 commerce in Milange relied on the (informal) export trade, particularly of clothing, which generated the Malawian currency with which to import local requirements such as beer, plastic shoes, sugar and rice. Despite this dependence upon cross-border trade there are no licences for export in Milange.

In Milange, as elsewhere in Zambezia, there is considerable uncertainty about the legal rights to commercial properties. The bulk of property takeovers by the government following independence were not secured in law. Most allocations to traders after the recapture of Milange in 1988 have been on a somewhat ad hoc basis, and tenure over certain

---

[13] In Milange there were, for example, claims that bribes from the Indian traders were responsible for the failure of Renamo to sack the town in late 1989 to early 1990, but this does seem unlikely.

properties is hotly disputed. One major issue is the degree to which local businessmen will have prime rights relative to the often more influential external associations rooted in Quelimane. This constrains their reconstruction efforts, and leads them to seek assurances of state commitment to their rights. There is considerable nascent interest in small-scale commercial farming in Milange, although by late 1991 there were only five formal applications. Actual operations were limited whilst the war continued. Although there are mechanisms to protect peasant land rights some competition for prime sites will be inevitable.

The small market operating in Milange traded mostly in locally produced fresh foods (such as bananas and boiled maize) and goods brought from Malawi (such as bread, matches, soap and especially dried fish). It grew rapidly from around ten stalls/day in 1989 to 35 in early 1991 and then stabilized. Traders in the open market were mostly young and of peasant origin and unable to raise loans. Many traders relied on the market as their main source of income, rather than combining it with such things as farming. Other forms of unlicensed commerce (all of which, like market trading, still pay taxes) were itinerant trade, petty store owning, and middlemen who usually traded (borrowed) goods for agricultural surpluses. Craft production such as carpentry, basketry, and tin smithing was also important.

The cumulative effect of all this commercial activity was to locate the motor of economic development away from the relief programme and the state, although it was initially these agencies and the state that provided commerce with the opportunity to expand. The rise of the market also reinvigorated the enthusiasm of Milange's population to become once more a cash-cropping peasantry; it may even have indirectly encouraged the increasing level of flight from the Renamo-controlled hinterland into Malawi. Whilst the relief programmes played an important role in creating the context for this trade, and sustaining a population upon which it could be based, it was above all the military security of Milange, and its border location, that initially enabled the rise of commerce, just as these same two factors have most enabled the return of so many of the refugees. Peace can provide both the conditions for the return of the refugees and the opportunity for a surge in purchasing power through peasant cash-cropping and commercial agricultural expansion to generate a local economic boom based on trading. To some extent, therefore, much of the activity of the business community prior to peace was just manoeuvring to obtain as good a position as possible in terms of premises and status; this was underlined by the lack of economic expansion between late 1991 and the coming of peace in October 1992.

This account demonstrates how by 1991 Milange town became an island of economic activity and commercial prosperity, surrounded beyond the garrison by an impoverished peasantry tied into a tribute system to support the Renamo war economy, with limited access to consumer goods through border markets. An intriguing feature of the economy of Milange is the historical changes over the last decade. Renamo fed off the fat – and later the carcass – of the state enterprises and the towns in its advance of 1982–86, and then focussed its full logistic requirements on the peasant tribute economy. But between 1988 and 1991 the under-supplied Frelimo military had to rely in part on scraping what little remained in the countryside they struggled to recapture (by stealing from the people they 'recuperated' from Renamo) as well as relying to an extent upon taxing relief aid in the government-held areas. Yet as the commercial economy grew in Milange in 1991 it was the business community who came to see it as their own obligation to support the government military, so as to enable them to realize their investments. Looking to the future in an abstract way, only a sustained economic advance may be enough to prevent a continuation – even elaboration – of a situation of a protected economy that purchases its security in islands and corridors, and an impoverished rural peasant economy preyed upon by 'self-help' military groups. And a sustained economic advance might require the breaking of the system of dominance by the commercial elite to release peasant purchasing power and cash-cropping potential, rather than see a return to forced labour and extortion for which Zambezia is historically so famous.

The Impact of Repatriation Planning & Programmes for Milange Refugees

This section looks at the planning and programmes of repatriation assistance to the refugees of Milange in the 1986–91 period, in the regional and national context. The argument traces the changing course of policies and programmes since the main refugee influx to Malawi in 1986, exploring the interaction between institutional requirements at local and national level on the one hand, and local realities on the other.

Repatriation Planning & Local Realities, 1988–91

Following the stabilization of government control of Milange town in mid-1988 the government and agencies undertook an exploration of possible repatriation measures. On the face of it this appeared highly logical. The refugees concerned had fled Mozambique because of their Frelimo affiliation, and Frelimo had now returned to Milange. The refugees were residing in crowded and difficult conditions a mere 5 kilometres from the government-controlled Milange town. The shift of relief provision and support services from Malawi to Mozambique could both help to rebuild Milange and reduce the pressures upon Malawi. Finally, the Frelimo-affiliated refugees had long articulated anxieties about their residence in Malawian camps and continually stated their desire to return. Many had indeed made the arduous journey to government-run camps in the province of Tete (see below); therefore they would surely welcome the chance to return to Milange. This section examines the kinds of provisions that agencies sought to make for this repatriation, and why such planning ultimately proved to have little impact on return movements.

Discussion concerning the return of the existing refugees immediately followed Frelimo's recapture of Milange. The first United Nations mission to Milange was undertaken by the World Food Programme on 15 July 1988, and the results communicated to Maputo, Blantyre (Malawi) and Quelimane (the capital of Zambezia). It included the Mozambique consulate, and encountered the gifted Military Administrator for Civilian Affairs, Capt. Kantumbianga, in Milange. The mission reported that 'consolidation of civil administration includes return of refugees from Mulanje area if security can be maintained', adding that the 'first returnee groups' should be the 'original land holders from Milanje [Milange]' (WFP, 1988a). In reference to the new refugee vintage who had fled the Frelimo advance, the report observed that

> Later integration of newcomer refugees in Mulanje since 2nd June pending rehabilitation of area by above group and obviously of political integration of so-called Renamo sympathisers (WFP, 1988a).

On the subject of repatriation the report concluded that the 'return of all refugees will need international assistance'. In practice, however, the pressing needs in Milange to supply the internally displaced and rebuild the most basic infrastructures of the administration took precedence over any assistance to return movements. This basic rehabilitation proved difficult to implement (and above all slow), although it proceeded faster than in most of the other small towns of Zambezia.

Even up to a year after reoccupation official repatriations to Milange were not undertaken because of the limited capacity of the authorities in Mozambique to absorb the

numbers involved. Two delegations of international relief officials and provincial government authorities to Milange town in February and July 1989 reported that as many as
22,000 to 25,000 refugees in Muloza had requested the district authorities for their immediate return but that this was 'indefinitely postponed' by the local authorities until 'regular
food supply and agricultural inputs could be guaranteed' (SCF-UK, 1989a; UNSCERO,
1989). At this time official efforts focussed upon simply meeting the needs of the existing
self-repatriates and displaced people in the town, and in the repatriation of several hundred
Milange residents who had earlier been transferred from the Malawi camps to Benga in
Tete (see below).

By the end of 1989 there was widespread recognition amongst the relief agencies gained
during field visits that the refugees had more complex attitudes towards repatriation that
were important and required a changed approach to planning. The Christian Council of
Malawi (CCM), for example, reported in December 1989 that 'naturally we try to encourage more to return home from the Malawi side but they prefer to wait until their own
home villages are liberated and safe' (CCM, 1989) and again in January 1990 'the 30,000
people at Muloza are still reluctant to return. Not until their own former villages are safe,
they say' (CCM, 1990b). UNHCR also briefed a Mozambique-based agency at the time
that the Muloza refugees 'were reluctant to go back to Milange town – they very much
want to go to their real homes', according to notes on their file for October 1989. It
appears that subtle changes in refugee attitudes had occurred during the year after reoccupation of Milange town, whereby refugees shifted from expressing an *en bloc* attitude
that they all should return as soon as possible to a diversity of views. One of the factors
which may have shaped this change was the greater security they now felt in the camps,
with Malawian official policy shifting considerably towards a pro-Frelimo stance during
1989. Furthermore, with the presence of Frelimo forces at the border post less than a kilo-
metre from the camp, they could easily obtain protection should they need it. Also
important, no doubt, was the requirement to shift from an abstract question of return to
making a concrete decision concerning whether to relocate to camps in Milange rather than
actual home villages in a situation where relief and economic wherewithal in Mozambique
were even more constrained than in Malawi. Security also continued to be an issue, with
regular Renamo attacks on the town, and rumours of major assaults being imminent.
Refugees were certainly prepared to take risks, but most took the security issue very
seriously.

Despite the changing attitudes of the refugees towards return the policy thrusts of the
relief agencies were increasingly towards repatriation as the objective. The Tripartite Commission (UNHCR, and the governments of Malawi and Mozambique) had agreed as early
as April 1989 on key strategies for the implementation of the December 1988 agreement.
These were to include the opening of three further transit points for repatriation in addition to that of Zobue, including the Mulanje–Milange border post. The commission, also
agreed to hold meetings to 'publicise the possibilities for repatriation in the refugee camps
and hosting areas with emphasis being laid on the voluntary nature of the programme'
(Tripartite Commission, 1989: 5). Meanwhile one of the stated objectives for the Christian
Council of Malawi's expanding Milange rehabilitation programme at this time was to
'increase the desirability of repatriation' from Malawi (CCM, 1989). The UNHCR and
its Mozambique counterpart, NARML, were clearly becoming obliged to take some
action on repatriation. Thus in June 1990 it is reported that they were now proposing to
bring 10,000 refugees to Milange (having initially proposed double that number), though
'the *administrator* had said that the infrastructure did not exist for that size of influx'. The
relief official reporting this proposal strongly supported this stance by the Milange local

government against the wider institutional pressures for action on repatriation. He reflected further:

> UNHCR/NARML have been trying to repatriate large numbers there since the place was liberated some two years ago . . . I have grave doubts about the possibility of the local structures coping with such a rapid increase, and the *Administrador* himself mentions that food supplies will have to be much better organised than at present. I hope for the sake of the individuals involved that this sort of mass movement doesn't occur (Aid Agency Memo, 1990).

During research visits to Milange in 1991 the administrator was loath to report directly misgivings about receiving returnees, perhaps because it is an important national priority. He would emphasize, however, the need to combine a return movement with prior investment in adequate infrastructure. In March 1991 he was hoping for the development of the Cunha site for UNHCR's still mooted 10,000 returnees, but this required, amongst other things, adequate provision of food, agricultural inputs and a new health centre. The Milange authorities have been using, in recent years, the working figure of 50,000 as the number of returnees they may anticipate from Malawi, a figure which they well appreciated was more than double the number of people Milange was precariously supporting even in 1991. The interaction between the UNHCR and the Milange local authorities also indicates another structural problem in contemporary repatriation programmes in Africa and elsewhere. This is that repatriation is nowadays occuring in situations of shattered infrastructure and economy where other agencies – and not the UNHCR – are the dominant external influences on rehabilitation (and, furthermore, as has been shown above, their effects may also be secondary to those of commerce). Thus the UNHCR has to handle institutional pressures for repatriation without access to the policy instruments (let alone resources) with which to create the conditions that can make it possible.

It is unclear whether the lack of local preparedness for the large-scale returns planned by the UNHCR in 1988–90 was actually responsible for the abandonment of these proposals, or whether other factors were at work. Events in mid-1989 for which documentation exists, however, suggest that overarching funding problems were more likely to have been responsible for protecting the refugees than the common sense of the institutions responsible. Essentially the sequence of events was as follows. Following a field trip to Milange with the responsible government officials SCF-UK was concerned about a possible '8,000 refugees [self-] returning to Milange from Malawi' in a situation of 'lack of tools and seeds and [the] planting season in two months'. The agency then pressed UNHCR and WFP in Malawi and Maputo for assistance (SCF-UK, 1989a). One month later, UNHCR responded that 'in view of our detailed financial situation and on-going influx of returnees to Tete and Manica Province which is considerably higher than originally expected, the assistance to returnees in Milanje [Milange] could be provided by UNHCR and SCF (UK) on 50 per cent basis mainly for sectors such as domestic needs and agriculture' (UNHCR-Maputo, 1989). It was thus under a reduced and joint programme that seeds, tools and the other items were obtained from Zimbabwe and Malawi and brought in later that year to assist both self-returnees and internally displaced persons, without any attempt to move more people back. The UNHCR's Zambezia Assistance Programme plan for May 1989 to April 1990 indicates that at this time it was essentially applying for the standard domestic items and agricultural inputs that were being provided to all recent arrivals in northern Mozambique whether self-repatriates or internally displaced persons, alongside the important inputs of grinding mills, warehouses, tents and vehicles for which there was rarely sufficient money available. It is not known what proportion of the $US341,000 requested in the plan was actually secured, but it was low. The United States

Government publicly reported that it was not prepared to contribute to these UNHCR plans 'because at present the security situation within Mozambique is not judged adequate to permit a safe and orderly return of significant numbers of the refugees' (United States Government Department of State, 1988: 2).

The progress of the Tripartite Commission for Repatriation in 1989 resulted in 'concerted visits to refugee camps in Malawi to encourage the refugees to return voluntarily to safe areas in Mozambique' (CCM, 1989) precisely at the time when their own attitudes towards returning were changing. A relief official who attended several of these meetings in Mulanje in 1989 commented that refugees were surprisingly vocal in their challenge to the visiting officials concerning the nature of 'voluntariness', 'safety' and its 'guarantee' back in Mozambique, despite the fact that officials of both countries strongly argued the case that it was time to return and that they could not be hosted permanently by Malawi. In the Chiringa camp, for example, he reported that new arrivals fleeing the Renamo-held zone after about five years of occupation strongly contested the official description of the situation in Mozambique as being safe. In early 1990 new influxes due to fighting in the border areas meant that the refugees were described as 'apprehensive' about any mention of return, though the CCM noted that Milange was one of the three areas of Mozambique that the government had declared as 'free zones' (CCM, 1990b). In such meetings in other parts of Malawi – and quite likely also in Mulanje – refugees were reported to regularly ask whether they would be allowed to return to their own home areas or to other relief camps.

The deliberations of the Tripartite Commission and the meetings that it organized with the refugees can be argued to have served several useful purposes concerning interstate relations and communication with the refugees themselves. However, they did not play much role in shaping the actual movements of people back to Mozambique or their assistance on return. The Christian Council of Malawi, for example, pointed to the contrast between official repatriation arrangements for Milange and the reality on the ground that

> officially refugees are not going through the border posts from Muloza refugee camp in Malawi. Those that go just walk across the Malawi–Mozambique border . . . we can say that returnees are using individual means to go into Mozambique. As such there is no accurate record of the returnees (CCM, 1990a).

According to an interview with the Director of NARML, Sr Fazenda, the 'spontaneous movement and voluntary return of populations' that was occurring was 'owing to financial problems with which the UNHCR is struggling' (*Noticias*, 1991). The elaborate plans for individual forms were never to be. Each returnee was supposed to sign 'to verify the voluntary nature of the repatriation', and then the forms, 'subject to the authentication by the Embassy of the People's Republic of Mozambique in Malawi', were to 'serve as a travel and identity document', having been distributed in seven copies to the United Nations and appropriate government units each side of the border (UNHCR-Blantyre, 1989). Indeed, reflecting on the scenario of a highly planned return in a situation of limited resources, the Director of NARML concluded that the approach had actually

> precluded effective control of the people returning to the country, 'because the program established by the UNHCR stipulated that the return of refugees was to be official and organised in nature' (*Noticias*, 1991).

By way of a conclusion for this part of the section, it is worth reviewing the impact of official repatriation planning and returnee programmes in Milange. Between 1988 and 1991 not one single refugee 'officially repatriated' from Malawi to Milange, despite all the institutional activity of meetings, delegations, camp tours and elaborate planning.

Furthermore, it is still unclear whether the programmes in Malawi to encourage repatriation influenced the numbers who actually self-returned. Whilst the strengthened economic situation of Milange town did in part enable return (and this was only partly the result of relief and rehabilitation programmes), the greatest factor promoting return to Milange was the government's ability to secure an increasing security radius for the town against Renamo attacks and to demonstrate itself likely to dominate Milange militarily in the foreseeable future. Even if the official repatriation programmes are described as having been 'facilitatory' in effect rather than actually directly achieving repatriation, it is difficult to argue that they have made much distinct impact. The self-repatriated refugees received assistance alongside the locally recuperated population, and largely in ways decided within Mozambique by the DPCCN, local government and the relief agency assigned to Milange by the provincial authorities, SCF-UK. The local authorities were (fortunately) able to prioritize the rehabilitation and development of Milange as a whole, rather than focus upon the relief and integration of returnees. As a function of its conceptual and managerial weakness, aid provided for the returnees by UNHCR essentially acted as a supplement to these existing programmes, as well as a few vehicles and staff to ensure their more effective implementation, rather than a discrete element with its own rationale. Though this was a more appropriate and effective contribution by UNHCR than the role it was playing on the official stage at the time of carrying out 'organized repatriation', what is important here is the lesson that planning for repatriation had no relevance in practice to the refugees and repatriates concerned.

The impact of rehabilitation programmes in Milange itself on repatriation appears to have been greater than that of formal repatriation programmes. As described above the rehabilitation activities played complex yet overall stimulatory roles in rebuilding the economy of the government-held areas, supporting people in need in these areas, and ultimately increasing government's military capacity to defend them against Renamo. Yet the rehabilitation programmes also played a wider socio-political and psycho-social role. This is how Alistair Hallam, one of the SCF programme managers (1988–90) perceived their impact in Milange:

> These [rehabilitation] inputs sent a strong message that the government did not expect to relinquish the district. This helped create a dynamic where refugees came back 'to have a look', and possibly encouraged some to stay. The good water supply and the mill were also very attractive elements of the programme. As more people returned more would become convinced that a return was viable, and it would become self-perpetuating. So we may not have had a direct influence on repatriations, but [we] must certainly have played a fairly major role purely in our presence and the messages this sent to the refugees in Malawi (personal communication, 1992).

Hallam did not consider this facilitating role as unambiguous, however. Acutely aware that SCF's Milange programme was generated and funded out of a general commitment to Mozambique and with little knowledge of the objective security situation in the districts they were working in, he was later to ask:

> Whether we *should* have taken on such a role at that particular time is a valid debating point, given the fragility of the local government at the time. It was not sure that the district could be defended, or that food or clothing could get through (personal communication, emphasis in the original, 1992).

Whatever the moral dilemmas, the rehabilitation role proved a greater contribution to successful return during the conflict than any amount of abstract planning of the relocation of refugees through formal repatriation instruments. It is also certain that the post-war return movements will rely more on the infrastructural and economic capacity established in Milange during the war, than on any new formal repatriation programme out of Malawi.

Post-War Repatriation Planning

The chapter now shifts to debate concerning the preparation of general repatriation plans and programmes for the anticipated post-war period. Due to the starting of the 'peace process' between Renamo and Frelimo in Rome in 1990, there was a considerable expansion in interest in repatriation not only by the UNHCR, but also amongst the non-governmental agencies working with Mozambicans in Malawi, including the Malawian agencies. A number of them either began, or greatly strengthened, cross-border programmes at this time, with different NGOs gaining *de facto* control in different border areas of Mozambique. It appeared that the NGOs might play a greater role in future repatriation exercises than the UNHCR because they were proving more capable of raising funds, designing programmes that appeared implementable to donors, and were in some cases keen to maintain their institutional interests with their programmes subsequent to peace, in that they would need to follow their beneficiaries to maintain their existing staff and programmes. In the case of Milange district, the obvious agency to take up the baton was the Christian Council of Malawi, which as explained above had been operating there since 1988, although by 1990–91 their cross-border programmes were on a small scale relative to developments within the district.

As early as 1989 the CCM started preparing preliminary plans for a programme of official repatriation under the Tripartite Commission framework across the Milange border, programmes that it wished to co-ordinate with the Christian Council of Mozambique with funding from the World Council of Churches and international church bodies (CCM, 1989). Planning was not detailed or well-advanced, however, and they noted, for example, 'at this stage we do not know what size such a programme might be, so the budget figures are nominal only' (CCM, 1989). Typically for such 'indigenous' non-governmental agencies, debate concerning these plans paid considerable attention to the local conditions in Milange and the attitudes of the refugees themselves. At the symposium in which this paper was first presented, Christian Council of Malawi delegates, for example, made interventions on the importance of listening to refugees and 'try[ing] to understand their expressed needs and intentions rather than trying to fit them into conceived plans'. They also stressed that the refugees' priorities were to return to their original villages, and that their principal concerns were likely to continue to be security-related. The CCM also emphasized the importance of working with refugees' own social networks from the camps for the process of rebuilding society through repatriation, notably the many small churches. Subsequent to the UNRISD Harare symposium, CCM hoped to further their planning with the Christian Council of Mozambique and their regional body on the basis of such principles, insights from the Harare symposium, and more fieldwork in the camps to identify modalities, though it is unclear how far this work proceeded. In fact documents stressing a similar approach were being prepared by other Christian organizations in the region, for example by Fr. Timmermans of the regional Catholic organization IMBISA, Christian Care in Zimbabwe, and also by Christian Aid in London. The Christian Council of Mozambique conceived of playing a central role in securing peace and reconciliation in the country, in addition to simply helping people physically return to their home areas (Muth, 1992). This refugee-centred and socially aware approach stood in sharp contrast to the concurrent preparations of other institutions, which will now be examined.

In order to contextualize the role of the UNHCR it is first necessary to identify that other major international institutions declared pòst-peace 'repatriation' as a central issue for Mozambique:

> such a mass return will become a major – perhaps *the* major – developmental issue, as Mozambique faces the enormous costs, in terms of both financial and human resources, involved in mass resettlement and productive reintegration of at least one quarter of the Mozambican population (World Bank, 1990a: 168–9).

In the face of such wide institutional interest, the UNHCR therefore needed to prepare a strategy indicating its jurisdiction and response. The UNHCR 'Emergency Contingency Plan' (which over time evolved into a somewhat modified 'Operations Plan') anticipated a future peace agreement would mean a 'complete or substantial degree of ceasefire' and thus provoke 'a massive influx of returnees back into Mozambique' of a voluntary nature, which could occur 'at any given moment' as a result of negotiations (UNHCR-Geneva, 1989: 1), leading to crisis as the local authorities would find themselves unprepared to cope with such numbers. According to this model, therefore, contingency planning for a short and massive operation was essential. Yet, despite apparent awareness that people would themselves start to move, the plan designated the physical transportation of people as the centrepiece. The point was to channel the million or so refugees who would leave their camps en masse immediately there was a cease-fire through just eighteen official transit/reception centres where they would be processed and assisted. The importance of these transit and reception centres in UNHCR's thinking is indicated by the fact that two-thirds of the US$40 million budget was to be allocated to this element of the programme (UNHCR-Geneva, 1989: 7). In all but one of these sites the contingency plan anticipated that the whole return movement through the transit centres would be complete within two months – and often in only a matter of days. It can be noted that international agency staff in Malawi reported that it was almost impossible to persuade the UNHCR official sent to draw up the repatriation plan to modify the approach in his blueprint from Geneva in the light of local conditions. Only under great pressure did he even agree to undertake some limited cross-border visits.

Thus the reasons for the structure of the plan need to be sought in the pressures and conceptions of Geneva and international fora, and not the realities of the Malawi–Mozambique border situation. It was by means of the rapid progress of returnees through the transit camps that the UNHCR involvement could be completed within a year as a celebratory contribution to political reconciliation – a much needed success story for a beleaguered institution under pressure to reduce the number of refugees. Furthermore, such rapid and complete movement was also needed to protect UNHCR from further public relations disasters. Their recent African experience was often of partial repatriation in a circumstance of institutional weakness, political uncertainty, and economic crisis. Indeed, during 1989, UNHCR officials sent from head office to the Malawi–Mozambique border were already warning of the dangers of what they called the 'Ethiopia/Somalian syndrome' emerging when there was large-scale repatriation, that is, the situation of double registration of people living on both sides of a border and moving backwards and forwards to survive on a whole network of assistance (UNHCR-TSS, 1989a: 3) and, indeed, in another report, alleging that some people were already doing this and buying cards from people returning to Mozambique to draw their rations (UNHCR-TSS, 1989b: 9). The planning for a mass, highly controlled movement in Mozambique is probably therefore also a reaction to a fear of such a protracted situation, with its high political and financial costs for the organization. It is even stressed on the very first page of

UNHCR's 1990 Appeal that both the April 1989 and October 1989 meetings of the Tripartite Repatriation Commission with Malawi discussed as a priority 'the retrieval of ration cards from returnees to facilitate relief operations on both sides of the border' (UNHCR-Geneva, 1990: 1). Thus a speedy and closely managed engagement was partly required to prevent refugees' own strategies from 'subverting' the operation. For example, so as to prevent people staying longer than the planned 24 hours in the reception centres, or returning for a second round of agricultural inputs, or suchlike, these camps would have 'family tents positioned in a rowlike manner to allow adequate control of arrivals and easy access of transport equipment' (UNHCR-Geneva, 1989: 7).

In fact, local pressures for the UNHCR to achieve repatriation have also gathered strength as Malawian villagers – initially willing to provide asylum – have found the growing numbers and the unending natural resource pressures increasingly too much to bear (Long et al., 1990: 12–13). The Malawi Government has presented this to its international donors in terms of pressures for repatriation. For example Malawi's Minister of Health informed the head of UNHCR during her visit in February 1992 that

> we must seize every opportunity for voluntary repatriation. This is most urgent because we do not want to have to turn back these refugees as is happening in other countries. But we shall be abusing the good nature of Malawian villages if we do not actively seek and implement voluntary repatriation now.
>
> You are aware that we discussed this issue in great detail at the meeting of the Tripartite Commission on voluntary repatriation in Maputo early this month. We appreciate the concern for security of the returning Mozambicans, we agree that the return must be voluntary (Ntaba, 1992).

The severity of the drought (especially in the southern region), and internal pressure for political change have further focussed attention on the refugee issue. Malawi has argued that without the reinstatement of developmental aid (that has been cut off by donors on the grounds of human rights abuses) it is not in a position to maintain the country's infrastructure and economy sufficiently to enable an increasing number of refugees to be catered for. Furthermore, the government has argued for increasing drought assistance for Malawians on the grounds that this will reduce resentment of the refugees and hence reduce the pressure for their repatriation. During 1992 the Mozambican authorities were thus obliged to identify areas of northern Mozambique to receive returnee populations even whilst the war continued, though such return movements never occurred before the peace agreement, due to the usual complications and inefficiencies.

The link between repatriation and development in the UNHCR's initial planning for Mozambique was limited to three points. First there was the possibility of the movement of population 'to their areas of origin or determined areas where they will be settled' (UNHCR-Geneva, 1989: 9),[14] with, second, the reception centres acting as 'the focal points or the nuclei for the reception intergration [sic] and further development of the returnee populations' (UNHCR-Geneva, 1989: 3). Thirdly it was envisaged that the UNHCR would, 'in collaboration with other agencies . . . assist in the creation of conditions to enable the returnees to initiate self sustaining activities' (UNHCR-Geneva, 1989: 2). However, UNHCR's role in the latter would be limited to the providing of

[14] UNHCR's repatriation mandate has traditionally been framed upon the right to go to one's home area or a place of choice, though as is indicated in this quote the HCR was not considering this essential in the Mozambican case. Documents from this 1989–90 period all avoid clear statements on this issue. The World Bank (1990a), for example, devotes thirteen pages to planning population distribution by addressing displacement and resettlement processes without explicitly dealing with policy regarding freedom of movement and settlement, except as regards peri-urban residents.

seeds, 'assorted agricultural hand tools' and 'selected household items such as buckets, blankets and cooking sets . . . to each head of family prior to departure' from the transit centres, assistance which would comprise one-third of the total repatriation budget (UNHCR-Geneva, 1989: 9). The exact manner in which reception centres would become part of longer term institutional development is not specified in these plans. The key interventions of a developmental kind at these centres (such as service provision), or in the surrounding rural areas concerned (such as roads), would clearly have to come from other activities outside this UNHCR plan. The closing section of the UNHCR plan recognized, however, that the success of the whole repatriation exercise would ultimately 'depend a great deal on how the districts would have been prepared to receive the additional popula-tion' (UNHCR-Geneva, 1989: 10), there being, unfortunately, no time or budget allo-cated for this in the 'emergency' framework of this plan between the signing of the cease-fire and repatriation commencement. The subsequent 'Operations Plan' sought to address this by a 'gradual and incremental' phasing-up of the programme with the volun-tary movement of 100,000 persons (three-quarters of whom were apparently expected to self-relocate) to new safe areas through new exit–entry points, prior to any peace agree-ment (UNHCR-Maputo, 1991: 3).

The UNHCR also came to recognize that integration of assistance to the repatriated refugee programmes with those for the more numerous internally displaced was essential in a situation where 'the extent to which the UNHCR mandate can be stretched [to the internally displaced] will . . . be only a partial solution' (UNHCR-Geneva, 1989: 10), so that, in their view, 'parallel planning' should occur for the internally displaced. This issue draws attention to the severity of the mandate constraints on UNHCR for situations like the one in Mozambique where both internally displaced and refugees are created by the same processes, and where 'development' is necessarily part of repatriation. This means in fact that within Mozambique many instititions have argued that returnee assistance should be co-ordinated within district and provincial rehabilitation and development planning under DPCCN/local government and line ministries, rather than vice versa. Experience from other African situations in this volume and recent activities like Operation Salaam for Afghanistan further encouraged the view that classic repatriation programmes do not contain the policy instruments that can significantly enhance returnees' livelihoods or national development. The World Bank stated this as follows at the Paris Consultative Group Meeting in December 1990:

> An end to the war will present a tremendous challenge to the Government to resettle several million displaced persons, refugees returning from abroad and ex-military personnel, and to pro-vide these groups with access to basic services and factors of production to enable them to resume economically productive lives. It will be essential that these problems are tackled through the effective implementation of a comprehensive development strategy focused on poverty reduction and rural rehabilitation, and not through special programs and initiatives (World Bank, 1990b: 4).

The UNHCR contingency plan for Mozambique was never to come to fruition, how-ever, the response of donors being such that it was never even formally presented for fund-ing. Even the US$6 million requested for ongoing repatriation and resettlement of 100,000 in the 1989–90 Emergency Appeal was not forthcoming, and the programme limped by with just US$1.5 million (*Mozambiquefile*, 1990b), providing reduced assistance to a smaller number of returnees. The request for US$7.7 million for 1991 'to ensure the availability of food and relief items, provide for their distribution, and guarantee the operations of UNHCR/NARML in the key provinces' was better received, obtaining about two-thirds of what was requested (Government of Mozambique, 1991: 53); but this was just a holding operation 'until conditions exist . . . for large-scale repatriation', which would require major resources from a still unfunded contingency plan (Government of Mozambique, 1990: 34–5). To seek to offset this persistent problem for 1992–93, the UNHCR sought a contingency stock from the WFP to feed 10,000 returnees for approximately three months (Government of Mozambique, 1991: 49).

The failure to raise funds for the general UNHCR contingency plan partly reflected the general constraints on forward planning in the disaster relief system, but it was also due to a diversity of views on the repatriation process within the donor and agency community in Mozambique.[15] Some suspected that peace negotiations would be a very slow process, and/or that continued banditry and economic collapse after a formal settlement would inevitably slow any return migration. Others were critical of the design of UNHCR's repatriation plan, particularly the commitment to an immediate physical relocation of the population into transit centres inside Mozambique, since they believed refugees could walk home whenever they wanted, and that if they were carried they would often be taken to places where the logistical capacity to sustain them would be lacking.[16] During late 1990, an informal group of around eight international agencies operating in Mozambique met in Maputo to review how they might respond to a demand for repatriation with the achievement of peace (the Mozambique Government was not involved in these discussions). The discussions of this committee played an important role in the generation of a new agency agenda for repatriation, and the reasons for this will now be elaborated.

The agency working group realized that the notion of a 'returnee emergency' was predicated on the untested assumption that the signing of a peace treaty would result in immediate mass repatriation. Thus they commissioned, in October–November 1990, a short study visit to refugee camps in neighbouring countries to investigate what the likely pattern of return would be, and how information might be provided to the refugees to prevent a massive influx before the situation inside Mozambique was deemed ready to receive them. This study reported that the refugees would not move quickly and en masse after a peace agreement, but would, in time, send members of families and social networks home to sort out whether life could be sustained, bringing back the rest of the family only when appropriate. Refugees expected to organize their own return movements mostly on foot. Thus the return would clearly be merely an acceleration of the pattern during the war, as has been described for Milange in this chapter, and would not be the sudden crisis envisaged by the original emergency plan. The team also concluded that the best way to communicate with the refugees would be through a combination of mass meetings, and the distribution of leaflets and posters to secure the message in writing. It was felt essential to communicate the limited institutional capacity of the repatriation programme directly to the refugees to supplement their own investigation and decision-making process.

During 1991 other United Nations agencies, the bilateral donors and the non-governmental agencies mounted sustained criticism of the successive drafts of the UNHCR plan in Mozambique on the grounds that the capacity to transport and process the

[15] A senior UNHCR official responded to the argument that the UNHCR plan was not funded because donor and agency staff considered it inappropriate, by stating that the Mozambique plan was little different in content, style or amount of detail from others that had been funded immediately for more geo-politically important parts of the world.

[16] One agency official interviewed was particularly emphatic on this point, alleging that the motivation behind the plan was to appear to be creating solutions in international circles, when the situation for the returnees on the ground would obviously be desperate.

returnees would not be available, and anyway the whole notion of transit centres lacked purpose. Originally eighteen reception centres were designated to receive the one million or so refugees from the six countries, process them during a 24-hour period, and send them on to their areas of settlement with an aid package (UNHCR-Geneva, 1989: 2–3). The pressure upon these few centres is revealed by the assumption that as many as 1,000 to 2,500 people would be transported through them per day (UNHCR-Geneva, 1989: 8). This was simply inconceivable under Mozambican conditions. Whilst it was anticipated 'that a certain number of the returnees will return spontaneously . . . it is expected that nearly all will [still] pass through the transit facilities prior to taking off on their own' (UNHCR-Geneva, 1989: 3), so that even those not transported would still have to be administered. Handling populations of this size would require unfeasibly rapid resolution of existing problems such as in water supplies at some of the centres (Government of Mozambique, 1990: 34), whose long-term usefulness was in doubt.

This criticism of the notion of creating infrastructure merely for transit facilities, which would anyway never be able to operate as quickly as planned for, led to a new concept in the final Operations Plan. Instead of refugees residing in the camps only for a single day before returning home, it was now reported that:

> It is expected that as conditions permit in Mozambique, returnees would proceed eventually to accommodation centres and districts of origin. Until that is possible, these 28 locations will provide medium-term integration for returnees (UNHCR-Maputo, 1991: 12).

These statements about holding refugees in centres for long periods resonated with the experience of settlements in the earlier wave of repatriation, which by this time was generally perceived negatively by the authorities and donors, on the grounds that it contributed solely to institutional dependence and neither to economic development nor to refugee well-being. Much repeated allegations by the representative of a major bilateral during the discussion meetings that such programmes would thus be acts of 'genocide' miss the point, however, in that they were essentially unimplementable, because insufficient returning refugees would even reach the sites to suffer from the fact that they would not be adequately supplied in the transit centres. The debate in Maputo, and the general expression of loss of confidence in the UNHCR plan by the major agencies in Mozambique, meant the Maputo office abandoned the plan, as its officials strenuously insisted in all encounters with other agencies and donors in late 1991. For 1992–93 it was officially stated that UNHCR had

> decided to consider [transit centres] only when returnees are obliged to wait in such centres for transport arrangements to move further inland. As a general policy, returnees will be encouraged to move straight to their places of origin or to areas where the Government will allow them to settle (Government of Mozambique, 1991: 51).

During the peace negotiations it became clear that the holding of elections in the post-war period would mean that the control of the locations of refugee return would have great political significance. The agreement signed between the ICRC/Red Crescent and Renamo and the government on 1 December 1990 explicitly 'reaffirmed that Mozambican civilians may move freely either from one zone to another within the country or from neighbouring countries to their places of origin, wherever they may be' (ICRC, 1990). In reference to the closing statement 'to their places of origin', it is understood – though not independently confirmed – that Renamo insisted that people be allowed to choose where they go, and stated that they would still consider camps and managed villages for repatriates as legitimate targets, presumably since such populations would be under

Frelimo and not their own control. This is then a further thorny problem awaiting technical planners, especially as the peace agreement explicitly provides Renamo with administrative rights in 'their' areas.

So as to resolve contradictions between the treatment of internally and externally displaced people, the Government of Mozambique and the United Nations agencies resolved in 1991 that during 1992–93 the UNHCR would play a role with returnees only for the first three months (previously it had been eighteen months: Polosa, 1991: 1) following their return before handing over responsibility to the local government and relief authorities.[17] Furthermore, 'all rations for the returnees and internally displaced persons shall be the same, both in quantity and contents' (Government of Mozambique, 1991: 48–9), although they would still be less than what is provided to the refugees when they are in Malawi.

How the populations would actually be transported to and from the reception or transit centres was never adequately resolved by the UNHCR plans. Initial procedures were dropped in later attempts to design logistics (UNHCR-Maputo, 1991), because of such things as the recognition of the need to first repair the roads, and wait for the dry season before such movements could be started. The Operations Plan was still to imply that all returnees would be transported by UNHCR. In fact, although this is not immediately apparent, the Operations Plan only budgeted for one-quarter of the return population to be transported by truck at a cost of c.US$2.5 million. It did this because it found that even moving this small proportion of the refugees would require nine months of continued activity for the two stages of the return operation, even if it were to go smoothly. Indeed, to demonstrate clearly how this 'final draft' of the Operations Plan was never an implementable document one merely has to note that it records in the small print that the internal transport costs and availability of transport should be investigated by the Maputo Office, underlining how the mechanisms for relocating people out of the transit centres had yet to be developed. Finally, this UNHCR plan identified ten further sites in northern Mozambique as 'settlement areas' for the returnees to be transported to and from the transit centres, apparently ignoring agreements that people would be free to return to their villages.

Unlike the UNHCR other assisting agencies concluded several years ago that, like it or not, most refugees will have to make their own way home, and generally on foot (UNDP, 1990). What little transport could be mobilized would have to be reserved for special populations, including those who have been moved far from the border and/or the point of entry into the country of asylum, people whose home districts or destinations inside Mozambique are very far from the border, and categories of people unable to walk long distances, such as the elderly and handicapped. In fact even according to UNHCR estimates, around 80 per cent of the refugees actually come from the border districts (UNHCR-Geneva, 1990: 2), and Malawian statistics do bear this out (UNHCR-Blantyre, 1990).

Alongside the UNHCR operational plan, the other United Nations agencies and the government bodies responsible for programmes of assistance for the returnees from exile and internal displacement designed terms of reference for a post-war planning programme that were presented to donors in Paris. This plan would be founded upon a detailed examination of the sizes of population movements likely on a district by district basis, and the documentation of the available infrastructure and resources in each area affected. This

---

[17] In the context of the 1991 (and 1992) drought, it is, however, essential that some returnees do receive food for longer even than the eighteen months, according to Sr Fazenda of NARML (*Noticias*, 1991).

information would provide a basis for anticipation of the actual rehabilitation and assistance needs, and enable their prioritization, and the plan proposed a participative process that could engage all relevant institutions (though not the returnees) so as to determine what each could contribute to the overall exercise of generating initial support and then sustaining development in the areas in question. Key features of the plan would also include the handling of the requirements of all sectors in the district and provincial planning process, and the integration of the exercise within the national development plan (UNDP, 1990). Furthermore, an important element to this approach is that there is no 'master plan' of priorities; rather 'the government will draw up general guidelines on priorities', according to Sr Baloi, the Vice Minister of Co-operation (*Southern African Economist*, 1991: 5). UNICEF, partly behind the terms of reference for this plan, proposed further studies which would examine the 'plans, priorities and aspirations for the post-war future' of the displaced people themselves as an input to such activities (UNICEF, 1991), indicative of the institutional movement against externally generated, fixed, and unresearched planning.

By 1990–91, long-established government concerns to link the emergency to national development (CENE/DPCCN, 1988) were finding increased expression by United Nations agencies, resulting in moves to make repatriation subordinate to wider programmes. Development planning in Mozambique was calling for the mobilization of counterpart funds from food aid sales for rural development and linking refugee resettlement to the priority district programme of focussed investment (World Bank, 1990a: 173). This kind of investment could also 'lure at least part of the peri-urban settlers back to suitably-endowed rural areas' and provide a motor to national economic development, as well as relieve the burden on the places of war-refuge (World Bank 1990a: 174). Discussion was moving towards linking the returnee programme with the public investment three-year plan, since the latter's focus upon agriculture, rural transport and other infrastructure was highly relevant. Mozambican government institutions such as the new INDER (national institute of rural development) and Acção Social (social action/welfare) also elaborated strategies – alongside the more established ministries – to handle the developmental and other needs of the displaced and returnee populations. Constrained by shortages of funding and personnel outside of donor-supported frameworks, these initiatives nevertheless threaten – in a healthy way – the notion of separate repatriation exercises. Finally, repatriation programmes were further to be brought under the overall relief and rehabilitation programme with its 'developmental' thrust as a result of the United Nations Inter-Agency Mission of October 1991 (headed by Mr Jonah), the United Nations General Assembly resolution of December 1991 calling for more co-ordinated involvement in the UN system, and Mr Priestley's UNDP Mission of February 1992 that reformulated the UNSCERO programme (Emergency Operations Committee, 1992: 2).

These developments between 1989 and 1991 meant that UNHCR thus lost the initiative both to NGOs in the countries of exile and to the major development agencies within Mozambique. Even certain bilaterals such as the Italians were stepping in with World Health Organization encouragement to examine cross-border co-ordinated programmes (WHO, 1990). Whilst the weakness of UNHCR partly reflected the hostility towards UNHCR in general by the Western donors in recent years, it became clear that an important reason was the poor credibility of UNHCR's plans and hence its inability to secure for itself a truly co-ordinating role. This led UNHCR in 1991 to seek new planning initiatives designed to reconsider the actual situation and needs on the ground; it was also essential that such planning reduce the domination of the larger and more powerful external country offices (especially Malawi) over the Mozambique office which would actually receive the returnees. The Norwegian Refugee Council played a central role in pushing for a 'regional plan' founded upon communication and co-operation between agencies and authorities in the different countries (NRC, 1991: 11). Unfortunately, however, their proposed regional conference 'to analyse the complexities of problems inside Mozambique, before the respective offices start drafting their repatriation contingency plan' (Government of Mozambique, 1991: 52) had to be postponed until 1992.

This NRC–UNHCR regional repatriation-planning workshop exercise was conducted in March 1992, and not only resulted in improved relations between UNHCR offices, and between UNHCR, NGOs and governments, but also led to a virtually complete reconceptualization of the relationship between repatriation and development on the one hand, and the manner in which repatriates would be handled in comparison to people who did not leave Mozambique. They proposed, for example, that

> repatriation be coordinated and integrated within a common strategy with national plans for the reintegration of the internally displaced people, and that return be transformed from a burden to a driving power for local and regional development (Emergency Operations Committee, 1992: 4).

Institutional activity was to have two phases, each of which was now conceived not as a logistical exercise of transferring refugees from one camp to another and giving a few hand-outs, but as a contribution to enabling returnees to rebuild their livelihood strategies.

> In the transitory or short-term phase, projects with immediate impact promoting the transition from emergency to development will be crucial. Their implementation should be through the sectoral departments at district level, NGOs and community structures, with support from the United Nations. Projects in this phase should focus upon food, services and income generation.
>
> In the second, or consolidation phase, emphasis should be on strengthening the absorption capacity and economy of the returnee areas and diversifying the economy. This phase should form a bridge with the transitory phase by including longer term and wider regional development, focusing on agriculture, education, health, water supply and income and employment generation' (Emergency Operations Committee, 1992: 4).

In the report to the Mozambique Government's Emergency Operations Committee it was furthermore stressed that, rather than following pre-ordained master plans, programme implementation would be based upon 'interdisciplinary assessment and planning teams' who would study the actual situation on the ground (Emergency Operation Committee, 1992: 5). On the basis of such reinvigorated thinking, UNHCR appeared to confirm the legitimacy of its co-ordination of the actual returning element to the programme, whilst the UNDP 'would have overall responsibility for coordinating rehabilitation and long-term reintegration during the post-war transitional and consolidation phases' (Emergency Operations Committee, 1992: 5). Nevertheless, despite these radical measures, it was still being argued that 'return would be mostly organised' and 'should include transfer of people' (Emergency Operations Committee, 1992: 3–4), though it appeared that such conceptions would probably be a marginal constraint on effective action when the time came. The report also drew attention to as yet little considered issues such as land mines and the special needs of vulnerable categories of the population (Emergency Operations Committee, 1992: 4–5). The initiative thus dealt with many of the criticisms of academics and field-based agency officials, and it appeared likely that this new framework would attract donor funding (especially Scandinavian), national governmental support and a desire on behalf of NGOs and other institutions to work in co-ordination. It was only unfortunate that progress with putting into practice this new approach was actually rather limited during 1992.

The post-war provincial planning seminar for Zambezia was held in October 1991 and addressed, amongst other things, issues surrounding the repatriation of people to Zambezia. The UNHCR draft repatriation plan, which the country office was at that time no longer actively promoting, was not discussed at this meeting, although the UNHCR field officer for northern Mozambique was present and offered much useful advice, beyond and in fact largely in opposition to this plan. The proposed repatriation plan of the provincial NARML delegate was constrained by wholly inaccurate figures concerning the numbers of potential returnees and their areas of origin,[18] and it was fortunate that one of the authors of this chapter was present during the meeting. This plan also hoped to bring all returnees through transit centres at major centres of the province, two of which were not even near the border, and this was generally rejected by the meeting in the face of the logistical constraints, as well as the lack of purpose to the exercise.[19] The UNHCR and several other delegates cautioned against attempts to establish transit centres and settlements, in part in the light of the Benga experience described below. Debate at the workshop did not resolve whether it was appropriate to allow complete self-settlement of returnees, or first to bring them through district-level authorities as part of a reintegration exercise: clearly this will have political significance in the context of transitional government and elections. Even by late 1992 this remained an uncertain issue, for, whilst the provincial governor and emergency programme had abandoned notions of transit centres, they were still the centre-point of the plans of NARML (the UNHCR counterpart body). The seminar also resolved that returnees should be handled through the same procedures as the internally displaced in the post-war period. The government's Provincial Commission for the Emergency in Zambezia had already officially ensured that there would be no preferential treatment in ration provision between returnees and the internally displaced, and that all would be assisted equally when they qualified as being 'in need' irrespective of the mandates of international organizations (interview with Sr Rocha, 1991).

The Zambezia Provincial Post-War Planning Workshop resolved that priority should be given to enabling people to get back to the land. The thrust of post-war programmes would be developmental, although it could not be made clear what kind of 'development' was envisaged beyond the re-establishment of basic infrastructure and services. The resources for such programmes are sorely lacking. Some attempts to prioritize requirements have been made, but it is clear that donor organizations will in practice be allowed to select projects from a general 'shopping list' format. The lack of Mozambique Government finance will probably render the provincial authorities more open than they would otherwise have been to cross-border operations into Zambezia by Malawi-based NGOs, as well as new initiatives from the NGOs within the province, despite the fact that this will lead to further institutional confusion. Zambezia does, as we have seen, have a substantial existing relief framework, which has developed fairly effectively its capacity to rehabilitate government services (if not to sustain them since it has no tax revenue base), and which is now tentatively exploring such things as participatory planning in the districts. The challenge facing government and the relief agencies in 1991 simply to sustain

---

[18] The UNHCR refugee survey figures for Malawi are available in Mozambique only unofficially through another international agency.

[19] It is possible that part of his problem reflected exposure to the UNHCR Operations Plan as it mentions Namacura and Mocuba as settlement sites for Zambezia, even though there are hardly any refugees in Malawi from these areas.

the current populations under their care made it long apparent that the needs and opportunities of peace would be much beyond their capacity. In Zambezia as elsewhere, the
future coming of peace was being described as likely to bring the arrival of a 'new emergency'. It is significant that hardly any assistance was provided to the several hundred thousand people in eastern and northern Zambezia who returned to their homes during
1990–91 due to the improvements in security.

Programmes of Temporary Settlement in Tete & Nicoadala

An important component of the efforts to support repatriated and internally displaced
people from Milange and other districts of northern Mozambique in the late 1980s has been
the establishment of agricultural settlements for their accommodation in special designated
areas during the years that western Zambezia was under the control of Renamo. Most
important have been several settlements in the Zambezi Valley in Moatize of Tete Province
(notably Benga), and settlements in the small and newly created (1986) Nicoadala district
adjacent to Quelimane city in Zambezia Province. This section will briefly review the
operation of these programmes and the lessons that they provide.

The agricultural settlement programmes in question were operationalized in late 1986
and early 1987, drawing much on Mozambique's ideology of development at that time
and the particular security situation then prevailing in northern Mozambique. Like many
African countries committed to modernization through massive state intervention (whatever their varied political leanings), Mozambique was convinced in the decade following
independence that the reorganization and state management of rural settlement was essential to transform what it saw as the economically constraining social relations of African
rural production systems and inadequate access to state services. The policy of communal
villages (aldeias comunais) was pursued across the country, though with limited and varied
actual implementation; and during the 1980s it became a major tool in the struggle to
counter Renamo's attempts to control the rural population (de Araujo, 1988; Geffray,
1990). It was therefore not surprising that Mozambican planners saw such settlements as
the natural policy response to returnees and internally displaced. Likewise the UNHCR,
which commenced field operations in the area around May 1987 (United States Government Department of State, 1988), generally remained convinced of the effectiveness of
agricultural settlement unlike most development agencies; this had always been their main
policy response to refugee movements in Africa, though it had nearly always failed in
practice, even according to official evaluation and criteria (Refugee Policy Group, 1986).
Amongst other things, settlements provided agencies with opportunities for effective and
targetted aid provision to a visible and discrete displaced population.

In addition to such ideological predispositions on the part of the planners, circumstances
in northern Mozambique in 1986/7 strongly promoted settlement formation as a policy
response. During 1986 Renamo had driven government forces in the region back to tiny
enclaves around the major cities. Whilst the vast majority of the population in Tete and
Zambezia lived under Renamo at this time, the number of people still dwelling with the
government – most of whom were displaced – far out-weighed the land and resources
available, and there was administrative and institutional chaos. The massive relief programme for the displaced was still developing. Government was faced with demands for
assistance from internally displaced populations, most of whom were key Frelimo affiliates
from the Renamo-held districts, and pleas from refugees in Malawi who were mostly
Frelimo supporters living in a country which was in 1986–87 being accused internationally
(and especially by Mozambique) of harbouring Renamo (Hedges, 1989; Vines, 1991).
Settlements for such returnees, it was believed, could be located in defendable areas and

guarded, and then provided with resources more easily. As the UNHCR appeared then to be a likely major new donor, and since it was believed that UNHCR would be able to generate donor support for 'repatriation' *per se*, it was only natural that the Benga settlement should be kept especially for repatriates with a discrete assistance regime as a form of aid additionality.

This early rationale of the agricultural settlement programme, despite being the product of circumstances in the mid-1980s, was to some extent maintained through to 1991 by policy inertia, and the continuing institutional need to find somewhere to locate returnees. Furthermore a number of international agencies came in to support agricultural, health and other services in the settlements, largely in their desire to respond to government priorities, and indeed sometimes against their better judgement. In fact, as will be shown below, by 1991 the Benga experience (in particular) was beginning to be seen nationally in a largely negative light. Yet it will be argued that, though it is true that events in Benga and Nicoadala indicate that such settlements will be an inappropriate response to the post-war repatriation and settlement requirements, there are reasons to see these settlement programmes as having contributed to the welfare of many northern Mozambicans trapped in the difficult late 1980s between the military weakness of the government they supported, and the pressures of exile in a neighbouring country.

One of the overarching problems of the settlement programmes was that, whilst they were constructed in the belief that they would be assured of the considerable funding they would need, this was simply not forthcoming. During these years, the UNHCR was coming under increasing pressure from donors claiming a loss of confidence in its programmes, and it proved extremely difficult to explain to potential donors why repatriation and building of rural infrastructure made sense whilst the war continued (United States Government Department of State, 1988: 2), not least an area without strategic importance to the West. Donors were not convinced – or convincible – of the needs of the pro-Frelimo and Jehovah's Witness vintages in Malawi at this time. Frelimo was losing the war in the mid to late 1980s partly because of state administrative and infrastructural collapse essentially due to lack of funds. But for donors the notion that investment in Mozambique would actually further peace was little understood, and/or attracted little sympathy. Furthermore, by the late 1980s the Malawi office of the UNHCR and the myriad of international agencies operating along Mozambique's borders proved a much greater force on the international stage than did organizations working in Mozambique, not least because of their relatively enormous budgets. The external agencies pointed to an accelerating influx and the lack of desire amongst most refugees to return under continuing war conditions. Therefore the external agencies served to further curb donor support to returnees to Mozambique. Unfortunately, the lack of forthcoming finance was not accompanied by a changed system of planning for the returnees. In late 1988, for example, a journalist found a government official trying to plan a resettlement in the far-distant Beira corridor in the centre of the country 'to receive 75,000 *deslocados* over the next few months – mostly people who would be returning from Malawi', despite a situation of great local military instability that made a nonsense of the plans (Finnegan, 1992: 94).

By February 1987 as many as 16,000–17,000 voluntary returnees were being accommodated in the three reception centres in Tete and in Benga, and 'a steady return is expected to continue' (UNHCR-Geneva, 1988: 29). The population was succinctly described as 'heterogeneous' and deriving both from Tete and from other provinces; and it comprised 'the families of subsistence farmers, plantation workers, artisans and junior civil servants', as well as returnee Jehovah's Witnesses originally from the Carico camp (UNHCR-Geneva, 1988: 29). Security has been a persistent problem of the Tete resettlements. Only months after its establishment, the Benga settlement had to be closed following an attack in early June 1987, and there was an attack adjacent to the open and unguarded Moatize II camp a few days later (MSF-B, 1987). The loss of investment, as well as the deaths, undermined the credibility of the programme, in the eyes of the non-governmental agencies involved (W. Dopcke, personal communication) and in the eyes of the donors, one remarking 'the ability of UNHCR and concerned governments to arrange safe transport and secure adequate facilities for returnees is extremely limited' (United States Government Department of State, 1988: 2). Ruiz, who visited the area for the United States Committee for Refugees, commented that:

> Security is particularly a problem at returnee centres because they tend to be small and scattered, and it is difficult for the government to provide more than a handful of soldiers to guard them. Also many returnee centers in Tete are in fertile areas, which enables returnees to harvest good crops, but also draws Renamo attacks (1989: 16).

Refugees in Malawi interviewed in 1989 expressed concern about these Tete settlements, arguing that they exposed people to Renamo attack, and that people lacked the freedom to settle where they chose; these stories were said to have emanated from ex-residents who had returned to Malawi for a second time after attacks. Similar problems have been recorded in villages for returnees from South Africa and Zimbabwe in the southern district of Chicualacuala (MIO, 1990a). The situation in the settlements in Nicoadala district in Zambezia has been somewhat different, however, with the problem being intermittent kidnapping of individuals and minor skirmishes together with frequent lootings, rather than major assaults.

The Tete settlements faced complex problems concerning the provision of assistance, including the amounts officially provided compared to other categories of displaced people and to refugees in Malawi, and a chronic underfunding of the programmes. These difficulties provide important lessons. In the late 1980s the rations for returnees under the UNHCR/NARML programme were larger that those provided by other donors through the DPCCN for the internally displaced in Mozambique. Returnees were also given preferential treatment in the distribution of cloth and cooking utensils. This led to friction and agency suspicion that some people left Mozambique for Malawi only so that they could receive more aid having returned. This problem was discussed by senior Mozambique government officials in Tete in 1989, and the then Acting Co-ordinator of the Emergency Programme, Sr Alfredo Gamito concluded that 'parallel logistics systems puzzle the people', and that this should end if possible (*Mozambiquefile*, 1989b). Yet it was only after the matter was specifically discussed in the December 1990 Emergency Programme funding application to donors (Government of Mozambique, 1990: 33–4) that the new provincial co-ordinator for the emergency and United Nations personnel in Tete finally ended this problem, by establishing one schedule for all those in Mozambique in need, irrespective of bureaucratic category. However, the amount of assistance officially provided returnees in Mozambique was still less than that rendered to the refugees when they were in Malawi, about which returnees were highly vocal (Ruiz, 1989: 16). The Tete Governor therefore took the view that 'they may prefer to retain the status of refugee and cross frequently back into Malawi' (*Mozambiquefile*, 1989a). UNHCR itself decided to 'recommend to WFP and UNDP/Mozambique that the basic ration in Mozambique be increased to the level of Malawi . . . in order that the food allowance in Malawi will not create a pull factor' (UNHCR-Maputo, 1991). Yet even the WHO and Ministry of Health have failed to bring the general level of rations in Mozambique up to minimum international standards, perhaps because changing it would be a complex task unlikely to produce greater resource allocations to Mozambique. This will then remain a problem for relief provision on the repatriation frontier, although deliveries are in practice sufficiently irregular and the amounts so small that the influence of these ration differences on actual refugee decision-making tends to be over-estimated (Wilson, 1991b).

It has not only been the officially lower rations for returnees than refugees that have created problems; general failures of funding and logistics have also been substantial. Only a quarter of the funds UNHCR requested in its 1989–90 appeal for these programmes was actually provided, a mere half of 'priority requirements' resulting in reduced assistance to a smaller number of those in need, and major cutbacks on basic infrastructural provisions (*Mozambiquefile*, 1990b; Government of Mozambique, 1990: 33). The food deficit in the 1990–91 period in Tete was for as many as 15,000 people, and the provincial NARML official in Tete argued that 'if there were efficient food assistance programmes, principally in the districts with the largest influxes of people, that would certainly increase the numbers who spontaneously returned from outside' (*Noticias*, 1990). Shortages of funds for the repatriation programmes also directly constrained the establishment of the settlements, and meant poor conditions for the returnees. There was clearly great suffering in the makeshift camps of the Moatize railway yards where 8,000 people gathered in 1987 (Fauvet, 1987); one group of 4,000 lived in such a yard from November 1986 to October 1987 (DPCCN, wallchart). A relief organization concluded of the conditions at the two returnee camps in Moatize in 1987 that:

> As a result, the situation of the camps, one dispersed in a village environment utilising the same [limited] water, woodland and space resources as the villagers, the other, in its enclosing fence, surrounded by the tracks of a railway, without any vegetation, does not seem to us adequate not only for a long term installation, not even for receiving new returnees (MSF-B, 1987: 12).

In August 1988 many of the repatriates dwelling in train wagons were taken to the reopened Benga camp, where about 5,000 people were located during 1988–89 (MSF-B, 1989). According to Hanlon (1991: 79) only one donor was prepared to assist with the establishment of irrigated agriculture in Benga in 1988, and it would provide only water tanks and roofing sheets produced by companies in its own country. During that year in Benga there were four Renamo attacks, and severe health problems (notably measles), and little camp organization during a long period of institutional conflict and inertia (MSF-B, 1989). Even in mid-1989 (at least some) people were still living in tents (Maier, 1989). Meanwhile a further 5,000 were being accommodated in train wagons and could not be moved because of lack of funds from Moatize to another planned settlement project 'for the fixation of refugees' at Chitima (interview with Director of NARML). Yet Benga was one of the few camps in the province where the soils were indeed conducive to farming (Brand *et al.*, 1989: 33), so that people could at least be able to make some kind of living for themselves, a prospect unlikely in many other sites in Tete which had unsuitable soil such as Changara (World Vision Mozambique, 1990: 4) and Fingoe (Donaldo, 1990; and field visit, 1991). Nevertheless, according to Belgian doctors the monotonous diet of maize and beans precipitated vitamin A deficiency, which had to be addressed in a limited fashion by MSF-Belgium distributing tablets to children and pregnant women; UNHCR had stated that it was not possible to widen the food rations supplied (MSF-B, 1989). Food shortages in these camps have been intermittent during 1989 and 1990 (Ruiz, 1989: 16; *Noticias*, 1990).

Despite the reported inadequate assistance, which usually promotes innovative livelihood strategies, MSF reported that Benga had 'a very lazy population which took advantage of their refugee status, and which didn't show any signs of [being] willing to improve their situation' (MSF-B, 1989). Possible reasons for this may have included that the people in the camp might have not wanted to be there any longer than necessary and had come on the understanding that it was a transit camp not a resettlement, and that any economic success would be subject to (and indeed encourage) Renamo attacks and looting. Furthermore, there was presumably a minimal sense of community or organization, and people were often in poor physical condition. These possible explanations notwithstanding, relief officials in Tete also insist that the Benga population realized that they were part of a special UNHCR-supported assistance programme, and used this to great effect to negotiate for increased aid. Some of the returnees, some relief officials have claimed, even refused to be relocated out of the programme when it was being wound down, ostensibly because they wished to retain that privileged status.

The agricultural resettlements also appear to have faced problems as modernizing 'development' institutions. The settlement in Nicoadala, for example, was slow to be established, and there are unconfirmed accounts that panic and abandonment followed attempts to mobilize residents to prepare the land prior to the visit of a senior government official. In Zambezia there is widespread fear amongst the rural populace of a return to the slavery–plantation economy; Vail and White (1980: 367) describe, for example, how the Lomwe of Alto-Zambezia refuse to plant or live near trees as a 'refusal to be associated with any plantation crop with its labour demands and destructive effects on the family', a reluctance to plant trees except for domestic use having continued to this date (Finnegan, 1992).

During the late 1980s the Tete settlements were increasingly seen by the authorities not as a permanent solution for development with returnees, but merely as holding centres whose capacity was itself threatened by logistical and security challenges. Former residents of Benga report that as early as January–April 1987 the population of three of the nine settlement zones were brought by air to Quelimane in their home province of Zambezia because, they insisted, the Frelimo party and Mozambican Government saw that people were suffering in Benga due to the lack of food, which could not be rectified in that location. According to these informants it was only logistical constraints that prevented the return of larger numbers. Whilst the majority of the population remained in Tete after the returns to Zambezia, as the security situation improved it is clear that the demands of many (though certainly not all) of the residents of Benga for return to their home areas also played a role in undermining the notion that this was to be a permanent settlement programme. In fact, many of the intended beneficiaries simply absconded from the settlements, and sought their own ways home or to other sites. In mid-1987, for example, less than a quarter of the returnees registered in the two camps in Moatize still dwelled on the sites (MSF-B, 1987: 2). Other residents continued to press for formal return movements to the delegations that frequented the project. It appears that the people themselves actually attracted significant funding for covering the costs of leaving the settlements from within Mozambique, even when the international agencies were reluctant to step in. The Mozambican Jehovah's Witnesses organization paid for many of its adherents to fly to other cities, though the activities of the Catholic Church were even more important in this regard. The Catholics flew large numbers of people of Zambezian origin to Quelimane in March 1988 and subsequently (especially in November 1989). Some other organizations were apparently also involved in these flights. (Unfortunately, some returnees were flown to Mocuba in late 1989, although many of them did not wish to settle there.) On arrival in Quelimane these internal returnees were settled in the resettlement zones of Nicoadala district, from where many were able to return to their homes following the advances of government troops and the Naparama popular militias in 1990 and 1991. By late 1991, when we interviewed people from this group, the largest remaining populations were from Morrumbala and Milange, which were the two districts still largely cut off by the war. Only people from those districts who had access to flights through relatives or other contacts had been able to return home.

With the growing recognition that Benga was only to be a transit camp, NARML and the UNCHR also began to emphasize the return of the people of western Zambezian origin to Milange via Malawi, the same route that many had come several years before when Renamo had dominated Zambezia. Several hundred returned by bus on this route to Milange in June 1989.[20] A journalist who interviewed them at the time found one man who had left his family in a border camp and gone to Tete on his own, an interesting example of how families split to secure opportunities. This man reported that 'she [his wife] wrote to me a few months ago and said people are going back to Milange, and they seem to be getting on fine. They are working their land again, she said, and we should return too' (Maier, 1989). In this case, therefore, an official repatriation exercise was used as part of a refugee household strategy. During 1990, NARML and UNHCR continued their efforts to get the Benga populations to their home areas, but they were frustrated by the lack of funding (*Mozambiquefile*, 1990b: 14; *Noticias*, 1990). Even the much cheaper overland journey from Benga to Milange (via Malawi) did not prove possible during 1990 (UNHCR-Geneva, 1991b), though in early 1991 some 503 Benga residents were returned to Beira (UNHCR-Geneva, 1991a); and/or 176 'returnees from Benga Transit Centre' were reported airlifted to Maputo, Zambezia, Nampula and Sofala 'by mid 1991' (Government of Mozambique, 1991: 49).

Clear lessons were being drawn in 1991 from Benga by government and relief officials. The institutional and financial costs of seeking to create formal agricultural settlements are unwarranted because the wish of most people to return home and settle themselves undermines their operation. Furthermore the establishment of settlements as 'transit camps' is extremely expensive in resources and contributes very little to any lasting institutional or infrastructural development. The establishment of a privileged client group for the UNHCR in a situation of general emergency not only constrained its operations but also led to the distorted allocation of resources. Finally, such settlement programmes in the context of continued instability did not attract sufficient donor funds, leaving the agency and especially the beneficiaries in an awkward situation. Reflecting on the settlements from the point of view of refugees' own livelihood strategies it might also be argued that the very process of creating a 'project' in a situation where the guerrilla movement preferentially attacks anything associated with the state puts the returnees at greater risk than allowing them to manage their own modus vivendi in Mozambique's tortured countryside. These critiques, whilst essentially valid, must not obscure the very real role played by the programme during the time it was created. In a situation where significant populations of refugees in Malawi felt that they needed to return to their country of origin for their protection and well-being, the programmes provided an essential space in a highly constrained military situation. It is true that they might have been able to do so more efficiently, but looking back on that period what is so remarkable is that people and institutions survived at all. Indeed, these programmes contributed to making continued allegiance to the government possible, such that between 1987 and 1989 Frelimo won back most of the ground lost to Renamo in 1985–86 in Tete and Zambezia provinces.

---

[20] In Milange we were informed that 500 had come at this time, but according to UNSCERO (1989) 348 people had been brought from Benga by July 1989, with another 187 to follow; and an SCF-UK (1989b) memo put the figure for the end of June and early July 1989 from Benga as low as 160.

Conclusion

This chapter has already been lengthy, and its conclusions are thus necessarily brief. Its thrust has been to demonstrate the diversity of local processes influencing flight and return movements, and the desires and abilities of refugees and returnees. Through the case study of Milange it has been possible to interpret the significance or otherwise of changes in the military and assistance programmes, and of planning by agencies, from the point of view of the strategies of the people themselves. Whilst the governments and agencies have lacked the understanding and adequately resourced policy instruments to design and implement repatriation plans that much influence movements, large numbers of refugees have in fact self-returned in a variety of ways, either successfully demanding assistance according to their own broad agendas, or returning without any formal aid. More effective planning and assistance therefore require an increased responsiveness to the returnees' initiatives and needs, and should be based on approaches securing – through protection and investment – the maximum effectiveness of the returnees' own strategies.

References

Africa Confidential (1991) 'Bandits of freedom fighters?', Vol. 32, No. 25, 20 December.

Aid Agency Memo (1990) Report on a visit to Milange [author uncited], 30 June.

Black, R., T. Mabwe, F. Shumba and K. Wilson (1990) 'Ukwimi refugee settlement: livelihood and settlement planning for Mozambicans in Zambia', unpublished report, King's College London, Refugee Studies Programme, Oxford.

Boeder, R. B. (1984) *The silent majority: a history of the Lomwe in Malawi*, African Institute of South Africa, Pretoria.

Brand, C., J, Wilding and V. A. Metcalf (1989) AgPack project evaluation, unpublished report, World Vision Mozambique.

CENE/DPCCN (1988) *Rising to the challenge: Mozambique emergency*, Maputo.

Chivilumbo, A. (1974) 'On labour and Alomwe immigration', *Rural Africana*, No. 24: 49–57.

Christian Council of Malawi (CCM) (Department of Aid and Relief) (1988) 'Church work with refugees in Malawi', unpublished report, Blantyre.

—— (1989) 'Sitrep of Milange, December 1989' in Relief Work Annual Report 1989, Blantyre.

—— (1990a) 'Sitrep of Milange, January 1990' attached to Relief Work Annual Report 1989, Blantyre.

—— (1990b) CCM relief work, January–June 1990; Blantyre.

Christian Service Committee (Malawi) (1988) Situation report, January–May 1988, unpublished, Blantyre.

Cisternino, M. (1987) Report on the situation of displaced Mozambicans in Malawi, until 12 June 1987, Comboni Missionary Society, Rome, unpublished.

Colson, E. (1971) *The social consequences of resettlement. The impact of the Kariba resettlement upon the Gwembe Tonga*, Manchester University Press.

—— (1980) 'The resilience of matrilineality: Gwembe and Plateau Tonga adaptations' in L.S. Cordell and S.J. Beckerman (eds) *The versatility of kinship*, Academic Press, New York.

Colvin, T. (1992) Visit to Malawi and Mozambique concerning the Evangelical Church of Jesus Christ in Mozambique, Ecumenical Consultancy in Africa Service, Harare, February–March.

Daily Times (1989a) 'Refugee surveillance course ends', Blantyre.

—— (1989b) 'Malawi needs more assistance for refugees', Blantyre, 10 October.

de Araujo, M. (1988) 'Dinamica das novas formas de redistribuicao da populacao rural em Mocambique', *Gazeta Demografica*, No. 3: 3–26, Maputo.

Donaldo, N. (1990) 'Effects of war on Maravia District described, *Noticias* (Maputo), 14 November.

DPCCN (1990) *News Bulletin*, June–July.

—— (1991) Relatorio sobre a visita nas provincias da Zambezia e Nampula, Maputo, September.

Dreze, J. and A. Sen (1989) *Hunger and public action*, Clarendon Press, Oxford.

Egan, E. (1991) 'Relief and rehabilitation work in Mozambique: institutional capacity and NGO executional strategies', *Development in Practice*, No. 3: 174–84.

Emergency Operations Committee (1992) CCPCCN/CENE Minutes, No. 162, 27 April.

Fauvet, P. (1984) 'Roots of a counter-revolution: the MNR', *Review of African Political Economy*, No. 29: 114–16.

—— (1987) *The Guardian*, report published in issue of 2 April.

— (1988) 'Malawi aiding rebels' *The Guardian*, 23 July.

Financial Times (1991) Supplement on Mozambique, 15 January.

Finnegan, F. (1992) *A complicated war: the harrowing of Mozambique*, University of California Press, Berkeley.

Geffray, C. (1990) *La Cause des armes en Mozambique: une anthropologie d'une guerre civile*, Karthala, Paris.

Government of Mozambique, in collaboration with the United Nations (1990) Update of the emergency situation in Mozambique, and provisional assessment of 1991 relief needs, Maputo, December.

— (1991) *Mozambique: emergency programme 1992–1993*, Maputo, November.

Hall, M. (1990) 'The Mozambican National Resistance (Renamo): a study in the destruction of an African country', *Africa*, Vol. 60, No. 1: 39–68.

Hallam, A. and S. Thomas (1992) 'Practice notes: associations as a means of organising small enterprises in war-affected areas of Mozambique. Reflections after four years of working with displaced people', with the Intermediate Technology Development Group, Nottingham.

Hanlon, J. (1984) *Mozambique: the revolution under fire*, Zed Books, London.

— (1991) *Mozambique: who calls the shots?*, James Currey, London.

Hansen, A. (1979) 'Once the running stops: assimilation of Angolan refugees into Zambian border villages', *Disasters*, Vol. 3, No. 4: 369–74.

Harrell-Bond, B. E. (1989) 'Repatriation: under what conditions is it the most desirable solution for refugees? An agenda for research', *African Studies Review*, No. 32(1): 41–69.

Hedges, D. (1989) 'Notes on Malawi–Mozambique relations, 1964–87', *Journal of Southern African Studies*, Vol. 15: 617–44.

Indian Ocean Newsletter (ION) (c.1989) 'Mozambique: the key sectors of the economy', France.

International Committee of the Red Cross (ICRC) (1990) Agreement on ICRC action in Mozambique, 1 December.

Kalemba, B., N. W. Kakusa and M. Shawa (1988) Ministry of Community Services Needs Assessment Survey for Displaced Mozambicans, Government of Malawi, 13–29 March.

Kunz, F. F. (1973) 'The refugee in flight: kinetic models and forms of displacement', *International Migration Review*, No. 7(2): 125–46.

— (1981) 'Exile and resettlement: refugee theory', *International Migration Review*, No. 15: 42–51.

Long, L., T. Cecsarini and J. Martin (1990) *The local impact of Mozambican refugees in Malawi*, US Embassy/US AID, Lilongwe, 10 November.

Maier, K. (1989) 'Refugees return as Mozambique tries to heal its wounds', *The Independent*, 25 July, London.

— (1990) 'Displaced peasants strain Mozambican aid', *The Independent*, 20 December, London.

Mandala, E. C. (1990) *Work and control in a peasant economy: a history of the Lower Tchiri Valley in Malawi, 1859–60*, University of Wisconsin Press, Madison.

Médecins Sans Frontières (Belgium) (MSF-B) (1987) Evaluation médico-sanitaire des populations 'retournées' dans le district de Moatize – province de Tete, unpublished report, Tete, June.

— (1989) Final evaluation of the medical activities in the Moatize District between July 1988 and June 1989, unpublished report, Tete.

Médecins Sans Frontières (France) (MSF-F) (1988) Annual Report, Blantyre.

— (1989) Monthly Report for Milange, December, Blantyre.

Minter, W. (1989) The Mozambican National Resistance (Renamo) as described by ex-participants, Ford Foundation/SIDA, March (also published in c. 1990) *Mozambique: a tale of terror told by ex-participants of Renamo and refugees*, African-European Institute.

Mozambiquefile (Maputo) (1989a) 'Waiting for repatriation: refugees in Malawi', February.

— (1989b) 'Security, transport and other problems', from AIM, 8 November.

— (1990a) 'Milange road opens', 24 September.

— (1990b) 'Malawi discourages refugees from returning home', October.

Mozambique Information Office (MIO) (London) (1990a) 'Continuing banditry', *News Review*, No. 191, 20 December.

— (1990b) *News Review*, No. 186, 2 September.

— (1992) 'Border closure threatens food security', *News Review*, No. 215, 9 January.

Muth, J. A. J. (1992) 'The Christian Council of Mozambique contribution regarded refugee towards [sic] voluntary repatriation of Mozambican refugees', First Country of Asylum and Development Aid, York University, Ontario, Canada and Malawi Government, paper presented in Blantyre, Malawi.

NELIMO (1989) *Relatorio do 1 Seminario sobre a padronizacao du ortografia de linguas Mozambicanos*, Universidade Eduardo Mondlane, Faculdade de Letras, Maputo.

Norwegian Refugee Council (NRC) (1991) Annual Report, Oslo.

Noticias (Maputo) (1990) 'Financial difficulties compromise repatriation', 31 December.

— (1991) 'Official gives repatriation figures', FBIS translation, 30 April: 8.

Ntaba, H. (1992) Speech printed in 'Minister explains impact of refugee problem in Malawi', *Daily Times*, Lilongwe, 28 February.

Nunes, J. (1992) Peasants and survival: the social consequences of displacement, unpublished report, SIDA, Maputo, Mozambique.

Palmer, R. (1984) 'Working conditions and worker responses on Nyasaland tea estates, 1930–53', *Journal of African History*, No. 25: 105–26.

Polosa, A. (1991) 'The returnee programme in Mozambique: an overview', unpublished, Oxford.

Refugee Policy Group (1986) *Older refugee settlements in Africa*, Washington DC.

Reynolds, P. (1991) *Dance civet cat: child labour in the Zambezi Valley*, Zed Books, London.
Ruiz, H. (1989) *Peace or terror: a crossroads for Southern Africa's uprooted*, United States Committee for Refugees, Washington DC.
Save the Children Fund (UK) (SCF-UK) (1988) Internal memos, July–December, Quelimane.
— (1989a) Report of Milange visit, 16 February, unpublished report, Quelimane.
— (1989b) Memo on Zambezia programme, 11 June, Quelimane.
— (1989c) Annual Report 1988–89, unpublished report, Quelimane, September.
— (1989d) Reconstruction and rehabilitation in districts liberated from bandit control, unpublished report, Quelimane, September.
— (1989e) Report on a visit to Milange, 9 October, unpublished report, Quelimane.
— (1989f) SCF internal memo, 28 February, Quelimane.
— (1990a) Report on visit to Milange, 30 June, unpublished report, Quelimane.
— (1990b) 1989 Emergency Seeds and Tools Programme in Zambezia Province, Mozambique, End Report for Comic Relief, June.
— (1990c) Wells for displaced and resettled populations, project proposal, Quelimane, mid-1990.
— (1990d) Annual Report for Zambezia, October 1989–September 1990, unpublished report, Quelimane.
— (1990e) Purchase of pick-up truck for cross border travel: Mozambique/Malawi, project proposal, Quelimane, late 1990.
— (1990f) Seeds and Tools Programme for 1990–91 agricultural season in three districts, Zambezia Province, unpublished report, Quelimane, July.
— (1990g) Report on visit to Milange, 10 May, unpublished report, Quelimane.
— (1991) Field report on Milange, 16–20 August, unpublished report, Quelimane.
Smith, S. (1990) *Frontline Africa: the right to a future. An Oxfam special report on conflict and poverty in Southern Africa*, Oxfam, Oxford.
Southern African Economist (1991) 'Picking up the pieces: Mozambique', June/July.
Thomas, S. (1992) 'Sustainability in NGO relief and development work: further thoughts from Mozambique', *Development in Practice*, Oxfam, Oxford.
Tolfree, D. (1991) *Refugee children in Malawi: a study of the implementation of UNHCR guidelines on refugee children*, International Save the Children Alliance and UNHCR, London.
Tripartite Commission (1989), *Agreed Minutes of the first meeting of the Tripartite Commission for the Repatriation of Mozambiquan Refugees*, Government of Malawi, Government of Mozambique, UNHCR, 2–4 April, Blantyre, Malawi.
UNDP (Maputo) (1990) Institutional contract for post-war planning: terms of reference, December.
UNDRO (Maputo) (1990) Mozambique: destabilisation and drought, Situation Report, No. 17, Maputo (Mozambique), 24 January.
UNHCR (Blantyre) (1989) Agreed minutes of the First Meeting of the Tripartite Commission for the Repatriation of Mozambican Refugees in Malawi, Blantyre, 2–4 April.
— (1990) Survey of districts of origin, unpublished mimeo, Blantyre, April.
UNHCR (Geneva) (1988) Mozambique: an emergency preparedness profile, Emergency Section, Geneva.
— (1989) Emergency contingency plan for the Mozambican refugees, Geneva, undated (late 1989).
— (1990) Programme of Assistance for Mozambican Returnees, Appeal 1990–91, Geneva.
— (1991a) Telex (in response to author's questions), 25 February.
— (1991b) Telex (in response to author's questions), 26 February.
UNHCR (Health Sector, Malawi) (1989) 'Briefing notes', Blantyre, January.
UNHCR (Maputo) (1989) Memo/Letter to SCF-UK, 28 July.
— (1990) Zambezia assistance programme 9 May 1989 to April 1990; Maputo.
— (1991) Operations plan: Malawi–Mozambique repatriation operation, final draft, UNHCR BO Malawi and BO Mozambique, January.
UNHCR (TSS) (1989a) Food nutrition assessment of Mozambican refugees, Nutrition Section, Geneva, 8–23 February.
— (1989b) Malawi: expanding income generating opportunities in refugee-affected areas through increasing demand, Income Generation Section, Geneva, January–February.
UNICEF (Mozambique) (1991) Terms of reference for a study of post-war planning from the perspective of rural communities, Mozambique.
United States Government Department of State (1988) *World Refugee Report*, Bureau for Refugee Programmes, Washington DC, September.
UNSCERO (Maputo) (1989) Report on returnees, 11–15 July.
Vail, L. and L, White (1980) *Capitalism and colonialism in Mozambique: a study of Quelimane District*, Heinemann Educational Books, London.
Vaughan, M. (1981) 'Social and economic change in southern Malawi: a study of rural communities in the Shire Highlands and Upper Shire Valley from the mid-nineteenth century to 1915', PhD Thesis, University of London.
— (1987) *The story of an African famine: Nyasaland 1949*, Cambridge University Press, Cambridge.
Vines, A. (1991) *Renamo: terrorism in Mozambique*, James Currey, London.
White, L. (1985) 'Review article: the revolutions ten years on', *Journal of Southern African Studies*, No. 11(2): 320–32.
— (1987) *Magomero: a portrait of an African village*, Cambridge University Press, Cambridge.

Wilson, A. D. (c,1961) 'Lomwe studies', unpublished manuscript.

Wilson, K. B. (1991a) 'Conceiving of the future amongst Mozambicans in Ukwimi refugee settlement in Zambia', unpublished report, Refugee Studies Programme, Oxford.

— (1991b) 'Repatriation and development in northern Tete: people's attitudes, current procedures and post-war planning: preliminary findings from field research in Angonia', unpublished report, Refugee Studies Programme, Oxford.

— (1991c) 'The new missionaries: review of *Mozambique: who calls the shots?*', *Southern African Review of Books*, July/October.

— (1992a) 'Cults of violence and counter violence in Mozambique', *Journal of Southern African Studies*, 18(3): 527–582.

— (1992b) 'Enhancing refugees' own food aquisition strategies', *Journal of Refugee Studies*, 5(2).

Wilson, K. B., D. Cammack and F. Shumba (1989) 'Food provisioning amongst Mozambican refugees in Malawi', unpublished report, Refugee Studies Programme/World Food Programme, July.

World Bank (1990a) *Mozambique: restoring rural production and trade*, New York, October.

— (1990b) Statement on current economic situation and the economic and social rehabilitation programme, Mozambique Consultative Group meeting, Paris, 10–12 December.

World Food Programme (WFP) (1988a) Report on WFP mission to Milange, telex, 15 July.

— (1988b) Follow-up report on Milange, telex, 8 August.

— (1988c) Follow-up report on Milange, telex, 5 October.

World Health Organization (1990) *Repatriation into north-east Tete: prospects and possible lines for action*, WHO-EPR, Maputo.

World Vision Mozambique (1990) Agricultural recovery programme for Tete and Zambezia Provinces, monthly report, May.

Zieroth, G. (1988) 'Fuel supply for displaced persons in Malawi, final report', Interdisziplinaro Projekt Consult GmbH, Frankfurt.

ZOA Refugee Care (1990) Policy, strategies, management report 1989–90, Blantyre.

Glossary of Acronyms

CCM	Christian Council of Malawi
CENE	Comissão Executiva Nacional de Emergência
CPE	Comissão Provincial de Emergência (Provincial Emergency Co-ordinating Body)
DPCCN	Departamento de Prevenção e Combate as Calamidades Naturais (Government relief agency)
EMOCHA	Empresa Moçambicana da Cha (the state tea company)
ICRC	International Committee of the Red Cross
INDER	Instituto National de Desenvolvimento
MIO	Mozambique Information Office
MSF	Médecins sans Frontières (either French or Belgian)
NARML	Nucleo de Apoio aos Refugiados e Movimentos de Libertação (Government agency responsible for refugees and returnees)
PRE	Programa de Reabilitação Economica
PRES	Programa de Reabilitação Economica e Social
PRM	Partiolo Revolucionario de Moçambique
SCF-UK	Save the Children Fund (UK)
SADCC	Southern African Development Co-ordination Conference
UNAMO	União Nacional Moçambicana (military faction now a registered political party)
UNDP	United Nations Development Programme
UNDRO	United Nations Disaster Relief Organization
UNHCR	United Nations High Commissioner for Refugees
UNSCERO	United Nations Special Co-ordinator for Emergency Relief Operations
WFP	World Food Programme

10 K.B. WILSON
Refugees & Returnees as Social Agents

The Case of the Jehovah's Witnesses
from Milange

Introduction

The preceding chapter on flight and return in Milange district of northern Mozambique discussed how refugees themselves – rather than the assistance agencies – have taken the major initiatives that shaped repatriation flows in recent years. Yet that chapter passed over one particular group of refugees from Milange, the Jehovah's Witnesses. The recent history of this religious community is quite extraordinary, and can be considered the 'exception that proves the rule' that refugees and returnees need to be understood as social agents rather than as simply victims or beneficiaries.

The objective of this short chapter is to explore how and why the Jehovah's Witness refugee group generated their own experience and dynamic of persecution, flight, exile and, ultimately, return. In part the uniqueness of this story reflects the different pressures on the movement from the Renamo guerrillas and the various governments of the region, each of which has persecuted the Witnesses in the past. But more important, however, is that the ideology and organization of this religious movement enabled its members to plan their flight and exile and so ascribe a totally different significance to the whole experience than the other refugees: basically it was perceived as one of continuity rather than disruption, and victory rather than frustration. The chapter also relates this remarkable degree of refugee initiative to the wider question of the role and impact of government and aid agency programmes.

Background

The Jehovah's Witness or 'Watch Tower' movement spread rapidly through Central and Southern Africa during the early colonial period, largely because it offered new ideologies and associations that both provided a sophisticated critique of the nature of colonial domination and also enabled people to live better in the changing socio-economic contexts of the period (Chirwa, 1984; Cross, 1973; Fields, 1985; Hooker, 1965). Whilst the movement regularly attracted suppression by the colonial authorities because it refused to accept the legitimacy of state authority, the persecution of Witnesses increased greatly following independence, due to the all-encompassing demands of the new African political leadership (Cross, 1978). Witnesses refused to respect the new symbols of nationhood (especially slogans and flags), and to participate ritualistically in mass political movements and parties. Indeed, for a variety of complex reasons the persecution of Witnesses, and the redistribution of their private and public assets, became central to the process of nation-building and government in these countries, particularly for the establishment of a strong party rank and file. The result of this was a series of seven systematic persecutions and subsequent mass migrations within and between Zambia, Malawi and Mozambique between the late 1960s and mid-1970s (Hodges, 1985). This appalling legacy certainly enhanced Witnesses' capacity to cope with persecution, migration and survival during the 1980s.

The Carico settlement – the place of residence for Milange's Jehovah's Witnesses – was initially established by the Portuguese authorities before independence in 1973 for around 10,000 Malawian Witness refugees, most of whom had arrived in 1972 and had been living with their brethren in border villages. After independence in 1975, the Frelimo Government rounded up another 10,000 Mozambican Witnesses in the central and southern provinces and relocated them to the north, choosing the Carico camp as the 're-education centre' for this group. By 1980 the more extreme oppression in Carico had ended, and the camp became a more open settlement, indeed, a major centre of crop production and commerce in the district. This situation was transformed by the arrival of the Renamo rebels in 1984, who tried to incorporate the Witnesses into their tribute economy and to recruit them into their struggle against the government. Elaborate displays of violence and systematic coercion, coupled with attempts at negotiation and persuasion spectacularly failed to win Witness support (Wilson, 1992). However, Renamo's assault set in motion a new wave of migrations and return migrations around Zambezia Province of Mozambique, into neighbouring Malawi, and across Malawi into Zambia and Mozambique's Tete Province.

The Scattering of the Witness Population & Survival in the Camps

A large proportion of the Carico population decided in 1985 to organize departure from Mozambique across Malawi (where the faith is proscribed) and into eastern Zambia and the Angonia district of Tete Province (Mozambique). Scouts were sent ahead to plan the routes, and to arrange networks of local Witnesses to receive, support and settle the Witness refugees during the clandestine movements that were to follow. The places selected for residence, Mlangeni and Sinda Misale, had both been areas of Witness refugee settlements on numerous previous flight movements over the past three decades. Most of those refugees who tried to reside in northern Tete soon had to leave for Zambia, since the war rapidly spread and they became once again identified by local Renamo supporters as refusing to contribute to the Renamo cause. After a period of one or two years in the Sinda Misale area, during which time the Zambia Red Cross had started to play a major relief role, the Witnesses were informed that they were to be relocated in a large agricultural settlement, Ukwimi, in Zambia's Petauke district.

Many of the Witnesses who did not leave Carico in this first group which traversed Malawi in the dry season of 1985 later found themselves obliged to organize refuge in Malawi. This group comprised some who had religious differences with those organizing the earlier departure, or who had not had the money for flight as far as Zambia or Tete, and/or had first sought to resettle themselves within Zambezia Province. There were also others who had originated in one of the small Witness populations outside of Carico such as at Chire in Morrumbala district. Departure of a determined group of Witnesses to an area of Malawi opposite the Carico settlement resulted in the creation of Chiringa camp in Mulanje district (Malawi) which Witnesses dominated in the 1986–89 period, and significant Witness minorities were found in Malawi's Muloza and Tengani camps which bordered Milange and Morrumbala districts respectively. There were other groups of Witnesses, not all of whom had been involved in complex migrations out from Carico, in many of the camps of western Malawi, especially in Dedza, Ntcheu and Mwanza districts. The Witnesses – characteristically – secured their asylum and organized their camp life with impressive vigour. The Malawi Government sought to restrict the Witnesses' religious activities to a varying degree through space and time, but was otherwise remarkably accommodating to their needs.

In addition to dwelling in the refugee camps, hiding their Malawian identity, a number of the Malawian Witnesses in Carico sought to return to their original homes and fields in Malawi during the Mozambican troubles of the mid-1980s. Indeed, many of these Witnesses successfully reinstalled themselves in Malawi village society, even reclaiming their land. At times this was because the local police had regained authority relative to the party, and refused to arrest Witnesses when they were brought in by party officials. However, there were a number of returnee Malawian Witnesses from Carico rearrested in Malawi at this time.

Witness movements out of the Carico settlement to other areas of Mozambique were many and complex in the mid-1980s, as the Witnesses attempted to create new communities that would be less subject to the targetted punishment then being meted out by Renamo in Carico. Some of these communities grew out of groups of Witnesses kidnapped by Renamo and taken south to Morrumbala district, where they either escaped or were released after refusing to collaborate. Although many of these communities survived the war, many Witnesses later also chose to take refuge in neighbouring countries as Renamo power spread.

The Frelimo forces also 'recuperated' some Witnesses, forcibly relocating them into the garrison towns, especially Milange itself, where two thriving congregations were thus established. Other Witnesses were taken by Frelimo soldiers to Morrumbala, where they spent eight months in perceived 'exile' before they managed to persuade the government to fly them 'home' to Milange (though most of this group were originally Malawians or from Mutarara in Tete Province). The government, however, only took the Morrumbala Witnesses to the provincial capital of Quelimane, and arranged for them to settle with other Milange exiles in Lobo in neighbouring Nicoadala district.

In addition to seeking refuge in other areas some of the Witnesses stayed in Carico or their new communities. Here the strength of their faith, and the threat that this provided to Renamo's hegemony, meant that the guerrillas eventually declared the Witness communities 'peace zones' which their soldiers were not supposed to enter (Wilson, 1992). By 1990–1 these areas even became islands of productivity and refuge for other Mozambicans fleeing the war.

Most of the relief officials and journalists who have encountered the Jehovah's Witnesses in exile in camps in Malawi and Zambia found that this group coped much better than other categories of refugees in both psycho-social and material terms. Finnegan, for example, who had travelled across Mozambique and through many Malawian camps, had clearly seen nothing like Chiringa which he visited in 1988, and described it as an 'extremely neat canico village' which was

10.1 *Jehovah's Witness congregation, Ukwimi refugee settlement, Zambia, September 1991 (K. Wilson)*

10.2 *Jehovah's Witness Kingdom Hall, Ukwimi refugee settlement, Zambia, September 1990 (K. Wilson)*

unusually well built. The huts were large, with separate cooking huts, separate shower huts with L-shaped entrances, granaries, gardens full of greens, wells with fences round them and stairways down into them, latrines that were clearly well reinforced (1992: 157).

These favourable observations have been borne out by the more detailed studies of Witnesses in the Zambian settlement, Ukwimi (Black *et al.*, 1990; Wilson, 1991a), in Malawi (Cisternino, 1987), in the Milange town camps (Wilson, 1991b) and in the other areas of northern Mozambique.

The reasons for the success of the Witnesses in the camps have included their long familiarity with persecution and camp life, an effective approach to handling authorities and agencies, an ideology that could ascribe purpose to exile and suffering, a strong community structure with a powerful mutual aid and welfare capacity, and economic skills, such as carpentry, useful in camps with low agricultural potential, which are organized around artisans' circles. In each of the camp settings, though to a variable extent, the Witnesses have proved capable of attracting new adherents among other refugees, local people, and have even converted soldiers and relief officials. In Ukwimi in Zambia in particular, they came to dominate the settlement's whole economy.

The Repatriation Movements

Introduction

Discussion of the nature and pattern of flight of the Witness community from Carico has introduced some of the complexity of any 'repatriation' process for them. Refugees of highly diverse origin had located themselves in camps in two countries, as well as becoming scattered within two provinces of Mozambique. Flight, far from simply rupturing existing social networks, had been a deliberate movement that actually utilized and strengthened them; rather than suffering destitution and alienation in the camps, the Witnesses interpreted persecution as evidence of their religious worth, and their economic endeavour transformed the conditions of life in exile from plight to relative wealth. Migration had taken many Witnesses to Malawi – their original home country, where most were still not accepted as citizens so that they presented themselves as Mozambicans, and these 'refugees' were primarily orientated towards a 'return to exile' in the absence of opportunities to reintegrate in the country of their birth. Most Mozambican Witnesses were meanwhile requesting 'repatriation', but not to the place where they had actually come from – a rural re-education camp – but to far distant cities and other rural areas. In fact their return and reintegration to those latter areas became possible in the late 1980s not because of changes in the conditions that made them refugees (for the war had worsened in Carico), but due to groundswell changes in Mozambique state policy towards religious movements such as their own (cf. Askin, 1988). Meanwhile the changing degree of religious persecution of the Witness refugees in the Malawi camps also had an impact on their desire to return to Mozambique.

Return from Zambia

Repatriation of Witnesses who had left the Milange camp for Zambia started as soon as international agency involvement provided a means to cross Renamo-held border zones of northern Tete to the safer cities beyond. When the refugees were offered the choice of repatriation or restriction to an agricultural settlement, a large number of the Witnesses – especially the more educated from the southern part of Mozambique – opted to

10.3 *Witness carpenter from Milange in Ukwimi, September 1991 (K. Wilson)*

10.4 *Some of the 5,000 Jehovah's Witnesses attending the annual convention, Ukwimi refugee settlement, Zambia, September 1991 (K. Wilson)*

go 'home', the place from which they had been forcibly separated for over ten years. A high proportion of the 415 voluntary repatriates to Maputo and some of the 48 repatriated to Tete during 1987 and 1988 were Witnesses; as were the bulk of the 87 repatriated to Maputo and some of the 400 who went to Tete in 1989 (*Development*, 1989).

The Witnesses of Ukwimi are an excellent example of how a group uses its social networks and communication channels to spread information about the possibilities and mechanisms of repatriation. Interviewing returnees in early 1989, for example, a camp official observed 'that the refugees have had letters from relatives in Mozambique telling them that the Watch Tower members are now allowed to practise their faith' (*Development*, 1989). During 1990 and 1991 Witnesses in Zambia reported to us details of the circumstances of returnees in Tete, Maputo, and even of friends who had gone on to Swaziland and South Africa after repatriation to Maputo. They made good use of radio services in Portuguese, Chewa and English and most were literate. The Witnesses were also able to make good use of the Red Cross message system, which became active in 1991. Individual Witnesses had the confidence and ability to obtain official permission to visit Malawi and Mozambique to visit relatives and friends and they brought back first-hand information. Obtaining this information led to decisions both to leave and to remain. Some who had declined to repatriate believed, for example, that some people had responded to repatriation missions with too much enthusiasm and naivety concerning the capacity of the government and UNHCR to get them home, noting 'some Witnesses got excited after receiving letters from friends and relatives in Mozambique who they hadn't seen for fifteen years', only to get stuck in the camps in Tete that are described in the previous chapter.

Repatriation of Mozambicans from Zambia was halted in 1989 due to lack of donor support for the UNHCR's repatriation operation, and, later, the reluctance of the Zambia UNHCR Resident Representative to return people to what he considered an ill-prepared situation. There were a number of Witnesses among the 400 registered returnees, whose lives were in limbo after October 1989 (Black *et al.*, 1990), and by September 1991 around a quarter of the Witnesses in Ukwimi in a small sample interviewed stated that they wanted to return immediately to their urban homes (Wilson, 1991a: 21). The main motivation for return was to unite with dependent relatives, though many also knew that they would secure a better livelihood in the cities of Mozambique than in Ukwimi settlement. In late 1991 a number of Witnesses had travelled without permission to Lusaka and were encamped at the office of Refugee Services in protest. Others were even demanding to be allowed to pay for their own repatriation. But the UNHCR in Zambia remained adamant up to late 1992 that it was not yet appropriate for them to return, and its view prevailed over the judgement of the UNHCR Tete office in Mozambique.

Return from Malawi

Though the Witness refugees in the Chiringa and other Malawian refugee camps were doing relatively well in the late 1980s, many of them also wished to return to Mozambique and rejoin their families and former communities. Cisternino (1987: 12), for example, whilst noting that 'being used to camp life they are the only group [of refugees in Malawi] looking relaxed, active and self-sufficient', nevertheless recorded that 'some skilled people are trying their best to move to towns or back to Maputo'. Their efforts were not in vain because, in May 1987, about 1,800 of the 3,000 Witnesses in Chiringa were indeed voluntarily repatriated under an agreement between the Malawi and Mozambican Governments, and with the guarantee of freedom of worship in Mozambique (Wooldridge, 1987). This was prior to the involvement of the UNHCR in the Tripartite Commission between these governments, and it is not clear how Witness lobbying achieved this agreement, although it appears the Red Cross may have been involved, although those officials asked deny knowledge of such a programme.

Repatriations from Malawi continued in late 1987 and from early 1988 to the end of the year, during which time the United States Government Department of State (1988: 2) reports that 3,000 Jehovah's Witnesses were returned to Mozambique. Indeed, by late 1988 most of the Witnesses had left their most important camp, that at Chiringa (MSF-F, 1988: 58–9). It appears that, as in other Witness return movements, the migration was fairly selective of southern and urban Mozambicans, with others wishing to remain closer to their home areas. As one said, 'Witnesses who were from this region did not want to go to Mozambique: they feared further displacement'. Other factors were also at work. One elderly and educated southern Mozambican from Chiringa reported that he had not registered for repatriation from Malawi because he had lost all his goods in the war and did not want to return to Maputo appearing to be poor after so many years in internal exile. He had resolved to work first, and if necessary fund his own return, so that when he arrived it would be well-dressed and with dignity. Whilst he had himself failed to raise the money to return, some other Witnesses did indeed fund their own repatriation to Tete and beyond from the Malawi border camps.

In 1988 there was a new refugee influx of poorly nourished people into Chiringa and the inadequate level of immunization of the new arrivals initiated a measles epidemic (MSF-F, 1988: 57). The resulting high mortality combined with other dissatisfactions encouraged further Witness repatriation to Mozambique, which in 1989, according to one aid official, included some movements by air, presumably because the worsened security situation in Tete prevented road transport (MSF-B, 1989: appendix 1). According to a Witness visitor to the camp, these poor conditions at Chiringa also fuelled the desire to come to Zambia, since in Zambia there were freedom of worship and less crowded and economically precarious conditions. But any substantial migration to Zambia for refugees registered in Malawi was not institutionally acceptable, though family reunions were possible, and during 1989 one Witness with asylum in Zambia was officially transferred to Malawi to be with his relatives.

Refugees from other Malawian camps such as Tengani and Muloza repatriated together with those from Chiringa between 1987 and 1989, though not all who hoped to return to Mozambique found it possible. Some Witness refugees in Muloza also complained that it had not been possible for them to join the repatriations of government officials arranged by the two governments in the months after Milange's fall to Renamo, and therefore they had been obliged to make their own arrangements.

The Witnesses repatriated from Malawi were mostly brought via Zobue to Tete city, with the other repatriated Mozambicans from Malawi. In the case of the Witnesses this was with the understanding that the sojourn in Tete was en route for Maputo and elsewhere (MSF-F, 1988: 58–9). It was only subsequent to some confusion following the arrival of one group of them in Tete that the UNHCR arranged for them to return to their homes in southern Mozambique, since they were first considered as potential residents for the special settlement schemes (see previous chapter). According to a reporter in the area at the time, this was on the grounds that their pacifist beliefs meant they could not form militias and so would not be safe in the Benga and Moatize resettlements (Wooldridge, 1987). Another journalist on the scene (Eddings, 1987) recorded that the

Witnesses were pleased that 'the government, now more comfortable with religious diversity, was helping them to move back to Maputo, the capital city – their original home'. Certainly the fact that they were Jehovah's Witnesses and not local people was indeed widely recognized by international organizations (e.g. UNHCR-Geneva, 1988: 29), and this ultimately ensured at least some differential treatment. Thus on 15 May 1987 those Witnesses who had been first sent to the agricultural resettlement in Benga were indeed repatriated to Maputo, after a very brief sojourn, and soon afterwards the camp was closed due to Renamo attacks (MSF-B, 1987).

The organized repatriation of Witnesses from the Malawi refugee camps continued in 1989-90, although at a lower level and over shorter distances. For example, between 400 and 600 returned in September 1990 to Angonia in Tete Province in the last official repatriation movement before the funding dried up (*Mozambiquefile*, 1990; interviews with relief officials in Malawi and Angonia). Many of this last repatriation were then reported as waiting for the opportunity to return to their home areas with the support of the government unit responsible for returnees, NARML, which acknowledged that they were from 'various provinces' (*Noticias*, 1990).

Witness Returnees in the Tete Transit Camps

Although some Witnesses did quickly leave the Tete transit camps for other areas, many of these earliest returnees remained in Moatize I and other camps for several years. (For a review of the wider experience of the Tete transit camps see the previous chapter.) In April 1989 a visiting agronomist to the Benga settlement noted that his 'informant came from Melange [sic] (Zambezia Province) in September 1987' and added 'people in camp come from all over Tete, Zambezia, Angonia etc. (some Jehovah's Witnesses)' (Brand *et al.*, 1989). Witnesses who had remained in the Benga camp complained to relief officials in 1988 and 1989 about their desire to go home and Witnesses in exile in Zambia told me that they had received letters from Benga reporting bitterly that some returnees had 'died stuck in these Tete returnee camps'. Some of the Witnesses even fled the armed attacks on Benga or the other settlements and ended up in the refugee camps of the Zimbabwe border (S. Makanya, personal communication).

The constraints on getting the Witnesses out of the Tete settlements and back to their homes possibly included the fact that conditions in their home province (Gaza) were still highly insecure (D. Keet, personal communication), as well as the underfunding and overwork of the responsible authorities. However, one relief official interviewed suspected that, in a situation of marginal official repatriation outside of the Jehovah's Witness group, UNHCR/NARML were anxious to secure a dynamic population for their settlements since these were supposed to be pilot projects to demonstrate to funders their capacity to handle the main repatriations anticipated with peace. The value of the Witnesses, who were not local, may have also been enhanced by the fact that they could not so easily self-settle locally (whereas such departure was very common amongst other returnee groups).

The Witnesses in the Tete settlements did not remain passive victims, however, for they found many ways to leave Benga. Large numbers were able to reach far-distant Maputo under their own steam in 1987-89, and presumably also other cities. A relief official responsible for air transport recalled that they would lobby very effectively for free lifts at Tete city airport. The Witness organization, who first reached Benga from Zimbabwe by bicycle when the war had stopped vehicle convoys, also raised money to pay for flights of some members stranded in Tete. A large group came to Quelimane from Tete by air in mid-1990, about half of whom had first returned from Ukwimi in Zambia prior to August 1988, and the other half of whom had left Malawi for Benga in 1987 and 1988. Interviews with members of this community of 262 Witnesses in Lobo in Nicoadala district in late 1991 suggested that they were coping remarkably well, although they had yet to establish 'homes' even by the standards of a group who have spent the last two or three decades living in camps. Whenever opportunities opened up for commercial transport to their home districts Witnesses would depart from Nicoadala, and return home unassisted. One even managed to reach Milange through an epic several-week journey by foot, boat and convoy via Alto Zambezia, Niassa Province and Malawi to get back to Milange, receiving en route help from local government officials, including some Malawi currency to pay for a ferry journey. Other Witnesses decided to join the general overland repatriation movements to Milange from Benga which were organized by NARML and UNHCR in the years after Milange was recaptured from Renamo, and which are described in the previous chapter.

Clamp-downs on Religious Activity in Malawi & Return Movements
Some self-returns of Witnesses from Malawi were directly related to clamp-downs on their religious activities in exile. An increased rate of return to Milange during 1991, for example, reflected a much more restrictive attitude towards the Witnesses in the Chiringa, Muloza and especially Tengani camps after February 1991. Chiringa saw seven Witnesses arrested for praying in secret in that month, though the subsequent arrivals from Chiringa stated that it was the lack of land and not the repression that had persuaded them to return. 'We have a custom of suffering for our God', they claimed flatly 'we cannot run away because of oppression'. Representatives of the remaining 800 Witnesses in Tengani, however, stated that they did decide to return to Mozambique because of heightened religious restrictions in Malawi, and the associated pressures on them from the authorities to depart. They stated that they had been under intensive surveillance since March 1991, and therefore had decided it was better to return to Mozambique. It had been agreed to make this return from Tengani in small groups so as to minimize the logistical pressures on their membership, and to ease the process of rebuilding their lives as a community in Milange. In the absence of formal repatriation assistance, the Mozambique Embassy had agreed to provide transport for 59 people to return in that month. (Unlike the other Malawi camps, Tengani is far from Milange.) However, by late 1991 difficulties faced by the returnees in Milange were discouraging further movements. These included the kidnap on 3 May 1991 of one of the returnees by Renamo, though he was later freed by the Frelimo counter-attack. Furthermore, despite an official agreement with the authorities in Milange that they were to be exempt, there were also continued attempts by elements in the Frelimo army to recruit the Witnesses for compulsory military service, as well as some other minor abuses by army personnel. Nevertheless, in late 1991 these 22 families of returnee Witnesses from Tengani were rapidly establishing themselves and had started to build their own 'Kingdom Hall'. They continued to prepare for the return of their fellow refugees from Tengani for when it would be considered that the time was right.

On the grounds that refugees must accept the 'law of the land' even the UNHCR publicly supported the Malawi Government's campaign to stop Witnesses worshipping during the latter half of 1991, particularly in the Chang'ambika camp, according to articles in the Malawi press and interviews with appropriate relief officials. Following these meetings a group of Witnesses from that Chang'ambika camp decided that they would not accept these restrictions and they self-repatriated to Mozambique (interview with a relief official in Blantyre, Malawi). This is presumably the same group as the

230 Witnesses reported to have arrived in
Zobue shortly afterwards, declaring themselves as expelled from Malawi and living
in precarious circumstances in a government centre in Mozambique, still very far
from what might be called 'home' (*Noticias*,
1991). The reasons for a changing government practice in Malawi towards the Witnesses are unclear, though they may reflect
the new instabilities in Malawi generated
largely by recent donor and internal pressures for democratization. Further influxes
of expelled Witnesses were reported in
northern Tete during May 1992 (*Noticias*,
1992), though later in 1992 the religious
restrictions on refugee Witnesses were said
by Witnesses resident in Milange to have
been reversed throughout Malawi, for reasons that are unclear. This liberalization
had reduced the number of Witnesses
returning from the Malawian camps into
Milange and other areas of Mozambique
once more. These events suggest, therefore,
that the processes stimulating repatriation
can be generated by a complex interaction
between the social and religious dynamism
of the refugees themselves, and events in
the 'home' and 'host' societies.

10.5 *Jehovah's Witness members in Milange,
Mozambique, September 1991 (K. Wilson)*

The Role of Repatriation Through
Official Channels

It is striking that Jehovah's Witnesses
dominated the small fraction of repatria-
tion during 1986–91 that has been undertaken as part of official programmes, despite
the fact that they are the most self-reliant and self-organized group of Mozambican
refugees. This fact even led to the NARML delegate in Tete to declare that this
demonstrated 'that Malawi only allows repatriation from its territory of Mozambican
"undesirables" ' (*Noticias*, 1990). In fact, however, it actually reflects a more complicated
relationship between the concerns of the authorities and a self-organizing movement.

Some of the reasons why Witnesses dominate the official repatriation movements are
illustrated by the Witnesses' own account of the 1990 return to Angonia. During 1987,
five Dedza refugee Witnesses were arrested by the Malawi Young Pioneers after crossing
the border to clandestinely attend a Witness gathering in Domue in Angonia district
of Mozambique. Negotiations followed, and in 1988 the Malawian authorities agreed
to release the five, on the grounds that the Witnesses agreed to return to Mozambique
under a repatriation exercise. This coincided with the official announcements of intended
repatriation programmes at meetings organized in camps throughout the country under
the Tripartite Commission. The Witnesses then held a meeting which decided to link

their return to the official programme, and to prepare their case for return and a list of returnees for presentation to the authorities. They also decided there that they should request the presentation to the Mozambican authorities of a formal declaration of their desire to return voluntarily, so as to protect them on the other side of the border. However, it then took two years for UNHCR and the Malawi authorities to make necessary institutional and transport arrangements for the return journey. Like many Mozambicans, the Witness informants suspected that the Malawian government stalled their return in order to maintain the emergency assistance programme to their country, though a more likely explanation for the delays is the institutional challenges of funding and negotiation.

During the two years that the Witnesses in Dedza waited to be repatriated to Angonia, it was officially recognized that tens of thousands of other Mozambicans self-repatriated into that province rather than attempt to go through the stalled official procedures. The potential ease of return is illustrated by the fact that the Angonia authorities, for example, recorded 43,659 returnees between 1987 and the end of 1991. Even those refugees who had not repatriated increasingly visited Mozambique for access to markets, services or natural resources during this period. Therefore the Witnesses could have easily self-returned, but they chose not to. Indeed, it is also noteworthy that, even when the official repatriation happened, many of the Witness returnees did actually also go on foot, because the transport provided was only available for two days at short notice, and many were not ready to go at that particular moment. In fact it is clear that the 'repatriation' programme was actually serving a 'protection' function, not one of relocation or reintegration, since they had used being legitimate returnees to effectively curb persecution for their religious affiliation. Even more ironic was the fact that the returnees were allocated to a special *bairro* distant from the Vila Ulongue town, in part because they were 'under UNHCR', and in part because they were perceived as a closed and an aggressively evangelical group; then, because of the inadequate aid in the early period, they managed to successfully return to Malawi from time to time to receive extra rations. Subsequently it came to pass in 1992 that the local Mozambican authorities even wanted to bring them closer to the centre of Vila Ulongue in order to use their industriousness to create official reintegration projects that would have a greater chance of succeeding.

Establishment of Returnees in Maputo

Those Jehovah's Witnesses who reached Maputo established highly successful congregations within a year of their first starting to return from exile (Maier, 1988). Interviews and observations by Jovito Nunes and myself in Maputo in 1989 and 1991 respectively suggested that they were also using their excellent woodworking skills to earn a relatively secure living in comparison to other recent immigrants to the capital. Meanwhile fellow Witness repatriates continued their migrations south into Swaziland and South Africa, following the social networks of their home areas abandoned fifteen years before, which had been restructured and relocated by the war and economic collapse. Interviews with Witnesses in Maputo in 1991 also indicated, however, that few Witnesses have been able to reach Maputo from Zambia, Malawi or the northern provinces since the large return movements in 1987–89.

Conclusion

The experience of the Jehovah's Witnesses in the war zone of northern Mozambique and the refugee and returnee camps across Central Africa throws important light on a wide variety of issues concerning the way in which refugees can be considered as social agents. The Witnesses, with their faith, courage and self-identification through collective action in the face of tribulation, lead us to most usefully question what really is meant by 'flight', 'repatriation' and 'reintegration' for people whose central experience has been as part of tumultuous relocations and whose sense of home and community is as a persecuted group. There is also much to ponder about concerning how the most self-reliant and self-organized group of refugees becomes the one most involved in official repatriation programmes, but in fact for entirely other reasons than their logistical usefulness.

References

Askin, S. (1988) 'All condemn Renamo except the Bishops', *The Weekly Mail*, Johannesburg, 15 September.

Black, R., T. Mabwe, F. Shumba and K. Wilson (1990) 'Ukwimi refugee settlement: livelihood and settlement planning for Mozambicans in Zambia', unpublished report, King's College, London, Refugee Studies Programme, Oxford.

Brand, C., J. Wilding and V.A. Metcalf (1989) AgPack project evaluation, unpublished, World Vision Mozambique.

Chirwa, W.N.C. (1984) 'Masokwa Elliot Kenan Kamwana: his religious and political activities, and the effects of Kamwanaism in South-East Nkhata Bay, 1908–1956', Department of History Seminar Paper, University of Malawi, March.

Cisternino, M. (1987) Report on the situation of displaced Mozambicans in Malawi, until 12 June 1987, unpublished Comboni Missionary Society, Rome.

Cross, S. (1973) 'The Watch Tower movement in South Central Africa, 1908–1945', DPhil thesis, Oxford.

—— (1978) 'Independent churches and independent states: Jehovah's Witnesses in East and Central Africa' in E. Fashole-Luke (ed.) *Christianity in independent Africa*, Rex Collings, London.

Development: Ukwimi Quarterly Newsletter (1989) 'Repatriation already?' Editorial, Vol. 2, No. 1, April.

Eddings (1987) 'The unending agony of a magic land', *The Washington Post*, Washington DC.

Fields, K. (1985) *Revival and rebellion in colonial Central Africa*, Princetown University Press, Princetown.

Finnegan, F. (1992) *A complicated war: the harrowing of Mozambique*, University of California Press, Berkeley.

Hodges, T. (1985) *Jehovah's Witnesses in Central Africa*, Minority Rights Group, Report No. 29.

Hooker, J.R. (1965) 'Witnesses and Watch Tower in the Rhodesias and Nyasaland', *Journal of African History*, Vol. 6: 91–106.

Maier, K. (1988) 'Religious revival in Mozambique', *The Independent*, 30 May, London.

Médecins Sans Frontières (Belgium) (MSF-B) (1987) 'Evaluation médico-sanitaire des populations "retournées" dans le district de Moatize – province de Tete', unpublished report, Tete, June.

—— (1989) 'Final evaluation of the medical activities in the Moatize District between July 1988 and June 1989', unpublished report, Tete.

Médecins Sans Frontières (France) [MSF-F] (1988) Annual Report 1988, Blantyre.

Mozambiquefile (Maputo) (1990) 'Malawi discourages refugees from returning home', October.

Noticias (Maputo) (1990) 'Financial difficulties compromise repatriation', 31 December.

—— (1991) 'Mais de 200 moçambicanos for expulsados do Malawi: autoridades deste pais accusam os repatriados de serem membros da seita "Testemunhas de Jeova" ', 12 November.

—— (1992) 'Refugiados moçambicanos expulsos do Malawi: por se recusarem a aderir ao partido de Banda', 16 August.

UNHCR (Geneva) (1988) *Mozambique: an emergency preparedness profile*, Emergency Section.

United States Government Department of State (1988) *World Refugee Report*, Washington DC. Bureau for Refugee Programs, September.

Wilson, K.B. (1991a) 'Conceiving of the future amongst Mozambicans in Ukwimi refugee settlement in Zambia', unpublished report, Refugee Studies Programme, Oxford.

—— (1991b) *War, displacement, social change and the re-creation of community: an exploratory study in Zambezia, Mozambique*, Refugee Studies Programme and Nuffield Foundation, Oxford.

—— (1992) 'Cults of violence and counter violence in Mozambique', *Journal of Southern African Studies*, 18(3): 527–82.

Wooldridge, M. (1987) BBC World Service radio report, 20 May.

11 CHRIS TAPSCOTT
A Tale of Two Homecomings

Influences of the Economy & State
on the Reintegration of Repatriated
Namibian Exiles, 1989–1991

Introduction

The implementation of UN Security Council resolution 435 in April 1989 marked the end of more than a century of colonial rule in Namibia and set in train a programme to repatriate some 45,000 exiles from neighbouring states and further afield. The repatriation of these exiles is recognized as one of the most orderly and well-managed operations ever to have been undertaken by the Office of the United Nations High Commissioner for Refugees. Yet, whilst the physical translocation of exiles was effected with considerable success, the process of reintegrating them into Namibian society, and into the labour market in particular, has proved to be one of the biggest disappointments of the entire independence process, and may in the longer run undermine efforts to forge a more equitable and politically stable society.

Most notable in that respect has been the marked differentiation that has occurred amongst repatriated exiles since their return. Expectations of the contribution which returnees would make to post-independence Namibia were high, and on one level these have been confirmed. Much of the leadership of the new government is drawn from the ranks of those repatriated, and many occupy key positions in the civil service where they enjoy the benefits of wage packages which are generous in comparison to standards elsewhere in Africa. However, despite high hopes of the future that awaited them after repatriation and national independence, the majority of returnees remain unemployed in the economically depressed rural areas of northern Namibia. The contrasts, frequently drawn, between those former exiles who have acquired employment and those who have not, thus serve to heighten disappointment and frustration with the present state of affairs.

The difficulties experienced by repatriated exiles can, to some extent, be ascribed to the limited mandate of repatriating agencies (which typically end with the physical translocation of refugees) and to a number of assumptions and presuppositions which underpinned the repatriation process. With regard to the latter, both the economy and state were taken to be dependent variables in the repatriation equation, since they were assumed to confront all Namibians (exiles and those that remained) alike. And yet, irrespective of how favourably disposed the SWAPO government may have felt towards returnees at the outset, the economy and the state have set the parameters in which the process of reintegration has been effected. These relate in particular to the capacity of the state administration to accommodate the needs of repatriated exiles and of the economy to support new work

11.1 *A transit camp in Angola for repatriating Namibians (UNHCR/19006/A. Gesulfo)*

11.2 *A reception centre for temporary accommodation of returned refugees (UNHCR/19097/L. Ward)*

seekers; they also relate to the impact of the policy of national reconciliation, introduced by the new government at independence, and its tendency to retain the status quo and reinforce social stratification.

While a number of studies have illustrated the universal complexities of repatriation pro-grammes (Rogge, 1991; Crisp, 1986) and have pointed out that a successful and relatively problem-free return is the exception rather than the rule (Coles, 1985), comparatively little has been written in the research literature on refugees on the socio-economic consequences of repatriation, and still less has been explicitly written on the impact of the state and state policies (however benign) on the process of reintegration. While the discussion which follows does not attempt to theoretize the impact of the economy and state in any systematic way, it does attempt to illustrate the importance of these two variables in analysis of the reintegration of refugees in the case of Namibia at least.

National Reconciliation & Social Stratification

Following elections to a Constituent Assembly in November 1989, the victorious South West African People's Party (the political wing of SWAPO), hitherto viewed by many Western governments as Marxist in orientation, surprised many observers with its con-ciliatory policies and its commitment to democracy and a free market economy. Most noteworthy was the introduction of a policy of national reconciliation, which was adopted in a concerted effort to overcome the ethnic and political divisions of the past and create a new Namibian identity.

Viewed from one angle, the pursuit of a policy of national reconciliation was both politically astute and economically necessary. Not only did it forestall the flight of much needed skills and capital, but it also minimized the potential for political destabilization by disaffected opponents. The policy of national reconciliation (mediated by a constitution which was forged through inter-party consensus), nevertheless, has done much to reinforce the status quo. In so doing, it has also strengthened trends towards social stratification amongst the indigenous population, and especially amongst repatriated exiles. In par-ticular, the new constitution served to entrench the status quo by guaranteeing the jobs and employment benefits of all civil servants in office at the time of independence. In so doing, it also ensured those entering the civil service after independence (including many returnees) of the generous wage packages which the colonial government had awarded its own administration.

In that respect, Namibian society in the colonial era was characterized by forms of struc-tured inequality which manifested themselves in severe income distribution skews and unequal access to productive assets and basic social services. The white settler community, together with a tiny black elite, comprised just 5 per cent of the population but in 1989 were estimated to control 71 per cent of the GDP. The bottom 55 per cent of the popula-tion, in contrast, controlled just 3 per cent of the GDP (United Nations, 1989). In the post-independence era there is evidence of a growing class stratification which transcends previous racial and ethnic boundaries. This observation relates primarily to the emergence of a new elite (comprising much of the existing white settler elite together with a new class of senior black administrators, politicians and business people), who inhabit an eco-nomic and social world largely divorced from that of the majority of the urban and rural poor. However, despite the fact that the vast majority of repatriated exiles were members of SWAPO, only a small minority have entered the ranks of this new elite.

Over and above the cadre of political and military leaders who grew out of the liberation struggle and who now occupy leading positions in the new government, the primary determinant of social and economic standing among repatriated exiles in the post-independence era appears to be education. Of the 40,000–45,000 Namibians who went into exile, a relatively small proportion (15 per cent at most) underwent comprehensive post-secondary training. The remainder were trained as soldiers or learnt rudimentary artisanal and agricultural skills in camps in Angola. Access to training, thus, was a key determinant in the social differentiation of exiles, not least in the employment opportunities which it has afforded in the post-independence era, but also in the lifestyles to which it accustomed many repatriated exiles. Although educated individuals by no means lived lives of affluence in exile, their expectations of the good life post-independence were clearly influenced by their years in Europe, the USA and elsewhere.

While the demands of the liberation struggle may have served to differentiate exiles to an extent, this tendency has been accentuated by the limitations of the Namibian labour market. In that respect, the single most important impediment to the full reintegration of repatriated exiles into Namibian society has been their inability to acquire wage employment. Registration of ex-SWAPO combatants in mid-1991 revealed that more than 16,000 were still unemployed. When taken together with non-combatants, this figure is likely to have risen to between 20,000 and 25,000 individuals, which would suggest that between 45 per cent and 55 per cent of all repatriated exiles were still unemployed more than two years after the first of them returned home.

The former exiles' re-entry into the employment market is severely constrained by the country's dependent and narrowly based economy. Despite its size, Namibia is not a richly endowed land. A significant proportion of the countryside is classified as desert or semi-desert, and ecological conditions in general are harsh. With the exception of certain regions, neither the climate nor the disposition of the soil is favourable for arable agriculture on any scale and this factor alone sets limits on the production frontiers of the country. The country's GDP is largely accounted for by four sectors: mining and quarrying (32 per cent), general government (18 per cent), wholesale and retailing (13 per cent) and agriculture and fishing (11 per cent). A tendency to greater capital intensity in both the mining and commercial agricultural sectors has increased the demand for skilled workers and, at the same time, has limited the potential for mass employment generation. At present less than half (43 per cent) of the labour force is in paid employment in the formal sector, with open unemployment between 25 and 30 per cent (ILO, 1990). Based on current estimates, the potentially economically active population is growing at a rate of 3 per cent per annum, and on this evidence Namibia faces a serious problem of employment generation. The task of reducing the backlog of those currently unemployed, while creating opportunities for repatriated exiles as well as the significant numbers of new work seekers entering the market annually, as a consequence, remains formidable (UNICEF/NISER, 1991).

At the same time, as a consequence of a distorted economy and as a legacy of apartheid rule (which limited access to higher education and skills training amongst the black population), there is both a critical shortage of skills (exacerbated by departing South Africans) and a severe problem of unemployment among the semi-skilled and unskilled. For those returnees with education and skills, demand generally exceeds supply and thus far there has been little competition for employment. The jobs which they fill, furthermore, tend to be in the urban areas (in the capital Windhoek in particular) where social services are relatively good and lifestyles are easier. The converse applies to those who have limited skills. Competition for employment is fierce, wages are low, and many are forced to eke out a subsistence in the rural areas where services are limited or non-existent.

In northern Namibia (which is home to more than 60 per cent of returnees) problems

11.3 *Some Namibians returned home from Angola in relative comfort, but the government have found their expectations hard to meet (UNHCR/19152/L. Aström)*

of employment generation are particularly acute. As a consequence of the limited resource endowments and underdevelopment of the region in the aftermath of twenty years of war, job opportunities are generally few and far between and, if anything, have diminished since the withdrawal of the South African forces in late 1989. Returning exiles have, thus, not only exacerbated the problem of unemployment, but must also compete for jobs with the local population, on terms which are less than favourable.

The fact that so many 'returnees' are living in scattered rural settlements throughout the region, moreover, has meant that the majority are isolated from major towns and from potential job markets. A further constraint to re-entry to the labour market is the fact that the skills which returnees do possess frequently do not match existing work opportunities in the north. For some, this implies that they should be looking for employment in other parts of the country and most probably in Windhoek. However, individuals' efforts to find employment elsewhere are often thwarted by shortages of cash for transport and travel expenses. Many returnees are thus effectively trapped in the rural areas.

A major premise of the repatriation programme was the assumption that returnees would be accommodated by their families. While this assumption was largely correct in that the majority of repatriated exiles were able to return to their family homes, what was not anticipated was the length of time they would have to remain dependent on the support of their families and the burden this would impose. Indeed, it is a seeming paradox of the entire repatriation programme that for many returnees their present welfare is determined less by their own ability (or their contribution to the liberation struggle) than by the income status of the families to which they returned. Those who returned to families which are comparatively better off have not only experienced better living conditions, but have had potentially better access to employment (through better access to cash and transport). Individuals who returned to aged or unemployed parents in contrast, for example, have received very little familial support. Similarly disadvantaged are individuals who have been unable to relocate their families which were scattered during the long years of war. The class dimensions of repatriation have thus been inescapable, whatever the extent of social equity in exile.

The decision to opt for a 'mixed economy' – in practice a capitalist economy – although in large part dictated by circumstance (Namibia's dependent economic status, and the collapse of support from socialist countries in particular), is also limiting the policy options open to the new government. While SWAPO controls the political arena, it does not control the economy which continues to be dominated by forces which vary in their support from indifference to open hostility. Consequently, in its efforts to promote the confidence of the business sector (which retains the ultimate sanction of disinvestment from Namibia), the government has moved extremely cautiously on issues of affirmative action, minimum wages and the question of land redistribution.

At the same time, within the private sector there has been a marked antipathy towards employment of returnees, who are seen as representatives of the ruling party. Linked to the above, the qualifications, experience and work ethic of individuals trained in socialist or Eastern Bloc countries have been the subject of scepticism among prospective employers, and have undoubtedly contributed to their reluctance to recruit returnees despite evident skills shortages in their firms. This attitude has placed added pressure on the already bloated public sector to provide employment and has made the efforts of returnees to reintegrate themselves infinitely more difficult.

The Constraints of Administrative Restructuring

At the same time, the SWAPO government faces further constraints in its efforts to transform Namibian society in that it has yet to fully 'capture' the state. As a consequence of the constitution, which guaranteed job security, middle management in the public service is still extensively controlled by civil servants from the former colonial administration. While most of these individuals have adapted to the new order, a number appear insidiously to be obstructing efforts to build a more egalitarian and non-racial society. In the months immediately after independence, many returnees complained of bureaucratic intransigence on the part of some civil servants both in processing job applications and in accrediting foreign qualifications – the latter applied especially to professions such as teaching, nursing and medicine. Others complained that incumbent officials displayed favouritism in their recruitment of new staff, and in particular that they discriminated against repatriated exiles.

Perhaps a more serious impediment to the reintegration of returnees, however, is the generally limited capacity of the state administration to implement development programmes in the populous northern regions. While this is a problem which confronts all sectors of the community alike, at present it appears to be affecting returnees most directly, not least because many lack basic productive assets, including access to land, implements and credit, to survive as subsistence farmers; expectations (and hence despondency) also appear to be highest amongst this group.

The situation has also been aggravated by the transition from the old regional administration to the new. In efforts to forge a more integrated society the former second-tier ethnic administrations have been disbanded by the government. In the process, the white officials who ran these administrations have either been transferred or, in most instances, have resigned from the service. The local officials who remain, perforce, tend to be junior staff with little or no administrative training. At the same time, the new officials appointed frequently have little experience and limited knowledge of the areas to which they have been sent. As a consequence, there is administrative confusion in many regional offices at a time when popular demands for government action are extremely high. To date no nationwide employment programmes have been embarked upon, and, due to administrative shortcomings, the 'Development Brigade' centres established in various rural areas have thus far failed in their objective of short-term job creation for ex-combatants. Fewer than several hundred returnees have been accommodated on the scheme, and donors are reviewing their continued support of the programme.

A lack of inter-ministerial co-ordination is a further problem within the new administration. The National Planning Commission, which was created to co-ordinate inter-ministerial activity and to promote inter-sectoral programmes, has experienced difficulties in recruiting appropriately qualified staff and in formalizing its activities. As a consequence thus far, comprehensive development planning at a regional or national level has been constrained and this in turn has limited inter-sectoral activity. This situation has, at times, lent itself to ad hoc interventions by both the government and donor agencies and, in certain instances, to duplication of effort. Such shortcomings inevitably limit the government's capacity to effectively utilize available donor aid, to implement new development programmes and, indirectly at least, to facilitate the reintegration of former exiles.

Problems of Social Integration

Problems of unemployment among returnees are compounding already existing problems of reintegration into Namibian society, including those of changes of lifestyle and of living standards. Most exiles were welcomed back by their families and the community as returning heroes who had brought liberation to the country. During this 'honeymoon period', many returnees found themselves overwhelmed with the generosity of family and friends, who donated gifts of clothing, food and money. Whilst this outpouring undoubtedly reflected the joy and pride of the community in their returned sons and daughters, it also reflected certain expectations about the future. In particular, many families believed that, with the return of family members educated abroad, their own fortunes would improve, both because of the salaries earned by the returnees and by means of the new opportunities which would open up through what was anticipated would be their influential positions in society.

The inability of returned exiles to acquire employment, thus, has been a source of considerable disappointment and embarrassment to themselves and to their families. Since their repatriation many returnees have had to rely heavily on the support of their families and friends for food, shelter and cash. This state of affairs is undoubtedly causing tensions within certain families (particularly those experiencing financial difficulties) and is stressful to the returnees themselves, some of whom have stated they constantly feel like beggars. A shortage of cash not only reinforces a sense of dependency on the part of returnees, but also, as intimated, hinders their efforts to find employment.

The returnees' inability to contribute to family income is also likely to have exacerbated problems of cultural readjustment. Under such circumstances, the behaviour of many young returnees has been a source of consternation to older members of the community. To some community elders, the manners and liberal attitudes of young returnees are symptomatic of a loss of respect for local culture. More seriously, in a community in which religious influences are strong, the disinterest of some returnees in attending church services, or, in certain instances, their professed atheism, is severely frowned upon. The independent attitude of repatriated women, too, has annoyed more traditionally minded members of the community, who view their behaviour as a challenge to local culture. Problems of social reintegration, however, appear to be decreasing with the passage of time.

The inability to find employment and to fully reintegrate themselves into Namibian society, nevertheless, has undoubtedly generated considerable psychological and emotional stress among many returned exiles. This state of affairs is particularly acute amongst those individuals who held positions of responsibility whilst in exile; the longer they remain idle, it would appear, the more their sense of personal worth is deflated. It is also evident that those individuals without families, or without family support, experience personal stress the most.

Many of the problems of morale and despondency amongst repatriated exiles also stem from problems of communication, or more properly the lack of communication, between returnees and both SWAPO and the government, particularly in the early stages of repatriation. Part of this confusion stemmed from a misunderstanding of the distinction between party and government. In the months of their return many returnees were clearly of the opinion that it was SWAPO, as a party rather than as government, which was responsible for job recruitment, training, etc. However, in a multi-party democracy and in pursuit of national reconciliation, the SWAPO government is portraying itself as the government of all Namibians. In so doing, with a few exceptions, it has avoided policies which directly favour the returnee community.

Political Consequences

Morale among repatriated exiles varies considerably according to age, education and levels of politicization. Older and better educated individuals seem more understanding of the range of problems which the new government is facing in bringing relief to the north. A small minority of young people, however, express strong feelings at what they feel to be a betrayal by party leaders. In particular, these individuals assert that the leaders in Windhoek appear to have forgotten about their supporters in the north and are taking care of their own interests first and foremost. Linked to this is the belief that national reconciliation is a one-sided process and that white settlers and former supporters of the South African regime are benefiting more from independence than those who had fought hardest for it.

An outburst of violence amongst former PLAN fighters in the Grootfontein district in 1991, following their failure to receive a government payout to all former combatants, is indicative of a broad-based frustration among many repatriated exiles. While the violence was confined to a small group of people, repatriated exiles constitute an important component of the population in Ovambo (the heartland of SWAPO), in terms of both their popular identity and their politicization. It is likely that as much as 50 per cent of the population in the region has close connections, of one form or another, with repatriated exiles; their opinions and influence on local thinking, as a consequence, remain significant. Whilst not probable, the possibility still exists that, with rising impatience, dissident returnees could, with promises of social and economic restructuring, be mobilized by forces wishing to destabilize Namibia. The experiences of countries such as Mozambique and Angola illustrate too well the costs of such strategies of destabilization.

References

Coles, G. J. (1985) *Voluntary repatriation: a background study*, UNHCR/International Institute for Humanitarian Law, Geneva.

Crisp, J. F. (1986) 'Ugandan repatriation programs in Sudan and Zaire: a critical examination', *African Affairs*, Vol. 86, No. 339: 163–80.

ILO (1990) 'ILO employment and training policy advisory mission', summary report, mimeo, Windhoek.

Rogge, J. R. (1991) 'Repatriation of refugees: a not-so-simple "optimum solution"', paper presented to an UNRISD Symposium on Social and Economic Aspects of Mass Voluntary Return of Refugees from One African Country to Another, Harare, March.

UNICEF/NISER (1991) *A situation analysis of children and women in Namibia*, Windhoek.

United Nations (1989) Memorandum on 'Provisional estimates of basic data for Namibia', mimeo, UN Statistical Office and Population Division, Windhoek.

12

ROSEMARY PRESTON
Returning Exiles in Namibia since Independence

Integration & Adaptation in Namibia One Year After Independence

By the first anniversary of Namibia's independence there was a growing literature on the planning and process of repatriating 43,000 Namibian refugees, which began in June 1989 and continued, as a mere trickle, through 1990. This included documents written for agencies implementing the return (e.g. RRR, 1989, 1990a, 1990b and 1991; UNHCR, 1990) and articles such as those by Mwase on repatriation, resettlement and rehabilitation (Mwase, 1990) and Gasarasi on Article 435 and the repatriation process (Gasarasi, 1991). Bush, Cliffe and Cooper have all written on the post-return, pre-independence election process (Bush, 1990; Cliffe, 1990; Cooper, 1990), while Simon has reviewed events leading up to and during the first year of independence, appraising their positive and negative implications for the consolidation of the new state (Simon, 1991).

In contrast, by the end of the first year, detailed information on the extent to which exiles had, without assistance, achieved social and economic integration was scarce. Reasons for this are various. They include not only the effect of the historically necessary time lapse between return and integration and the dispersal of those returning to all corners of the land (with the majority, 33,000, in Ovamboland in the far north of the country), but also the policy decision not to differentiate returners from stayers.

However, whatever the policy, it became quickly apparent that the experiences of reinsertion for returning exiles and adjustment to their presence on the part of those who had remained behind were qualitatively different. By early 1990, voice was being given to some of the difficulties encountered. In the special issue of *Refugees* celebrating the return to Namibia, a case study from Ovamboland revealed the embarrassment felt by returnees at being kept by families who had remained behind and their disappointment at the lack of economic opportunities and infrastructural support in the land of their dreams (Williams, 1990).

By April 1990, a national nutrition survey had found that 7 per cent of returnees had found formal sector employment and that no more than 36 per cent were active in subsistence production. This left 57 per cent who were described as economically inactive (Coghill, 1990). Independently, the Otto Benecke Stiftung, which had provided vocational training scholarships to Namibians in exile, found that only 10 per cent (of the 270

260

12.1 *A joyful reunion in Namibia, 1989 (UNHCR/19098/L. Aström)*

for whom they then had information) had obtained employment by the end of 1990 (Otto Benecke Stiftung, 1991).

Observations such as these, their own review of secondary sources (a UNICEF survey, newspaper accounts, UNHCR statistics) and in-depth interviews with a small number of people who had returned to Ovamboland led Tapscott and Mulongeni, in the one micro-level study undertaken during the first year of independence, to challenge two of the assumptions upon which the repatriation was based: (i) that those returning would be accommodated by those members of their families who had remained in Namibia; (ii) that the economically active would be absorbed into the private and public sectors of the labour market. This latter assumption had been made in the light of (iii) the anticipated skill deficit that would arise as settlers unable to reconcile themselves to independence emigrated to South Africa; (iv) the knowledge that many exiles had received some education or training (Tapscott and Mulongeni, 1990).

Tapscott and Mulongeni listed a series of reasons for the limited integration of returnees into the labour market during 1990. They included the lack of knowledge of how to go about finding employment; lack of access to job information via radio or newspapers; delays in reaching prospective employers once word came about vacancies or the possibility of work. The lack of funds to cover the cost of transport to job interviews was seen as a further impediment (Williams, 1990). Other problems encountered were thought to include the lack of adequate fluency in English or Afrikaans (the lingua franca), a failure by employers to recognize qualifications and experience obtained in many countries abroad (especially in Eastern Europe, Cuba and parts of Africa) and employer discrimination against returnees in general on account of their assumed support for SWAPO. To this list should be added the fact that fewer than the anticipated number of settlers returned to South Africa and the effects of global recession combined to reduce the number of employment opportunities available.

The low levels of economic integration in the early months generated strong, often uncomprehending, resentment. This derived partly from envy of the few who were appointed to government and other secure positions and anger at their conspicuous affluence. This resentment was aggravated by obstacles to employment encountered by those with unaccredited professional qualifications. Complaints were of unfair written tests (on grounds of language and theoretical limitations, and unchanged racist preferences on the part of employers (*The Namibian*, March 1991).

Even worse was the situation of the many who felt betrayed after years of sacrifice and hardship. As fighters or refugees, they had been fed promises of the opportunities to come with independence and return to Namibia. As fighters or refugees their every need had been met. Their every action had been regulated by people with authority in the party. With their return they expected that the party would continue to provide, failing to see that the party in government had different priorities from the party in opposition, leading the fight for liberation. They were unaware of the pressures that would lead to *laissez-faire* principles dictating the process of national consolidation and so waited in vain for a personal call from the party to assume their designated role in building the new state.

Disillusion on this scale brings problems or, at best, compromises. During the first year, it became apparent that, for many, economic difficulties were exacerbating those in domestic arenas. As commonly observed in the case of migrant labour, many of those returning found it difficult to resume or assume (in the case of the young) productive and social roles in their communities of origin. They did not identify with community culture, particularly in subsistence producing areas. Men with nothing to do to alleviate their distress are seen to take to drink, violence or crime. Women accustomed to leadership in exile were soon observed to suppress their skills so as to achieve community acceptance (Tapscott and Mulongeni, 1990), in ways reminiscent of post-war Zimbabwe a decade ago (Simon and Preston, 1992).

Former fighters demanded compensation and the demonstrations that they held in Windhoek in pursuit of their claim were widely reported in the first months of 1991 (*The Namibian*, March 1991). Extensive coverage was given to government embarrassment when South Africa agreed to compensate its former soldiers before arrangements for SWAPO fighters were in place. After prolonged public exchanges, former combatants on both sides received some compensation, but not before some of the fund was diverted as seed money for veteran Development Brigades. Those who joined were to be trained in either agriculture or construction, prior to being given sustainable income-generating opportunities. In the case of those expecting to take up farming, this was to be through the assistance in the development of co-operative enterprises. It was planned that those with building skills would be given preferential access to public sector construction tenders.

In spite of media pressure at the time of the first anniversary of independence, SWAPO had not explained or excused the protracted detention of hundreds of its supporters in 1982 and 1983. Conspicuous among those detained was the high proportion of non-Ovambo party members and known intellectuals. Some of these last appear to have been rehabilitated since their release and were given senior positions in government or in the private sector. But the fate of the majority, in particular their state of health, is not known. Many are still missing (*The Namibian*, 7 April, 1992).

At least some assistance has been given to school children who returned from other countries and to the disabled. Emergency schools were opened for one year to enable refugee children to continue their education in English, with their peers, at the levels they had reached in exile. An adoption programme was set up to find homes for orphaned children, among whom several hundred returned from East Germany and other socialist countries. Problems were reported with those who experienced a severe culture shock. Many spoke only German (which few of their adoptive families understood) and had difficulties in accepting the minimal standards of living in their new homes. Several, unable to adapt, abandoned their adoptive families. Some are now in children's homes and orphanages.

The disabled, especially those requiring longer term care and rehabilitation, required special arrangements. Twenty-five retarded and 17 blind children were accommodated and provided with nursing and training at existing church medical facilities at Engele in Ovamboland. Up to 100 physically disabled, including war wounded, were initially catered for at Nakayele, another church centre in Ovamboland. Those unable to rejoin their families were being trained in market gardening (RRR, 1991).

After one year of independence, without any significant research having been carried out, the label returnee had served to create a new, but differentiated category of Namibian: one who was capable of articulating in some cases its needs, in others its frustrations. Through the media, its interests have been kept in the public domain, sometimes evoking a response from government. At the same time, this publicity has served to obscure the processes by which stayers and returners have learned to interact. It has blocked the expression of needs by other categories, as seriously or still more seriously affected by the war, to the extent that they are hidden from view and ignored.

Alongside such difficulties, which can be seen in social, economic and military domains, and uncertainties about how to resolve them, there was, by the first anniversary of independence, a continuing optimism that the new Namibia would establish itself in the family of nations and, with the good will of multi- and bi-lateral aid arrangements, achieve an acceptable standard of well-being for all its people.

The Situation After Two Years

During the second year of independence, there have been several studies published giving information about some aspects of the situation of those who returned to Namibia in 1989 and after. Without exception, they have undertaken very limited analyses, restricting themselves to reporting on returnee location and employment statuses. Explanations for this include the fact that the studies were not primarily concerned with the situation of war-affected people and the nature of the sampling frame meant that the numbers of returnees included were small.

These studies do confirm that, by late 1991, as many as 25 per cent of those who returned from exile were living in Katatura, but not the extent to which this percentage is a product of secondary or circular movements after return. It seems likely that difficulties of adaptation to life in communities abandoned in adolescence one or two decades previously may have produced a stepwise drift down the rural kinship network, ending in a decisive move towards town (Tamas, 1992).

The most recent draft employment percentages (Table 12.1) suggest that many more returnees have found at least partial employment than was the case a year previously. Returnee men have as yet inferior access to regular employment compared to men who stayed, but there is virtually no difference between the two in respect of the fully unemployed. With women the reverse is the case. There is no difference between returners and stayers in access to regular employment, but significantly more returners declare themselves to be fully unemployed than do women who remained. There is no hard information about the processes by which these patterns are achieved, but inevitably some speculate (Tamas, 1992).

A small survey of businesses in the Oshakati/Ondangwa nexus found that one-third of the employers ($N = 63$) had taken on returned exiles, most in skilled or semi-skilled capacities. This was at a time when many businesses were being forced to cut back on staff. The data do not reveal the proportion of returnees in relation to other staff in these businesses, but it is unlikely to be high. In the public sector, it is being reported that fewer than 10 per cent of 60,000 public servants are returned exiles. Of these only a tiny proportion are in senior executive capacities.

By March 1992, branches of the Ministry of Labour and Manpower Development (MLMD) had registered 2,800 skilled or semi-skilled returned exiles as being without work and without credit for their skills. Both the MLMD and the Ministry of Education are developing systems that will, at least in future, facilitate credit transfer in a less restrictive way than the South African system hitherto employed. In particular the intention is to shift the requirement for the Grade 10 school leaving certificate, as a prerequisite for formal sector skilled and professional employment, to acceptance of recognized, frequently higher level, post-secondary qualifications and experience.

In a small study ($N = 9$) of the employment expectations of Namibian students preparing for a post-graduate degree in Britain, it was found that none were certain about their career prospects on return in 1993. Several expressed a willingness to take whatever job was offered, not necessarily in teaching. Only the two men interviewed had, independently, a clear strategy of how they would set about finding the work that they wanted. Several of the women were restricted to locations where they had housing or families to support. Among the group, there was a common feeling that, as time went by, their record as fighters, exiles and above all as SWAPO activists was likely to work against them in the labour market. Such feelings were causing severe existential problems.

With one exception, overt intervention during the second year of independence has continued to be minimal. In 1991, under the Directorate of Resettlement and Rehabilitation,

Table 12.1 *Employment status of stayers and returnees, August 1991*

| | Men | | Women | |
	Returnee	Stayer	Returnee	Stayer
Regular Employment	30	53	30	30
Underemployment				
casual	4	7	6	7
unemployed with smallholding or other business	43	25	50	42
Fully Unemployed	15	14	14	20
Total	Not given			
Sample Size	2,000 households selected from census enumeration districts			

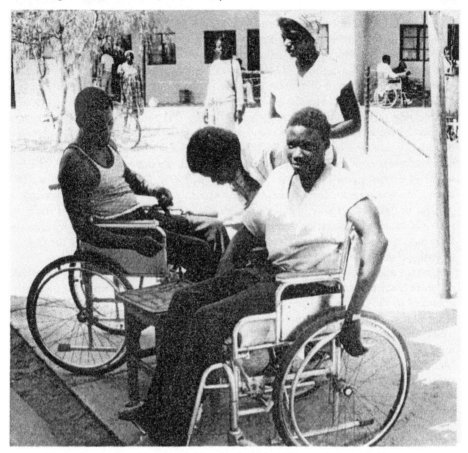

12.2 *The war of independence has left a large number disabled (UNHCR/19095/T. Williams)*

schemes were initiated to assist returned exiles, veterans and some others without means of subsistence in their places of origin. This may be because their families are lost or because their politics are at variance with those of the family who remained. Located in different parts of the country, the resettlement schemes provide each household with a plot of land and training opportunities in horticulture and livestock production. In the north they include settlements at Mangetti, Bagani and Oshiveli. There is one at Tsintsabis near Tsumeb and in the Goababis area at Drimopsis. Several cater for the semi-nomadic San people who, having been coerced into supporting the South African defence forces, were effectively abandoned without means of subsistence when the fighting ceased. There are also settlements for the disabled at Marienthal and Gibeon in the south and also at Tsia near Rundu in the north.

Linked to some of these resettlement schemes are the Development Brigades for ex-combatants which have now opened in several locations. Instructors have come from Cuba, but it seems that there are problems with curriculum development and equipment delivery.

Consultant reports on the various schemes directly affecting returned exiles and fighters suggest weaknesses in project planning and design, which are affecting donor willingness to provide funds and so the quality of project implementation (Symacon, 1991). Questions have also been raised about the quality of care and relevance of training at the centres for disabled returnees at Nakayele and Engele (Allison, 1992).

So far, there has been one reported case of damages awarded to a civilian for crimes of war by South African fighters (*The Namibian*, April, 1992), but overall, in the background, the rumblings of discontent continue. It was informally reported that, early in April 1992, a delegation of former SWAPO officers had met with the Minister of Defence complaining that without work they were starving (Preston, 1992). There are tales of conflict between former SWAPO and Koevoet members within the Development Brigades. Those who worked as teachers in Kwanza Sul and Nyango refugee settlements have received no credit in Namibia for their work and, unemployed, see former pupils in senior government positions (Pakleppa and Hango, 1992). Problems of substance abuse, criminality and mental illness amongst those seriously affected by the war, whether as civilians or fighters, are now beginning to be seen as symptoms of war-related stress and post-war failure of expectations. In one report, in what may come to occur with greater frequency, a man assaulted a former SWAPO fighter seeking vengeance for the death of a relative (Lubbe, 1992).

A recent documentary film, *Cucu's People*, televised on the second anniversary of independence (Pakleppa and Hango, 1992), caused discomfort among sections of the population ill-atuned to the problems of the north and the fate of frustrated returnees. The purpose of the film was to draw attention to the efforts of a local NGO, the Namibia Development Trust, at encouraging participatory approaches to community reconstruction and development. At the same time, locating exile within the context of a long tradition of migrant labour, not only did the story of a post-war Ovambo village feature some of 120 returned exiles without work, it highlighted the residual despair among those who stayed and their experiences during the war as a buffer between the opposing military forces. Overall, however, the damages to the resident civilian population, white as well as black, have been given minimal publicity and remain invisible in the post-war popular press.

References

Allison, C. (1992) Notes of interview, 5 May, Windhoek.
Bush, R. (1990) 'The Namibian election process: just about free and fair', *Review of African Political Economy*, 45/46: 151–7.
Cliffe, L. (1990) 'Namibia postscript: the election results', *Review of African Political Economy*, 45/46: 157–8.
Coghill, B. (1990) 'Household health and nutrition survey in Namibia', Report of a survey in Katatura and selected northern areas of Namibia, April–May, UNICEF, Windhoek.
Cooper, A. (1990) 'UN-supervised elections in Namibia: a critical analysis', *Without Prejudice*, Winter: 45–69.
Gasarasi, C.P. (1991) 'UN Resolution 435 and the repatriation of Namibian exiles', *Journal of Refugee Studies*, Vol. 3, No. 4.
Goldlust, J. and A.H. Richmond (1974) 'A multivariate model of immigrant adaptation', *International Migration Review*, Vol. 8, No. 2: 193–225.
Lubbe, A. (1992) 'Ex-PLAN man persecuted', *New Era*, 1, 40.
Mwase, N.R.L. (1990) 'The repatriation, rehabilitation and resettlement of Namibian refugees at independence', *Community Development Journal*, Vol. 25, No. 2: 113–22.
Namibian, The (1991, 1992) Various issues, Windhoek.
Otto Benecke Stiftung (1991) Annual Report, 1990.
Pakleppa, R. and I. Hango (1992) *Cucu's people*, New Dawn Videos, Windhoek.
Petola, P. (1992) 'Organised labour in post-independence Namibia', doctoral thesis in progress, University of Helsinki.
Preston, R. (1991) Notes of interview with Dawson Sanangore, Director of the Department of Social Welfare, Zimbabwe, March.
—— (1992) Notes of interview with Festus Nahola and Kandindime Nehova, SWAPO HQ, 7 April.

Refugees (1990) Various issues, UNHCR, Geneva.

Repatriation, Resettlement & Reconstruction Committee (RRR) (1989, 1990a) *Council of Churches in Namibia/Repatriation, Resettlement & Reconstruction Committee weekly newsletter*, CCN/RRR, Windhoek. (Supplement to *The Namibian* during the repatriation exercise.)

— (1990b) *Narrative reports*, CCN/RRR, Windhoek.

— (1991) *Mission accomplished*, CCN/RRR, Windhoek.

Simon, D. (1991) *Independent Namibia one year on*, Conflict Studies 239, Research Institute for the Study of Conflict and Terrorism, London.

Simon, D. and R. Preston (forthcoming) 'Return to the promised land: the repatriation and resettlement of Namibian refugees, 1989–1990', in R. Black and V. Robinson (eds) *Geography and refugees: patterns and processes of change*, Belhaven Press London.

Symacon (pvt) Ltd. (1991) Update on missions report on the Namibia Development Brigade project, SIDA, Windhoek.

Tamas, K. (1992) 'Repatriated Namibian exiles: political, economic and social integration', paper presented at NISER, 6 May.

Tapscott, C. and B. Mulongeni (1990) '*An evaluation of the welfare and future prospects of repatriated Namibians in Northern Namibia*, NISER, Windhoek.

UNHCR (1990) *Namibia repatriation operation: lessons learned survey*, Geneva.

UNRISD (1991) Symposium on social and economic aspects of mass voluntary return of refugees from one African country to another, Harare, 12–14 March.

Williams, T. (1990) in *Refugees*, May.

13

KWAME ARHIN
The Reaccommodation of Ghanaian
Returnees from Nigeria in 1983 & 1985

Large-scale migration from Ghana to Nigeria started in the mid-1970s and reached its peak in the early 1980s at a time when the Ghanaian economy was in severe decline and Nigeria was experiencing an oil boom. Skilled, semi-skilled and non-skilled personnel were in great demand in Nigeria, and both air and lorry fares to Nigeria were relatively cheap. It was also possible to travel on foot. Ghanaian migrant workers were protected by a Protocol of the ECOWAS (Economic Community of West African States) Treaty signed in Lagos in 1975, which allowed free movement in a member country for a maximum period of 90 days, within which a traveller could formalize a longer stay.

The Ghanaians who migrated to Nigeria belonged to one of two basic categories: legal and illegal immigrants, which generally corresponded to skilled and unskilled personnel. The legal/skilled personnel mostly had placements in organizations and sometimes even had their passages paid before they went to Nigeria. They included university teachers, doctors and paramedical staff, engineers, surveyors and draughtsmen, members of the legal profession, air pilots and mechanics. They were generally not affected by the expulsion orders of 17 January 1983 and 10 May 1985, and were not included in the figures of 900,000–1,000,000 (1983) and 90,000 (1985) as the estimated numbers of Ghanaians who were to be repatriated from Nigeria as illegal immigrants.[1] The illegal, semi-skilled and unskilled migrants were scattered throughout Nigeria, in the kinds of jobs that Nigerians were said to scorn. A report in *West Africa* described the life of some unskilled migrants in Lagos in the following way:

> A visit to the Ghanaian village of Ijora revealed an area of filth, stench and squalor. Ijora is a sprawling area of one mile radius, and almost all the buildings are wooden structures suspended on wooden poles. Underneath these wooden structures, the liquid is stagnant and anything imaginable is dumped there. 4,000 of the 5,000 inhabitants are Ghanaians.
>
> Ghanaians in Ijora have kept links with home. Ghanaian music blares from loudspeakers amidst the aroma of Ghanaian food. Ghanaian reading materials abound and believe it or not one can get Ghanaian dailies 24 hours old. The dailies which sell for one cedi in Accra, are 40 kobo at Ijora. Walk for 200 metres and one is bound to hear all the major Ghanaian dialects.
>
> Certain types of Ghanaians live at Ijora. They are usually labourers, roadside hawkers, drivers, prostitutes, or unemployed. Some of the unemployed have formed themselves into criminal

---

[1] See Final Report on Emergency Operation 346 and Expansion of Emergency Food Aid for people affected by drought and bush-fires: Office of the National Mobilization Committee, Accra, 30-9-86.

gangs known as 'jagudar'. The fact that the work of some able-bodied men at Ijora is to peel cassava and help pound fufu in chop-bars is indicative of the level of unemployment. (*West Africa*, 24 January 1983)

It is clear from the passage that the Ghanaian migrants regarded themselves as temporary residents in Nigeria. Most of them visited Ghana when their short-term targets had been attained: the acquisition of money and scarce goods such as radio and TV sets, lorries or cars. Even while in Nigeria, the migrants still lived, at least partly, within the 'moral order' of their natal communities.

The Manner of the Ghanaians' Return to Ghana

It was not so much the enforced return of the illegal immigrants as the manner in which they were expelled that turned them into 'refugees'. As in most Third World countries, the Government of Nigeria had no efficient ways of registering people who arrived from Ghana. Moreover, given the country's need for unskilled labour, the authorities were prepared to turn a 'blind eye' to the presence of the Ghanains. When, for both economic and political reasons, the government was no longer prepared to tolerate the migrants' presence, it simply announced through the media a two-week deadline within which all aliens had to obtain valid documents or leave the country. The announcement was apparently welcome to the Nigerian public at large who reportedly tried to enforce it through the threat or use of force. Acts of molestation, reportedly, included beatings by Nigerian 'hoodlums' and police, who forced the victims to abandon their property. Nigerian employers allegedly took advantage of the general panic, and cut or refused to pay salaries and wages due to the migrants.

The combination of public and state hostility heightened the feeling of insecurity of the migrants, leading to overcrowding at reception and departure points: the airport in Kano, the Mohammed Mustala airport and the Apapa docks in Lagos. In addition to air and sea transport, there was the possibility of road transport, but for a period, following the announcement of the deadline for the departure of the 'aliens', Nigeria closed her border with Benin, and Ghana closed hers with Togo. There was, therefore, heavy demand for air and shipping services. The waiting and the physical struggle to secure these services, as well as the conditions of travel on the ships during the Lagos–Tema passage, produced fatigue and illness among the migrants. Air travel was also restricted because the Nigerian authorities would not, at first, permit other airlines than those of Ghana and Nigeria to operate on the Accra–Lagos route. The problem of transportation was eased when the Nigeria–Benin and Ghana–Togo borders were opened, and migrants could convey themselves in their own vehicles. For the 'evacuation' Ghana mobilized Ghana Airways, the national air-carrier, and the Ghana Air Force as well as the National Shipping Line. The Nigerian Shipping Line also played a part; and migrants used their own vehicles, where they had any.[2]

Whereas the Ghanaians had migrated to Nigeria individually or in family units over an extended period, in 1983 and 1985 they were forced to return en masse, within a restricted period, and by limited means of transportation. It was these conditions of

---

[2] Report by Commodore Steve Obimpeh, Chairman of the National Mobilization Committee (NMC), 6 May 1985: Office of the NMC. My own sister's son brought his own truck from 'Agege' in 1983.

enforced return that evoked both national and international response, and turned the return of the migrants into a 'refugee problem' worthy of international support.

The year 1982–3 may go down as one of the worst in the economic, social and political history of Ghana. The Provisional National Defence Council (PNDC), which assumed power by a coup d'état on 31 December 1981, had not then succeeded in gaining international economic aid. It was uncertain of its own ideological position, and seemed to favour an anti-Western or anti-capitalist orientation. It was after a fruitless search for economic support from Russia and the Eastern Bloc that an approach was made to the International Monetary Fund (IMF) and the World Bank for support.

Meanwhile, Ghana's economic problems were aggravated by drought and 'bush-fires'. The near-collapse of basic infrastructure, road and railways, undermined the PNDC's efforts to move pangas, seed and fertilizer to the rural population.[3] There were threats of massive redundancies, lay-offs and unemployment in both the private and public sectors owing to shortages of raw materials for the factories, arising from lack of foreign exchange. The export sector – the cocoa, gold, manganese and timber industries – was reported to be in 'a state of almost total collapse'. Ghana was reaping a harvest of a long period of over-employment in the state-owned enterprises, the civil and public services (*West Africa*, 19 and 26 December 1983).

It was in these conditions that, following conversations with the IMF and the World Bank, the PNDC announced a drastic adjustment in the exchange rate of the cedi, a sharp curtailment of subsidies on imported items that Ghanaians had long regarded as 'essential commodities', and a sharp reduction of credit. As a *West Africa* correspondent summed up, all this was done

> against a backdrop of 10 years of 'disaster, hardship and dislocation', less rain in 1983 than for the past 48 years, real incomes at 17 per cent of the 1972 level, and a black market rate of C100 to US $1 after devaluation. 1983 was a year of management by inaction and fruitless recourse to the Eastern block (*West Africa*, 19 and 26 December 1989).

Thus, even as the Government of Ghana formalized its response to the crisis caused by the return of the migrants, and the international community organized its aid programme for Ghana, many of the migrants sought to return to Nigeria, so that they could escape from an apparently hopeless situation. Some of them succeeded in regularizing a further stay. Others risked a stay without 'papers' and were re-expelled in May 1985.

After the announcement of the 'quit order' on 17 January 1983, the Government of Ghana set up task forces to deal with the various aspects of the returnee problem,

Task Force	Project
Ministry of Transport and Communication	repatriation
Ministries of Labour and Social Welfare	transit
Ministry of Interior	accommodation
Ministry of Local Government	screening and rehabilitation.

These task forces were later replaced with (i) the National Co-ordinating Committee (NCC) and (ii) the National Mobilization Committee (NMC). The NCC was placed under the PNDC Co-ordinating Secretary, now the Chairman of the Committee of

---

[3] As in Note 2 above.

Secretaries (the equivalent of a Prime Minister), and asked 'to execute medium- and long-term plans for the rehabilitation of Ghanaian deportees'.[4] The National Mobilization Committee, in turn, took over the task of 'rehabilitating' the 'deportees' but regarded it as part of the general task of mobilizing the unemployed youth of Ghana in the productive sectors of the economy, including construction and agriculture.[5]

The first task of these committees was to transport the migrants to Ghana and to ensure that they found their way to their various homes. Following the announcement of the deadline, the Ghana High Commission in Lagos negotiated the establishment of reception centres as gathering points for the migrants, prior to their transportation to Ghana.

For internal transportation from the Togo border to Accra, from the Ghanaian seaport at Tema to Accra, and from Accra to the regional capitals which were designated as points of dispersion, the government ordered all government agencies to make buses and other vehicles available to the National Evacuation Task Force (NETF); the government agencies included ministries, departments, boards and corporations, and state financial institutions. The Evacuation Committee also made appeals to private commercial and industrial establishment for donations of vehicles. Individual transport owners and those organized in the Ghana Private Road Transport Union (GPRTU) volunteered buses for the 'evacuation exercise'. Since it was a period of acute shortage of fuel, the Ministry of Fuel and Power had to make special arrangements for the supply of fuel to the vehicles engaged in the evacuation.[6]

The first task of the task forces and the committees was to set up reception committees at the Ghana–Togo border, at Tema harbour, Accra airport, the Trade Fair Site and in (1985) the El-Wak Stadium at Accra.[7] The job of the reception committees at the points of entry was to receive and help transport or direct the migrants to first aid centres, where they could be medically examined and, in case of need, treated for fatigue or minor ailments. A special Medical Task Force consisting of medical practitioners, drawn from the Ghana Medical Association (GMA) and normally based at the Government Hospital at Korle-Bu in Accra, volunteered to examine and treat the migrants. Examination and treatment were administered in part at the Tema harbour but mainly at the Trade Fair Site. Migrants had to register, giving details of name, home town, region, profession and complaints of losses of property incurred in the course of the journey. For registration, medical examination and treatment, migrants were expected to stay at the site for 48 hours. They were then placed in groups on the basis of their regions of origin to facilitate group transportation to the regional capitals (*Daily Graphic*, 3 February 1983).

The reception committees consisted of personnel drawn from the Ministries of Health, Labour and Social Welfare, the Immigration and Customs Services of the Ministry of Interior, and the Red Cross Society. For their work the committees required medical supplies, bedding and food for first aid services to the migrants. The second task of the National Committee, therefore, was to procure these materials, if possible, from

[4] Report by Commodore Steve Obimpeh, dated 6 May 1983; also Report by Commodore Steve Obimpeh on 'The Repatriation of Ghanaians from Nigeria, 0-02, Exodus 85' dated 21 May 1985, Office of the NMC, Accra.

[5] Reports as in Note 4.

[6] Ghanaian press reports. Report by Commodore Obimpeh, 6 May 1985, NMC Offices.

[7] Ghana press reports, *Daily Graphic* (DG) 12, 20, 21 April; 6, 7, 9, 20 May; 1, 2, 5, 11, 13, 23 July; 25 August; 28, 29 September; 22, 25, 27, 31 October 1983.

voluntary contributions both at home and abroad; and, towards this end, they made a worldwide appeal.

The response to the appeal may be described as overwhelming. There was a spill-over of aid beyond the requirement of the 'returnees' to the needs of the Ghanaian public at large; aid donors not inclined to respond to political appeals were prepared to give to Ghana for humanitarian reasons. A reason for this was that the international media coverage of the expulsion and the manner of the Ghanaians' departure from Nigeria had already aroused great sympathy for Ghana. Consequently aid flowed from all over the world. This must be seen against a background of extreme hardship and business stagnation within Ghana.

The co-ordinator of international assistance was the Resident Representative of the United Nations Development Programme (UNDP) in Accra. After the immediate emergency period, food aid to Ghana was channelled through the World Food Programme (WFP) whose representative worked in close collaboration with the Chairman of the National Mobilization Programme.[8]

Distribution of drugs, food and clothing was made through national, regional and district sub-committees made up of the representatives of several organizations including Committees for the Defence of the Revolution (CDR), the army, the Civil Defence Organization (CDO), the police, the Ministry of Health, the Red Cross, and Ghana Private Road Transport Union (GPRTU). The CDRs and CDOs in particular were supposed to oversee the distribution of various goods from the national capital to the regional, district and village centres for the benefit of the returnees. They are para-governmental organizations called 'revolutionary organs' and said to represent the ordinary people. They are hierarchically organized, with national, regional, district, town/village branches and corresponding command structure.

Economically, the foreign donations certainly enriched Ghana beyond her expenditure on the 'refugees'. The returnees opened the doors to external aid for Ghana in a way that might otherwise not have been the case. The return of the migrants did initially aggravate the problems caused by drought, bush-fires, and economic slump. But, ultimately, the international goodwill it evoked, and the material aid it attracted, prevented Ghana from being overwhelmed by those problems.

The Social Aspects of the Reaccommodation of the Returnees

Since the Ghanaian migration did not result from social or political conflict, the reaccommodation of the returnees did not pose much of a social problem. The returnees resumed the statuses that they had had before migration; that is, they went back into their old jobs, found new jobs, or went abroad 'in search of greener pastures'. Those who remained unemployed were largely those who had always had this problem.

As far as can be gathered from media reports and personal observations, the public were sympathetic to the plight of the migrants. Many Ghanaians had benefited from the migrants' stay in Nigeria in the way of remittances of money and scarce consumable

[8] Report on WFP Emergency Assistance to Ghana 1984 1346 Exp. 1 and 11 by Commodore S. G. Obimpeh, Chairman NMC, 30 September 1985, Offices of the NMC; also a letter from J. F. Mableh, WFP Representative to Mr P. V. Obeng, PNDC Co-ordinating Secretary, of 26 January 1984, Office of the NMC.

goods. Consequently the media reported a rush of relatives to Tema harbour and the airport to welcome expected relatives. Between Tema and Accra, along the coastal road, the townsfolk offered water, food, and fruit to migrants who were on their way to the reception centre at the Trade Fair Site. In the regions, the traditional councils of chiefs organized reception committees and offered tracts of land to the 'returnees' for collective farming. The public response to the appeal of the National Rehabilitation Committee for donations in cash and in kind was highly favourable.

The government had medium- and long-term plans for dealing with the problem of resettling the migrants. In the area of employment, the Ministry of Labour and Social Welfare was directed to ensure the placement of returnees in their previous jobs, if possible, and into other jobs in establishments where there were vacancies.

The long-term plan for rehabilitating the migrants was conceived as part of the general plan for mobilizing the unemployed youth for work in construction, cocoa cultivation, cottage industries, co-operative farming, and rural housing. Returnees were urged to register with the District Secretaries (the government's political representatives in the districts) in order to be drafted into the revolutionary work force known as 'the Mobisquads' (*Daily Graphic*, 2 February 1983).

To ensure a favourable public response to the government's efforts, the Head of State addressed the National House of Chiefs at Kumasi, the capital of the Ashanti region. He urged public sympathy for the migrants, and appealed to the chiefs, as custodians of communal lands, for the donation of tracts of land to individuals or groups of returnees who wished to go into farming.

There were reports of favourable response to the appeal by the Government of Ghana for aid to the returnees. Chiefs in the Ashanti and Brong Ahafo regions were reported to have granted 405 and 20 hectares of land to the returnees for farming (*Ghanaian Times*, 23 February 1983).

Within the framework of the government's plans, the regional administrations also made their own. The Greater Accra Regional Administration, for example, set up a Resettlement Committee of sixteen members, under the chairmanship of a former Government Resettlement Officer. The committee was reported to have kept records on all deportees residing permanently in the Greater Accra region, and worked through government agencies and private organizations to help place them in gainful employment in either industry or agricultural ventures.

These plans were admirable, but, in Ghana, in spite of the recurrence of military regimes, people have generally shown great aversion to governmental regimentation. The plans simply remained on paper.

After the registration and medical examination exercises, the migrants generally went about their own business and were soon absorbed into their natal communities or former places of work. Those who brought their own vehicles into Ghana helped to relieve the acute transportation problem of the country. Those who settled back in their old jobs could only be distinguished from others in their possession of better clothing or exotic gadgets, including tape-recorders and TV sets.

The 'returnees' apparently developed feelings of solidarity, solidarity taking diverse forms in different parts of the country. In one locality they formed a 'Young Farmers Co-operative Society to embark on food production' (*Ghanaian Times*, 23 February 1983). In another, they joined the young men of the town in sinking wells (*Ghanaian Times*, 10 March 1983). Another group of returnees formed a labour gang to rehabilitate a well that was 'the only source of water in the town' (*Ghanaian Times*, 12 March 1983), while

13.1 *The Ghanaian social structure is still capable of absorbing its own (T. Allen)*

another decided to engage in food farming (*Ghanaian Times*, 26 March 1983). Others 'decided to devote their Tuesdays on work aimed at saving the land around Akroso railway lines from erosion'. The report also stated that 'it was disclosed by the chairman of the association [of returnees] that members had cleared five hectares of land for cultivation of cassava pepper and garden eggs [aubergines]. Cassava sticks, pepper and garden eggs seedlings valued at C5,000.00 were purchased by the association through individual contributions' (*Ghanaian Times*, 15 June 1983).

But these co-operative movements were short-lived and did not survive the successful attempts of the returnees to travel abroad in order 'to seek greener pastures'.

There were scattered reports in 1983 of some migrants being involved in anti-government demonstrations and engaging in violent crimes. But these too were short-lived and involved an insignificant proportion of the migrants.

Conclusion

As a general rule, the economic and social aspects of the resettlement of returning migrants depend on the causes of migration or 'flight' from the country of origin. The causes also determine the extent of disruption of normal economic and social life and the degree of social dislocation. In Ghana, the migration was gradual and clearly targetted: people fled an economy brought to near collapse by a combination of economic and political factors. What made the return of the migrants unusual was its abrupt and massive character; and it was these startling characteristics that posed a problem and also provided an international solution. There were only temporary problems of 'reaccommodation'. The Ghanaian social structure, though not the economy, was and is still capable of absorbing its own.

14

NICHOLAS VAN HEAR
Forced Mass Repatriation of Migrant Workers in Longer Term Perspective

With the mass exodus of Arab and Asian workers from the Middle East in the early 1990s following the mass expulsion of Ghanaians and other West African migrants from Nigeria in the early 1980s, the world has seen two great episodes of migrant worker mass exodus in less than ten years. While there are many differences between the two episodes, there are also significant parallels – not least the involuntary return of large populations from regionally dominant, oil-fired economic centres to their labour-supplying peripheries. Does then the longer term experience of Ghana following the mass return in the early 1980s hold any lessons for countries like Jordan, Yemen and other Arab and Asian states that received large numbers of returnees during the Gulf crisis of the early 1990s?

This brief chapter suggests that the consequences of such episodes for countries receiving returnees may not all be negative, and, indeed, in the longer term, mass returns may ultimately turn out to be beneficial. Arab and Asian countries affected by mass returns in 1990–92 in the aftermath of the Gulf crisis might draw some comfort from Ghana's experience in the 1980s, where the mass return of about one million migrants appears to have been followed by a positive turnaround in the country's economy.

It was reported that, by 1985, two years after the first mass expulsion to Ghana, several hundred thousand returnees were engaged in agricultural work, and teaching and health posts vacant before 1983 had been filled (Ricca, 1989). The large increase in agricultural labour power, coinciding with better rains, is thought to have boosted food crop production, revived Ghana's ailing cocoa output, and may well have assisted the country's economic recovery in the second half of the 1980s. These improvements may in turn have helped to convince donors to continue backing Ghana's Economic Recovery Programme.

Five years after the first mass return of expellees, Ghana was in much better economic shape than at the time of the expulsion. According to World Bank and IMF figures, Ghana staged a substantial turnaround in its fortunes between the early and the late 1980s (World Bank, 1990). Commonly cited Ghana government figures indicate annual growth in GDP of more than 5 per cent in the second half of the 1980s, until 1990 when growth slowed to 3.3 per cent (Kapur et al., 1991). These figures should be interpreted with caution. Adopted as a model reforming economy by the World Bank and the IMF in the 1980s, Ghana continued to receive large amounts of assistance in the form of credits from these and other institutions; there were doubts about the basis, the costs and the sustainability of the recovery (see, for example, Toye, 1992). Nevertheless, it is generally accepted that there was a recovery in Ghana's economy from the mid-1980s.

276

While there were many other contributory factors, at least some of the credit for this recovery was arguably due to the returnees. It is very difficult to determine to what extent the mass return of migrants contributed to the economic improvements. At the very least it may be said that the returnees were not a net burden. The evidence is not conclusive, but since it is likely that they contributed substantially to Ghana's labour-scarce rural economy (Tabatabai, 1988), it is plausible to argue that returnees helped to bump-start the revival of agriculture and the economy more widely in the second half of the 1980s.

This argument is lent support by various local-level studies. One such investigated the coping strategies of a small town in southeast Ghana between 1983 and 1989 (Dei, 1992). The town absorbed nearly 300 returnees, increasing its population by 5 per cent. Well over half of the returnees engaged themselves in agriculture locally (others dispersed themselves elsewhere in Ghana or abroad). They farmed individually and co-operatively using land held communally, bought or rented. Some, in response to favourable market conditions for food crops, engaged themselves in lucrative new ventures growing tomatoes and beans. Others may have helped to remedy shortfalls in the availability of hired farm labour in the area.

14.1 *Directly or indirectly the return of migrants to Ghana in the 1980s helped boost the Ghanaian economy (T. Allen)*

The mass return of migrants from Saudi Arabia and other Gulf states to Yemen in 1990–1 was of the same order as that to Ghana – about 800,000 people compared with a total population of just under 12 million (Van Hear, 1991 and 1992). While Yemen's economy was in a parlous state and many returnees remained in severe straits, the mass return may eventually turn to the country's advantage, although there was little sign of this two years after the mass return. There was nevertheless potential for a positive contribution given the skills that Yemeni migrants acquired while abroad, and the demand for labour in the repair and maintenance of the terraced farms on which Yemeni agriculture depends.

The movement of about 300,000 Palestinians and Jordanians from Kuwait and other Gulf states to Jordan in 1990–1 was proportionately of about the same order as the mass return to Ghana – about 7.5 per cent of the total population (Van Hear, 1991 and 1992). Here again, while Jordan's economy was in poor shape before the crisis, the return of skilled people and substantial capital could eventually prove beneficial. There was indeed a large inflow of capital as returnees recovered some of their assets and entitlements from Kuwait; the most obvious manifestation of this was the building boom that was visible in almost every corner of the capital Amman from late 1991.

It would be foolish to underplay the very different circumstances that obtain in the early 1990s compared with the early 1980s – not least adverse world economic conditions and the disposition of international donors. But if the right conditions can be generated – requiring judicious intervention nationally and internationally – the Ghanaian case appears to suggest that there is at least the potential to turn to advantage the mass returns to Arab and Asian countries of the early 1990s.

References

Dei, George (1992) 'A Ghanaian town revisited: changes and continuities in local adaptive strategies', *African Affairs*, Vol. 91. No. 362: 95–120.

Kapur, Ishan, Michael Hadjimichael, Paul Hilbers, Jerald Schiff and Philippe Szymczak (1991) *Ghana: adjustment and growth, 1983–91*, IMF, Occasional Paper 86, Washington DC, September.

Ricca, Sergio (1989) *International migration in Africa. Legal and administrative aspects*, ILO, Geneva.

Tabatabai, Hamid (1988) 'Agricultural decline and access to food in Ghana', *International Labour Review*, No. 127: 6.

Toye, John (1992) 'World Bank policy-conditioned loans: how did they work in Ghana in the 1980s?', in Chris Milner and A. J. Rayner (eds), *Policy adjustment in Africa. Case studies in economic development*, MacMillan, London.

Van Hear, Nicholas (1991) 'Forced migration and the Gulf conflict, 1990–91', *The Oxford International Review*, 3, 1, Winter.

—— (1992) *Migrant workers in the Gulf: update*, Minority Rights Group International, London.

World Bank (1990) *World development report, 1989*, Oxford University Press, Washington DC.

TERENCE RANGER
Studying Repatriation
as Part of African Social History*

Much of the discussion at the UNRISD Harare symposium was about the *difficulty* of carrying out research on past and present refugee repatriations. There were grave problems of access, severe shortages of sources. And, of course, this is a general dilemma for Africanist historians and social scientists. The past is acutely sensitive, let alone the present. It is a truism that sources are inadequate – censored, suppressed, destroyed.

I have been working, as have many of my students, on the social history of the Zimbabwean guerrilla war. Everyone begins such research haunted by the opening pages of Julie Frederikse's *None but ourselves*. An ex-Rhodesian army soldier tells her:

> 'Whew! A lot of stuff went up in smoke in this country in early 1980. A helluva lot. Salisbury was surrounded by a little cloud of black smoke . . . When the city incinerators were all full, they sent us off to the crematorium for more burning.'
>
> Frederikse asks: 'What was destroyed?', and he replies in words that send a shiver through any historian: 'The past.'[1]

And yet the social history of the war *is* being written. I found myself, when working in Makoni district in 1980 and 1981, that the habits of literacy were so hard to break

*Author's note. The concluding remarks reproduced below are a tidier version of my oral summing up at the UNRISD Harare symposium in March 1991. They still relate to the conference presentations and discussions rather than to my reflections on the chapters in this book as digested in tranquillity. I have also made no attempt to comment on the latest developments in the repatriation of refugees in Southern Africa – though as I write I learn that the UNHCR has authorized the beginning of organized voluntary repatriation to Mozambique. My justification is that the points I was concerned to make at the end of the conference still seem to me to need saying. Indeed, they struck some of the delegates at Harare as all too little related to the then immediacies of the refugee crisis or to the urgent need for practical recommendations. Because there had been debate during the conference about sources, methods and approaches – with government and agency representatives criticizing academics and vice versa – I chose to focus my summing up on these questions. Now that some of the immediate policy issues so hotly debated at the Harare symposium have become less controversial, the underlying research issues still seem important. To summarize a summation, what I wanted to say was that there was nothing more important than research on refugees and on repatriation *except* to ensure that such research did not compound the plight of refugees and repatriates by cutting them off from the social history of rural people in general. This is a message which gained in importance at the UNRISD Addis Ababa Conference on Repatriation in the Horn in September 1992, where speaker after speaker sought to erode such categories as 'refugee', 'returnee', 'stayee', and where the local UNHCR representative sought to escape the restrictions of his mandate so as to attack the whole issue of rural poverty and grassroots political impotence. So I choose to end this book as I chose to end the Harare symposium and to speak as a social historian. Since that is what I am, my remarks will perhaps gain in authenticity whatever they lose in immediacy.
[1] Julie Frederikse (1992) *None but ourselves. Masses vs. media in the making of Zimbabwe*, Ravan Press, Johannesburg, and James Currey, London: vi–vii.

that both blacks and whites had kept diaries or letter-books – even if they had to bury them in the backyard.[2] Sister Janice McLaughlin has discovered astonishingly detailed Catholic diaries, as well as pioneering the use of the prolific Zimbabwe African National Liberation Army (ZANLA) Archives.[3] Professor Ngwabi Bhebe has drawn on the remarkable records of Swedish Lutherans and Swedish relief agencies.[4] Many scholars have tapped oral memories of the war.[5] Even Rhodesian records have not all been destroyed in the great cloud of smoke in early 1980. In these days of photocopying and duplication it is hard to destroy *every* copy of *every* document and files survive in police stations and administrative offices throughout Zimbabwe. Moreover, many white Rhodesians were reluctant to destroy the records of their own 'achievements' during the war. I have myself been shown by an ex-Rhodesian army officer, now in Australia, numbers of operational security files. One of my students has been shown materials on the planning and construction of Protected Villages and on counter-insurgency; and has had access to an overall Security Force operational diary.

So one has to lay alongside the truism that the sources are inadequate the paradoxical counter-truism that the sources are abundant. And this is certainly as true for the study of Zimbabwean (and other) refugees and repatriation as for any other aspect of the war. At the Harare conference after all, a wide range of sources has been used. Stella Makanya used confidential reports submitted to the Zimbabwe Project from visitors to or residents in the Zimbabwean refugee camps in Zambia and Mozambique; Christian Care, however patchily, *has* preserved records; I was able to cite written materials produced by Zimbabwean refugees in Dukwe Camp in Botswana; there are subject files on refugees in district administrative offices; Professor Bhebe's Swedish sources have many things to say about refugees; Jeremy Jackson made use of oral testimony from ex-returnees. And from outside Zimbabwe the conference was presented with the varied fruits of fieldwork – of Tim Allen's life as an extra mouth to feed among returnees on the Sudan/Ugandan border; of the interviews carried out by Jovito Nunes and Ken Wilson among Mozambican refugees in Malawi, Zambia and Zimbabwe. And we had less formal but extraordinarily revealing sources – children's drawings, camp songs.

In short, refugees are as available for research as any other rural Africans, indeed, more available than most. Refugees are a 'problem', addressed as such by agencies and in innumerable memoranda. They generate an archive. Moreover, all too often, refugees are literally available to researchers, gathered together in huge concentrations with all too little to do. One can interview refugees as one can no longer interview guerrillas. The problem, then, for research on refugees or on repatriation is neither access nor scarcity of sources. The problem, as for other types of social and historical research, is how to generate, how to evaluate and how to use the data.

---

[2] Terence Ranger (1985) *Peasant consciousness and guerrilla war*, James Currey, London.
[3] Janice McLaughlin (1991) 'The Catholic Church and the war of liberation', Ph.D. dissertation, University of Zimbabwe.
[4] Ngwabi Bhebe (1993) *ZAPU and ZANU guerrilla warfare and the Evangelical Lutheran Church in Zimbabwe*, Skotaville, Johannesburg.
[5] Norma Kriger (1992) *Zimbabwe's guerrilla war. Peasant voices*, Cambridge University Press, Cambridge; David Lan (1985) *Guns and rain. Guerrillas and spirit mediums in Zimbabwe*, James Currey, London; Ken Manungo (1991) 'The role peasants played in the Zimbabwe war of liberation with special emphasis on Chiweshe district', Ph.D. thesis, Ohio University; Irene Staunton (ed.) (1990) *Mothers of the revolution*, Baobab, Harare, and James Currey, London; Richard Werbner (1992) *Tears of the dead. The social biography of an African family*, Baobab, Harare.

At the conference at least *five* dimensions of this problem manifested themselves. These were:

(i) The tension between the urgency of crisis and the deliberation of research. Refugees are seen as the product of crisis; their situation is abnormal; repatriation will resolve the crisis and restore normality. Hence, there is not time for thorough research. In this context, it is not so much that there are few sources. The objection is that *it takes too much time* to generate the sort of sources being used, for instance, by social historians of the Zimbabwean guerrilla war.

My answer to this objection is simple – perhaps unrealistically so. First, the 'refugee crisis' has gone on so long in many parts of Africa that it has become totally unrealistic to see their situation as a short-term emergency. This was the case Tim Allen argued against the NGOs in the Sudan/Uganda border area which go on year after year with 'emergency measures', while in effect becoming the standing administration.[6] It is also a case that can be argued against over-hasty and inevitably superficial research. Unhappily there has often been all too much time to generate evidence and to think hard about it. And, second, the very extremity of the refugee situation demands *good* research rather than bad.

(ii) But what is 'good research'? During the debates at the conference researchers have been challenged by government and agency representatives on two main grounds. One has been that governments want specific proposals rather than 'academic analyses', the other that researchers should privilege certain sources over others. In particular, an objection was raised that some researchers had focussed on 'secondary sources' – i.e. the voices of refugees themselves – at the expense of 'primary sources', i.e. the documents produced by governments.

I shall say more about 'academic analyses' versus specific proposals below. At this point I will content myself with saying that repatriation is bound to be so complex and varied a process that it must require sound general analysis of the recipient rural societies at least as much as specific policy recommendations. As for 'primary' and 'secondary' sources, historians generally – in Britain as well as in Africa – have moved away from formal state documents to confidential government correspondence, and from that to the range of evidence I have described above. To adapt George Orwell, one might say that all these sources are 'primary' but that some are more 'primary' than others. In any case, there is an inconsistency between governments demanding policy-directed insights from researchers and at the same time expecting them to make most use of materials already produced by those governments themselves. Above all, the refugee situation is so much the product of gross imbalances in power, including the power of communication, that researchers have a particular duty to correct these as much as they can by listening to and recording 'the refugee voice'.

(iii) Yet the third expression of the difficulty in using sources was directed explicitly to 'the refugee voice'. During the conference Ayok Anthony challenged the researchers who particularly relied on refugee oral testimony. Why should we suppose, he asked, that this amounts to 'the truth'? Were not refugees – or returnees – ignorant of many of the larger factors that bore on their situation? Were they not subject, perhaps particularly subject, to rumour and fantastic speculation about the causes of their

---

[6] Allen's research findings will be available in a companion volume to this one (T. Allen (ed.) (forthcoming) *In search of cool ground: displacement and homecoming in northeast Africa*, James Currey, London).

15.1 *Returned refugees in northwest Uganda, 1988 (UNHCR/no number/J.M. Goudstikker)*

misfortunes? Did they not have ethnic and religious and ideological and political axes to grind? Were we to suppose, in any case, that researchers could gain the confidence of refugees and returnees enough to be trusted with their real thoughts? All these and other difficulties led Jovito Nunes to confess his own doubts about refugee sources to the conference.

And, of course, such doubts are well taken. But they are doubts which reinsert refugees and returnees into the general stream of the study of history and society rather than remove them into some special problematic category. The more we insist that refugees and returnees are agents rather than helpless victims, the more we restore them to a history in which they must necessarily reveal, like everyone else, their capacity for deceit and fraud and force as well as for endurance and courage. Suffering does not make people admirable – though whether they are admirable or not makes no difference to the need to end suffering. One can certainly take a different view theologically. Thus the Jesuit General, Pedro Arrupe, believed that God was manifested especially in refugees and sent Jesuits to camps in Zambia and Mozambique to 'witness'. This they did in the double sense of sharing the suffering and of documenting it. These admirable Jesuit reports, full of empathy, constitute an invaluable historical source, but one which the researcher must evaluate as sceptically as any other. And this perpetual scepticism is the solution to the 'difficulties' of refugee testimony as well. We confront here the general problem of evidence rather than any particular dilemma and it is a problem which can be resolved by means of the best practices of social historians rather than by any special rules for refugee studies.

(iv) There is thus plenty of evidence which can be evaluated according to well-established conventions. But the evidence is uneven. In the study of refugees and returnees, as in the study of African rural society generally, it is easy to be too satisfied with the richness of the data for some things and to forget the paucity of the data for others. In the case of refugees, of course, the camps generate a mass of evidence. We know much less of 'refugees' who have melted into the host population. But it is not only visibility which determines data. In the case of Zimbabwe, we know a great deal about the refugees who ended up in camps in Mozambique and Zambia, remote and inaccessible though some of these camps were, and hardly anything about the rural people who fled to Salisbury or Bulawayo, visible though these were in their plastic encampments. The urban refugees were not the concern of any political party or liberation movement; no Jesuits lived among them; no Scandinavian evaluations were carried out. Similarly, they are easy to overlook when we come to consider post-war repatriation. *Their* return to the countryside was accomplished neither by successful UNHCR planning nor by ZANU/PF conscientization. It was a complex process of individual and family negotiation and the payment of fines to those who remained in the countryside and bore the brunt of the war while the refugees from 'plastic city' 'lived it up' in the towns.

(v) So far as external rather than refugee evidence is concerned, there is the problem of the great shift in responsibility for local administration and welfare provision. In many parts of Africa – the Sudan/Uganda border, great stretches of Mozambique – it is now the NGOs that administer and provide facilities rather than governments. This has many worrying implications but one that is easy to overlook concerns data for research. Governments have a tradition of preservation of and eventual public access to the documents they produce. NGOs have no such tradition. Oxfam, which has just celebrated its 50th birthday, has no archive and no plans for one. This is a problem, like all the others, which concerns research not only on refugees but on all types of rural experience and change.

So much, then, for the question of sources. But what about the question of method? Of the unit of analysis? At the Harare symposium, Jovito Nunes explained that his dilemma was not merely how to evaluate refugee testimony, but how to combine this view from below, intense but limited, with 'the global dimension' – a task he felt all the more difficult because each researcher is trapped within the assumptions of their major discipline. I would want to restate this question so as to get rid of a polarization between the refugee/returnee microcosm and the 'global' macrocosm. And just as I have argued that sources for refugee studies are similar to and can be evaluated within the context of sources for African rural society in general, so I want now to argue that Jovito's methodological dilemma is best seen as the dilemma of every student of African rural society.

Having written about Southern Rhodesian/Zimbabwean history as a whole, for instance, I turned after 1980 to focus on one district – Makoni. When I explained this shift of focus in a public lecture at the University of Zimbabwe, I was accused by some of 'mere historicized anthropology'. I was suggesting, so I was told, that there might be a possible contradiction between the Zimbabwean state and local peasantries, whereas the only true contradiction was between all the people of Zimbabwe and global capitalism. My students today, or those carrying out case study research in Mozambique, face similar criticism, though nowadays it is more likely to be expressed in the jargon of 'civil society' than of 'world system theory'. The theory of civil society is a theory about how to relate associational life to the state – but it is a theory which all too often excludes rural society as incapable of civil association. What both the Marxist and the Liberal problematics have in common, therefore, is that they both exclude the specifics of the rural experience from their Grand Narratives. Hence they offer us no helpful way to conceptualize the actual interactions of the local, the national and the 'global'. We have to find ways of studying rural experience in all its density and particularity without closing off an 'ethnicity' or a district from wider networks of national and regional interaction. We have to work out, in short, what Steven Feierman calls 'the strategies for dealing with an unbounded local society.'[7]

I strongly recommend to anyone working on refugees – clustered in their own camp microcosms – or on returnees, as they go back to this or that remote rural 'home' – that they read Feierman's *Peasant intellectuals*. It seems to me to be a model of how to restate and rethink Jovito's dilemma. Thus Feierman begins by admitting that, during his first fieldwork on 'the Shambaa' or northeastern Tanzania, he was content to work with the classic anthropological cultural/ethnic unit. Later, as he read the political economy studies emanating from the University of Dar es Salaam, with their emphasis on the penetration of the logic of colonial capitalism into the most seemingly remote and 'traditional' rural societies, he came to see the inadequacy of any bounded unit of study. Yet the political economy studies did not help him to resolve the dilemma because they had nothing to say about rural culture and consciousness. Anthropological studies were strong on the local; political economy insisted on the unbounded. What was needed was a way of combining the two.

Feierman writes of the pressing need still to understand the local in ways which are very relevant to the study of refugees and returnees:

---

[7] Steven Feierman (1990), *Peasant intellectuals. Anthropology and history in Tanzania*, University of Wisconsin Press, Madison and London.

Within African peasant society, analyzing the links between domination and peasant culture opens up a difficult problem of the scale – the extent in space – of the things being studied. Local cultural forms (the rituals or narratives of a particular place) deserve to be given special weight, yet the framework of domination can never be understood within narrow boundaries . . . If we begin from the assumption that peasant discourse is local and the organization of power national, then change can be shaped in only one direction: the powerful colonial or national state shapes the fragile and helpless local culture . . . The contrasting impressions of national power and local helplessness are less the products of data and more the consequences of an analytic framework . . . We must systematically shift the angle of vision, changing the analytic approach.[8]

Feierman's way of doing this is to privilege what he calls local 'intellectuals', defined not so much in terms of the excellence of their ideas as in terms of their pivotal position between the local, the national and the global. These men (and a few women) select from local ideas and 'traditions', fusing them with externally derived ideas, and hence modifying both sets in the process. In this way local societies learn how to relate to the national and the global and also how to exercise some purchase on these externalities. In this way one can add culture and consciousness to political economy.

Now you may be thinking that this sounds all too airy-fairy. Do refugee camps have culture, tradition, intellectuals? Do returnees know how to relate to the national and the global or how to exercise some purchase upon them? Is this not a case in which the model of external power and local helplessness persists because it is grounded in data as well as in particular analytic frameworks? Well, yes, and yet also, yes, but. We heard often enough during the conference that what is crucial is what refugees 'know', how they define the 'home' to which they will be repatriated or return, how they perceive authority. We have also heard that the helplessness of refugees *is* to a large extent an illusion and even an illusion which refugees can exploit as part of a total strategy. (Like the Mozambican men who crossed the border into Zimbabwe; left their families in camp so they could get food, clothing and shelter; and then went off to seek employment in one or other sector of Zimbabwe's rural economy.) The helplessness of returnees is even more of an illusion since no-one doubts that governments and agencies will play a relatively minor part once Mozambicans begin to return 'home'.

So 'ideas' become crucial; so does 'camp culture'; so does the 'culture of survival' in rural areas close to borders, which, for decades, if not centuries, have pursued policies of controlled flight and return. If we return for a moment to one of the problems of evidence discussed above – namely how to evaluate the testimony of refugees – then it becomes clear that one cannot do so as though refugees are atomized individuals. We need to know how what they say relates to 'camp discourse' and to the discourse of their home areas. There *are* intellectuals in refugee camps – like the spirit mediums who occupied special locations in Zimbabwean refugee camps inside Mozambique, or the independent church leaders who proliferate in Mozambican camps inside Zimbabwe. Nor do these represent merely the escape into irrational religion which refugee trauma induces. Fay Chung has described how spirit mediums in ZANU/PF camps inside Mozambique took care to understand the 'global' dimension of the struggle, cross-examining her, for instance, about China's support for the guerrilla war. She has also described how these mediums made use of 'traditional' ideas about the shedding of innocent blood or abstention from sex during a campaign in order to develop a critique of the ZANU 'veterans' who imposed harsh 'discipline' and commandeered refugee girls. In this way the mediums were acting just like Feierman's 'peasant intellectuals'. We

[8] *Ibid*: 4–5.

know a great deal about how mediums innovated intellectually so as to 'localize' guerrillas during the liberation war; we are just beginning to discover their role in 'repatriation', in the return of refugees from Mozambique, from the towns and from the 'keeps' to the rural 'homelands'. We are also beginning to learn about the uses of religion in rural Mozambique.

Hence, if we cannot separate 'the Shambaa' from territorial and global interactions, no more can we separate refugees and returnees from 'peasant history' – by which I mean that we cannot separate them either from 'peasants' or from 'history'. The present crises, on which researchers focus – with all their new experiences and innovative responses – are moments in the flow of history, drawing on long-standing memories of migration and reintegration. This is certainly true for flows between Zimbabwe and Mozambique, as Jeremy Jackson emphasized in Harare; it is equally true for flows between Mozambique, Zambia and Malawi, or for flows between Uganda, Sudan and Ethiopia. And, while it is sometimes only the erection of colonial frontiers which turns migrants into 'refugees' or 'returnees', there are all too many pre-colonial instances of flight rather than a migration.

Of course, we need precise particulars of the refugee and returnee here and now, but we also need the perspective of history, the context of rural sociology, and the insights of discourse theory.

I am not suggesting, of course, that the conference ignored complexities of classification. The simple monolithic notion of 'voluntary repatriation' was broken down into at least five categories. These were labour migrant returnees who became refugees in the crisis of return; returning displaced persons; returning dispersed persons; exploited villagers, who are 'refugees in situ', and whose desired 'return' is to the restoration of 'normality'; and, in Tim Allen's paper, constantly oscillating refugee/returnees. There were also many sub-divisions in the political context of return: anti-colonial refugees returning after political victory; defeated or persecuted political factions returning under amnesty; 'returnees by force', as in the Chad case; repatriation into continuing violence of those displaced by violence in the first place.

How, then, do these complex classifications relate to the historical dimension on which I have so strongly insisted? At the conference a simple model was suggested which runs as follows. The end of colonialism saw a nationalist return in political triumph, the most triumphant example offered to us being that of Algeria. By contrast, post-colonial refugees, the product of internal violence and the collapse of institutions, and victims of extreme poverty, usually return back into situations of instability and immiseration, and with no political event or victory to mark the moment of return. This is a useful model, but it is certainly an incomplete one.

It misleadingly identifies *types* of refugee/returnee situations with *periodization* between colonial and post-colonial regimes. Yet we can find examples of the second type of flight and return during the colonial period, as for example in colonial Mozambique, where rural peoples regularly fled from institutional violence and as regularly returned into a fundamentally unchanged situation. And we can find examples of the first type developing in the post-colonial period, as for example in contemporary Mozambique, where 'voluntary repatriation' is taking place in the context of a profound political and ideological change. (The development of 'democratic' electoral processes in Africa means that returnees will be mobilized as voters just as they were in Algeria, Zimbabwe or Namibia at the coming of independence.)

Moreover, this simple model is also confusing because it separates out processes which can certainly co-exist. Indeed, the papers on Uganda presented revealed both types of return taking place. Those on the Luwero Triangle are really dealing with a mini-Algerian, Zimbabwean, Namibian situation. The Triangle had been the heart of rural support for Yoweri Museveni's National Resistance Movement; his government is seen as 'their' government, able to mobilize relief for them from an international community relieved at last at a decent regime in Uganda. But Tim Allen's Madi are in a very different situation, as distant from this government as from its predecessor, and continually moving to and fro from violence into violence.

This leads me to another topic which needs to be seen in historical perspective – frontiers. Tim Allen suggested that there was a crucial difference between returning to 'heartlands' and returning to frontier areas. Governments take heartlands seriously and know that they have to satisfy their inhabitants; frontier peoples remain literally peripheral. Tim also suggested that frontier peoples often have different definitions of 'home', with some frontier societies actually defining themselves in terms of movement. You will remember that he said: 'Movement is normal. It is the frontier that is peculiar.' I think it is important in studying return to trace the developing 'peculiarity' of frontiers. And here I *am* suggesting a periodized contrast – between pre-colonial, colonial and post-colonial states.

We are all familiar with the idea of arbitrary colonial frontiers cutting their rectilinear way across Africa, disrupting flows of trade and communication, turning rivers into barriers rather than highways, turning points of contact into underdeveloped peripheries or the enclosing border of reified ethnicities.[9] At the conference we were given many examples of colonial disruptions of pre-colonial flows. In Kwame Arhin's presentation in Harare we heard of 'intra-migration that goes centuries back'; Nunes and Wilson gave us a 'sense of the permanence of migration', in more senses than one, emphasizing that 'migration became a central feature of Lomwe society over the past 150 years' and offering fascinating details of Lomwe traditions and techniques of migration. All these flows were disrupted by colonial boundaries.

And yet most colonial borders were *not* intended to be impermeable. They deliberately disrupted indigenous flows of trade so as to establish European dominance, but *labour* was intended to cross frontiers, as Jeremy Jackson's chapter makes clear. In colonial regional labour systems borders played the role of 'sifters' of labour rather than as barriers to its movement. Colonial borders were defined zones of power or weakness in the 'game' of colonial pursuit or supply of labour. So South Africa made its treaties with Mozambique for labour in exchange for remissions of cash and for railway and port concessions. Southern Rhodesia, frustrated, sought to obtain its 'share' of Mozambican labour. Thus in colonial Rhodesia there was a different response to the incursion of Mozambican refugees than in contemporary Zimbabwe. In 1917, refugees fleeing from the Portuguese repression of the Makombe Rising were welcomed across the border

---

[9] Since I delivered this concluding address I have read Thomas Spear and Richard Waller's *Being Maasai*, James Currey, London, 1993, which seems to me to contain one of the best analyses of the colonial transformation of a frontier. In this case it was a frontier internal to what became the colonial state of Kenya – the frontier between 'Maasai' pastoralists and 'Kikuyu' cultivators. In his chapter, 'Acceptees and Aliens: Kikuyu Settlement in Maasailand', Richard Waller shows how the original 'frontier' was a zone of necessary and fruitful interaction between two types of economy, with much interaction and intermarriage across it. Under colonial closure of expansive opportunities and of ethnic identities, it became the boundary of increasingly defined and narrow ethnicities. It also became the setting for frontier criminality – smuggling, 'incursion', etc. Colonialism criminalized cross-frontier transactions and criminalized ethnic identity, regarding 'Kikuyu' as alien to Maasailand, rather in the way in which Zimbabwe came to criminalize nationality and to define 'Mozambicans' as aliens.

15.2 *Refugees from Mozambique being transported to work on farms in Zimbabwe* (The Herald *and* The Sunday Mail, *PO Box 396, Harare/William Mafunga*)

and given land, not through any principle of benevolence but in the pursuit of labour (and to embarrass Portugal in the hope of getting Rhodesian forces along the Beira Corridor).

Colonial 'permeability' often changes with African independence. New governments ban migrant labour flows to South Africa, as happened both in western Zambia and in Malawi; land shortage and unemployment undercut the receptivity of host governments and communities; much more developed ideas of 'national identity' make migrants seem more and more 'foreign' and change ideas of 'home'. Return becomes 'repatriation'. The most spectacular examples of 'labour-border wars' after independence come from West Africa, with mutual expulsions and enforced repatriations. But in many other parts of Africa borders have hardened and formalized, defining otherness yet more sharply.

Zimbabwe today relates to Mozambique in some ways irrespective of frontiers. 'Refugees' under Zimbabwean protection exist as much in the Beira Corridor as within Zimbabwe itself. Yet at the same time the border has hardened. After decades of Mozambican labour migration into Zimbabwean commercial and communal agriculture, after centuries of interaction of kin and shared speech, Mozambicans today are defined very clearly as aliens and as potential spies. Moven Mahachi, when Minister of Home Affairs, publicly regretted that Zimbabwe does not have South Africa's guts or morale and hence cannot erect an electrified fence along the border with Mozambique. Mahachi's remark was provoked by Renamo raids into Zimbabwe (themselves, in fact, a function of continuing cross-border economic activity and directed towards punishing defaulting partners in smuggling). But imagine the electrification of this and other frontiers and one can see the multiple consequences of the hardening of frontiers on many things we have been discussing – the foreclosure of Jacksonian 'opportunities'; increasing Arhin-style 'returnees'; profoundly affecting response to refugees and further emphasizing 'encampment'; defining repatriation solely in territorial/nationalist terms, as many returnees do not.

And this in itself raises another set of topics that need to be historicized. How *do* 'returnees' perceive 'home'? How do they define 'identity'? The answer to these questions is critical to understanding mechanisms of 'integration', to assessing the prospects of 'innovation' by returning refugees. Hence these questions are central to refugee studies. But I want to argue that they can only be answered in the context of the general social historical literature on identity.

Needless to say, the concept of 'repatriation' derives from the idea of a 'patria', and this in turn implies that an individual's primary identity, rights and obligations derive from membership of a 'nation'. The nation encapsulates 'home' in terms of language, culture, rights to citizenship and land. Yet this is precisely what is at stake in many contests which generate refugees and returnees – in the Southern Sudan, in northern Uganda, and so on. Even in effectively operating nation-states, where the idea of return to one's 'country' is a national as well as a local sentiment, that idea co-exists and sometimes conflicts with many other senses of identity and entitlement. Thus in Zimbabwean resettlement policy the state's nationalist 'global' definition of priority settlers – refugees and landless from anywhere in Zimbabwe – clashed with the 'ancestral' claims of Communal Area peasants who wanted lost 'home-lands' returned to them. In such a context 'returnees' sometimes opted for one definition of identity and entitlement, becoming settlers on government schemes, and sometimes opted for another, rejoining other peasants in the Communal Areas or 'squatting' with them on the lost lands.

Any study of repatriation or return needs, therefore, to look closely at such multiple ideas of identity and entitlement. It needs also to be aware of the 'mythic' or 'ideological' element, not only in the idea of 'nation', where it is obvious enough, but also in so-called 'traditional' identities. The same 'Shona' peasants who appeal to ancestral rights, whose claims to land are rooted in the graves of the founders, whose chiefs claim to descend from the first conquerors and civilizers, are in fact recent descendants of regular massive movements of population to and from regions and areas.[10] Thus with people who – unlike Tim Allen's mobile Ugandans – construct their identity in terms of permanance and rooted ancestral continuity, one needs to study how 'home' is constantly re-created after movement. It is the idiom rather than the place which constitutes home. Even for these 'rooted' groups, then, 'home' is not so much a place as an idea.

Similarly, group identity itself is ideological. A great body of work for Eastern and Southern Africa has documented the processes of 'inventing' and 'imagining' ethnic

---

[10] D. N. Beach (1980), *The Shona and Zimbabwe, 900–1850*, Mambo Press, Gweru and Heinemann, London.

identity.[11] This process has gone on throughout the processes of colonial conquest, labour migration, peasantization. It goes on throughout the process of flight and 'return'. Thus Wendy James has said for 'the Uduk' that before their constant wanderings between Sudan and Ethiopia they had little sense of a distinct ethnic identity. During their wanderings their ethnic identity came to *consist* in being refugees. Now that they have been given enough land in Ethiopia to recommence cultivation they will be able to combine a new ethnicity with a return to an earlier core idea of identity – self-reliant subsistence. For the Uduk the restoration of this possibility was more important than an actual physical return to the place where their refugee wanderings began.

'Healing', about which there was much discussion at the symposium fits in here as well. It is often not about cleansing a community or reintegrating an individual, but about re-creating 'home', claiming the land in a new area. If agencies want to assist 'repatriation' it is often not so much a matter of identifying the exact place of departure as identifying and understanding the processes of 'making' home and 'imagining' identity. Nor is this a matter of privileging 'tradition' against 'modernity', 'tribe' against 'nation'. It is dynamics not statics that need to be understood.[12] And if all this sounds too nebulous to be of immediate concern to hard-pressed agencies, let me give an example from the work of Christian Care on Zimbabwe's eastern border. Incoming Mozambique refugees refused to erect huts at one camp site because it had not been 'cleansed' and its spiritual 'owners' had not been propitiated. On inquiry Christian Care were told that it was state land, 'and governments don't have spirits'. So the agency carried out complex oral traditional research, sifting rival ancestral claims until it arrived at a plausible spirit ownership. Propitiation rituals were then carried out and the huts built. (I don't know under what obligations to the chiefly lineage concerned this placed the refugees.)

The same principle is true when we turn from the return of whole groups and look at the integration or reintegration of individuals and families into rural societies. Here, almost by definition, we are talking about innovation rather than statis. But such innovation is not in itself a new process. African rural societies were integrating immigrants and reintegrating returnees long before anyone was defined as a 'refugee' or a 'repatriate'. The 'ancestral' Shona chieftaincies, with their immemorial homelands, were made up by the constant recruitment of incoming strangers – as hunters, diviners, warriors, clients of the chief – who were given wives and imagined as kin. Where notions of difference *were* maintained, and one grouping asserted identity and privilege as indigenes over another, incoming population – as in southern Malawi over the centuries – long-standing rituals and ideologies defined the relationship. The existence of these mechanisms helps to explain the generosity of the receiving societies of southern Malawi to the latest waves of Mozambican immigrants. What we have to understand here, in the context of contemporary refugee studies, is not so much how to create new mechanisms of integration

[11] Among many others see Leroy Vail (ed.) (1989) *The creation of tribalism in Southern Africa*, James Currey, London; John Lonsdale (1992) 'The moral economy of Mau Mau', in Bruce Berman and John Lonsdale, *Unhappy Valley. Book Two: Violence and Ethnicity*, James Currey, London; Terence Ranger (1993) 'The invention of tradition revisited', in Terence Ranger and Olufemi Vaughan (eds), *Legitimacy and the state in twentieth-century Africa*, St Antony's/Macmillan London.

[12] These remarks, made at the Harare Conference, gain greater force now that there is a great debate in Mozambique about 'civil society', the state, and the reconstruction of the rural areas. To over-simplify, intellectuals in the capital seem to be moving from an endorsement of 'modernizing' interventions in the countryside, such as consolidated villages, to a rediscovery of 'tradition'. There is a danger that this rediscovery will produce artificially static notions of identity and location. There is a great need in Mozambique, particularly on the eve of a massive repatriation, to understand the ideological and processual character of identity, location and 'tradition'.

as in what ways the latest incursions have transformed, and perhaps overwhelmed, the old.[13]

I was very glad that Professor Arhin introduced the question of migrant labour returnees. As became clear from his paper, Ghanaian labour migrants were familiar with long-standing processes of reintegration before that great crisis in interstate relations which turned them overnight into 'returnees' and 'repatriates'. In some ways, indeed, they must have thought that it was Christmas when the crisis produced such uncharacteristic behaviour as chiefs actually offering them land instead of demanding prestations, and families actually weeping with joy at their return and the prospect of the end of caṣh remissions! The literature on Southern Africa, too, is replete with illustrations of the processes by which labour migrants were repetitively reintegrated. The great missionary anthropologist, Junod, described how in early twentieth-century Mozambique returning labour migrants were isolated in special huts for ritual cleansing before they could be reintegrated with society. Many other studies described elders seeking to tax and control returning labour migrants, with the latter seeking to evade and retain, sometimes breaking off to found their own village, sometimes grouping together to accuse the elders of witchcraft and themselves in need of cleansing. (Thus Junod also described how in southern Mozambique – aggrieved by their constant stigmatization by the elders – returning labour migrants supported the Murimi movement in 1915 which swept away all the charms and medicines of the elders.) This reminds us of what is equally true for returning refugees – that reintegration is a dynamic, contested process of power and inequality. A great deal depends upon who lays down the terms for reintegration.

These labour studies are very relevant to contemporary concerns with repatriation. For one thing they remind us not to make too great a distinction between 'normality' and 'crisis'. Even in Arhin's case, routine patterns underlay the apparently abnormal response. He tells me that the chiefs' promise of land was purely rhetorical. No land was actually given! If in some cases, as with southern Malawi today, huge increases in scale break down long-standing patterns of integration, in other cases the differences are more in terminology than in process. The refugee/repatriation situation is only partly unprecedented and very largely precedented.

And of course there are precedents not only for 'normality' but also for 'crisis'. Take, for example, the great contemporary crisis of subsistence, of drought and dearth, which may have precipitated refugee flight and will now limit and condition the possibilities of return. There are, of course, splendid books about droughts now. But there is much to learn about migration, acceptance, return, negotiated reintegration, etc. in a historical study like Megan Vaughan's account of a late colonial famine in Nyasaland, with its added bonus of a sophisticated gender dimension.[14]

Now, everything I have said affected the discussions at the Harare symposium about returnees as a source of innovation. Some of the participants emphasized this very strongly – for Chad or for Uganda, for example. Yet we have to be careful not to fall

---

[13] The work of Matthew Schoffeleers has been crucial to understanding these southern Malawian processes. His long studies of the Mang'anja cult of Mbona – brought together in *River of blood. The genesis of a martyr cult in southern Malawi*, Wisconsin University Press, Madison, 1992 – have described, among much else, ritual processes of subordination of immigrants to the minority 'owners' of the land. He has reflected on the apparent recent collapse of these processes in 'Economic change and religious polarisation in an African rural district', in W. Beinart (ed.) (1985) *Malawi. An alternative pattern of development*, African Studies Centre, Edinburgh. See also E. C. Mandala (1990) *Work and control in a peasant economy: a history of the Lower Tchiri Valley in Malawi*, Wisconsin University Press, Madison.
[14] Megan Vaughan, *The story of an African famine: gender and famine in twentieth century Malawi*, Polity Press, Cambridge, 1987.

here into the besetting sin of 'development planning'. That besetting sin is to imagine that everything up to today, up to one's intervention, is 'traditional', unchanging, backward. The moment of development intervention is the moment of challenge to stasis, the moment when modernization at last begins. This is a notion held, for example, by Zimbabwean development planners who persist in regarding Zimbabwean peasants as subsistence traditionalists despite a century of engagement with the market. It is easy to combine this tendency of development thinking with the idea that the refugee crisis is totally new. Then one can readily imagine that refugees will by definition have been shaken out of 'tradition' and that they must return as innovators. Yet, as I have been arguing, so much of this has happened before. The innovative potential of returnees reminds me irresistibly of the literature on labour migration or on the return of African servicemen after the Second World War. If African rural areas have gone on looking 'traditional' despite all these returns, it is partly because planners have not looked at them closely enough and partly because sustained, progressive change requires backing and capital. Rural innovators, whether returnees or not, cannot work miracles by themselves, or as ready tools for outside interventions. They need structures of localized power and decision-making, a supportive rather than a commandist state.

So students of repatriation must learn not to over-privilege *their* particular change, not to see it as the moment of transition from pre-modern to modern. Repatriation is an instant, if a very important one, in the *real* process of modernization, which extends over centuries of adoption of new crops, of exchange of ideas, of contestation of identities and rights, of flexible innovation and invented tradition.[15]

The time has come to draw *my* conclusions from all this social history and to deliver messages to agencies and to states. So here goes:

(a) Agencies and states need to hear the 'voice from below'; to understand the 'cultures of perception' both of refugees and of the societies to which they return. But this understanding needs to be *dynamic*, seeing identity as fluid, 'tradition' as a means of innovation. As Tom Colvin told us, agencies must not expect or impose traditional group categories on a situation where fluid new assertions of identity and community – themselves a mirror of more general rural processes – emerge. He instanced new churches as relevant communities of belonging and we heard how the Mozambican refugee camps in Zimbabwe are also full of little congregations each under their own 'bishop'. Yet these are not a function of refugee trauma: the changing relations to kin, church and state which they imply are amply documented by studies in rural communities way outside the refugee camps.

(b) Agencies must facilitate what returnees 'want' while realizing the complex, conflictual and sometimes contradictory character of their desires. Usually it is better to let the returnees themselves work out the contradictions than to seek to tidy things up from above.

(c) As for states the lesson is that refugees are not just 'available' for modernization or mobilization. The Algerian case presented to the symposium and summarized in Chapter 4 was impressive in its testimony of shared collective and directed achievement after the war and the return of refugees. But it was alarming for its denial of pluralism and its insistence on modernization from above – in the end with the predictable consequence

---

[15] For a magisterial account of the long duration of change see Jan Vansina (1990) *Paths in the rainforests. Towards a history of political tradition in equatorial Africa*, James Currey, London.

15.3 and 15.4 *Is it a Utopian dream to want open borders and an internally generated pluralism for African states? Refugees from Mozambique in Malawi, 1990 (UNHCR/no number/S. Errington); returned refugees arriving home in South Africa, 1991 (UNHCR/21085/L. Gubb)*

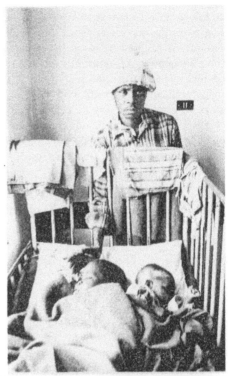

of failure. In the context of rural social history, 'pluralism' is not just a trendy liberal slogan but the major fact of historical reality. Kwame Arhin made a pleasantly patriotic comment in his presentation at the symposium. Having described governmental plans for the reintegration of returning labourers, he writes: 'These plans would have been admirable in any other country. But in Ghana people have generally shown great aversion to governmental regimentation.' Well, I would like equally patriotically to claim the same for Zimbabweans as I am sure most of you would claim for your own nationals. Nor is this just peasant bloody-mindedness. 'Governmental regimentation', whether colonial or independent, has historically thrown up great roadblocks to progressive change, obstructing the multiple and fluid processes of rural invention and imagination.

(d) At the symposium, there was much talk about plans and someone sensibly said that there are many kinds of plan. Hooray, then, for little plans – district development plans, which really rather than rhetorically originate from below; local repatriation plans which reflect the real dynamics of reintegration. Down with huge mega-plans, far beyond the possibility of implementation. When one speaker was trying to use the microphone he complained 'It works when I hit it but not when I talk' – the slogan of frustrated modernizers through the ages! Returnees are not microphones, not even to be talked at rather than beaten. They should constitute part of a relaxed, multiple modernization.

(e) Finally, let me assure states that I am *not* anti-state. How could I be when I am above all a pro-Zimbabwean peasant man, and when today Zimbabwean peasants, faced with the threatened withdrawal of state services under the slogan of 'liberalization', are clamouring for their retention or return? Of course, legitimate, autonomous, tolerant African states are essential for the satisfactory working out of the rural processes I have been describing. These have been processes of pluralism in the African sense rather than in the cant sense of political conditionality – to come at last to the hope expressed by some participants that in this summing up I would confront the present.

My own Utopian scenario for the 1990s is the same as that of Peter Nyoni of Oxfam and the spokespersons of other Zimbabwean NGOs at Harare – an internally generated pluralism, internally recognized and arbitrated, internationally supported with aid. It is my scenario for peasants and labour migrants as well as for refugees and returnees. Its achievement certainly requires *more* state intervention than the IMF wants – to continue to protect industry, to allocate land fairly, to stimulate rural production with services and subsidies. I see no reason why this cannot be combined with state acceptance of multiple but not exclusive identities. I see no reason why it cannot be combined with effective representative structures of local government. All this would legitimate the state and such a legitimated state could afford to be tolerant. It would be defined by its frontiers but not corseted by them, allowing its citizens to go out for labour if that is essential to their strategies of survival and investment, receiving in-migrants from other states as a potential resource rather than as dangerous aliens. Moven Mahachi said recently that even when peace returns to Mozambique the border would always be there, always a danger. I do not see that it has to be. A border can be a zone of interaction and possibility rather than a zone of mutual fear and suspicion.

In this Utopia – which at least has the advantage of building on the processes of rural Africa as we have come to understand them – states would not generate 'refugees'. Repatriation across such borders could be natural, gradual. It is a long way, I know, from current realities but even a historian has to end a discussion of homecoming and home-making with a dream of the future.

Additional Bibliography
Compiled by John R. Rogge

Barber, M. (1986) 'Resettlement in third countries versus voluntary repatriation' in B.S. Levy and D.C. Suscott (eds) *Years of horror, days of hope: responding to the Cambodian refugee crisis*, Associated Faculty Press, Millwood, N.J.: 301–4.

Barton, M.S. (1985) 'Repatriation from Djibouti: end of the organized phase', *Refugees*, No. 13: 11–12.

— (1986) 'Argentina, returning from exile', *Refugees*, No. 25: 20–2.

— (1987) 'Voluntary repatriation: what are the prospects?', *Refugees*, No. 39: 12–13.

Barudy, J. (1988) 'Going home: emotional crisis or a new life?', *Refugees*, No. 57: 41–2.

Billard, A. (1987) 'Haiti: hope, return, disillusion', *Refugees*, No. 39: 13–18.

— (1987) 'A swinging door: repatriation and migration', *Refugees*, No. 39: 19–20.

— (1987) 'Repatriation or integration', *Refugees*, No. 47: 33–4.

— (1987) 'Making up for lost time', *Refugees*, No. 48: 10–13.

— (1989) 'Afghanistan: Operation Salam', *Refugees*, No. 61.

— (1989) 'The eve of departure', *Refugees*, No. 66: 17–18.

Brooks, P. (1987) 'Repatriation to Ethiopia: a journalist reports', *Refugees*, No. 42: 30–1.

Buehler, H. (1984) 'Voluntary return from Djibouti', *Refugees*, No. 5: 39.

Burrows, R. (1985) 'Returnees in Laos', *Refugees*, No. 17: 32–3.

Bush, K. (1990) 'Preparing for the future', *Refugees*, No. 76: 16–17.

Casella, A. (1988) 'Soubanh Srithirath, Laotian Vice-Minister for Foreign Affairs answers questions on voluntary repatriation', *Refugees*, No. 53: 13–14.

Cerquone, J., (1983) 'Repatriation: a troubled, favoured solution', *World Refugee Survey 1983*, United States Committee for Refugees, Washington, DC.

Crisp, J.F. (1987) 'Voluntary repatriation: the hope of thousands of African refugees', *Refugees*, No. 47: 21–9.

— (1989) 'Going back to Burundi', *Refugees*, No. 60: 9–12.

— (1989) 'Namibia: great expectations', *Refugees*, No. 72: 11–12.

— (1990) 'A model operation', *Refugees*, No. 75: 30.

— (1990) 'UNHCR in action: returnees from around the world', *Refugees*, No. 75: 21–4.

Crisp, J. and T. Williams (1989) 'Together again', *Refugees*, No. 70: 22–4.

Cuny, F. (1990) 'A conceptual framework for analysing the repatriation process during unresolved conflict', unpublished paper.

Gorman, R. (1984) 'Refugee repatriation in Africa', *The World Today*, October: 436–43.

Goudstikker, J.-M. (1987) 'Northern Uganda: returnees settle in', *Refugees*, No. 38: 16.

Groves, R. and L. Hardy (1990) 'Time to go home', *Refugees*, No. 72: 12–14.

Hansen, A. (1981) 'Refugee dynamics: Angolans in Zambia, 1966–1972', *International Migration Review*, Vol. 15: 175–94.

Hooper, E. (1987) 'Ugandans leaving Sudan', *Refugees*, No. 45: 11–13.

—— (1987) 'From Zaire to Uganda: the end of an operation', *Refugees*, No. 45: 13–15.

Hudson, H. (1985) 'Uganda: returnees in the North-West', *Refugees*, No. 36: 17–18.

Hutchinson, M. (1985) 'Ethiopia's returnees – what chance for rehabilitation?', *Refugees*, No. 20: 9–11.

—— (1986) 'First organized voluntary repatriation movement to Ethiopia', *Refugees*, No. 24: 34–5.

Jambor, P. (1990) 'Breaking a vicious circle', *Refugees*, No. 72: 10–11.

—— (1990) 'Voluntary repatriation of the Indochinese refugees', *Refugees*, Vol. 9(3): 7–9.

Lamb, S. (1986) 'Refugees and returnees in Ethiopia', *Refugees*, No. 33: 9–10.

—— (1986) 'Djibouti: voluntary repatriation resumes', *Refugees*, No. 34: 9–10.

—— (1986) 'Ethiopia: returnees from Djibouti', *Refugees*, No. 35: 32–3.

—— (1987) 'Next stop: home', *Refugees*, No. 44: 20–2.

—— (1987) 'Guatemalan exiles and returnees', *Refugees*, No. 44: 30–1.

—— (1987) 'Return and reintegration', *Refugees*, No. 44: 32–3.

—— (1988) 'After all these years', *Refugees*, No. 53: 27–9.

MacDonald, H. (1986) 'Papua New Guinea voluntary repatriation: a long, slow process', *Refugees*, No. 29: 32–3.

Niwa, T. (1989) 'Repatriation: the human dimension of the Khmer border population', Annual Conference of Indochinese Displaced Persons in Thailand, CCSDPT, Bangkok.

Ortiz, R.D. (1987) 'Return flight from exile', *Refugees*, No. 44: 27–9.

Paringaux, R.-P. (1987) 'Mozambique – the repatriation train', *Refugees*, No. 42: 27–8.

Refugee Policy Group (1991) *Repatriation: Cambodia – a time for return, reconciliation and reconstruction*. Refugee Policy Group, Washington, 42 pp.

Reynell, J. and T. Jackson (1990) 'The myth of voluntary repatriation', unpublished position paper, CCSDPT, Bangkok.

Rogge, J.R. (1989) 'Repatriation: its role in resolving Africa's refugee dilemma', *International Migration Review*, Vol. 23: 184–200.

Skari, T. (1985) 'Spontaneous return to Ethiopia', *Refugees*, No. 19: 9–12.

Stainsby, R.A. (1988) 'The seven principles of voluntary repatriation', *Refugees*, No. 57: 33–4.

Standley, L. (ed.) (1990) *Back of the future: voluntary repatriation of Indochinese refugees and displaced persons from Thailand*, CCSDPT, Bangkok.

Stepputat, F. (1989) 'Repatriation: persisting doubts among Guatemalans in Mexico', *Refugee Participation Network*, No. 6: 5–8.

Telford, J. (1988) 'Return to Mesa Grande', *Refugees*, No. 57: 40–1.

UNHCR (1985) 'Promoting voluntary repatriation', *Refugees*, No. 21: 5.

—— (1987) 'Voluntary repatriation of refugees', *Refugees*, No. 44: 5.

—— (1988) 'Afghanistan: preparing for repatriation', *Refugees*, Special Issue, December: 27–9.

—— (1988) 'Helping refugees to go home', *Refugees*, Special Issue, December: 35–6.

—— (1989) 'Repatriation and root causes', *Refugees*, No. 60: 5.

—— (1990) 'Repatriation: policy and principles', *Refugees*, No. 72: 10–11.

Index